The Experts Shiver
for
WANTED UNDEAD OR ALIVE

"Wanted Undead or Alive is a fascinating, far-ranging analysis of the nature of evil and those who rise to fight it . . . in real life, in pop culture, in literature, and in legend. A must-read for those who want to dive deep into the reasons for why we are fascinated by monsters . . . and love those who make it their business to take them down."

> —Rachel Caine, author of the *Morganville Vampires* series

"Wanted Undead or Alive is a riveting chronicle of all things that drop fangs in the dead of night. All aficionados *must* have this in their library!"

> —L. A. Banks, *New York Times* bestselling author
> of The Vampire Huntress Legends series

"Jonathan Maberry and Janice Gable Bashman probe into pop culture's Heart of Darkness, and what they find is both fascinating and thought-provoking. This book is a great addition to the library of anyone who's ever wondered why vampires are popular, ever dressed in a Klingon costume, or ever pondered the boundary between bad and evil."

> —Charlaine Harris, creator of True Blood
> ⬤⬤⬤⬤ ⬤⬤⬤⬤ novels

"Wanted Un⬤⬤⬤⬤ ⬤⬤⬤⬤⬤⬤⬤⬤ fending off
the fearsome ⬤⬤⬤⬤⬤⬤⬤⬤ ⬤⬤⬤⬤ght. Weird,
insightful, an⬤ ⬤⬤⬤⬤⬤⬤⬤

⬤⬤⬤⬤⬤⬤⬤ertainment

Also by Jonathan Maberry

NONFICTION

They Bite (with David F. Kramer)

Zombie CSU

The Cryptopedia (with David F. Kramer)

Vampire Universe

FICTION

The Wolfman

Rot & Ruin

The Dragon Factory

Patient Zero

Bad Moon Rising

Dead Man's Song

Ghost Road Blues

WANTED
UNDEAD
OR ALIVE

VAMPIRE HUNTERS
AND OTHER KICK-ASS ENEMIES OF EVIL

JONATHAN MABERRY
AND
JANICE GABLE BASHMAN

CITADEL PRESS
Kensington Publishing Corp.
www.kensingtonbooks.com

CITADEL PRESS BOOKS are published by

Kensington Publishing Corp.
119 West 40th Street
New York, NY 10018

First printing: September 2010

10 9 8 7 6 5 4 3 2 1

Printed in the United States of America

Library of Congress Control Number: 2010925000

ISBN-13: 978-0-8065-2821-2
ISBN-10: 0-8065-2821-4

From Jonathan . . .
This is for the real-world heroes—firefighters,
members of law enforcement, doctors, soldiers
in the field and returning veterans, teachers, aid workers,
hospice care workers, staff and volunteers at shelters,
anyone on the front line fighting for civil and human
rights; and, as always, for Sara Jo.

From Janice . . .
To all the real-world heroes and the heroes in my life,
especially Sam, Howard, Mom, and Dad—may you
always continue to inspire.

CONTENTS

Acknowledgments		xi
Introduction: **That Whole "Good and Evil" Thing**		1
1.	**The Roots of Good vs. Evil**	5
2.	**Heroes and Villains**	18
3.	**It Didn't Start with Van Helsing**	35
4.	**Hunting the Fang Gang**	59
5.	**Fangs vs. Fangs**	93
6.	**Legendary Heroes**	99
7.	**Did You Use Protection?**	156
8.	**A Priest and a Rabbi Walk into a Crypt . . .**	171
9.	**Who You Gonna Call?**	208
10.	**Pulp Friction**	229
11.	**Spandex to the Rescue**	261
12.	**Children Shouldn't Play with Dead Things**	299
13.	**Real Evil**	318

Appendices

A. The OFCS Top 100 Villains of All Time   **355**

B. Spirit Superstitions   **359**

C. The Top 40 Genre Movies of All Time   **365**

ACKNOWLEDGMENTS

This series has been a massive undertaking and there have been a host of people who have generously provided information, assistance, insights, and support. Thanks to Sara Jo West, Don Lafferty, Tony Finan, Jessica Price, Sam West-Mensch, Brandon Strauss, and our good friends in the Horror Writers Association (www.horror.org). Special thanks to David F. Kramer, Stephanie Lechniak-Cumerlato, Online Film Critics Society.

INTRODUCTION: THAT WHOLE "GOOD AND EVIL" THING

Paul Gustave Doré, *Cain Kills Abel*

To many, Cain's killing of his brother Abel was not only the first murder, but also the first crime. Whether the story is true or merely a parable used to make a point about morality, the need for laws, and the sanctity of life, it allows us to take a hard look at the enormous consequences of the act of violence.

Depending on whom you talk to—or which spiritual path you follow—the struggle between good and evil is either the oldest conflict known to man or the second oldest. If we factor evolution into the mix, then the oldest struggle is for basic survival—food, shelter, and safety from natural predators. But once early man had something of a handle on those, back during those first hours of leisure time huddled around cook fires in caves, the struggle against evil began. With the advent of a belief in a larger world— God or gods, demons, monsters, and elemental forces—the struggle became a battle. The rise of religion turned the battle into an outright war, and the development of philosophy transformed that struggle into an art.

Now, here at the beginning of the second decade of the new millennium, we see this conflict played out in countless forms. It shows up in politics, in the friction between ideologies, in sports, in pop culture, in war, in dating, and just about everywhere else. Where there is no obvious evil (a serial killer, a tyrant's attempt at ethnic genocide, etc.) we personify natural disasters so that tsunamis and hurricanes become evil. We demonize sickness so that the process of treating a disease becomes a fight against death— as if death was a conscious being with a personal stake in it.

Funny thing is, we humans kind of groove on the conflict. The fight between good and evil, whether as an external battle against a monster or an internal struggle against temptation, makes for great storytelling, and we are certainly a storytelling species. Storytelling is in our nature, a fact we've known since the earliest humans learned how to mix pigment and paint on cave walls.[1]

In *Wanted Undead or Alive*, we'll explore a number of variations on this eternal struggle. The central theme will be the fight against supernatural evil, but along the way we'll investigate personal evil (what Joseph Conrad labeled the "heart of darkness"), temptation, corruption, ideological clashes, and more. There's certainly no shortage of examples of conflict in the human story. We should probably feel bad about that, but it's in our nature to accept

---

1. Arguably this suggests we are also natural graffiti artists. But that's a different book.

that evil exists and to believe, or at least hope, that something good (or less evil) will step up to oppose it.

Along the way we'll talk with all kinds of people, from clerics and politicians to pop culture experts and the guy on the street. Insights on the struggle come in all forms and frequencies.

This book is meant to be browsed, so don't feel guilty about jumping around. Guilt is a form of shame, which in turn is based on the belief that you've done something wrong. "Wrong" is the opposite of "right," and that's just another tweak on the whole good and evil thing. We don't want you to feel bad. Just enjoy the ride.

THE ROOTS OF GOOD VS. EVIL

Paul Gustave Doré, *Lucifer, King of Hell*

The name "devil" derives from the Greek word diabolos, which means "slanderer" or "accuser." As a concept, the devil symbolizes all of the baser, negative emotions and desires such as temptation, evil, greed, and hatred, and is antithetical to the higher virtues. Most cultures have some kind of devil figure, a diametric opposite of the God/creator force.

EVIL 101

So . . . what exactly is evil?

In simplest terms, evil is a label given to anything that is deliberately immoral, cruel, harmful, or unjust. Evil is different from "bad," and that difference is entirely built upon intent. Easy examples: Losing control of a car and running over a puppy is bad. Deliberately chasing it up onto the lawn and running it over is evil.

Most evil, however, is conditional on a point of view and situational variables. Take the puppy example. If the puppy is rabid and is about to bite a toddler in a sandbox, then driving a car over it is a good act, even a heroic one. But by this same example, is the puppy now evil for wanting to bite the kid? From one point of view it was deliberately intending to bite the toddler; from another it can easily be argued that the dog was not capable of normal behavior because of the active symptoms of a disease known to create erratic behavior.

The sound you hear is a big ol' can of worms being opened up.

This argument can be extended in a lot of directions. If we replace the puppy and toddler with a man and a woman, then if the man stabs the woman to death is he evil? If he deliberately wishes to degrade and harm the woman, we'd all pretty much agree that, yeah, he's evil. But what if the killer is a psychotic driven to violence by a brain tumor or an imbalance of brain chemistry? The evil label is hard to pin to that because "choice" seems to have been edited out of the equation, or at the very least the power of personal choice has been severely weakened.

This is why most states will incarcerate and treat a homicidal maniac rather than execute him. Then you have the question of nature versus nurture. Is a person who commits evil disposed to do so because of the way he's organically wired? Or does it require one or more negative influences to shove a person toward the dark side? Case studies of many violent and degraded serial murderers reveal that they were the victims of abusive childhoods. Is that enough? If we're asked to accept a bad childhood as the gun from which the evil adult "bullet" is fired, then why aren't all abused people evil? Or . . . even most of them? Why don't all people with chemical imbalances or brain tumors turn to mass murder?

The nature versus nurture argument, particularly as it relates to evil, seems to be lacking a crucial third component: choice. Choice is a central component to the unique makeup of the human mind.

The Root (Word) of All Evil

In Old English is was *Yfel*; in German it's *Übel*, in Dutch it's *Euvel*. The exact meaning is uncertain, though linguists and historians believe it dates back to early words for "transgression," or sin.

Even a person who feels a powerful call from his or her internal darkness can make a choice whether to answer or ignore.

And it is choice, you see, that gives us an understanding of evil. Without choice evil does not exist because evil itself is a choice. Evil isn't the action, it's the intention behind the action.

UNDER THE INFLUENCE

In many cultures evil is something a person does only when under the influence of a negative spiritual force such as the devil or a possessing demon. This extends into most forms of supernatural belief. It's easier to understand—and even accept—the reality of an otherwise ordinary person doing an evil act if we accept that a demonic force drove him to it. Especially if he was driven to it against his will, which makes the comforting argument that the natural inclination of people is to resist or oppose evil rather than perpetrate it.

This logic can be broadened to accept that all harmful acts occur because an evil force makes it so. Evil is seen in disease and storms and catastrophes of all kinds, and for many people this is a strangely comforting thing.

We can see it in the rationalization for infant mortality before sudden infant death syndrome (SIDS) was understood. Many of the world's vampiric beliefs are built around the unexpected death of a child—a child who dies in the night with no visible marks, no pre-existing health conditions, no other logical reason. For the parents of such a child, especially those in preindustrial cultures hundreds of years ago, the need to have an answer to this inexplicable tragedy was of first importance. The unexplained is unbearable; it erodes confidence and faith and sanity, particularly when it involves so significant a loss as the death of someone so innocent. There must be a reason.

So what was it?

In the absence of a physical cause—bite or disease or a bad fall—the grieving parents looked elsewhere for an answer. Simple folk could simply not accept that God had killed their young and sinless child. So . . . if not natural causes and not God, then there must be some unnatural cause that is antithetical to the loving and benign nature of God. In order to restore some semblance of balance, of justice to their world, they had to accept the possibility that there was something out there that wanted to do harm to their child, which had in fact done harm.

Hence the birth of malevolent and predatory monsters.

If they could accept that some kind of monster came under cover of darkness to do deliberate harm to the child, then this—however horrific and tragic—made a kind of sense. There are enough parallels in nature to give it sense: animals hunting and killing one another. The leap from the knowledge of animal predators to a belief in supernatural predators is not that big.

Such beliefs even persist into modern days. After 9/11 some televangelists declared that it was God's punishment on gays that led the al Qaeda to commit their terrorist acts.

Yes, take a moment here to admire the scope of that stupidity.

Which brings up another twist on the good and evil thing. For some individuals, the supernatural intrusion is on the part of a holy entity—God, an angel, etc.—against one or more humans who have embraced evil. This thinking has been the basis for every "holy war" in history in that one or both sides feel that they have been empowered and mandated by the Eternal to go lay a smackdown on the [*fill in the blank*—infidel, unholy, heretical, whatever].

There is enough evidence to support the contention that many organized religions have fostered beliefs in evil. It's good church politics and it's a great sales tool. Depending on your own personal beliefs it may even be true.[1]

---

1. And the authors of this book are *so* not going to debate the validity of any religion. That's a whopping big can of worms, and it's also beside the point.

Good vs. Evil

"The most effective good versus evil storytelling I've been a part of was *Pan's Labyrinth*. So complex and so reminiscent of the wrestling of childhood demons we all had to conquer. Being involved with the Hellboy world has also involved fleshing out a struggle of an inherent evil within us that we have the choice to overcome or not . . . Good and evil battle it out in our hearts every day. Watching or reading fantasy stories where these forces have names and faces inspires us to go back home and finish that battle of our own." —Actor Doug Jones plays Abe Sapien in the Hellboy films, among other roles.

The belief in supernatural evil has flickered a bit in modern scientific times, as seen in the case of SIDS. Nowadays we know that SIDS exists, even if we don't understand everything about it. Because we know that SIDS exists there seems little to support the old belief that an invisible vampire is the cause of these tragedies. Similarly, an understanding of catalepsy, catatonia, porphyry, rabies, and other medical disorders can account for many of the incidents of the dead rising, erratic behavior, skin pallor, and other symptoms that are commonly attached to monsters like vampires and werewolves.

THE PHILOSOPHY OF EVIL

Western philosophers have tended toward a different view of evil, seeing it as an expression of base human emotions such as greed, anger, frustration, resentment, envy, or lust. In Plato's *Dialogues*, Socrates (c.469–399 B.C.) observed, "From the deepest desires often come the deadliest hate."

The great philosopher also said, "The only good is knowledge and the only evil is ignorance." This view that evil was an expression of human ignorance is easy to understand when we view human behavior. Humans tend to fear what they don't understand, and fear of a thing very often leads to violence toward that thing.

Socrates also viewed retribution as a source of evil, as he eloquently stated: "One who is injured ought not to return the injury,
for on no account can it be right to do an injustice; and it is not
right to return an injury, or to do evil to any man, however much
we have suffered from him."

This philosophic view of evil is more centered on human weakness and failure than on any supernatural force or deliberate mali-
ciousness.

Sociologically speaking, evil is a useful way for science to quantify
aberrant behavior. The more comfortable word among sociologists
and psychologists, however, is "sociopath." This is a person who
demonstrates extreme self-serving behavior, an apparent lack of a
conscience, and a marked inability to empathize with others.
Sociopaths generally feel no remorse for harming other people and
seldom demonstrate any restraint in doing so. Though many do
possess enough control to be careful when avoiding implication,
as seen in the actions of so many serial killers.

However, sociopathic personality disorder—previously called
psychopathic mental disorder—as a label or explanation is frequently called into criticism by the general public, law enforcement, and the clergy because it "appears" to be offered as an
excuse (though not a justification) for very bad behavior. Some
researchers even hold that this label holds no more real weight
than the label of "evil"; and again here we cross over into the question of whether the sociopath is a product of nature or nurture, or
whether his actions are motivated purely by choice. This debate
has been raging since the early days of Freud and Jung and there's
no light at the end of that philosophical tunnel.

And this ties to a viewpoint presented by the Dutch philosopher
Benedict de Spinoza[2] (1632–1677), who said, "So everyone, by the
highest right of Nature, judges what is good and what is evil, considers his own advantage according to his own temperament . . ."
A view that suggests that the difference between good and evil is
merely one of personal inclinations.

Choice.

2. Benedict de Spinoza, *Ethics*, translated by Edwin Curley, Penguin Classics, 2005.

Why Write About It?

"It's at the core of our lives. Statistics tell us that we all cross swords with some form of evil at some point in our lives—maybe in nothing more sinister than getting shortchanged by a cashier, or having a wallet lifted by a pickpocket. But if we're unlucky, we come face to face with the kind of uncompromising evil that makes supernatural evil seem mild. Evil exists, and we all know it does. Storytelling helps show us that we can face it and survive." —Rachel Caine is the *New York Times* and *USA Today* bestselling author of the Morganville Vampires, Weather Warden, and Outcast Season series.

DEVILISH DUALITY

Most cultures in which a belief or understanding of evil can be found view it as one-half of a philosophic whole; the other being good. This duality—the eternal struggle of good versus evil—takes many forms.

It's fair to say that evil cannot exist without good. If nothing else, it's a form of measurement. You can't have up without down, hot without cold. One state is defined by the distance from its opposite. A Catholic view holds that God cannot exist without the devil, that they are inseparable. And although this doesn't actually square with scripture, it's both a compelling argument to reinforce faith and a simple explanation for the way in which the universe works.

A more new age viewpoint is that the universe is composed of positive and negative energy, always in motion and always seeking balance. This view of an energetic relationship between the extremes is an attempt to excise human emotions and personification from the natural order. This philosophy isn't new, of course, but it serves as the secular name for the concept of yin and yang.[3]

---

3. Yin and yang does not always relate to religions such as Taoism, but has an older connection to Chinese science and medicine. The religious connection is newer and therefore the concept is often mistaken as an aspect of religion.

Evil Impulses

"We all have the capacity to be good, evil or a combination of both. Do we act on our evil impulses is the ultimate question. There is a fascination and repulsion with people who are so monstrous. On the flip side, we fantasize about being a true hero—someone who has superpowers or is able to cure a deadly disease and save the world. That is why endless TV shows, films and novels are about superheroes and villains. We all like to see the good guy win even though we may secretly identify with the bad guy." —Ellen Dubin portrayed Giggerota the Wicked on *Lexx* and appeared in *The Collector, Highlander: The Raven,* and *Forever Knight.*

This belief is known as "moral dualism," and the key concept is that there is a constant and eternal struggle between opposite forces. Call them good and evil, light and dark, benevolent and malignant, or order and chaos.

WWJD?

Clerics, philosophers, cops, and judges have wondered whether good and evil are defined by cultural customs and laws or by our shared humanity. An argument can be made that virtually all cultures view murder, rape, child molestation, and torture as evil.

Except when they're not. Or, at least, except when they are permitted or sanctioned.

Murder is considered evil because it isn't permitted by law. The law defines it, not the act. A person killing another person is not always evil. We know that from every war ever fought. We know it from self-defense. We know it from state-sanctioned executions. We even know it from euthanasia. So . . . it's not the killing that defines it as evil, but the transgression of a law written by humans.

Many people kill. Some enjoy the hell out of it and are rewarded for it. A suicide bomber, though viewed as evil by the families of

Chad Savage, *Nightmare Visions*

"Any good story is based on some sort of conflict, and the simplest conflict possible is good vs. evil—even toddlers can understand that one, hence fairy tales. The storytelling gets more complex as we get older, but when you boil 'em down, they still usually have pretty well-defined Good Guys and Bad Guys. I think that's why stories that fall into gray areas are so disturbing to us—stories that end on a morally neutral (or amoral) note are often very jolting. As a culture, we like to see evil punished, maybe because we know in real life that often doesn't happen."
—Chad Savage is the artist behind Sinister Visions, Inc., a full-service visual design studio catering to the horror, Halloween, and haunted house industries.

the survivors, is regarded as a great hero by the followers of his own ideology. A preacher presiding over the funerals of the victims of terrorism will shake his fist and speak of the evils of such actions; while on the other side of the world another cleric will praise God and speak of the heavenly reward for the killer. Same person. Is he evil or good?

A soldier who kills the enemy is a hero. A soldier who continues to kill the enemy after a cease-fire is announced is a murderer.

If someone kidnaps a random person, straps him to a chair, and inflicts torture on him, we view this as evil. Yet during times of conflict governments have given official approval for torture. It's interesting to note that torture isn't generally called that by the sanctioning government. Since we—and the general public—associate torture with evil, we don't want to regard ourselves as evil, and therefore we give it a more acceptable label. During the Bush administration torture was called "enhanced interrogation techniques." Has a much cleaner ring to it, though I doubt the subjects of the torture appreciated the difference.

And that raises a conundrum. Call it the Jack Bauer paradox, and unless you've been living in a cave you're probably aware that Jack Bauer is the lead character on the Fox television show *24*. Jack is undoubtedly the hero, but he has done some questionable things during his race against the clock. The argument goes like this: We absolutely will not torture. Never, under any circumstances. Okay, fair enough. It's a view most sane and moral people would agree to without reservation. Except . . . what if there was a nuclear bomb set to explode in the center of a densely populated city and one person, a terrorist, knew where it was. The clock is ticking and hundreds of thousands could die, but everyone could be saved if someone can get to the bomb in time. Every second matters. Would it be acceptable to torture the terrorist for the information so that all those lives could be spared?

Most people would pick up the pliers or wire the terrorist's testicles to a car battery if it meant saving all those lives. If anyone insists they wouldn't, put a polygraph cuff on them and tell them that their own family would die in the blast as well. Then ask if they wouldn't cross that line.

This is what philosophers have labeled an "acceptable evil" or a "necessary evil." Jack Bauer isn't a bad guy, but the scriptwriters keep putting him in positions where there are no other doors left open and only "hard choices" are left. So . . . under those circumstances, what would Jack do?

What would you and I do? If it meant saving a hundred thousand orphans from being murdered, I think Mother Teresa would have gone medieval.

That's necessary evil. No one has yet been able to come up with anything approaching an answer to this conundrum.

UNNECESSARY EVIL

Some evil acts can be labeled as temporary insanity or crimes of passion, and maybe they are. These labels cover everything from popping a cap in an unfaithful spouse to road rage.

Take that up a notch and you have multiple individuals committing antisocial or violent acts—mass hysteria, the mob mentality. Psychologists have made careers out of explaining and defending this kind of behavior. But when we turn the dial all the way up to ethnic genocide, can there possibly be an explanation or have we crossed the line from a momentary lapse of reason into true evil?

"Genocide" was coined by Raphael Lemkin during the Nuremberg Trials; it is the systematic and deliberate destruction of an ethnic, racial, religious, or national group. It's not a spur of the moment thing. It isn't the end result of a frustrating screaming match or a riot over a soccer game. It's cold and calculated. It's a choice, and that makes it evil. We've seen it happen. The Srebrenica Massacre of July 1995 resulted in the slaughter of an estimated eight thousand Bosniak men and boys, an atrocity carried out during the Bosnian War by units of the Army of Republika Srpska under the command of General Ratko Mladić. A year earlier in Rwanda, a Hutu power group known as the Akazu perpetrated the mass murder of Tutsis and Hutu political moderates; and over the course of one hundred days they slaughtered an estimated eight hundred thousand people. Some estimates put the number higher, at a million victims, a number equal to 20 percent of the total Rwanda population.

These massacres were years in the making, as was the Nazi Final Solution and other campaigns of genocide. Not rash acts, but cold choices.

It makes you wonder why we look so hard for our evil to be of supernatural origin. We humans seem to be pretty talented at it without demonic help.

MONSTERS (AND THE PEOPLE WHO HUNT THEM)

However, the belief in supernatural evil persists. Exorcisms still occur. Hauntings are investigated. People wear charms against evil. Congregations pray for protection against unspecified harm.

It can be argued that the belief in monsters persists as much because of pop culture as because of ignorance. Possibly more so. Books, movies, comics, TV, video games, and all of the other forms of entertainment continue to showcase vampires, werewolves, vengeance ghosts, demons, dark gods, and other unnatural nasties.

Scaring the bejesus out of people is big business. If you're reading this book you grasp that concept. You probably have horror movie DVDs at home, maybe some dog-eared Stephen King novels. Shows like *Supernatural* and *Fringe* are on your TiVo, and a lineup of American remakes of Japanese horror flicks are in your Netflix queue.

Go ahead . . . admit it. You like being scared.

Maybe . . . you even like to imagine what it would be like to be the monster. A lot more people empathize with Dracula than Van Helsing. The monsters are more fun.

In *They Bite*,[4] authors Jonathan Maberry and David F. Kramer explored the darkness from the point of view of the monster,

---

Does Good Win or Does Evil Fail?

"In general, good survives in my books by holding to its principles . . . by believing in the things that I want to believe in, in my real life. Evil fails, when it fails (which, truthfully, is most of the time), by underestimating the good guys' willingness to sacrifice their lives. Because that's what heroes are: people who, without regard for their own safety, are willing to sacrifice themselves to save the day." —Rachel Caine is a bestselling author.

---

4. *They Bite: Endless Cravings of Supernatural Predators* by Jonathan Maberry and David F. Kramer, Citadel Press, 2009.

tracking the creatures from folklore and myth, through urban legend and into pop culture.

This companion book takes the other view by examining who (and sometimes what) stood against the coming of the darkness, who defended the helpless against the night predators, and who chased away the ghosts and exorcised the demons. We're talking about the good guys, the heroes, the vampire hunters, exorcists, ghost hunters, priests, witch doctors, and other often unsung heroes in the never-ending battle between good and the darkest evil.

Grab a stake, polish your crucifix, load your pistol with silver bullets, and let's go hunting.

2 HEROES AND VILLAINS

Scott Grimando, *Dragon Slayer*

"The Dragon Slayer was done for an Epic Poem I wrote for my book, *The Art of the Mythical Woman, Lucid Dreams*. The Hero sets out to prove her worth in battle donning the armor of her father who had no sons. Even the dragon underestimated her quickness and agility." —Scott Grimando is an illustrator and conceptual artist.

HOLDING OUT FOR A HERO

We've always had heroes and villains. In the earliest days the hero was the caveman who throttled something and dragged it home for dinner. The villain was the brute in the next cave who throttled the hunter and stole the intended dinner.

From another view, the hero is God and the villain is the devil, and everyone who came afterward and embraced light or darkness are wannabes. To the ancient Greeks a hero was a kind of demigod, a half-breed offspring of a human and a god who was born with special powers or knowledge and who often had the support of a god. That's not how we use the word today. By modern popular definition a hero is a person who shows courage when faced with a problem. This could be someone showing poise and determination during a fight against cancer or a soldier on a battlefield running to rescue a wounded comrade. Firemen entering a burning building are heroes. So are cops. A lot of people are heroic at different times in their lives, some more visibly than others. There is big, dramatic heroism and small, quiet heroism.

In storytelling, heroes tend to be a bit larger than life. They are the ones who stand up to threats that other people cannot face. Heroes slay dragons or hold a bridge against a horde of foes. Because of stories we tend to think of heroes as having big muscles, square jaws, and a will of iron.

But that's a skewed view of heroism. If you're big and tough, well trained and resourceful, then fighting the enemy is not that much of a stretch. If you're small and weak and have no special training, standing up to danger is viewed as a much grander undertaking. This is, of course, an absurd view, because a few ounces of lead in a sniper's bullet can plow through a muscular chest as easily as that of a ninety-pound weakling. Heroism is relative; it's based on the individual's emotional and psychological makeup—more so than on physical attributes.

The media tends to warp the word, using it for all the wrong reasons. They call sports stars "heroes," confusing the word with "idols." Hitting a home run may make fans adore you, but it isn't heroism. Running into a burning house to rescue someone is

Chris Kuchta, *Evil Dead*

**"In *Evil Dead III: Army of Darkness*, the conflict between Ash
and the Deadites is one of the most iconic examples of good vs.
evil/hero vs. villain. It resonates with viewers in both a visceral
and epic way, by showing the resolve and determination of the
hero, overcoming the forces of evil by severing it at its head. The
chainsaw representing the sword and the Deadite representing
the classic dragon shows undertones of the classic hero's journey, but accomplished in a contemporary world. Like Perseus
and Medusa or Beowulf and Grendel it will never get outdated."
—Chris Kuchta is an illustrator and art instructor at the Kuchta
Academy of Fine Art and Illustration. He has done work on films
such as *House of the Wolfman* and for *Blood Lust Magazine*.**

heroism. So is standing up for a friend who is being bullied. Or
saying "no" in the face of threat and intimidation.

Heroes are also defined by measuring what they do against what
they stand to lose. A mother who stands between her children and
a rabid dog is a hero. If she fails, she might lose her life and more
critically (to her) the lives of her children. If that same person was
faced with the rabid dog when no helpless children are involved,

the same situation might end differently. She might lose more easily; she might not find the inner reserve necessary to rise to the demands of the moment.

But we know that the extraordinary can happen. It has happened.

Heroism is also situational, and this is one of the really weird and inexplicable aspects of modern-day humans. On any given street in any big city in the world, most people not only pass one another by without acknowledgment, but they will growl, snarl, and snap if one of the other pedestrians intrudes into the bubble of their personal space to ask the time, directions, or the generosity of a quarter. And yet, let a terrorist's bomb go off, those same people will often risk life and limb to rescue injured strangers from burning debris.

Many people go their whole lives without ever encountering the kind of circumstances that will allow them to access their inner hero. Some hear the call of the moment and fail through fear, unshakable insecurity, cowardice, or some social bias that makes them withhold rather than reach out. And yet there are those people who are called by the moment, perhaps by the voice of destiny, to step up and show their mettle. Myth, history, and fiction are filled with the everyman who becomes the hero, or the green youth who discovers in his heart an iron resolve. Circumstance can make or break.

The HBO miniseries *Band of Brothers* (2001) showcased this beautifully, presenting a variety of characters who, under the intense and varied pressure of combat, discover weakness or strength. That series is probably one of the most accurate, poignant, and powerful presentations of ordinary heroes.

In world myth, the hero's journey—eloquently described by Joseph Campbell in his 1949 book *The Hero with a Thousand Faces*—is built around this process of discovery. Also known as a "monomyth," this is a common story form in which the hero-to-be begins in the ordinary world and is drawn into an adventure, experience, or journey during which he faces a series of challenges, tasks, and trials. Sometimes he faces these alone (Indiana Jones, Spider-Man); sometimes he has companions (Luke Skywalker, Dorothy Gale). The process of facing and dealing with each challenge expands the hero's mind, deepens his understanding of the world, and makes him stronger. Ultimately the hero must face a major challenge, a make-or-break moment that often has a lot riding on it: the hero's life, the lives of others, perhaps a kingdom, maybe even the fate of the world. The bigger the stakes the more drama in the story.

Some people, in life and in myth, are born to be heroes, and their journey is all about discovering and then embracing their destiny. These characters often have some special gift or ability that gives them an edge so that when they face their challenges they can draw on this inner resource and win the day. That's the case with Hercules, King Arthur, Wolverine, and Leelu from *The Fifth Element* (1997). These heroes are often willing to fill that role.

Unwilling heroes may also possess gifts or be chosen by destiny to rise in a time of crisis. Bilbo and Frodo Baggins were unwilling heroes. So was Harry Potter. There is usually a moment, however, when they man up and do what has to be done.

There are also antiheroes—people who seem unsuited for the role, often because of attitude issues or personality problems such as cowardice or self-absorption, but who nevertheless find that inner spark when the chips are down. Han Solo is a great example. At the end of the second act of *Star Wars: A New Hope* (1977) he was ready to take his reward and bug out, but a pesky conscience brought him back into the fight, and in the nick of time.

More tragic antiheroes are those who resist the call of heroism, or are even villains for a while, but who rise to the moment, often at their own expense. Annakin Skywalker's heroism surfaced in the last few minutes of *Star Wars: The Return of the Jedi* (1983), and—sadly—he died. Antiheroes often have a short life span once they've reclaimed their better nature.

A switch on the antihero is the kind who is viewed as a hero only by one side in a conflict. Certainly Joan of Arc was viewed as a heroine by the French people, but the English burned her as a witch. Hans-Ulrich Rudel was the most highly decorated Stuka dive-bomber pilot of World War II, and the only person to be awarded the Nazi Knight's Cross with Golden Oak Leaves, Swords, and Diamonds. To the Allies, however, he was a monster. During the Depression, gangsters like John Dillinger were hailed as heroes by the common man. Everything is relative.

Some people make great personal sacrifices that do tremendous good, but they do it without guns or bulging biceps, and often they fly under the radar and seldom get hung with the label of hero. Mother Teresa, Mahatma Gandhi, Rosa Parks, the Dalai Lama, and the host of unsung people working without applause to combat poverty, disease, and ethnic genocide in third world nations.

OPPOSING EVIL: CHOICE, DESTINY, OR RIGHT PLACE/WRONG TIME?

In the supernatural world heroes are often pitted against challenges no ordinary mortal is meant to face. Hunting a vampire, slaying a werewolf, driving unclean spirits from a house or from a possessed person—these are challenges that separate heroes from the vast majority of humanity (who would rather run for the hills—and sensibly so!).

What makes someone take that stand?

Sometimes it's love. When evil invades the home and targets one or more family members, it provokes a response that's been hardwired into us since we were lizards. "Defend the species" is a primal response. "Defend a loved one" is simply the most recent coat of paint on that ancient reflex. Defending a loved one does, however, require more active choice than simple species protection because with higher mind comes rationalization and considered self-interest. There are people who will flee in the face of attack even if it means leaving their loved ones to die. Yes, it can be argued that self-preservation is as old an impulse as species defense, but we can overcome it in order to defend others. Opting to save one's own life instead of someone else's is a choice. Tragic, surely; even understandable in certain circumstances . . . but it isn't heroic.

A hero may oppose the threat even if he believes that it's hopeless, or that he'll die in the process. Heroic choices don't always stand up to close logical scrutiny. But damn if they don't elevate the spirit.

Given a choice, a hero will opt to do some research, prepare some weapons or charms, maybe call on a few dozen buddies to help storm the castle. That's another benefit of higher mind: strategic thinking. And common sense . . . let's not forget common sense. A hero with some horse sense is likely to end the night as a live hero rather than a dead one.

Sometimes heroism is determined by pure chance and a mix of bad luck (having to confront a monster at all) and good luck (living to talk about it). This kind of hero usually has no prep time, no encounters with cryptic mentors, and no chance to get up to speed. The moment looms and the person reacts, and through some action wins the day. The reason this person gets to be the "hero" is largely based on survival: he either has defeated the monster or saved someone else from the big bad. A person who merely "escapes" is not a hero—just a lucky s.o.b. who should now go out and buy a fistful of lottery tickets.

FIGHTING EVIL

A hero is often defined by his enemies. A person who fights a vampire the size and approximate strength of, say, Tickle Me Elmo is not likely to be rated among the greatest champions of all time. When St. George fought a fire-breathing dragon, that one made the record books. For stories to have real pop—be they mythic, biblical, or fictional—there has to be a Big Bad, and the bigger and badder the evil the more profound the struggle. It's what makes a character into a hero. Beowulf fought Grendel and got serious points, but when he fought Grendel's much more powerful mother, he became a much greater hero. That he later died while fighting a dragon (which also died) gives his life story a real "wow!" factor.

In more modern heroic stories there is often a bigger power gap between hero and villain. Luke Skywalker versus Darth Vader, Clarice Starling facing down Hannibal Lecter, and Indiana Jones against the entire Nazi army are examples. Wits, resourcefulness, pluck, luck, and maybe some useful personal knowledge are common among the modern hero. Even when the hero is immensely tough—Spider-Man, for example—the villains tend to be an order of magnitude tougher, like the Rhino or the Hulk.

People who believe they are empowered by God (or whoever is

driving their particular belief system) can make formidable heroes. They can also be villains, depending on the point of view. During the Inquisition the Church was ostensibly the "hero" in a protracted battle against supernatural evil; however, in retrospect we can see that the Inquisition's actions were a campaign of corruption resulting in a slaughter of innocent people.

The burden on the hero who faces the supernatural is first to determine if the enemy is actually unnatural. Not an easy thing. A large part of the hero's challenge, then, is studying the creature, devising a series of tests to establish its nature, determining which weapons will work against it, and then actually killing the thing. For this reason the smallest portion of virtually any monster story involves actually killing the monster.

Most of it is the hunt.

VILLAINS—NATURAL AND UNNATURAL

Villains are the bad guy. Whether human, monstrous, alien, spiritual, or other, the villain is the person or being whose aim is to do some kind of harm. Real-world villains range from vicious dictators like President Robert Mugabe who has been accused of a laundry list of human rights violations to a snatch-and-grab thief who robs a convenience store.

Some villains are reluctant, and many are villains only from the perspective of political or ethical ideology. This is the case in every war ever fought.

Some villains fill that role briefly—perhaps a momentary lapse in which they succumb to greed or lust or one of those other pesky Seven Sins. Some are opportunists who see something and grab at it. The 2008 financial collapse was filled with bad guys of that kind.

Some villains, on the other hand, revel in it. Villainy is their choice. They groove on the negative energy released from their actions. This, sadly, is a pretty large category that includes child molesters, rapists, mass murderers, corrupters of youth, and many others.

Movies—perhaps more so than novels—are often structured to present the villain as the most interesting character. Filmmaker John Carpenter (*Halloween, The Thing, The Fog*) agrees and shared his views with us: "The villains always have the best parts. Darth Vader had the best part in *Star Wars*, the Wicked Witch had the best part in *The Wizard of Oz*, everybody loves villains. And these guys are just actors in makeup, but we all love them. They have a power to them. They're strong. Everybody knows about them. So they become incredibly familiar. It's hard to get people riled up and scared by them anymore because they're so familiar to us. For Halloween we dress up as scary characters, but we love them, we enjoy them and celebrate them. That's what movie storytelling's all about."

So . . . why the great love affair with the bad guys? "The reason we bond so much with the movie villain," says Carpenter, "is that we secretly want that kind of freedom, to be able to break all the rules. Especially when we're young. That's what we long to do, we want to break the rules. That's the appeal of horror films in general. Especially when they're on the edge. We go in there and we want a thrill. We want to get out of normal society. But as you get older, and become more responsible it becomes less fun."

It's interesting to note, however, that very few people ever regard

---

Creating Fictional Villains

**"I think the key to any villain in fiction is to make him human. He may do evil things, but he's still a human being and he reacts to the world in a very human way, although with a complete lack of impulse control. My character of Vincent, in *Whisper in the Dark*, for example, feels that he has been wronged. That after he has worked so hard to make a name for himself, creating his "art," some impostor has come along and stolen his thunder by, more or less, taking credit for his work. At least that's the way Vincent sees it. He sees the impostor as a plagiarist—and a bad one at that. So he's very human in his reaction, although he goes about getting revenge for this insult in ways that most of us wouldn't think of. Or maybe we'd think of, but wouldn't act on."
—Robert Gregory Browne is an AMPAS Nicholl Award–winning screenwriter and the author of *Down Among the Dead Men* (St. Martin's, 2010).**

themselves as evil. Wiretaps of conversations between members of organized crime families bear this out. You rarely get statements like, "Hey, let's go out and do some evil stuff." Though that would really make court cases a lot easier.

However, in myth and storytelling there are plenty of villains who delight in simply being evil. That's a club that has Satan as its chairman emeritus and includes Baba Yaga, quite a few dragons, the occasional ogre and troll, vampires, child-eating forest hags, and others. When it comes to child-eating hags there's no moral gray area, and heroic slayage is both acceptable and encouraged.

However, these days it's all about the gray area. Even a monster like Hannibal Lecter—a mass-murdering cannibal who was voted the second greatest villain of all time (after Darth Vader[1])—was a character people actually *liked*. In Thomas Harris's chilling novel, *Silence of the Lambs* and Jonathan Demme's nail-biter of a film, Lecter was charming, likable, even admirable in certain ways. We rooted for him to escape from his captivity, and the warden was made to look like the villain. The character's charisma blinded us to the bare facts that the warden was justified in maintaining the harshest security standards because the prisoner was an incredibly dangerous monster. But gray areas are at the heart of modern storytelling.

True Evil

"All of my films have tackled 'good vs. evil' to some extent. The most obvious is probably *Pink Eye*. There is a masked killer who is a victim to government testing—so the killer is not the true evil, the government is. They drug this man to the point of insanity; he escapes an asylum and kidnaps my character. I am just a nice girl trying to keep my family together and I end up tied to a bed . . . I won't give away the whole story because there are some twists in there. All real good vs. evil stories are morally convoluted because nothing is ever truly black or white."
—Melissa Bacelar is an actress, model, producer, and animal activist.

---

1. See Appendix A for the 100 greatest movie villains of all time.

New York Times bestselling author Rachel Caine shared her view on crafting these "gray area" characters: "I can't really warm up to characters who are just one thing or another. Black or white. Real people don't fall into those categories, and for me, the characters I create have to be realistic, if not real. My characters make mistakes. Bad choices. Sometimes, they compromise their ideals for short-term gains. I have a hard time making stock heroes or stock villains without mussing them up a little bit—most of my villains have redeeming qualities, and most of my heroes have less admirable ones. It just makes them more interesting to me."

A lot of modern horror and fantasy fiction explores those gray areas of evil and villainy, and that makes for some fascinating reading. It also allows the writers to throw some curves at the reader. Few things are more boring than a completely predictable villain. When it's hard to make a clear distinction as to whether someone (or something) is a villain, it infuses the encounter with paranoia, tension, and real scares.

Monsters as Social Commentary

"Zombies in storytelling are all about social commentary, not about evil. They are the perfect vehicle for allegory. To the writer, zombies can represent anything they want them to, but nothing works better than tapping into what a society is afraid of at any given point in history. A zombie trying to destroy a family barricaded away in a farmhouse could represent the decline of marriage or the destruction of the housing market. A band of the undead overrunning a city, with the way our country is now, may represent the terrorists that have been working to destroy our freedom. The zombie oozes no sexuality, like the vampire. There are no undertones there. It is not meant to seduce you, but just flat-out ruin everything you value. For a writer delving into zombies, they leave a lot of room for commenting on society and tuning into the frequency of what scares us as a collective group." —James Melzer is the author of *Escape: A Zombie Chronicles Novel* (Simon & Schuster, 2010).

MINDLESS EVIL

Monster stories of all kinds, from mythological tales of hydras and sea serpents to folktales about werewolves to modern tales of zombies, often present all threats as evil. That's not always accurate and it isn't fair. Evil is measured by intent not by the degree of harm done. It can't be judged according to body count because a fighter pilot in war who sinks a ship may be responsible for the deaths of hundreds of enemy soldiers, but that's the nature of war. Dracula only killed a handful of people in Bram Stoker's novel and yet we can all agree that he's evil.

The challenge in determining whether something is evil or merely dangerous crops up a lot when talking about monsters. *The Creature from the Black Lagoon* (Universal, 1954) is an animal and a natural predator. Are we right in calling such a creature "evil" because it kills humans? It isn't breaking any set of laws that apply to its species. No more so than a scorpion or a snake. The mistake is to equate "dangerous" with "evil."

Zombies are another good example. In George A. Romero's classic 1968 film, *The Night of the Living Dead*, the zombies kill over and over again without remorse. By the second film in the series, *Dawn of the Dead*, zombies had killed nearly every man, woman, and child on the planet. They are certainly threatening, relentless, and unnatural. So . . . does that make them evil?

Almost certainly not. Zombies, according to the Romero model, are unthinking. They are dead bodies that have been reanimated. They walk; they can use very simple tools (we see them picking up bricks or pieces of wood); they can problem-solve in a limited way (the zombie who attacks Barbara in the graveyard picks up a brick to try to smash the window after he has been unable to open the door using the handle). They can even pursue. And yet Romero— and other writers in the genre like novelists Max Brooks (*World War Z*), Joe McKinney (*Dead City*, 2006), and Robert Kirkman's ongoing comic book *The Walking Dead*—have clearly established that there is no personality, no emotions, no higher consciousness of any kind.

"Zombie stories are like a photograph in that they capture a society in a moment of time and freeze it there," observed the late

Billy Tackett, *Dead White & Blue*

"When I painted Zombie Sam I thought I'd piss some folks off. That didn't happen. The broad range of people that have become *Dead White & Blue* fans continues to amaze me. My Zombie Sam image is embraced equally by both the political left and right! I've sold shirts to both anti-war protestors and to soldiers voluntarily heading off to Iraq. Everyone seems to be able to put their own spin on him and personally I love it!"
—Billy Tackett is an illustrator and creator of the popular *Dead White & Blue* series of images where he zombifies iconic American images.

Z. A. Recht, author of The Morningstar Strain, a duology of zombie novels. "No further progress will be made. Nothing more will be manufactured. Life will go on—mostly—but the society has broken a cog and stopped in place. What remains are the echoes of that society, and now that it's frozen, and we, the survivors, have become something more, we can look back at it and really see what we were. It also forces the human characters to expose them-

Zombie Appeal

"Zombie stories appeal to a wide set of groups on a lot of different levels. There are the darkly beautiful feelings of hopelessness and bleakness that run rampant in the genre, but there's also the fantasy escapism of being one of the last people alive with everything left to you but also being free from the rules of a civilization that no longer exists." —Eric S. Brown is the author of *Season of Rot* (Permuted Press, 2009) and *The War of the Worlds Plus Blood, Guts and Zombies* (Coscom Entertainment, 2009).

selves: a greedy person might successfully hide behind a curtain in a civilized society, but in an anarchic one, they will have to be openly greedy and grab what they can when they can . . . Similarly, a generous character might be open-handed to the extent that they do not eat enough. The situation forces the morality of the character, for good or ill, to surface and take over. A person's morals—their principles—are the cornerstones of their personality, and I truly think that in an extreme situation, an individual will tend to revert to these cornerstones almost unconsciously, and cling to them."

"You cannot judge zombies in a moral sense," argues Dr. Kim Paffenroth, associate professor of religious studies at Iona College and author of *Gospel of the Living Dead: George Romero's Visions of Hell on Earth* (Baylor, 2006). "Before the modern era, there was talk of something they called 'natural evil'—things we'd call natural disasters or just facts of life (earthquakes, fires, diseases, etc.). Zombies would seem to fit there. It also means that zombie tales have to go one of three ways, it seems to me: either they humanize the zombies and give them more of a sense of mind and soul, or they treat them as a natural disaster (which makes some zombie movies look more like disaster movies than monster movies), or they have to focus on the evils committed by human survivors against one another."

Jacob Kier, the founder and editor of Permuted Press, one of the most successful publishers of zombie and apocalyptic fiction, agrees. "The classic Romero-style zombies are neither good nor

Night of the Living Id

"Freud described the id as 'The dark, inaccessible part of us that has no organization, produces no collective will, but only a striving to bring about the satisfaction of instinctual needs.' That sounds like a zombie to me. At least the reanimated dead we've come to know and love over the past four decades. Creatures not driven by any agenda or motivated by any amoral sense, but operating completely on instinct. Zombies are all id, just like newborn children. True, most children aren't born with the instinct to consume the flesh or brains of their parents, but that's no justification to label zombies as evil. They're just a collection of involuntary drives and impulses demanding immediate satisfaction." —S. G. Browne is author of *Breathers*: *A Zombie's Lament* (Broadway Books, 2009) and *Fated* (NAL, 2010).

evil, they're driven by pure instinct. You wouldn't call a shark that attacks a human 'evil,' so neither would you call a Romero-style zombie evil. There as dangerous as a tsunami but equally innocent of malicious intent."

Though, admittedly, it might be hard to remember that when a zombie is chomping on your arm.

"Blameless," Kier adds, "does not equal 'harmless.'"

Part of the popularity of zombie and apocalyptic stories stems from the joy of seeing people survive against overwhelming odds. Seeing a great bit of ingenuity is thrilling in any context, but in an apocalyptic scenario the opportunity for ingenuity is boosted to a whole new level. Take the ultimate survival challenge combined with the new level of freedom due to society's collapse and out pops a whole new horizon of solutions to all manner of problems. Go ahead and take an axe to the staircase. Build a wall out of wrecked cars. Construct catwalks between rooftops. Trap and train the zombies (or aliens, or infected). Nuke a city to eliminate just one person (or creature, or building). Fight to get into prison. Fans of the apocalypse eat up these scenarios that can only really play out in a world that's already gone to hell.

THE MISUNDERSTOOD MONSTER

Along with the mindless evil we have the misunderstood monster, a creature who is dangerously innocent. Innocent because he, she, or it lacks the emotional maturity or cultural awareness to grasp the concepts of right and wrong or good and bad. Dangerous because they may be equally unaware of their own strength or unable to control their own nature. Yet these monsters differ from the mindless variety because they can think (to a degree) and feel (again, to a degree), and they are often confused, hurt, psychologically damaged, or too alien for their own good.

The classic example is Frankenstein's monster. He has no true identity; he's a composite being with a damaged brain. Many literary scholars have debated over whether such a creature would have a soul—though I tend to think so. The possession—or lack thereof—of a soul was never the creature's issue. It was his damaged brain and awareness of his hideous and unique nature. This was most poignantly portrayed by Boris Karloff in the James Whale movie of 1931. Karloff gave humanity to the creature and highlighted its pitiable state.

Universal Pictures made a number of films with a similar theme. In both versions of their take on werewolves, *The Wolf Man* (1941) and *The Wolfman* (2010), Larry Talbot is a tragic figure who is by no means evil and is unable to control the violence of

---

Misunderstood Monsters

"I always sympathize with the monster, because the most interesting ones are simply misunderstood when you get right down to it. They really just want one thing: love! All the classics like Frankenstein's monster, Dracula, and the Wolf-man are simply looking for a hug from a lovely gyno-American! I have always wanted Frankenstein's monster to live, and instead of a little girl with a daisy, I made sure Toxie caught the blind eye of a gorgeous blond bombshell!" —Lloyd Kaufman is president of Troma Films and creator (with Joe Ritter) of the Toxic Avenger.

Twas Beauty Killed the Beast

"King Kong was always my favorite. He was taken away from what he knew, his home and life, to a place where he was a monster, a novelty and a tragic victim of his captors. The love story is there to humanize the beast so we can relate better with his loss and solidify the monster to our own perspectives. Most great stories involve a monster who is a hero and a hero who is a monster." —Doug Schooner is an artist, poet, and animator.

the monster that lives beneath his skin. Each morning following the full moon, when Talbot becomes aware of what the werewolf has done, he is torn by remorse. Genuine remorse.

King Kong is another twist. Kong has the intelligence of a great ape, or perhaps a smidge more, but he isn't a human and cannot reason (we assume) like a human. However, he shows compassion when protecting Anne Darrow from pterodactyls and tyrannosaurs, and he believes he's protecting her when he breaks out of the New York theater and carries her to the top of the Empire State Building. At the same time, the mayor, the governor, and the flyers from Roosevelt Field are justified in doing what they do to protect the city from the monster. They kill him the way they would kill a lion loose in the streets. Has either character acted with evil? No. The true villain of the piece is Carl Denham, the blowhard showman who captures Kong and brings him to America. Every death in the movie can be laid at his feet, and yet none of the film versions really paint him as evil. Corrupt, self-important, egocentric . . . but not evil; yet he shows no remorse for all the deaths he's caused. It's weird, and it's also disturbing.

3 IT DIDN'T START WITH VAN HELSING

Alan F. Beck, *Draculmouse*

"The image of the old classic black-and-white horror movie characters being portrayed is charming and hilarious. Imagine little mice dressed up in little suits acting out the scenes of grand horror films. I can hear Draculmouse saying in a squeaky voice: 'I do not drink . . . wine.' And . . . vampire bats are essentially flying mice, so it's not even that much of a stretch."
—Alan F. Beck is an award-winning artist and illustrator whose work is exhibited at science fiction and fantasy conventions coast to coast.

FANGS A LOT

Along with ghosts and demons, vampires are incredibly common in the beliefs and legends of cultures worldwide. Even today there are people who believe that vampires exist, and people who believe that they are vampires. However, here in the modern twenty-first-century Western world we tend to have a somewhat distorted image of what exactly a vampire is.

In world myth and legend, vampires come in all shapes and sizes, from the stereotypical pale-skinned risen corpse to fiery balls of light. Even the label "vampire" is only used here for convenience because vampirism isn't limited to the bloodsucking living dead. In fact barely a third of folkloric vampires are hematophagous (bloodsuckers).

With each cultural twist on the vampire model the vampire hunter is also tweaked. Rarely are the hunters sophisticated and learned scholars like Abraham Van Helsing. More often they're clerics of one kind or another, or family members who are driven to heroic extremes in order to put their risen relative to final rest and thereby protect the rest of the family. There are also professional monster hunters and even monsters who hunt other monsters. It takes all kinds to spin this weird world.

NATURE OF THE BEAST

So what is a vampire?

About the only overarching similarity between the disparate vampire types is that they are, by their nature, *takers* of something precious that we do not want to share. The blood drinkers are the most famous of this group, but many vampires attack humans in order to feed off life essence, breath, or sexual essence. A few feed on emotions, others on faith, fidelity, and even knowledge. And quite a few vampires are necrophagous (flesh eaters).

Many vampires spread disease and pestilence. In fact the word "nosferatu" means "plague carrier"—not "undead" as Bram Stoker mistakenly insists in *Dracula*. It's very common for plagues and diseases to be blamed on some evil spiritual force.

Some vampires can affect the weather, causing mists and storms.

The Romanian Varcolaci was reported to be able to cause eclipses, though this would involve forceful rearranging of the solar system and would probably result in the destruction of Earth . . . so we can discount that as one of the taller tall tales.

Not all vampires are dead. Some are risen corpses, sure, but there are living vampires, vampire gods, and otherwise ordinary humans who transform into vampire-like creatures at certain times.

About half of the world's vampires are theriomorphs, or shape-shifters. Funnily enough, it's exceedingly rare for any vampire to turn into a bat. More often they turn into fireballs, birds of various kinds, insects, dogs, dragons, cats, and a host of other critters. But bats? Not really. Shape-shifting in wolves is also rare, and is probably an overlap with werewolf legends.

It's impossible to create a definitive list of vampiric powers or vulnerabilities because they vary from culture to culture. Most vampires from folklore do not fear sunlight or the cross. Stakes won't kill them, they can cross running water, mirrors are irrelevant, and they don't have to obtain permission before entering a house.[1] Those qualities were added to the lore of the vampire by writers in order to make the vampire more mysterious, more directly tied to universal good and evil, and in some ways more vulnerable.

The connection between vampires and religion varies, too. When fiction writers began telling tales of vampirism, they took the position that supernatural beings were in direct opposition to the church and established new "traditions" to retell the stories of vampires in relation to purely Catholic concepts. For example, the idea of a vampire trading blood with its victim to create a new vampire was a twisted variation on the ritual of communion, where Christians drink wine that symbolizes the blood of Christ and as a result are "reborn." The transformation from human victim to newborn vampire taking three days is clearly modeled after the three days it took Jesus to rise from the dead after his crucifixion.[2]

Such concepts have since been adopted as established legend largely because most people learn about vampires through books

---

1. Except in the case of the *Vrykolaka* vampire from Greece and Macedonia.
2. And, to be accurate, this is only two days. Jesus died on Friday and was buried; he rose from his tomb on Sunday. Two days.

and movies rather than from a study of folklore. As a result, the classic elements of the "Hollywood" vampire have become the new folklore, and since folklore itself is mostly a collection of stories told and handed down, an argument can be made that these changes are as valid as anything told around a campfire or spoken of in folk songs. No argument. Writers have long been called the new mythmakers.

These new myths are nicely thought out, too. Dracula has more or less become the Bullfinch's Mythology of vampirism for the modern age. This is not to say that were no connections between early vampire beliefs and religion. There certainly were and they took very many forms. Using religion as a weapon against evil is not confined to Christian countries or even to the Christian era. Vampires are tied to various religions around the world, from widespread religions like Hinduism, Buddhism, Judaism, and Islam to the less common religions of the druids and Native Americans. In every country, vampire stories have been influenced by religious beliefs and popular fiction so that the original folkloric beliefs are often muddied, and in some cases, entirely lost. This makes it very difficult for the vampire slayer to know the nature and specifics of his unnatural enemy because he cannot trust most of what is "popularly" believed.

And, before we get hate mail . . . the vampires discussed in this chapter are subtypes of the monster paradigm. Our remarks here do not refer to those persons who embrace vampirism as a real and valued part of their lifestyle. Our focus is strictly on the supernatural monsters that prey with malicious intent upon humans.

On Mythology

"Humanity created mythology to answer unanswerable questions, to give voice to our innate human vulnerabilities. Film, TV and Literature are just a continuation of that very basic human need to express ourselves and our fears."
—Amber Benson played "Tara" on *Buffy the Vampire Slayer* and is the author of *Death's Daughter* (Ace, 2009) and *Cat's Claw* (Ace, 2010).

WHAT MAKES JOHNNY BITE?

The process by which a recently dead body becomes a vampire is up for debate. Every culture has its own take. Here are some examples from around our dark planet:

Animal interference

- ▸ In Chinese and some Slavic folktales a vampire is created when a cat or dog jumps over a fresh grave.
- ▸ Elsewhere in the world corpse-jumping is tied to humans strolling across a new grave, or birds, stray animals of all kinds, and even insects.
- ▸ In China, tigers are believed to possess what was known as a "soul-recalling hair" that hooks part of the spirit when it crosses over a grave.
- ▸ The corpse-jumping phenomenon stems from the belief that the spirit of the dead can snatch a portion of the life of any living creature and use it to rekindle its own unnatural life.
- ▸ In Western Europe if a black cat or a white dog watches a funeral, then the corpse will rise.
- ▸ Conversely, in Russia, if a white dog wanders through the graveyard, then the dead will not rise.

Marked for damnation

- ▸ Being born with a caul—an amniotic membrane covering the face—in some cases indicates the presence of evil within the newborn. Vampire species created through this means[3] include the Wume of Togo, the Nachtzehrer of Germany, the Strigoi of Romania, the Upier and Ohyn of Poland; while in other cultures it's a sign of great positive spiritual power.
- ▸ On the peninsula of Istria, both the Croats and Slavs believe that a caul is a sure sign that the child will either become a

---

3. Though this is given as a cause for many of these vampires, it is by no means the *only* method of vampiration found in these cultures.

good-natured and heroic kresnik, or a foul and vampiric kudlak.[4]

▸ Some cultures believed that a child born with teeth was destined to become a bloodsucker. This includes the Neuntoter of Germany, Viesczy in Russia, the Upier and Ohyn of Poland.

▸ Red hair was seldom viewed as anything but a sign of trouble in days gone by. This idea got kick-started when some genius decided that Judas was red haired. As a result, a cult of red-haired vampires called the Children of Judas was purported to terrorize parts of Serbia, Romania, and Bulgaria.

▸ You'd think that being born with a physical deformity was enough of a burden, but in many cultures such people were reviled as having been marked by evil. This is one of the most common prejudices associated with the belief in vampires, and it occurs all throughout Europe, Asia, and Africa.

The Caul of David Copperfield

"I was born with a caul, which was advertised for sale, in the newspapers, at the low price of fifteen guineas. Whether seagoing people were short of money about that time, or were short of faith and preferred cork jackets, I don't know; all I know is, that there was but one solitary bidding, and that was from an attorney connected with the bill-broking business, who offered two pounds in cash, and the balance in sherry, but declined to be guaranteed from drowning on any higher bargain. Consequently the advertisement was withdrawn at a dead loss . . . and ten years afterwards, the caul was put up in a raffle down in our part of the country, to fifty members at half-a-crown a head, the winner to spend five shillings. I was present myself, and I remember to have felt quite uncomfortable and confused, at a part of myself being disposed of in that way. The caul was won, I recollect, by an old lady with a hand-basket. . . . It is a fact which will be long remembered as remarkable down there, that she was never drowned, but died triumphantly in bed, at ninety-two."
—from *David Copperfield* by Charles Dickens

---

4. A common abbreviation for Vorkudlak.

Good days, bad days

▶ The day on which a child is born impacts everything from astrology to damnation. In a number of countries being born on a holy day was seen as an insult to God. (As if the child or the mother had a choice!)

▶ Being born on a Saturday—the biblically dictated day of rest—was also viewed as an insult. The Ustrel of Bulgaria, for example, is a person damned to an unlife of vampirism for daring to be born on the Sabbath. Conversely, in Greece, a person born on that day is destined to fight evil. (See the entry on the Sabbatarian in chapter 4.)

Oh, baby

▶ This one is really disturbing. In India, the Philippines, Southeast Asia, and a few other places, a stillborn child is believed to linger on Earth as a vampire—either a bloodsucker or some kind of essential vampire. The Pontianak of Java and Malaysia is one such tragic monster; others include the Bajang and Langsuir of Malaysia, the Ekimmu of Assyrian and Mesopotamian belief, the Ohyn of Poland, and the Pret of India.

▶ In many of the same countries the mother of the dead child is likewise doomed, particularly if she dies during childbirth.

Repent, sinners!

▶ One of the most reliable ways for a person to become a vampire is to die unrepentant. Many cultures hold this to be the case, and it's particularly true if the sinner dies while engaged in a violent act, or dies as a result of violence.

▶ Suicides are also damned souls, according to Western beliefs. A suicide is doomed to return as a ghost or a vampire, or some unpleasant combination of the two.

▶ Murder victims are also in trouble. Dying by any kind of violence apparently tethers the soul to this world as a pernicious spirit of one kind or another.

Christa Campbell, *Vampire and Hunter*

"As an actress I love exploring both dark and light characters because it's part of our human nature. Though . . . at the end of the day I prefer to see good win over evil."
—Christa Campbell has appeared in *2001 Maniacs*, *The Wicker Man*, and *Blood: A Butcher's Tale*.

▶ A person who dies craving revenge sometimes gets the chance by rising from the grave.

If you have to do it over, you have time to do it right the first time

▶ Improper burial rites are tied to the creation of many species of vampires, such as the Callicantzaro of Greece, the Mrart of Australia, the Chindi of the Navajo, the Doppelsauger of Germany, the Langsuir of Malaysia, the Nelapsi of Czechoslovakia, the Tenatz of Bosnia, the Kathakano of Crete, and the Pret, Churel, and Gayal of India.

▶ Burial customs take two forms: those that honor the dead and those that protect the living against the dead. Most folks are familiar with the former, but the latter procedures are even more crucial, especially in areas where vampirism has been known to flourish. Preventative steps include:

- binding the limbs of a corpse so that it cannot move.
- burying a corpse upside-down so that it faced hell rather than heaven. (Very likely this came about when it was generally viewed that the world was flat and that heaven and hell were physical places. Otherwise we'd have vampires tunneling through the earth to the other side. Jules Verne could have had fun with that.)
- chopping the body into pieces and wrapping each piece in a separate shroud. (Granted this seems excessive, but there are no reports of pieces rising from the grave, so take that for what it's worth.)
- cremating the body. Fire not only purifies, it simplifies.
- driving long nails through the limbs of the dead to further immobilize it.
- filling the coffin with splinters of hawthorn or other rose-wood.
- laying a sprig of holly on the throat of the corpse.
- placing sickles or scythes near the grave to frighten off the evil spirits that sought to possess the corpse. Though . . .

how an edged farm tool was supposed to harm a noncorporeal spirit is anyone's guess.

- placing a block of wood between the teeth to prevent the newly awakened vampire from chewing his way out . . . or chewing on his own flesh in order to gain enough strength to burst free from the coffin.
- placing a coin in the mouth to pay the toll across the River Styx. A very Greek practice.
- placing a wax cross and piece of pottery with the inscription "Jesus Christ conquers" in the coffin.
- placing garlic in the coffin.
- placing pictures of family members in the coffin to remind the dead of love and family honor.
- placing pictures of saints in the coffin to remind the corpse of its obligation to faith.
- putting the deceased's shoes on the wrong feet so that they will become confused when they try to walk.
- using a metal coffin and sealing it with melted lead.

BATS OF A FEATHER . . .

Even though most vampires are not identical there are certain themes that pop up in different cultures—and not always in cultures where one can easily trace the flow of information through the expansion of population or the exchange of information. The sheer coincidence of these similarities makes for wonderfully creepy speculation. If vampires from the ancient culture of China and the pre–Marco Polo Europe share similarities it makes us go "Hmmmmm—how is that possible?"

For example, there are a lot of connections between vampire subtypes and counting. Vampires around the world seem to possess an obsessive compulsive need to count items found on the ground. In Europe they love to count seeds, in South America it's straw, in China it's rice. Go figure.

Some of these similarities are a little easier to understand, such as pallor and a foul stench, both of which are typical of dead bodies and decaying flesh.

Eighteenth-and nineteenth-century folklore influenced and was influenced by emerging pop culture. Writers of the era began tossing bloodsuckers into poems, plays, short stories, art, and novels, starting with Heinrich August Ossenfelder's poems "The Vampire" (1748) and "Lenore" (1773); and then spreading like a literary plague with Johann Wolfgang von Goethe's "Die Braut von Corinth" ("The Bride of Corinth," 1797), and works by Samuel Taylor Coleridge, Lord Byron, John Polidori, Sheridan le Fenau, Bram Stoker, and many others.[5]

Most of these writers added new elements to the story—as writers will—to build mystery and suspense, to elevate the level of threat, and to set the stage for new dimensions of heroism on the part of the protagonists. As a result some of the more romantic elements of the vampire story have been either amped up or introduced to an audience who more or less viewed fiction as being directly based on reality. This genuinely confused the issue of what is and is not a vampire, particularly from the European view, and as the film industry blossomed, that view became the most common take globally.

Those vampire qualities that best suited the needs of dramatic storytelling got more play. For example, a large percentage of vampire movies and books uses a vampire's inability to cast a reflection as a nice trick for establishing that a person is actually a vampire. Notable moments include the ballroom scene in *The Fearless Vampire Killers* (1967) and the disco scene in *Fright Night* (1985). However, the lack of reflection is fairly rare in folklore and is usually tied to those species of vampire who are actually ghosts rather than reanimated corpses.

The connection between vampires and mirrors, though mostly fictional, is grounded in older beliefs, however. In many cultures it was believed that the soul is somehow projected out of the physical body and can be glimpsed in reflective surfaces. The superstition of bad luck resulting from a broken mirror came from the belief that breaking one's reflection damaged one's own soul. In some cases the soul became outraged that its physical counterpart would

5. For more on the history of vampire fiction see *They Bite: Endless Cravings of Supernatural Predators.*

allow the mirror image to be broken and would punish that person with bad luck.

The ancient Romans, who were the first people to develop glass mirrors, believed that the entire human body was completely renewed every seven years; hence their attachment to the belief in seven years of bad luck for breaking the image of the current body. In other cultures the length of time varied from seven hours all the way to seven generations of the family line.

According to some of the movies, vampires cannot cross running water. The myths suggest that running water is symbolic of self-renewing purity and therefore an impure thing cannot cross it. In the Christopher Lee flick *Dracula Prince of Darkness* (1966), the titular count falls through a break in a patch of ice and the rushing water beneath kills him. Sounds great until you think of all the streams, rivers, and oceans that have been crossed by bandits, murderers, and whole armies of pillaging brigands. And, let's face it, Dracula came to England by ship. Lots and lots o' running water.

There are several vampires who actually live *in* water. The Kappa of Japan and the Animalitos of Spain are water-dwelling demon-vampires, as are the Green Ogresses of France.

Sunlight is one of the elements of vampirology that has almost completely emerged from pop culture. In folklore, and indeed in most vampire fiction prior to the early twentieth century, vampires were night hunters but could walk around in daylight without harm. The Upierczi of Poland, for example, rises at noon and hunts until midnight. The Bruja of Spain lives a normal life by day and only becomes a vampire at night, as do the Soucouyan of Dominica and the Loogaroo of Haiti. It wasn't until F.W. Murnau's 1922 silent film, *Nosferatu: A Symphony of Horror*, that sunlight became fatal to vampires. Thereafter it became a staple of vampire fiction to the point that people generally believe that all vampires always fear sunlight—despite the fact that Dracula strolls around in daylight in Stoker's novel, *Dracula*. It's a clear sign that more people have seen the movies than read the book.

Oddly enough, the Chiang-shih vampire of Chinese myth *does* fear sunlight. It's also one of the few vampires that take the form of a wolf and cannot cross running water. In these ways this Asian monster more closely fits the pop fiction model than do the many vampires of Europe. Go figure.

On the subject of vampire strength, nearly all of the sources—from folklore to the most current direct-to-video fang flick—seem to agree: they are stronger than humans. Nearly all of them are at least twice as strong as a human, and some are a great deal stronger. The Draugr of Scandinavia, for example, is a vampiric ghost that inhabits and reanimates the bodies of dead Viking warriors, creating a monster so strong that no weapon can harm it. The Chiang-Shih of China actually entertain themselves by ripping their victims limb from limb with their bare hands, as do the Callicantzaros of Greece and the Czechoslovakian Nelapsi. That strength gives vampire hunters serious pause, and significantly increases the difficulty of confronting one. Fair fights aren't a major theme in supernatural folklore.

Some vampires do not need physical strength to kill their victims. The Jigarkhwar of India and the Russian Eretica both possess lethal stares. Conversely, the Aswang vampire of the Philippines is best defeated by engaging it in a staring contest and waiting until it backs down and slinks away.

The method by which a person becomes a vampire is also in some dispute. The idea of trading blood—a vampire must bite its victim and then offer its own blood—was started in *Dracula* and is now popularly believed to be the case. Not so, however. For the most part, all that is required for a person to become one of the undead is to die in a horrible fashion—violent deaths, suicides, hangings, battlefield deaths, murders, stillbirths, death during delivery, death by plague, and so on. Being born under a curse can also lead to a vampiric life, including being born with teeth, born with a caul, born between Christmas and the New Year, being born out of wedlock, being a seventh son or daughter, or even being born on Christmas day. In some rare cases a person returns from the dead if they were bitten by a vampire, without having had to drink the vampire's blood. In more than a few cases, if a werewolf dies it comes back as a vampire. That's not something seen in movies, which is a shame because it makes for a nice and very frightening twist.

Another power that vampires possess that is never addressed in

Vampire Tunnel

Built in 1918 by British soldiers, Vampire Tunnel lies deep below the ground near Ypres, Belgium. According to Andrew Curry in his article "Under the Western Front" (*Archaeology Magazine*, July/August 2009), "no one is sure why World War I mapmakers named the dugout after the bloodsucking creature of the night, but it may have had something to do with the pale, silent soldiers who crept out of the tunnels under the cover of darkness." Intended to house troops, the dugout was never completed; the Germans attacked and captured Vampire Tunnel before the British could make use of it.

movies or books, but is extremely common to vampires around the world, is the spread of disease. Vampires are frequently plague carriers, and either infect with their bite or carry with them a pervasive air of pestilence that can wither humans, livestock, and crops. After all, the dreaded word "nosferatu" means "plague carrier."

FIEND FINDING

Identifying the resting place of a vampire is a crucial skill for vampire hunters. Not all of the world's vampire species are undead Einsteins. Most are mindless or near mindless monsters that rest in their graves because they lack the imagination to book a room in Motel 6, or because they are compelled to do so for some reason tied to their supernatural nature. In either case, they are fairly easy to find. Or are they? Most cemeteries have a number of fresh graves. Hopefully not all of them contain vampires. Digging up every dead body in order to drive stakes or lop off heads is likely to result in some violent resistance on the part of disgruntled relatives. Can't blame them. Furthermore, not all vampiric attacks are perpetrated by vampires who have risen from the dead. Folklore is filled with stories of vampires who are not actually dead or were never human beings.

On the other hand, in regions where revenants are common, the graveyard is a good place to start. In such cases there are several useful ways to locate the correct grave. Here are some examples:

Grave concerns

- ▶ Leading a white horse through a cemetery will result in the horse reacting violently to a grave where evil lies. In Europe this method required a white stallion, and sometimes a stallion that is still a virgin.
- ▶ Another variation requires that a virgin human (generally a teenage girl, and occasionally nude[6]) rides a white horse through a graveyard.
- ▶ An Eastern European version has the vampire hunter leading a virgin boy through the graveyard. And there are lots of variations of the whole virgin/graveyard thing.
- ▶ In some Western European countries the horse doesn't need to be a virgin (or bearing one) but it does need to be black. In Albania, however, it definitely has to be white.
- ▶ Discovering open ditches, holes, or other disturbances of the ground are viewed as suspicious. They might be the routes by which monsters travel from the grave to the surface world.
- ▶ In parts of the Appalachians, dead birds found around a grave will indicate evil, especially if they are carrion birds.
- ▶ Conversely, in Asia, the presence of live birds around a grave indicate that a monster is in residence.

He looks so natural

- ▶ The appearance of a corpse is often a tip-off. For example, disinterred bodies that are flushed and healthy looking are considered to be well-fed vampires.
- ▶ Ditto for corpses with blood on their mouths.
- ▶ A body that shows no signs of normal decomposition is another red flag.

---

6. A sociologist would have a field day with that particular variation.

Necrolysis

There is a likely medical basis for corpses having a ruddy or healthy appearance. It's a phase of decomposition called "necrolysis," which is the separation or exfoliation of necrotic tissue, often leading to a temporarily ruddy appearance to dead flesh.

Vampire CSI

▸ The presence of a vampire in the neighborhood can be deduced by the signs of its predation. Typical evidence would be bite marks that are too large to have been made by bats or other animal predators.

▸ The unexpected death of livestock is regarded worldwide as being unnatural. Though, to be fair to vampires, there are a lot of monsters in world folklore that prey on animals.

▸ Crop failures have long been attached to vampire beliefs, particularly if the poor harvest is the result of plant blight.

▸ Disease outbreaks in humans have also been associated with vampires for many centuries. Remember, the frequently used label for vampire—nosferatu—means "plague carrier."

MAKING THE DEAD DEADER

So, how do you kill a vampire?

In most legends and popular tales, vampires are hunted by Joe Ordinary rather than a professional. It's the family of a risen vampire who usually has the burden of disposal. Or villagers (with or without pitchforks and torches).

However there were—and are—people who claim to be professional vampire hunters. These pros vary from clerics, for whom fighting all manner of evil is an expected part of the job; to people whose destiny aims them at the undead; to half-vampire offspring with a real case of parental resentment.

If the nature of the vampire is frequently misunderstood and the qualities of a vampire vary from region to region and culture to culture, the problem of knowing how to kill them becomes extraordinarily tricky.

THE UNKINDEST CUT

Beheading is a fan favorite, and it doesn't require a sanctified sword or sacred axe. Anything with a heavy blade and a sharp edge will git 'er done. When in doubt, decapitate.

The trick, of course, is getting close enough to a vampire to swing a sword or an axe. Many vampires are enormously strong and unnaturally fast. Most vampire hunters are content to wait until the vampire is asleep and helpless in its grave before playing slice and dice.

A few vampires are not vulnerable to the blade, however. Notable among them is the Draugr, a demonic spirit that enters the grave of a fallen Viking, inhabits its flesh, and then rises as a virtually indestructible monster. The creature is immune to any weapon. Only a hero whose heart is pure and is in good standing with the gods of Valhalla can stand up to the Draugr with any hope of victory, let alone survival. But the hero needs to defeat and destroy the monster in empty-handed combat.

WELL—THAT STINKS!

Many cultures ascribe spiritual qualities to garlic (*allium sativum*). Most often garlic is held to be something good and wholesome, and true to its use in herbology, it's used as a blood purifier. It has antibacterial and antiparasitic qualities, and there is solid thought that these attributes could prevent the kinds of infections that lead to delusions and other psychosis related to disease.

In variations on the vampire-destroying ritual of Exorcism, garlic is usually placed in the mouth of the monster in order to purify the connection between the flesh and the spirit, which thereby eliminates tainted spiritual energy.

However there's an early Christian belief that when Satan left Eden, garlic plants grew from his left footprints and onion from the right. In Islamic beliefs, the Koran says: "Whoever eats onions,

Jason Beam, Eternal Empress

"This piece is *Eternal Empress*, and features supermodel Christy Hemme. Christy is a very power person who exemplifies the qualities of beauty, strength, and intensity. I can think of no better qualities for a vampire queen. And, perhaps no more frightening qualities as well." —Jason Beam is a photographer, artist, and illustrator.

garlic or leeks should not go to the mosque because his breath may disturb the angels and the people."

Garlic's protective qualities, however, far outweigh any occasional connection to evil. In fact, garlic is used as a protection against many kinds of evil throughout Europe and Asia, and is hung on doorways and windows to ward off vampires, werewolves, evil witches, ghosts, and demons. In Bavaria, for example, the Blautsauger is kept from entering a house by smearing the windows and doors with mashed garlic. In some countries, including Bavaria, garlic paste is lathered onto livestock to keep them safe from vampiric attack.

WHAT ABOUT A POINTED STICK?

The stake through the heart business is a tricky one because it does appear in folktales of vampires from all over the world, but it is not used to kill the undead. Despite the quick, clean "dustings" shown on *Buffy the Vampire Slayer*, or the bloody stakings in so many vampire films, the stake was not generally a weapon used to actually destroy a vampire[7] but a tool in a more elaborate exorcism. In cases of ritual destruction of a vampire, a stake (of wood or metal) was driven through the body (chest, stomach, wherever) of a resting vampire. This did not end the vampire's life (or un-life) but rather pinned the vampire either to its coffin or to the ground, preventing it from rising. Once restrained in this fashion, the vampire slayers would decapitate the creature, often filling the mouth with garlic. The corpse was then either re-interred or burned. It is the decapitation and burning, not the staking, that does the job.

BURN, BABY, BURN

There are few constants in vampire disposal, though by far the great majority of the world's many vampiric creatures fear fire, and that puts a new topspin on the adage that "fire cleanses." Fire destroys the physical remains to such a degree that there is nothing

---

7. The Kozlak of Dalmatia is the only vampire that will perish from a staking.

substantial left to reanimate. And it's widely believed that even hellish evil is destroyed so long as it is burned while inside a reanimated human body.

Like most aspects of monster hunting, incineration has been frequently ritualized. In the Czech Republic, for example, when the vampiric Nelapsi is burned, the ashes are spread over fields and along roads as a final charm against evil. In Romania, the ashes of a destroyed Strigoi are mixed with water and fed to the members of the Strigoi's surviving human family to cure them of any sickness or evil taint. Here are some other variations on fire as a weapon against evil.

Need fire: This custom, also known as "wildfire," appears throughout Europe. To begin the process all of the other fires in a village are extinguished and a new fire is ignited by the ages-old tradition of rubbing two sticks together or using the rope-and-stake method. The new spark is blessed according to local traditions, some of which are not exactly textbook Christian, and many of which significantly predate the Christian era. Once the fire is burning, all other candles, torches, and cookfires are lit from it, either directly or in a kindle-down-the-lane method. In this way all of the fire in the village starts from the same source. The need fire is used to ignite a bonfire in the center of a field on which green branches and leaves have been thrown to produce a thick and visible smoke. If there is a blight on the livestock that is believed to be of supernatural origin, then all of the livestock are walked through the smoke. In most cases the villagers walk through the smoke as well, thereby receiving a purifying blessing. If it is discovered that a single fire burned in the village that was not started by this fire, then the magic fails, and in some cases invites more and terrible evil into the village. This is a serious offense. A need fire created in the small village of Quedlinburg, Leipzig, in 1855 was spoiled by a small night candle left burning in the local parsonage. Even smoke from a cigar or a pipe lit by a match is enough to spoil the effect.

Bone fire: A variation of this ritual involves cremating any livestock believed to be infected by a vampire, or even the bones of a vampire itself. Or, lacking the actual monster, then effigies of evil things such as vampires, witches, and werewolves are thrown into the fire. The body is completely burned, with the blaze stoked until even the toughest bones are reduced to ash. This type of sacrifice actually gave the blaze its name: bone fire (though over the years the name has been bastardized to the more common "bonfire"). In a ritual similar to the need fire, once this fire has burned down and cooled, the villagers will quickly walk through the smoky ashes, purifying themselves of any taint of evil. Livestock and even family pets are likewise driven through the ashes to remove any taint of evil from each living thing in the village. A small part of the fire is kept aside and allowed to burn, and when everyone has passed through the ashes, embers or tapers from this special fire are carried to each person's home and used to reignite the hearth fires. Then the ember is extinguished and kept as a talisman against evil. The remaining ashes from the bonfire are scattered along the roads as a final defense against supernatural forces. In some cases, the ashes of a torched vampire are mixed with pure water and given to members of the vampire's living family as protection against a similar fate.

- ▸ Variations on need fires and bone fires abound, though often the direct connection between the blaze and the spiritual protection afforded to the people is not consciously considered. For many, a bonfire is a place to party; and yet the shared experience takes us back to some tribal bonding ritual that is itself a defense against the unknown.

- ▸ Common fire rituals include:
  - *January 6.* Bonfires are lit to celebrate the Epiphany day. Straw witches dressed in old clothes are thrown into the fire to ward off evil and remove it from the community.
  - *January 6.* The last day of the Icelandic Christmas season sees bonfires lit for good luck and prosperity.
  - *April 30.* The residents of Limerick, Ireland, build bonfires to celebrate Beltane, the day that marks the midpoint in the sun's progress between the spring equinox and summer solstice. Since the Celtic year was based on both lunar and solar cycles, it is possible that the holiday was celebrated on the full moon nearest the midpoint between the spring

equinox and the summer solstice.[8] Though this celebration is primarily held in Limerick, it was originally widespread throughout the Celtic lands and there is some movement to restore it to common practice.

- *May 1.* On a more mundane level, Slovenians build bonfires on this date to celebrate Labor Day.
- *June 21.* On midsummer's night eve, a pagan event is celebrated with a bonfire in honor of the summer solstice.
- *June 23.* In Denmark, the bonfires are held on the night of June 23, combined with the burning of a witch made from straw and clothes.
- *June 24.* On the celebration of the solemnity of John the Baptist (holy day in the liturgical calendar that begins with the vigil on the evening before the actual date of a feast in celebration of Jesus or a saint), and on Saturday night before Easter, bonfires are lit throughout continental Europe. A similar festival, known as "Bonfire Night," is held on June 23 in Ireland and other Celtic countries.
- *October 31.* In Ireland bonfires blaze in celebration of Halloween.
- *November 5.* England lights up on Guy Fawkes Night (also known as Bonfire Night, Cracker Night, Fireworks Night, Bonny Night), the annual celebration of the foiling of the Gunpowder Plot in 1605 that nearly resulted in the blowing up of the Houses of Parliament, in London, England. It's celebrated by blowing a lot of (smaller) things up . . . and by setting lots of fires. Funny Old World.
- *December 31.* Iceland celebrates the coming of the New Year with a good luck bonfire.
- *Bon-bi.* Bonfires lit throughout Japan to welcome the return of the spirits of the ancestors, to encourage them to linger in order to offer protection and guidance.
- *The eve of Lag Ba'Omer.* Bonfires are lit throughout Israel to celebrate Sefirat Ha'Omer (or, the Counting of the

---

8. The precise astronomical date for this is closer to May 5 or May 7, but this varies from year to year.

Omer), which is a verbal counting of each of the forty-nine days between the Jewish holidays of Passover and Shavuot.

▸ *Lohri:* In the Indian state of Punjab, the festival of Lohri is held to celebrate the victory of good over evil. Men and women perform Giddha and Bhangra, popular Punjabi folk dances, around a bonfire. Children go from house to house singing songs, and people reward them with gifts of money and food. The revelers build bonfires, then go three times around the blaze, giving offerings of popcorn, peanuts, rayveri, and sweets. Then, to the beat of dhol (the traditional Indian drum), people dance around the fire.

▸ *Bhogali Bihu:* In Assam, a state in northern India, the Bhogali Bihu harvest festival is celebrated to mark the end of the winter paddy harvest. On the night before the festival, people fast and pray, and thatched pavilions are put up around the countryside. As a sign of the festival having begun, the pavilions are set on fire at dawn.

GOING FORMAL

Throughout Europe (and indeed much of the world) there is a formal method of disposing of vampires called the Ritual of Exorcism. There are scores of variations on this ritual; but the basic plan works like this:

▸ The vampire hunter is accompanied by at least one able-bodied assistant (and ideally by a bunch of tough guys with sharpened staves, torches, axes, and other useful weapons).

▸ Once the resting place of a vampire is located, the tomb or grave is opened.

▸ As soon as the monster is exposed, one or more of the assistants use long stakes or sharpened staves, preferably of hawthorn, to pierce the body and pin it to the ground or against the bottom of the coffin. The stakes do not kill the vampire, though the hawthorn—which is believed to have positive spiritual qualities—renders the monster temporarily helpless. A long stake is driven through the vampire's body, pinning it to the coffin or to the ground. This stake does not need to pierce the heart; and most species of rosewood are believed to have a similar effect.

▸ The lead vampire hunter usually steps in at this time and cuts off the vampire's head with a sword, axe, bone saw, or anything else that will get the job done.

▸ Fresh garlic is stuffed into the vampire's mouth and sprinkled liberally throughout the coffin. The purifying qualities of the garlic break the bonds between the demonic possessing spirit and flesh.

▸ The arms and legs of the corpse are bound to prevent movement.

▸ A corncob, block of wood, or other object is used to prop open the vampire's mouth so that it cannot bite.

▸ Long needles are driven through the extremities of the vampire to further immobilize the creature.

▸ The coffin is resealed and buried again.

▸ If, somehow, the vampire rises again, then the vampire hunters dig up the corpse and burn it to ash. That usually does it, but it's a last result because not all cultures or religions permit cremation.

Brinke Stevens, *Vampire Lovers*

Actress Brinke Stevens has been a fan favorite "Scream Queen" and has appeared in scores of horror films, sometimes as the enemy of evil and sometimes as a creature of the night.

Identifying a vampire is only part of the problem, and it's the smallest part. The real challenge is getting rid of the monster. Sadly, vampires are a bit harder to kill than movies would have us believe. Deus ex machina doesn't get much play in folklore. Vampires don't conveniently fall into icy streams or trip over their capes and land on jagged pieces of wood that just happen to be lying about.[1]

Besides, as we've learned, most of the Hollywood methods of disposal don't work. So, when you have to do a job right, you call a pro.

MEET THE PROS

Batak: Centuries ago the vampire species known as the Pontianak flourished on the isle of Sumatra, as well as in Malaysia and Java; nowadays they are all but extinct thanks to a kind of witch doctor/vampire hunter called a Batak. The Batak has the power to reclaim the soul of a person lost to vampirism, a feat accomplished through prayer and the use of rare herbal medicines.

The Batak blends precise amounts of special herbs and garlic into a broth, praying over it as it comes to a full boil. The concoction is then forced down the vampire's throat and it has the virtue of forcing the separation of all that is natural from anything unnatural, and thus the demonic spirit is cast out and the human soul is allowed to once more take possession of the body. Other medicines and rituals are then used to restore the victim to normal health.

The Batak uses a similar ritual if a person has been killed by a vampire. The corpse will not be returned to life, but the victim's immortal soul can return to its body and can thus be properly buried in sacred ground.

The Batak also gives advice or prepares medicines to combat other physical or spiritual maladies, including a treatment to allow a barren woman to conceive and safely carry a baby to term. This

1. And isn't it odd that movie vampires never fall onto wood and impale their arms or legs or stomachs? It's always the heart. Very convenient.

is especially important if it's believed that the woman is barren as a result of a curse or negative supernatural influence.

Dhampyr (also **Dhampir**, **Dhampire**, **Svetocher**, etc.): Some people are born lucky, some are as far from that as is possible to get. The Dhampyr of Gypsy legend is a prime example. The Dhampyr is the offspring of a mating between a vampire and a human. Unions of that kind only end happy in fiction, never in folklore. The Dhampyr is a cursed being. He is destined to relentlessly hunt evil, a job that is as hazardous as it sounds. And although the Dhampyr is born with some supernatural abilities, he is also doomed to die young, and to die painfully as his bones slowly disintegrate into a gelatinous goo that ultimately collapses.

The Dhampyr's powers vary according to different folktales. In most, however, he has the ability to sense evil and is thus able to seek it out, even when the source of evil is an evil ghost. One of the Dhampyr's most common enemies is the Mullo, a vampire-ghost with enormous dark powers that include the spreading of blight and plague, the destruction of harmony, the encouragement of sinful behavior, and the ability to drain life essence from its victims.

Since the Dhampyr is unable to live a normal life, he travels from town to town seeking out evil, but in order to survive he charges for his extermination services. Once employed, the Dhampyr uses his psychic powers to locate the unseen monster, at which point the Dhampyr begins a strange ritual dance during which he uses sharp whistles and strange body movements to lure and then engage the Mullo. The Mullo remains unseen during all of this, so all that the villagers see is the Dhampyr twitching, whistling, and moaning. There has, of course, been speculation that this is all based either on a misunderstanding of epilepsy or outright chicanery. Even so, Dhampyrs have been active even into the twentieth century. The last known professional killing by a Dhampyr was reported in 1959, in the Yugoslavian province of Kosovo.

Djadadjii: The Djadadjii is a professional monster hunter from Bulgaria and neighboring lands who specializes in vampires who take the form of spirits or poltergeists. The Djadadjii's most common enemy is the fierce krvoijac, a vampire created when a person dares to smoke tobacco or drink alcohol during Lent. Forty days after burial, the sinner's bones melt and then reform into the unholy form of the Krvoijac. The forty-day resurrection is thought to be Satan's perverse mockery of the forty days Jesus wandered in the wilderness before beginning his ministry, which itself is the basis for the forty days of Lent. This new body is immortal unless ritually killed, and possessed of enormous physical strength. The Krvoijac smashes its way out of its coffin and tears apart the grave in order to escape. In appearance it's much like the traditional revenant: pale rotting flesh, sunken eyes, and horrible breath.

When a Krvoijac is believed to be in the vicinity, a Djadadjii is called in. The Djadadjii baits a trap for a spirit-vampire by placing the vampire's favorite food in a bottle to lure it in, then uses religious icons and casting spells to draw the vampire's spirit into the bottle. Once the vampire is trapped therein, the Djadadjii throws the bottle into a fire to destroy the creature. Once this has been accomplished, the monster's human remains, some of which are still in the grave, resume ordinary form and continue with the regular process of decomposition. The village is safe, and the Djadadjii heads off to find other monsters to fight.

Glog: In and around Bulgaria vampire hunters in general are often called Glogs. It comes from the local word for "hawthorn," the wood favored by vampire slayers for their stakes.

Kresnik (also **Krsnik**): Like the Dhampyr, the Kresnik of Serbia, Bosnia, and Slovenia, and the Croatian peninsula of Istria, is born to be an enemy of evil; however, this unnatural birth has an even more unnatural twist. The Kresnik has an evil counterpart: the Kudlak. Children of that region born with a caul are destined to become one or the other. Such children are watched closely because it is rarely clear which path in life they will take: good or evil.

The term "Kresnik" is drawn from the root word krat, meaning "cross." Kudlak is likely an abbreviation of the southern Slavic word, *vorkudlak*, a general term for vampires in that region.

Both Kudlak and Kresnik possess vast supernatural powers: they can shape-shift into various beasts, and even become birds and fly.

The unfortunate whose path leads them to the dark ways of the Kudlak will grow up with evil alive in his heart and will do all manner of harm while still a living being. Even if that person leads a normal and sinless existence during the day, at night the soul of this tainted being will leave the body and roam the night wind in the shape of a locust, night bird, bat, or a wolf, attacking the innocent, sometimes killing outright, sometimes amusing itself by maiming or tormenting its victims. The Kudlak can also cast spells over the community, resulting in crop failures, bad weather, stillbirths, and other calamities.

When the living Kudlak finally dies (whether naturally or through violence), it will rise again as an undead revenant, a true vampire. Then the real reign of terror will begin.

If fate chooses to let a person born with a caul become a kresnik, his destiny will be to become a champion and protector of his people. He, too, can leave his body and adopt the form of an animal or a bird, but his sole purpose is to seek out the Kudlak and destroy it in any of its evil guises. The Kresnik is fierce and strong and can confront the Kudlak in either its living or undead form.

The popular Slavic legend of the brothers Mutimirov is a classic tale of the struggle between these two supernatural beings. The children were both born with cauls over their faces. One brother, Matej, was born an hour before midnight on a Saturday. His twin, Dmitar, was born nearly three hours later, early Sunday morning. The boys looked identical, acted the same, and were both raised to be millers like their father, Mutimir. When the boys reached puberty, Matej began straying from his duties and constantly argued with the elders of the family. His aunts, both of whom were old and wise, believed that Matej was beginning to display signs of spiritual corruption, and they feared that he would become a Kudlak. Eventually he became so wild that he was sent away to live with a relative, a harsh man named Ninoslav who was asked to put the fear of God into the boy.

Meanwhile Dmitar grew to be a very quiet and respectful young man. He worked hard alongside his father, fell in love, and married. His brother, Matej, was allowed to come home for the wedding, but was made to sleep in the barn rather than the main house.

A week after Dmitar was married his wife was found murdered, her body drained of blood and showing signs of great violence.

Matej was immediately arrested for the crime and thrown into jail pending the arrival of a priest-exorcist.

But once the exorcist arrived and examined the young man he announced that Matej was the Kresnik and that his mannerly twin, Dmitar, was actually the Kudlak. The priest confronted Dmitar and his vampiric nature emerged. Dmitar attacked the priest and members of his own family. Only the timely arrival of Matej saved them from being killed.

Matej and Dmitar fought in the woods outside the village, and the fury of their battle uprooted trees and caused well water to boil. The battle lasted three nights, during which the moon was eclipsed three times and cows yielded blood instead of milk.

On the fourth day of battle, a few hours after midnight, Matej overcame Dmitar and staked him to the ground with a sharpened stave of hawthorn. The priest was able to perform the exorcism despite his injuries. It was completed just as Dmitar died, which meant that the young man's soul had been saved.

Matej became a hero to his people. His uncle Ninoslav was praised for having helped the boy find his true destiny, and together the uncle and the Kresnik traveled throughout the region seeking other vampires to destroy.

Sabbatarian and the Fetch Dog (also **Sabbatianoí** in Greece; **Sâbotnichav** in Bulgaria): In the Mediterranean, a Sabbatarian is a person born on a Saturday who has the power to cure illness, sense the presence of evil, and combat monsters in the physical and spiritual world. A handful of folktales of the region suggest that the sabbatarian is a kind of Dhampyr, the result of a human-vampire mating, but overall this doesn't seem to be the case.

The Sabbatarian is often accompanied by the Fetch Dog, a spirit that acts like a supernatural hunting hound. In some versions of the story the Fetch Dog is invisible, trotting through the spirit world to sniff out evil for its master; in other tales the dog is visible while the Sabbatarian is unseen. For this reason, stray dogs are seldom chased away or mistreated in the Greek isles; in fact they're often treated kindly and given food because it's possible they're helping to save the village or town from an unseen monster.

In some legends Sabbatarians are purported to eat meat from

sheep killed by a wolf as this is supposed to give them the courage to face the creatures they encounter. And they do need courage, because their most constant foe is the dreaded Vrykolaka.

The Vrykolaka is the most well-documented vampire in Greece and Macedonia. Legends of it persisted well into the nineteenth century. The Vrykolaka is a vampire created when a person has either committed suicide (a mortal sin resulting in damnation), or dies a violent death (resulting in an unquiet spirit filled with rage and confusion). A grossly immoral—or amoral—person was also a likely candidate for becoming this species of vampire.

The name "vrykolaka" loosely translates as "wolf-pelt," "wolf-skin," or "werewolf," which is odd since this species of vampire does not share any obvious qualities with werewolves.

The Vrykolaka gains vast powers as it grows older. It is very hard to identify, and few methods of destroying it are known. Oddly, it's the only known vampire species who can't enter a house uninvited. Instead, the creature stands outside and calls the name of its desired victim, hoping either for an invitation inside or for the person to come out. The monster possesses extraordinary charisma, which results in people making what seems like obvious blunders in personal safety and opening the door. Oops.

The Vrykolaka's method of attack is pretty damn direct: it leaps onto its victim, slams him to the ground, and then uses its own massive body to smother the unfortunate being. In some accounts the Vrykolaka is invisible and the victim merely feels a crushing weight on his chest. People who have escaped the vampire's attack describe symptoms very much like those of a heart attack: a great weight on the chest, shortness of breath, and pain.[2] Other reports describe the monster as a fierce blood drinker.

The people of the island of Chios in the Aegean Sea (reported to be the birthplace of the poet Homer) believe that placing a cross made from wax or cotton (or both) on the lips of a corpse can help prevent the corpse from becoming a Vrykolaka. A priest can increase

---

2. A likely link to "sleep paralysis," the probable basis of the Old Hag legend in which a (sometimes seen) force crushes the breath out of a sleeping person.

the odds of preventing the creation of a Vrykolaka by taking a shard of pottery, preferably from a bowl belonging either to the family of the deceased or to the local church, inscribing JESUS CHRIST CONQUERS on it, and burying it with the corpse.

Greek scholar and theologian Leone Allacci, also known as Leo Allatius (1586–1669), wrote extensively about the Vrykolakas in his treatise, *De Graecorum Hodie Quorundam Opinationibus*, Cologne 1645:

> The Vrykolaka is the body of a man of wicked and debauched life, very often one who has been excommunicated by his bishop. Such bodies do not, like other corpses, suffer decomposition after burial nor fall to dust, but having, so it seems, a skin of extreme toughness becomes swollen and distended all over, so that the joints can scarcely be bent; the skin becomes stretched like the parchment of a drum, and when struck gives out the same sound.
>
> This monster is said to be so fearfully destructive to men that it actually makes its appearance in the daytime, even at high noon, nor does it then confine its visits to houses, but even in the fields and in hedged vineyards and upon the open highway it will suddenly advance upon persons who are labouring, or travelers as they walk along, and by the horror of its hideous aspect it will slay them without laying hold on them or even speaking a word.

Strong and dangerous as it is, the Vrykolaka can be killed by dousing it with boiling water, a tactic that destroys its hunting senses of smell, touch, and sight. This method is used most often when trying to keep the creature from breaking into a house, or if one happens to discover the monster's resting place. The creature can also be crippled by driving a long nail through its stomach while it sleeps (attempting this method while it is awake is generally fatal to the would-be slayer). The nails must pierce the spine as well as the internal organs so the creature cannot rise to feed. If the coffin is weighted down with rocks the creature will soon starve to death and the evil demonic spirit will depart, leaving only a regular corpse behind.

Enter the Sabbatarian.

Once the Fetch Dog has sniffed out the presence of the monster in a village, the Sabbatarian begins a campaign to foil the creature.

Chad Michael Ward, *Unholy Trinity*

"What happens when the thing we place our trust and faith in becomes the very thing we fear? *The Unholy Trinity* gives us a dark view of what happens when religion becomes corrupted."
—Chad Michael Ward is a southern California–based artist and photographer.

He spreads birdseed outside of the doors and windows of any house believed to be targeted by the Vrykolaka. Often this results in the creature (with typical vampiric obsessive compulsive disorder) lingering to count every last seed. Place enough seeds and the process takes all night.[3] The Vrykolaka's powers diminish quickly if it doesn't feed. The Sabbatarian waits for the creature to become weakened and distracted, and then it attacks. To dispose of the monster, the Sabbatarian favors the brutal tactic of nailing it to the wall and letting it perish from hunger. Though no one can actually see the monster, there is usually a strong smell of rotting flesh after a couple of days.

Sometimes the Sabbatarian will lure the vampire with a trail of droplets of sheep's blood. He places a pile of dried mullet on the floor of the barn, and once the Vrykolaka is engaged in his obsessive counting, the Sabbatarian stabs it repeatedly and then nails it to the wall of the barn.

Sons of the Shepherd: At the height of the Holy Inquisition, a splinter group of clerics began hunting vampires under the blanket name of the Sons of the Shepherd. These vampire hunters carried hawthorn staves that were sharpened at one end and tipped with silver at the other. The silver tip was typically carved to resemble a shepherd's crook. Several of the Sons would use the sharpened ends to pin down a suspected vampire, while their leader would use the heavy silver shepherd's crook to bash the vampire's brains in. The Sons maintained that the silver's purity broke the tethers that bound the demonic spirit inside the vampire to the energies of hell. For each soul they "saved" via this method they claimed that a scar was carved onto Lucifer's flesh.

The Sons of the Shepherd were one of the rarest vampire-hunting groups and very little authenticated documentation can be found regarding them. If they lasted longer than a few years, then they managed to cover their tracks pretty well. That . . . or they ran afoul of some vampires who didn't like getting bashed by disgruntled former monks.

Vampirdzhija: The Vampirdzhija is both a general term for professional vampire hunters in Bulgaria and a specific kind of slayer. This more specific kind of Vampirdzhija is very similar to the

---

3. Some legends insist that the Vrykolaka counts the seeds at the rate of one per century. Even given the nature of most supernatural monster stories this just seems silly.

Djadadjii in that he possesses special abilities to locate evil, and carries holy icons useful for protection (of himself and the people under his charge). The Vampirdzhija is usually a monk skilled in magic—some of which is not precisely Christian. The Vampirdzhija is able to perform spells that enable him to see and detect vampires that no one else can perceive.

Legends tell of them squaring off against the Obour and the Ustrel, as well as other pernicious night hunters. Sometimes they are invisible, and at others they assume the appearance of children, but the Vampirdzhija isn't fooled. He can see through glamours and other spells and can use his magic to draw the creature into a specially prepared bottle, which is then thrown on a fire.

VAMPIRE HUNTERS IN POP CULTURE

"Why do people love vampires so much?" reflects bestselling author Rachel Caine. "I get asked that question fairly frequently, and it's one I struggle with. It helps to remember that vampires have traditionally been 'the monster under the bed,' something to be truly loathed and feared and destroyed; it's only once we began to put a truly human face to them and make them a reflection of aspects of our own personalities that we began to find them sympathetic. But now that we have, they tend to be great reflective mirrors of what we fear, or what we want—Dracula might have represented repressed Victorian sexuality, but what does the Hammer Films Dracula represent? I would argue the changing culture, which at the time was becoming more accepting and permissive of sexual issues. The spectrum kept broadening, making vampires both more monstrous on one hand (*30 Days of Night*), and heroic/romantic on the other (*Forever Knight, Moonlight*, the entire genre of vampire romance, including *Twilight* and its sequels). I love that there's so much variety available in that one odd storytelling niche."

So . . . if you're going to write about vampires or make flicks about the fang gang, you have to have some interesting and capable heroes in the mix. Bram Stoker set the bar pretty high with Abraham Van Helsing and his crew, but other writers, comic creators, and filmmakers have added nicely to the lineup of heroes who hunt these immortal monsters.

Professor Van Helsing: The most famous vampire hunter in fiction is the Dutch metaphysician Abraham Van Helsing, the wise curmudgeon who led the fight against Dracula. He is described by his student and protégé, Dr. Seward, in this way:

> He is a seemingly arbitrary man, this is because he knows what he is talking about better than anyone else. He is a philosopher and a metaphysician, and one of the most advanced scientists of his day, and he has, I believe, an absolutely open mind. This, with an iron nerve, a temper of the ice-brook, and indomitable resolution, self-command, and toleration exalted from virtues to blessings, and the kindliest and truest heart that beats, these form his equipment for the noble work that he is doing for mankind, work both in theory and practice, for his views are as wide as his all-embracing sympathy."
> —from *Dracula* by Bram Stoker, chapter 9

BUFFY THE VAMPIRE SLAYER

Pop culture icon Joss Whedon has made a career out of creating multifaceted and believable characters who face challenges that are never clear-cut choices between good and evil. The good guys face inner conflicts and often stray into darkness or have come from dark places and are struggling to deserve the right to walk in the light. His characters and stories are among the most potent influences on modern supernatural and science fiction storytelling. Foremost among these is Buffy Summers, a teenage girl who discovers to her dismay that she is destined (or perhaps fated) to be the embodiment of an ancient spirit that imbues her with enormous physical powers in order to fight evil. The character was first introduced in a mediocre 1992 movie over which Whedon had little creative control and then given a reboot in a brilliant TV series, *Buffy the Vampire Slayer* (1997 to 2003), which starred Sarah Michelle Gellar. Supported by a growing though motley crew of friends (unofficially dubbed the "Scooby Gang"), Buffy fought vampires, demons, aliens, robots, and all manner of evil. She even died a couple of times doing it, though it's hard to keep a good slayer down. When the series was canceled, Whedon authorized (and occasionally wrote) a follow-up series in comic book form.

The Buffy Effect

"Before *Buffy the Vampire Slayer* there was a real lack of quality supernatural or horror style programs on network television. By utilizing his own pop culture savvy writing style without ever looking down on either the audience or the genre, Joss Whedon managed to make the things that go bump in the night palpable to viewers that may never have watched a horror film before. Without *Buffy the Vampire Slayer*, there would be no *Supernatural* or *True Blood*."—Andy Burns is editor-in-chief of the pop culture website Biff Bam Pop! (www.biffbampop.com).

What marked this series was its blend of wacky pop culture–infused humor, deep and intelligent character development, and insightful storytelling that explored the big bad, the big good, and a whole lot of gray areas in between. Throughout the series, Whedon and the other writers pulled no punches when addressing issues of moral conflict, the challenge of redemption, and the burden of heroism—and this latter theme is never given a shallow coat of white paint. Being a hero is a bitch, especially when the big bad is so bad that often there is nothing to indicate that good will (or, indeed, can) triumph.

The show also presented episodes of such daring and storytelling integrity that they rose above virtually everything else on television (broadcast or cable). One of these, "The Body," explored the unbearable evil of ordinary human frailty by having a regular character die of natural causes. After having seen countless deaths by

The Whedon Touch

"These shows set the standard for exploring specific vampire culture. The Buffy characters learn to live with vampires—as a threat, and as a part of life. This really set the precedent for shows like *True Blood*, which explore vampires as an entity rather than simply employing them as a literary contrast to humanity or mortality."—Tara M. Clapper is a freelance writer.

vampire bite or demonic attack, the death by brain cancer, and the manner in which it was presented, was tremendously shocking and it leveled the playing field by showing that there are some things over which even the most powerful hero has no control. Absolutely brilliant.

Actor Chris Morse observes, "At the end of the series, when faced with an enemy that she can't defeat, Buffy enlists the aid of her best friend, Willow—a powerful Wiccan—to change the nature of the 'Slayer' destiny by awakening the same power in every girl on Earth who carries the potential of being the next Slayer. Suddenly Buffy has an army of Slayers, and they kick some serious undead ass. Joss Whedon's creations are almost single-handedly responsible for returning the vampire to the mainstream. Not only bringing the bloodsuckers back, but even altering the rules of vampirism and making those new rules standard. Nowadays can you even imagine a vamp being staked without it disintegrating into a puff of dust?"

Angel: Joss Whedon and David Greenwalt created a spin-off of *Buffy* that featured the character, Angel, an Irish vampire who had been one of the most feared and destructive monsters on Earth for more than a century but who is "cursed" by Gypsies who return his human soul to him so that he has to confront the reality and remorse of all the harm he's done. Angel (played by David Boreanaz) is tormented by remorse and retreats into solitude and suffering for decades before finally meeting and falling in love with

---

Supernatural Role Model

"Buffy brought a whole new meaning to what it was to be the underdog and still fight the good fight. Here you have a high school girl no more than 5' 2 with super strength and attitude who doesn't run from her problems but faces them head on. I feel it empowered young women to stand a little taller and to face the obstacles in their lives."—Chris Duffner is a diehard Buffy fan.

Dark Fantasy

"*Angel* has been a huge influence on the Dark Fantasy genre, maybe more so that *Buffy*. There have been a lot more supernatural detectives recently than young monster slayers."
—David Carroll has written gaming material for the Buffy, Demon, and All Flesh Must Be Eaten RPGs.

Buffy. Their love is so powerful that Angel rises to embrace a destiny he did not know was waiting for him: to be the champion who would stand against the forces of evil during the Apocalypse. The show lasted five seasons and, like *Buffy*, was continued in comic book form.

Spike: A supporting character in both the Buffy and Angel TV series, who was a vicious and murderous vampire for over a century and who became a significant enemy of Buffy. When Spike

Immortal Influences—The Buffy Effect

"The overall impact of Buffy and/or Angel—Buffy changed everything. I think the more distance we get between the end of that series and the present day, the more we forget just how much impact it had. Yes, Laurell K. Hamilton's influence was part of the foundation for the new urban fantasy movement, but Buffy was the true catalyst. My agent at the time was telling me, while I was working on Buffy novels, 'you've got to come up with your own spin on this,' but I didn't want to do it because it would have been so transparent, and obviously I'm much more interested in more personal and imaginative inspiration. But purely from a commercial standpoint, refusing to do that was foolish, because by the time the series ended, an entire generation of novelists had adopted Buffy as their inspiration. There's a great deal more to it than that, but the existence of urban fantasy as its own category really begins with Buffy."—Christopher Golden is the author of numerous Buffy and Angel books and comics (some with Amber Benson, who played Tara on *Buffy*).

(played by James Marsters) is captured by a secret anti-demon military unit called the Initiative and implanted with a chip that prevents him from attacking humans, the weakened Spike seeks out Buffy for protection and support. As he regains some of his power, he continues to work with Buffy and then falls in love with her. They begin a torrid and illicit affair, and when she ultimately rejects him because of his reemerging demonic nature, he undergoes a series of terrible trials in order to have his soul returned to him. Like Angel, Spike is a vampire with a soul; unlike Angel, Spike chose to have it restored to him, which is arguably a mark of greater nobility. Spike returns to fight alongside Buffy, and though they don't rekindle their love, they do forge a deep friendship. Spike dies saving Buffy and the whole world from an attack of super-vampires from a demon dimension. The world is saved, and Spike returns from death (though still as a vampire) to become an uneasy ally of Angel's.

Faith: Like Buffy Summers, Faith LeHane (Eliza Dushku) is a girl who was born with the potential to become the one true slayer and protector of Earth. When Buffy is killed (temporarily), another slayer is automatically empowered. The first new slayer after Buffy was Kendra, a Jamaican teenager, but she is killed by Drusilla, one of Buffy's most dangerous enemies. The death of Kendra activates the next in line, Faith. The thing is . . . Buffy was only dead for a few minutes, and so there are now two living slayers.

The character of Faith was all about moral conflict. Faith was the product of an abusive childhood and was emotionally and psychologically damaged and eventually strays into the dark side. She becomes a murderous agent of evil and opposes Buffy. In a deadly battle, Buffy defeats her (though it's a close call), and after lingering in a coma for months, Faith regains consciousness and goes to work as an assassin for Wolfram & Hart, an evil law firm based in Los Angeles. Her first target is Angel. In the hands of lesser writers, the character of Faith could easily have become just another sexy bad girl, but Whedon and company excelled in telling stories about the gray world between the moral poles. Faith attacks and tortures Angel's friends and tries to kill him, but Angel is able to fight her to a standstill and essentially allows Faith's inner conflict to be

Len Peralta, *Horrible Humor*

"I consider humor to be the best defense against all things horrible. I find it's more natural to laugh frightening things off, than to scream and cower in fear. I think about that whenever I am creating a new piece. By cushioning the macabre nature of the subject matter in a humorous, almost lighthearted approach, it allows the viewer to pull the hands away from their face and explore their fears more easily."—Len Peralta is an illustrator from Cleveland, Ohio, and the host of the weekly podcast Jawbone Radio.

the weapon that defeats her. Angel understands that the path to redemption is a rocky road—after all, he's one of the greatest mass murderers in history. Faith turns herself in to the police and goes to prison, willing to pay for the crimes she's committed.

However after a couple of years a massively powerful force rises to threaten the entire world, and Faith breaks out of prison to save the world, first by standing with Angel, and then by joining Buffy in a battle against the first evil—the being who invented the concept of evil.

Like Angel and Spike, Faith knows that even great acts of heroism are not quick fixes for having done great harm. She accepts that she will be working on her own redemption for a long time, possibly forever.

Willow and Tara: When we first meet Willow Rosenberg (played by Allyson Hannigan) she's a painfully shy teenage computer nerd whose most common social interaction is to be the butt of a cruel comment by the popular girls. In the Buffy series, Willow undergoes one of the most fascinating processes of change in all of pop culture. Over the course of seven years, the character discovers her own importance—not as a physically powerful hero, but (first) as a support system for Buffy, often providing crucial and timely information as well as friendship and moral support. Later, Willow begins experimenting with magic and witchcraft, and over the

---

What I Did for Love

"I don't think it always had to do with good or evil . . . I think it had to do with love. Buffy sends Angel to hell to prevent the Apocalypse and in doing so loses the love of her life. Willow goes mad with heartbreak at the loss of her beloved Tara and turns evil to exact revenge on Warren who had shot Tara. Faith turns evil and helps the mayor because he is the only person who ever treated her as something other than a tool to be used and discarded. Are each of these things good or evil? Put yourself in these shoes . . . does it make you bad for wanting to be loved?"
—Chris Duffner is a Buffy fan.

Vampire Chic

Lucienne Diver tackles the good and evil question from the point of view of character flaws. "Well, my heroine is a bit of an anti-hero really, at least at first. Gina calls herself the 'fashionista of the damned'—think the big-haired girl from high school with the reputation turned to the dark side by the class chess champ turned vampire hottie. Her priority at first has nothing to do with saving the world, but with finding a way not to go through eternity a total shlub. I really had fun knocking her off her social pedestal and watching her claw her way back to the top. In the process, she becomes more human than she ever was with a pulse. Gina manages to fight the vampire vixen turning her classmates into cannon fodder and trying to make time with her boyfriend and look great doing it. In a way I do tackle the theme of redemption, but Gina's still got a way to go before she's completely on the side of the angels."—Lucienne Diver is the author of the young adult novel *Vamped* (Flux, 2009).

---

course of the next couple of years blossoms as the most powerful witch on the planet, a course that leads her into dark places as she struggles with a destructive addiction to the "high" of being powerful. Willow also explores her conflicted sexuality and ultimately settles into a loving relationship with Tara (Amber Benson), an equally shy young woman she meets in college. Tara is also a witch, but not as powerful as Willow; however with a great deal more self-control.

The importance of these two characters extends well beyond the confines of the show, and they've become cult icons through novels, comics, and conventions. *Buffy* writer Christopher Golden shared his insights with us. "I don't think *Angel* has nearly the cultural importance that *Buffy* has. It was good, no doubt, but *Buffy* transcended the usual restrictions of television. Not only did it change pop culture, finally institutionalizing and normalizing the female-action-hero thing that *Terminator* and *Aliens* had begun, it changed the worldview of young women and girls who watched it . . . and of many boys as well. The fact that Buffy made the decisions, that even Giles—the father figure—and the other

Empowerment Through Evil

"Most of our films don't have clear-cut heroes and villains. *A Feast of Flesh* is a good example of this. We have vampires and vampire hunters, traditionally evil and good respectively, but in this film the vampires are the ones that help a confused young woman out of a bad situation to become a stronger person."
—Amy Lynn Best is a horror film actress, producer, and director.

males around her all deferred to her, that somehow worked on *Buffy* in a way it hadn't worked in other films and TV. It changed the way people looked at themselves. That may sound like hyperbole, but it isn't. In e-mail, at conventions, at book signings, I talked to these people, to young women, and heard it directly from them. And, of course, there's Willow and Tara. Young women struggling with their sexuality saw the acceptance of that relationship on *Buffy*, saw that it was presented as love, and it gave them peace. Many times, signing with Amber, I heard girls and young women tell her that she and Alyson Hannigan saved their lives. Several times, I saw crying women tell her that they had been thinking about suicide, and that Willow and Tara convinced them to live. Television did that. I don't think you can quantify that."

The Watchers Council: In the universe of Buffy (fans call it the Buffyverse), the slayers are taught, advised, guided, and studied by the Watchers Council, a group of humans who are devoted to fighting supernatural evil. Their mission is guided by the belief that there will always be one girl in all the world who would be born with the powers to be the slayer. The watchers try to locate all potential slayers and watch over them—sometimes from a distance, sometimes training them before they manifest as the active slayer.

Buffy Summer's watcher is Rupert Giles, a low-level sorcerer and former bad boy who became a rather stuffy and tweedy scholar. Giles also serves as a father figure for Buffy, and their relationship becomes a metaphor for the parent-child relationships, with all of the challenges and complexities inherent in that dynamic.

Rob McCallum, *Zombie*

"I think Zombies frighten people because the whole process of coming to terms with death excludes being prepared for a dead person to stand up and probably try and eat you. Being eaten is also something we find scary. The combination of walking dead and eating you seems to work well."—Rob McCallum is an internationally known award-winning storyboard, concept, and comic artist. He's worked on many horror films and has drawn many zombies.

Like all characters in the Buffyverse, the members of the Watchers Council are hardly squeaky clean, even when they are fighting for the right goal. Some of their methods are questionable and even vile, which nicely parallels the methods used by governments and military groups who are sometimes faced with finding ways to combat an enemy in battles where no rules apply. Whedon and company frequently explored the issue of how difficult it is to identify that invisible line in the sand that separates acceptable actions from those that are as morally polluted as the methods used by terrorists and criminals. This topic was never given an easy fix, and many of the questions were left unresolved—leaving it to the viewer to decide where "right" ends and "wrong" begins.

OTHER HUNTERS

Quincey Morris, Jonathan Harker, Dr. John Seward, and Arthur Holmwood: In Bram Stoker's *Dracula* (1897), these men, along with Abraham Van Helsing, hunted and killed Count Dracula. At first, it was Jonathan Harker who decided to kill Dracula after Dracula almost turned him into a vampire during a business meeting at Dracula's castle. But then the other men joined in the fight. They sought to avenge the death of the woman they each loved, a woman they had to kill—in order to save her soul—after Dracula made her a vampire. But in the fight against evil the good guys don't always survive—this time it's Quincey Morris who sacrificed his life for the greater good.

Dr. Julia Hoffman: While not a vampire hunter per se, Dr. Hoffman was a medical doctor who specialized in rare blood disorders at the Windcliff Sanitarium in Collinsport, Maine. The character was a key figure in the celebrated TV show *Dark Shadows*. Dr. Hoffman discovers that one of the Collins family, Barnabas, is a vampire, and when we first meet her, the doctor is clearly interested in defeating what she believes is an evil presence. But as the story develops she comes to believe that vampirism is a disorder of the

---

Dark Romance

"The key component of the success of *Dark Shadows* that so many other shows have missed is romance. *Dark Shadows* came out of the '60s gothic romance revival—it was not strictly about horror. This special combination has been rediscovered recently and helps contribute to the success of two modern vampire franchises—True Blood and especially the Twilight saga."—Daniel Seitler is a career bookseller, freelance writer, illustrator, and bibliographer.

Dark Conflict

"Unlike most vampire characters—in fact unlike even many characters on *Dark Shadows*—Barnabas grew as a character. He started as a monster, then became a sympathetic victim and ultimately a hero of sorts. He was also a reflection of the '60s fascination with outsiders and anti-heroes. In the 1960's era of *Dark Shadows*, traditional values were being questioned. The idea of evil characters was provocative at that time and the characters' moral faults often made them more sympathetic. It should be said though that ultimately the show was grounded morally by the Collins family who represented all that was decent if not in the world—certainly in Collinwood."—Daniel Seitler is a bookseller.

blood that might have a cure. Ultimately she begins working with Barnabas—who is desperately trying to control his dark urges.

Dr. T. Eliot Stokes: An occultist on the show *Dark Shadows*, who befriended the Collins family and Dr. Julia Hoffman, who he later learns is attempting to use medical science to cure Barnabas Collins of vampirism. Believing that vampires are supernatural evil and cannot be cured, Stokes directly opposes Barnabas and tries to kill him. Unfortunately he is overpowered by Barnabas, drained of blood, and transformed into a vampire.

Dr. Martin Hesselius: In 1847 Dr. Martin Hesselius came onto the scene, and the literary world was introduced to a new kind of doctor—an occult doctor—in J. Sheridan Le Fanu's *In a Glass Darkly,* a collection of supernatural tales. Although Dr. Hesselius is deceased, his medical cases and observations make up these stories and are related to the reader through a narrator. In a bold move by Le Fanu, Dr. Hesselius took the standard doctoring of the time and expanded the line between reality and the supernatural to include the possibility that ghosts could exist and influence people—and that they were not necessarily hallucinations or symptoms of illness. Le Fanu's stories ("Green Tea," "The Familiar," "Mr. Justice Harbottle," "The Room in the Dragon Volant," and

"Carmilla") first appeared in magazines and were later published together in book format in 1872. Some believe that Dr. Hesselius was the inspiration for many literary characters, including Van Helsing.

Belmont Clan, Morris Family, and Adrian Farenheights Tepes: Dracula believes he is destined to take over the world, and it's up to the vampire hunters to stop him. The action is fierce, the stakes are high, and the courage and strength to fight is strong. But it takes a leader to win the war against Dracula. He's intent on ridding the world of all humans, and he'll do whatever's necessary to win the war. It's a war that takes place in the Castlevania series of video games, but a war nonetheless. It's a battle where humans are pitted against vampires. And, it's a battle to the death.

Throughout time, the Belmont Clan (including those of the Morris family who are somehow related) has taken responsibility for defeating Dracula. Once again, they are called upon to fight this evil with their vampire killer whip. Of course the clan doesn't go at it alone. Adrian Farenheights Tepes, also known as Alucard, is Dracula's son but he's also half-vampire, half-human and he's out to seek vengeance for his mother's death. So, he joins up with the Belmont Clan to defeat Dracula.

Blade: Fighting all things supernatural, especially vampires, was Blade's specialty. This Marvel superhero—created by writer Marv Wolfman and penciller Gene Colan in 1972—was a dhampyr (half-vampire) who slew vampires with teakwood daggers and other weapons. Immune to vampire bites and possessing the ability to detect supernatural entities, Blade first battled evil in *The Tomb of Dracula #10* and appeared in dozens of comics thereafter, including the 1998, 2002, and 2006 Blade series; Blade: Crescent City Blues series (1998); and Blade: The Vampire Hunter series (1994 and 1999). A trilogy of films (*Blade, Blade II,* and *Blade: Trinity*) featured Wesley Snipes as this great vampire hunter. Guillermo del Toro directed the first and second films, and fans and critics loved the action and the story, particularly the fact that Blade's character was flawed and grew emotionally throughout the film. Whether Blade's in comics or film, this is one kick-ass vampire hunter. Let's just say we're glad we're not vampires.

D: This vampire hunter is also a dampher (the son of Dracula and a woman) and possesses both physical strength and supernatural powers. He's a strong and formidable hunter, one of the strongest in the world, and one who resorts to using his supernatural powers only when absolutely necessary. His world is a postnuclear one in the year A.D. 12090, a place where vampires and humans once coexisted but is now fraught with evil as the vampires feed on humans to exert control over the world. It's up to D to stop the vampires (and other demons); the humans depend on him.

D, the main character in the Vampire Hunter D novels, was created by writer Hideyuki Kikuchi and illustrator Yoshitaka Amano and was first published in Japan in 1983 and in the United States in 2005. Although at least twenty D novels were published, not all are available in the United States. The year 1985 saw the release of the anime film *Vampire Hunter D*, a film appreciated for its character-driven storyline rather than an action-driven one, although there's certainly no lack of action when fighting vampires. A sequel, *Vampire Hunter D: Bloodlust*, was released in 2001.

Karl Kolchak: He may have been a seedy reporter in a bad suit, and he may have been scared of just about everything, but Karl Kolchak was one of the most fascinating, intrepid, and ultimately heroic characters ever to face down a bloodsucking monster. Introduced in 1972, in *The Night Stalker*, one of the most popular TV movies of all time, Kolchak (wonderfully portrayed by Darren McGavin) is a down-on-his-luck reporter for a Vegas paper who stumbles onto the biggest story of his life: the person killing showgirls is actually a vampire. No one believes him, of course, so Kolchak goes vampire hunting. The movie was as funny as it was truly frightening, and it spawned a sequel the following year, *The Night Strangler.* Kolchak, having been chased out of Vegas and now working in Seattle, discovers a serial killer who needs to kill in order to live forever. A weekly series was launched in 1974 and despite high production values and some really terrifying moments (just say "Kolchak" and "zombie" to anyone in the know and watch the reaction), the show was canceled after only twenty episodes. An attempt to reboot the series in 2005 fell flat. The character was created by Jeff Rice for a

Unsung Hero

"Kolchak is an anachronism, the archetypal old-school reporter in the true film noir sense of the term. Every time his story is withheld, he saves the day and gets charged with arson, or is kicked out of town by crooked civic types, we feel a little of that kick to the posterior too. Kolchak says it himself in *The Night Stalker* film to his girl, Gail Foster, as they discuss how many times he's been fired in how many cities, Carl sitting slouched on a chair sipping his glass of sour mash bourbon: 'I'm becoming extinct in my own lifetime. . . .' "—Lawson Welles is the writer, director, producer, and star of *Cricket Snapper*, released in 2009, and is currently editing *Schreck: Hitler's Vampire.*

novel that went unpublished until after the first movie. Richard Matheson (author of *I Am Legend*) wrote the scripts for both movies. The show and character have become cult favorites and spawned comics and additional novels. It's no stretch to say that Kolchak was the seed from which shows like *The X-Files*, *Supernatural*, and *Fringe* grew. According to comic book writer and Kolchak expert, Bill Spangler, "Chris Carter, creator of *The X-Files*, regularly said in interviews that he was heavily influenced by *The Night Stalker*. Carter and his creative staff formally acknowledged that influence when McGavin appeared on two episodes of *The X-Files* as Arthur Dales, the first FBI agent to be formally assigned to the X-Files section."

Rayne: This female vampire hunter is one kick-ass hero—she's got attitude, great looks, and a pair of blades that can slice and dice the most evil of vampires. Defeating enemies is her forte, and she doesn't let the fact that she's half-human and half-vampire get in her way when it comes time to take down those evil bloodsuckers. She's on the hunt for her father—a vampire who killed her family in a twisted attempt to force Rayne to bond with him. And she's not stopping until she finds revenge. Of course she must battle Nazis, monsters, and other beasts.

Rayne is a character in the BloodRayne video games (BloodRayne, released in 2002 and BloodRayne 2, released in 2004). Both video games were praised for the storyline and the game play. Of course gamers, especially the males, would probably admit that part of the attraction to the game is this hot, scantily clad female hero. While the 2005 film *BloodRayne* had a host of stars on board (Ben Kingsley, Michelle Rodriguez, and Kristanna Lokken as Rayne), critics and fans couldn't seem to find a nice word to say about it.

David Christman, *Eating for Two*

"The tragic monster is always misunderstood. Those who would call themselves pious and just will most likely see its great acts of kindness and selflessness towards what it cherishes the most as wicked."—D. E. Christman is an artist and designer from Philadelphia who loves all things dark and creepy; he makes a living through his company Grendel's Den Design Studio.

That didn't stop the production of *BloodRayne II: Deliverance,* which was released straight to DVD in 2007, or *BloodRayne 3: Warhammer,* scheduled for release in 2010. With the games such huge hits, it's difficult to imagine how these films flopped. But what's important to remember is that Rayne gets the job done. And who can argue with that?

Anita Blake: Talk about strong women vampire hunters. Anita Blake has it all—she brings the dead back to life, she controls zombies, and she hunts and kills murdering vampires—and it's all part of her job. She's a strong woman who is trained in the martial arts, who knows how to effectively handle guns and knives, and who has an astute mind. What Anita lacks in height—she's under 5' 4"—and brawn doesn't deter this vampire hunter from succeeding.

New York Times bestselling author Laurell K. Hamilton created Anita Blake, the main character in the Anita Blake: Vampire Hunter series (eighteen books as of February 2010). The first book in the series, *Guilty Pleasures,* was published in 2002. Marvel Comics and the Dabel Brothers adapted this novel into the first title in a comic series, *Anita Blake, Vampire Hunter: Guilty Pleasures,* in 2006. Other books were also adapted into comics—*Anita Blake, Vampire Hunter: The First Death* (2007); *Anita Blake, Vampire Hunter: The Laughing Corpse* (2008); *Anita Blake, The Laughing Corpse—Necromancer* (2009)—and fans were thrilled. In books and in comics this is one tough female we wouldn't want to face in a showdown.

E-Branch: In Brian Lumley's E-Branch trilogy (*Invaders, Defilers,* and *Avengers*), Harry Keogh defends the world against evil. Harry uses his powers to speak to the dead and uses their knowledge— especially the ability to time-travel, which he gleaned from a mathematician—to aid his fight against the nasty necromancer Boris Dragonasi who can control the dead. Unfortunately, Harry dies in the fight.

Years later, vampires attempt to conquer Earth, and it's up to the E-Branch to stop them. Jake Cutter, like Harry, possesses the ability to communicate with the dead and was chosen by Harry's

The Necroscope Universe

"Right from his earliest beginning, his infancy and childhood, the hero of the books, Harry Keogh—the eponymous Necroscope—has known evil: the pain of his mother's cruel death, the hatred in his stepfather's heart, the bullying of the school yard . . . right up to his adulthood: the monstrous necromantic murder of his mentor, the almost palpable, radiant evil of his nemesis, Boris Dragosani, the loss of his wife and infant son in an alien dimension. To live—to be able to live with himself—Harry has to fight, and in fighting he literally defines everything that is good. But just as there is black and white, there is gray. While for day and night, there's dawn and dusk. And so of course there's something—perhaps a touch—of the gray and the dusk in Harry, too. For after all, the Necroscope's motto is "An eye for an eye. . . ."
—Brian Lumley is the author of the international bestselling Necroscope novels.

spirit to be his successor in the fight against the vampires. Scott St. John and Nathan Kikulu also aid in the fight.

Dean and Sam Winchester: When you're Dean or Sam Winchester, it's only natural to hunt demons and supernatural beings. The two brothers—with the help of their father and a demon-killing Colt revolver—hunt down their mother's murderer. Throw in shape-shifters and mistaken identities and these guys have a tremendous fight ahead of them. Later, after the death of their father, Sam and Dean must hunt down hundreds of demons that escaped from hell. And if that's not bad enough, Dean dies and is tortured in hell for years, then hurts others to avenge his pain. But this demon hunter isn't pure evil; in fact, he turns to the good side once again when his memories are erased (supposedly). Sam, who has powers from a demon, drinks blood to forge those powers and tortures and kills demons. But in addition to having to kill demons, there is a greater power lurking in the background for these hunters. Demons want to make Sam evil and it's up to Dean to stop them before it's too late.

Dean and Sam Winchester are the protagonists on the television series *Supernatural* that began in 2005 and remains in production at the time of this writing. The show was created by Eric Kripke, stars Jensen Ackles and Jared Padalecki as Dean and Sam respectively, and has been nominated for over a dozen awards.

Victoria Gardella: So your debut into society is approaching, you're living in London, and it's the nineteenth century. What's a person to do when she realizes for the first time that she's a vampire hunter? For Victoria Gardella, the answer was easy. Figure out a way to hunt vampires at night and pretend she's just a normal woman during the day. Of course, it's not as easy as it seems, for vampire hunting is serious business . . . and so are societal duties.

Peter Mihaichuk, *Succubus*

"I always thought of this piece as 'evil' contemplating its defeat of 'good'—a bittersweet feeling indeed. This was a commission for the Modern Church of Satan."—Peter Mihaichuk is an artist, production designer and illustrator.

But if Victoria Gardella Grantworth, the protagonist of the Gardella Vampire Chronicles series written by Colleen Gleason, doesn't take out the vampires, then they may take out society and turn everyone into vampires. And if that happens we imagine the women will drink blood in those dainty little cups instead of tea. Victoria Gardella manages to do it all at a time when women tended to move through the world without making much of a fuss, when tea and crumpets were often the highlight of the day, and when men held all the power . . . at least in public anyway.

Abraham Whistler, Abigale Whistler, and Hannibal King: Heroes— and vampire hunters—need their sidekicks. Especially when they're battling vampires and demons in the underworld. And Blade, the protagonist of the Blade movies, has all the help he needs in Abraham Whistler, a mentor who joined with Blade and taught Blade how to hunt and fight vampires. Whistler, played by Kris Kristofferson, is no youngster, but it's his knowledge of the vampire world that gives the pair the edge they need to kick some serious vampire butt. When Whistler supposedly dies in the third film (*Blade Trinity*), Blade teams up with a pair of hunters who call themselves the Nightstalkers—Abigail Whistler (Abraham's daughter played by Jessica Biel) and Hannibal King (a former vampire played by Ryan Reynolds). The Nightstalkers are human and Blade isn't immortal, so they really must know their stuff to survive. But that's not a problem for this team. They've got smooth martial arts moves and a mastery of weaponry—skills that enable them to face the most powerful of vampires and stop them from taking over the world.

Steve "Leopard" Leonard: This guy's not a vampire hunter—not in the true sense of the word as we've described the others here—but he does hunt down his best friend Darren (who has turned into a vampire) and tries to kill him. Not very nice, especially for a guy whose best friend became a vampire's assistant just so he could save Steve's life.

Steve "Leopard" Leonard is a character in Darren Shan's Cirque du Freak series. Always fascinated by vampires, Steve can't believe it when he encounters one at a freak show; he'd do anything to become a vampire. But when Steve gets a fatal spider bite, the boys turn to the vampire for help—he's the only one who can save Steve. But there's a catch and it's a doozy—Darren must become a half-vampire. Jealousy turns Steve into a vampire hunter—the worst kind, the kind that turns on his best friend and tries to kill him. And when that fails, he seeks revenge hunting the vampire that was once his friend. The first three books of the twelve book series were adapted into the film *Cirque du Freak: The Vampire's Assistant* (2009).

Carlisle Cullen: The Twilight series of books by Stephanie Meyer sent teenage girls rushing to the bookstores and swarming the movie theaters. Why? Vampires. Carlisle Cullen is a vampire hunter who first appeared in *Twilight* (Little, Brown Young Readers 2005). Not only does he hunt vampires, werewolves, and other unsavory creatures, but he's good looking too. At first life seems simple for Carlisle . . . well, as simple as life can be for a vampire hunter anyway . . . but then Carlisle's attacked by a vampire and transformed into one. He goes from hunting vampires to being one of the hunted. And if that's not bad enough, he hates what he's become and despises the idea of feeding on humans, so much so that he tries to kill himself on numerous occasions. Ultimately, he becomes a doctor to control his lust for blood, but he's still not satisfied. He's one lonely guy, so he transforms two people into vampires to keep him company until the end of time.

Peter Facinelli plays Carlisle in the films *Twilight* (2008), *The Twilight Saga: New Moon* (2009); and *The Twilight Saga: Eclipse* (2010), each of which is based on one of the first three books in the series. The fourth film, *The Twilight Saga: Breaking Dawn* (2011) is in production at the time of this writing. Although it is not known if Facinelli is reprising his role for this film, we'd bet on that in a minute, especially since the Twilight books and films are such incredible hits.

Robert Neville: When you think you're the only remaining man left on Earth following a pandemic, the last thing you want to see is vampires, especially vampires that were once humans. But that's exactly what happens to Robert Neville, the protagonist in Richard Matheson's *I am Legend* (1954), a novel that inspired the vampire and zombie genres. Neville has a choice. He can fight back or let

Zombie Popularity

"I think the modern zombie has become an even more compelling apocalyptic avatar than the nuke. The flesh-eating zombie is a true American monster—relatively young, yet easily on par with Old World standards like the vampire in its cultural significance. And George Romero's simple yet ingenious template allows for countless different takes on the ghouls, both dark and fun."—David Dunwoody is the author of the zombie novel *Empire* (Pocket Books, 2010).

---

his death mean the extermination of the human race. For Neville it's simple—slaughter vampires at night and hunt for a cure for the bacteria that turned everyone into vampires during the day. In fiction, as in the real world, things don't always go as planned, and for Neville that means dying rather than becoming a new legend, the only human among a race of vampires.

Matheson's book was made into three films: *The Last Man on Earth* (1964) starring Vincent Price; *The Omega Man* (1971) starring Charlton Heston; and *I am Legend* (2007) starring Will Smith. An untitled prequel is in development and set for release in 2011 in which Will Smith reprises his role as Neville. Of the three completed films, *The Last Man on Earth* follows the book most closely, but each film captures the essence of Matheson's work.

Damali Richards and the Guardian Team: When it's your mission to hunt vampires and you're the one who is called to do so—the only one in the current millennium—you had better be prepared to answer the call. That's exactly what Damali Richards did. Vampire huntress at night, hip-hop artist by day, Damali is one tough woman. She's smart. She's attractive. And she's got the skills to slay vampires. With her special dagger (Madame Isis) and the help of the Guardian Team—a group of six heroes each equipped with his or her own special powers—Damali Richards battles to save the world from evil.

Damali Richards is the protagonist in L.A. Banks' bestselling the Vampire Huntress Legend series. *Minion*, the first book in the series, was published in 2003 (St. Martin's Griffin), and the most recent and last book in the series, *The Thirteenth*, was published in 2009.

Special Deputy Jameson Arkeley: The protagonist of David Wellington's novel *Thirteen Bullets* (Three Rivers Press, 2007) thought he had it made. He'd already saved the world from the vampires and killed all but one in a bloody battle . . . at least that's what everyone thought until a new rash of vampire killings occur. But the surviving vampire couldn't be responsible; she was on life support. So there had to be someone . . . something . . . out there that survived. Something that was threatening human existence. Something Special Deputy Jameson Arkeley had to kill before it was too late.

Armed with a Glock .23 loaded with thirteen hollow point bullets (hence the title of the book), Special Deputy Jameson Arkeley is tasked with hunting down the last remaining vampires. But it's not an easy job—these vampires are abnormally strong and possess the ability to survive nearly anything. That doesn't deter Jameson from his quest to kill the vampires, and he's more determined than ever.

Francis Tsai, *Demon*

"I think storytelling is a fundamental part of being human. Even cave paintings express a need to convey a story, or at least an idea or concept. Good vs. evil is a pretty good basis for telling a story—a good story is all about resolving a conflict, and what bigger conflict is there than good vs. evil?"—Francis Tsai is a freelance illustrator and concept designer for Marvel Comics, Warner Bros., and Wizards of the Coast.

GHOULISH GOOD GUYS

Monster hunters come in all shapes and sizes. Not all of them look like Peter Cushing (or Anthony Hopkins, depending on your favorite Dracula movie). Some aren't even human. In later chapters we'll discuss how the clergy (of all faiths) deal with evil, follow some ghost hunters, profile serial killers for the FBI, and even journey back in time to the age of legendary heroes and gods.

But for the moment, we're going to talk about those rare vampires, werewolves, ghosts, and other supernatural creatures who hunt other monsters.

Benandanti: Although there are a lot of good-guy vampires in fiction and film, you seldom hear about any good-guy werewolves. The common view of the werewolf is that of a slavering, unthinking animal whose entire raison d'être is wholesale slaughter, which, admittedly, isn't a model that lends itself to the concept of "good guy." Yet there was once an entire race of heroic werewolves: the Benandanti.

Benandanti (Italian for "good walkers") were theriomorphs, meaning they could change readily from human to animal and back again. When preparing to fight evil, they most often took the form of a wolf and in that form were able to channel the better qualities of the natural wolf: loyalty, intelligence, and a desire to kill only in defense. The Benandanti who chose to assume wolf form adopted the nickname the "Hounds of God."

The Benandanti possessed the ability to sense evil spirits— witches, evil werewolves, vampires, even ghosts—and could sometimes harness the forces of nature to combat them. In a pitched battle between a Benandanti and an evil werewolf, the Benandanti might summon fierce winds, driving rain, earthquakes, and even lightning strikes.

Some Benandanti engaged in battles only on the astral plane, entering into comalike sleep states that allowed them to astrally project their spirits into other dimensions to seek out and combat the supernatural. They envisioned their astral forms riding into battle on strangely mutated goats, giant cats, or fire-breathing horses. Their astral selves were armed with sticks from fennel, a plant that is widely held to have many wholesome curative properties. The

Benandanti were most active in agricultural areas, largely because they possessed a special talent for defeating those supernatural forces that cause crop blight, plagues, and famine. The Benandanti themselves were believed to have potent healing powers as well.

These intrepid hunters lived in secret for untold centuries before coming to the attention of the Inquisition in the sixteenth century. Unfortunately the Inquisition saw them not as doers of good but as witches or werewolves themselves. Many people were executed because they were avowed (or suspected) Benandanti.

One trial had a different outcome. In 1692, an eighty-year-old resident of Jurgenburg, Livonia, named Theiss claimed to be a Benandanti. He told the court that he and a band of other shapeshifters descended into hell to fight a coven of witches that were causing famine in the area. The judges were astounded by the story of Theiss and his fellow "hounds of God," and though church law demanded that any supernatural beings be punished, they sentenced him to a mere ten lashes.

Those Benandanti who survived the Inquisition went into hiding until the latter part of the twentieth and early twenty-first centuries. The advent of new age mentality created a more accepting climate for the Benandanti. They have become regarded as being similar to Wiccans; part of the earth's natural healing process. Though no modern Benandanti claim to fight werewolves and vampires, they still bless crops and claim to be able to turn aside blight and plague.

Good vs. Evil?

"Good triumphs over evil or evil triumphs over good? Life is just not like that and stories that paint such a black-and-white picture of the universe are rarely satisfying. Even to go with something as popular as Stephen King, is Carrie White good? Evil? She's human. Jack Torrance? The house? I find when a story has been reduced to such blasé labels as good vs. evil that my attention wanders quickly. As human beings we scheme, deceive, divert, to get things we want, to have things our way. Is that 'good'?"—Shade Rupe is the editor of *Dark Stars Rising.*

Persons destined to become Benandanti were born with a caul over their face, an event that heralds supernatural qualities of many kinds in various cultures. There is one long-standing custom of the Benandanti that still lingers: mothers of children born with a caul often save that amniotic membrane. When the child grows up and accepts the task of being a Benandanti, she wears the caul in a charm around her neck.

Negrinho do Pastoreio: This is one of those tragic stories that probably has some roots in the truth. The story, known as Negrinho do Pastoreio ("The Little Black Boy Who Tended the Pasture"), has it that during the days of slavery in Brazil a young black child was beaten by his master because he had lost a race on one of the master's horses. The abused child was then ordered to watch over a small herd of horses, but they managed to escape—not a surprising occurrence considering the child was recovering from a savage beating. The boy, fearing another round of abuse, lit a candle and went searching for them, and as he went he prayed fervently to the Virgin Mary. Droplets of wax from his candle fell upon the ground. The boy rounded up the horses but became hopelessly lost in the night-shrouded hills; however, when he turned around he saw that each droplet glowed with a heavenly light. A gift from the Virgin to light his way back.

However the son of his master was a wicked little brute who liked to see the slaves suffer. He let the horses run free again, knowing that the blame would fall solidly on the black child. It did. This time the master beat him senseless and tied him down over an anthill. The master returned three days later, expecting to find a corpse ravaged by ants and scavengers, but the boy appeared to be in perfect health. There was no sign of insect bites and no trace of the savage beatings. The boy stood there with the herd of horses . . . and right next to him was the Virgin Mary. Paintings of the scene show her with a typically beatific smile.[1]

From that day forward the slaver did not lay a hand on the boy (though in some versions of the story, the child died and returned

---

1. But we like to imagine a fairly pissed-off Mary, perhaps gloating at the shock and awe she was inspiring in the slaver.

to life free from bondage). Since then, the boy has become a kind of saint that people call upon when something precious is lost, much in the same way as people call upon Saint Anthony. However, the Brazilian oral storyteller, Cedro Araújo, shared a different version of the story with us: "In my village of Alter do Chão," he says, "the Black Boy is a protector spirit. Whether we are chased by drug runners or criminals or haunted by the Cuc,[2] we pray to the Virgin Mary to send the Boy. When he comes, he sends biting ants, stinging flies, and all manner of insects against those who would harm us."

Stregoni Benefici: Reformed vampires get a lot of play in pop culture. The majority of them are male and they have the appeal of being genuine bad boys (often with a very dark past) and yet they're now on the side of the good guys. A beautiful woman is often in the mix here, usually as the X-factor that either drew the vampire from the dark side, or whose love keeps him on the straight and narrow.

In the legends of vampires the story is far less romantic. Case in point is the stregoni benefici or "beneficial vampire." These are creatures who were captured by monks or priests and then "reformed" according to the church laws of the day. The laws we're talking about here were grouped under the heading of the "Holy Inquisition." In simpler terms, the priests tortured the vampires until they recanted their devotion to evil and embraced eternal service in the name of Jesus.[3]

From that point forward this "beneficial vampire" was used as a supernatural hit man against other vampires as well as witches, werewolves, and anything else the Church deemed a threat. Can we get a hallelujah, brother!

There were, of course, other ways that a vampire could reform and become a stregoni benefici. Dying from a vampire's attack was a popular method; and perhaps dying at the hands of a monster created some kind of spiritual outrage that couldn't be satisfied until some manner of redress was obtained. Another legend

2. A female monster of Brazilian folklore.
3. And don't get us started on how the Inquisition rationalized torture in the name of a person who, according to the scriptures of that religion, preached only nonviolence.

suggested that a vampire who willingly performed an act of contrition would be redeemed and officially forgiven by the Church. Though still trapped in a kind of undead limbo, the vampire is at least on the side of righteousness.

The characters Angel and Spike from *Buffy the Vampire Slayer* (1997–2003) and *Angel* (1999–2004) fit the description of stregoni benefici pretty well. In Angel's case, his redemption is forced upon him by Gypsies as punishment for his savage attack on their village. They restore his soul in order to make him suffer—quite literally—the torments of the damned. Spike, on the other hand, goes seeking the restoration of his soul even though he knows how painful it will be. Both become champions fighting against the very kinds of evil they perpetuated.

In another TV series *Forever Knight* (1989–96), the lead character (played by Geraint Wyn Davies) was an eleventh-century vampire who had gone by many names over the centuries. Now reformed and helping protect humans against others of his kind; by day he was officially Nick Knight, a homicide detective, and by night he was secretly a crime-fighting (and evil-fighting) hero. With the help of a medical examiner friend he sought a cure for his vampirism while continuously facing his past.

Author Stephanie Meyer's enormously popular Twilight young adult series presents another reformed vampire in the person of Carlisle Cullen who believes that the process of becoming a vampire magnifies all the emotional and psychological qualities of a person. Since he was a compassionate person prior to becoming a vampire, he becomes even more so during his undead life.

6 LEGENDARY HEROES

Vince Proce, *Dragon War*

"This piece I did for the Dungeons & Dragons Draconicom is a good example of good vs. evil but it is hard to determine which side is good and which side is evil. And these days the lines of good and evil have been so blurred. It's the antihero who is really the everyman hero. The hero has, in many modern stories, had to do something really bad to help something really good. It's the whole 'kill one to save a thousand' theme that is everywhere now."—Vincent S. Proce is an artist and illustrator who has done extensive work for Midway Games, Dungeons & Dragons, Magic: The Gathering, and other high-profile fantasy projects.

What Makes a Good Hero?

"Honor. Loyalty. A willingness to sacrifice, both themselves and the ones around them. Openness to temptation, but incalculable strength. A single-minded vision to combat evil, to fight the good fight, to look into the abyss, tread carefully along the razor edge, yet not succumb. And a sense of humor in the face of despair."
—J. T. Ellison is the bestselling author of the Taylor Jackson thriller series, including *The Cold Room* and *The Immortals*.

CHAMPIONS AND HEROES

We all love a good hero—a champion who triumphs over obstacles, who perseveres when hope seems lost, and who manages, somehow, to emerge a better person on the other end of the struggle. Some heroes are all-powerful beings, especially superheroes and mythological heroes. Others are ordinary men and women who rise up to an occasion, often at great personal sacrifice, to help others in need.

Heroes fight for many things, including justice, equality, and safety. They face great challenges and formidable foes. They must use intelligence, wit, or physical strength to defeat the enemy; it's a difficult task, however, and one entrusted to only the most capable hands. Although we often think of heroes as indestructible, as all-powerful beings that can tackle any evil and survive, that's not the case for all heroes. Some heroes perish in their quests but become immortalized in the minds of those they helped and in the culture of their society. They become bigger than life, and the legend often changes as time passes, creating an even more impressive hero.

The definition of a hero varies from person to person, nevertheless it is easy to recognize a hero when we see one. Let's take a look at some of the heroes in myth, folklore, fiction, and real life.

ANCIENT MYTHOLOGICAL HEROES

Mythological heroes are found in many cultures throughout time. Their names may be different, but their deeds are similar—heroic actions that lead to success, actions so important to the culture that stories surrounding these deeds are related from generation to generation. Mythological heroes play an important role in society, not because they are all powerful or possess incredible strength, but because they represent what is good in the human race, the ability and willingness to help others, and the fortitude to persevere in the face of adversity when all signs seem to indicate the impossibility. As the myths move through the generations, some stay true to the original tale; others become distorted and overexaggerate the importance of the hero's deed. But regardless of the myth, heroes serve an important purpose. They challenge people to face evil when evil confronts them, they give people hope when they are faced with tremendous odds, and they give people strength to persevere in difficult situations.

The ancient Greeks depended on their heroes, many of whom performed heroic deeds while on a quest to defeat evil. Hercules, one of the most famous Greek heroes, was a warrior who, as a young man, defended Thebes from an army. As a reward Hercules married King Creon's daughter and bore children with her, but she soon made him crazy and he murdered his family. So that Hercules could obtain redemption for his sins, King Eurystheus of Tiryns gave Hercules the Twelve Labors to complete, a task that took him twelve years and included killing the ferocious Nemean Lion; defeating the nine-headed Hydra; stealing Queen Hippolyte's golden belt; swiping apples protected by Ladon, a hundred-headed dragon; cleaning stables covered with thirty years of dirt and debris in one day; and killing the murderous Stymphalian birds. Hercules also had to capture: the Ceryneia's hind without killing or hurting the deer; the dangerous Erymanthian Boar; the Cretan Bull; King Diomedes' man-eating horses; the monster Greyon's cattle, and the vicious beast Cerberus from the Underworld, which was the most dangerous and difficult task of all.

Hercules appears in plays by Euripides, Sophocles, and Seneca and is quite the hero in popular culture, especially in films of the 1960s. During this decade, there were many films on the subject, including *The Loves of Hercules* (1960), *The Three Stooges Meet Hercules* (1962), *Hercules Against the Mongols* (1963), *Hercules vs. the Molloch* (1963), *The Triumph of Hercules* (1964), *Hercules*

Against the Sons of the Sun (1964), *Hercules Against the Barbarians* (1964), and *Hercules and the Princess of Troy* (1965) starring Gordon Scott, who also played Tarzan.

Later, Arnold Schwarzenegger portrayed Hercules in the 1970 cult film *Hercules in New York* where Hercules moves to New York and fights the Mafia for his girlfriend. And Lou Ferrigno's portrayal of this mighty hero in *Hercules* (1983) was nominated for five Razzie Awards, including worst picture. Interestingly, Ferrigno went on to star in *Hercules II* (1985). There's also the Disney animated film *Hercules* (1998), a classic action-adventure comedy and musical that portrays Hercules attempting to regain his immortality.

In television, Hercules appears in *Hercules: The Legendary Journey* starring Kevin Sorbo, which ran for four seasons (1995–1999). In Marvel Comics, Hercules is a fictional superhero who loves to battle. Created by Stan Lee and Jack Kirby, Hercules first appeared in 1965 in the *Journal into Mystery Annual #1*. And, the Topps Company, Inc., produced a five-issue Hercules comic book in 1996 (*Hercules: The Legendary Journeys*), which was based on the above-mentioned television series.

Like Hercules, Odysseus (Ulysses) was a Greek hero who accomplished great feats. His adventures are related in Homer's epic poem *The Odyssey*, one of the world's oldest poems, written around 650 B.C. Odysseus was the king of Ithaca who, during his ten-year journey back home following the Trojan War, fought the Cyclops Polyphemus, the Sirens (dangerous nymphs whose seductive singing lured men to their death), Scylla (a monster with six heads), and Charybdis (a monster capable of sinking ships by fiercely churning the water).

Odysseus is a frequent hero in popular culture. In *Dante's Inferno* (part of the *Divine Comedy*, written in the 1300s), Odysseus encounters Dante near hell and relates what happened on his final voyage. Odysseus also appears as a Greek commander during the Trojan War in William Shakespeare's *Troilus and Cressida* (1602).

More modern instances of Odysseus in fiction are found in *Ilium* (Eos, 2003) and *Olympos* (Eos, 2005), written by Dan Simmons. In these books, "metahumans" have recreated the Trojan War on a futuristic Earth. In David Gemmell's Troy series (Ballantine Books, 2006) King Odysseus is a famous storyteller. And, in Rick Riordan's *The Sea of Monsters* (Miramax, 2006), the second book in the Percy Jackson series, the main character, Percy Jackson, encounters many obstacles during his journey that are similar to those faced by Odysseus on his way home following the Trojan War.

In film, Odysseus can be found in *Ulisse* (1954) starring Kirk Douglas, *Helen of Troy* (1956), *Troy* (2004), and *Odysseus and the Isle of the Mists* (2008). But it's in television where Odysseus appears most frequently. Four episodes of the 1965 classic *Dr. Who* feature Odysseus: "Horse of Destruction," "Death of a Spy," "Small Prophet, Quick Return," and "Temple of Secrets." And, in the episode of *Xena: Warrior Princess* titled "Ulysses" (1997), Xena and Ulysses fall in love when Xena helps Ulysses fight Poseidon's forces so that Ulysses may return home.

In 1986 the television cartoon series *Ulysse 31* hit the air. In this series, which takes place during the thirty-first century, Ulysses is a married space explorer and pilot journeying home from the planet Troy. Another television cartoon series, *The Simpsons*, portrays a version of *The Odyssey* in "Tales from the Public Domain" (1992). Homer, the least heroic member of the Simpson family, pretends he's Odysseus when reading an overdue library book. As Odysseus, Homer fights evil on his journey home to his wife. In true Simpson fashion, Homer/Odysseus takes out the trash when he arrives home. Several other television shows or made-for-TV movies feature Odysseus, including *Helen of Troy* (2003), the miniseries *The Odyssey* (2004), and *Hercules: The Legendary Journey*, a series that ran from 1995 to 1999 and starred Kevin Sorbo as Hercules and Steven Weber as Odysseus.

Another well-known Greek hero is Jason, leader of the Argonauts, who set out with his men on a seemingly impossible journey to find the Golden Fleece and take it from a dragon that never slept. Possession of the magical ram's wool would enable Jason to recapture his position as leader of his kingdom. To everyone's surprise, including Jason's uncle who had stolen the kingdom from him, Jason and his men succeeded in their quest. Third-century poet Apollonius of Rhodes recounts the brave tale of Jason and the Argonauts in

Ray Harryhausen

Without Ray Harryhausen some of the greatest movie scenes wouldn't exist. Harryhausen revolutionized the world of film-making with his stop-action animation sequences. Dinosaurs and beasts shared the scene with humans in *The Beast from 20,000 Fathoms* (1953). While common today, this technique was unique for its time. Harryhausen also created a giant octopus monster in *It Came from Beneath the Sea* (1955) and created sequences for *The 7th Voyage of Sinbad* (1958), *Jason and the Argonauts* (1963), *The Golden Voyage of Sinbad* (1974), *Clash of the Titans* (1981), and more. He has inspired countless filmmakers and won an honorary Oscar (The Gordon E. Sawyer Award) in 1992 for his contributions to the film industry.

Argonautica, as does the Roman poet Ovid in his classical text *Metamorphoses* (first published in A.D. 8).

The Columbia Pictures film *Jason and the Argonauts* (1963) tells the tale of this great quest and uses stop-motion animation to create the monsters. In one famous scene seven skeleton warriors attack Jason and the Argonauts. Legendary animation expert Ray Harryhausen created the special-effect sequences for this film, but because the process was slow and Harryhausen preferred to work alone, a half second of elapsed film time could take a day to shoot. Harryhausen's work on *Jason and the Argonauts* is considered one of the greatest special effects achievements of all time.

The tale of Jason and the Argonauts is told in the television movie *Jason and the Argonauts* (2000) and the film *Jason and the Argonauts: The Kingdom of Hades* (scheduled for a 2010 release), where Jason and his men embark on a perilous journey home after capturing the Golden Fleece.

Other Greek heroes include Perseus, who slew the Gorgon Medusa and engaged in other dangerous feats, and Theseus, who defeated the Minotaur and later became king of Athens. The 1981 film *Clash of the Titans* portrays Perseus's battle with Medusa. Books such as *Perseus (Gods and Heroes of the Ancient World)* by Daniel Ogden (Routledge, 2008) and *The Legend of Perseus Volume*

I by Edwin Sidney Hartland (Adamant Media Corporation, 2000) also recount this myth. Theseus's battle with the Minotaur appears in Jim Henson's 1990 television series *The Storyteller—Greek Myths: Theseus and the Minotaur/Orpheus and Eurydice* and in the 1975 short film *Errand in the Maze*. In books, Theseus and the Minotaur appear in *The Helmet of Horror: The Myth of Theseus and the Minotaur* by Victor Pelevin (Vintage Canada, 2007); *Graphic Myths and Legends: Theseus Battling the Minotaur, a Greek Myth* by Jeff Limke and John McCrea, illustrator (Graphic Universe, 2007); and *The Hero and the Minotaur* by Robert Byrd, illustrator (Dutton Children's Books, 2005).

Lastly, Achilles, considered the most fearless warrior in Greek history, was a legend in the Trojan War and demonstrated his valor and strength on many occasions. Unbeatable, he couldn't be injured, unless his enemy struck him on the heel, an injury that meant death. Over time, that vulnerable tendon that connects the calf muscle to the heel became known as the Achilles tendon. Achilles appears in Homer's epic poem the *Iliad* and in Euripides play *Hecuba* (where Achilles is a ghost), written around 424 B.C. In addition, Achilles appears in many poems and numerous works of art, and he is a character in William Shakespeare's *Troilus and Cressida* (1602).

In other areas of pop culture, the Marvel Comics character Captain Marvel possesses the courage of Achilles. Achilles also appears in the video games Rise & Fall: Civilizations at War (2006) and Rise of the Argonauts (2008). Films portray Achilles within the context of the larger Greek stories, such as the Trojan War, with Achilles as one among a cast of many. Some of these films include *Ulysses* (1955), *Fury of Achilles* (1962), *Helen of Troy* (1956), and *Troy* (2004), where leading actor Brad Pitt portrays Achilles.

Although King Arthur was a British hero, he is known throughout the world and has become part of the universal mythology shared among cultures. King Arthur was one of the greatest and most legendary knights, a man who, with the help of the Knights of the Round Table and his magical sword, Excalibur, fought twelve major battles, the last of which mortally wounded him. King Arthur appears frequently in pop culture, and mention of his bravery dates back to as early as 1275 when a fearsome warrior is compared to King Arthur in the Welsh text *Y Gododdin* written by the poet Aneirin. Arthur's story was told in the *History of the Kings of Britain* by the medieval writer Geoffrey of Monmouth and in Sir Thomas Malory's *Caxton Morte d'Arthur* (1485), one of the first works John Steinbeck read and one that influenced him to write *The Acts of King Arthur and His Noble Knights* (1976), in which he modernizes the stories of King Arthur.

More modern written accounts appear in *The Story of King Arthur and His Knights* by Howard Pyle (1902), *Arthur* (Book III of the Pendragon Cycle) (Buchet Chastel, 2000) by Stephen R. Lawhead, and *The Tales of King Arthur* by Daniel Randall and Ronne Randall (Barnes and Noble, 2004). *Camelot 3000* (DC Comics, 1982–85) is a series written by Mike W. Barr and drawn by Brian Bolland that takes place during the year 3000. Here, King Arthur must save Earth from aliens. The Atari video game by the same name was based on this comic. In another comic, *Mage: The Hero Discovered* (Comico, 1984), written by Matt Wagner, the main character, Kevin Matchstick, possesses the soul of Arthur Pendragon, otherwise known as King Arthur.

Films and made-for-TV movies featuring King Arthur include *Knights of the Round Table* (1953); *Camelot* (1967), starring Richard Harris as King Arthur; *King Arthur, the Young Warlord* (1975); *The Legend of King Arthur* (1979); *Excalibur* (1981); and *The Legend of King Arthur* (2004). There's also a British television series, *King Arthur and the Knights of Justice* (1992) and a video game, The Legend of King Arthur (1996).

Of course, other cultures have their mythological heroes, too. And they certainly are abundant and varied. In Native American legends the Hero Twins—Hunahpu and Xblanque—are key figures in the battle of good versus evil. These heroic warriors engage in a series of tasks assigned to them by the gods of Xibalba, and the quality of life on Earth is dependent upon their success. Luis Oropeza's 1998 play *The Marvelous Adventure of the Hero Twins* recounts this story. For the Blackfoot people, the hero Kutoyis made it his mission to rid the world of evil by destroying both men and monsters who harmed others. Zuni Indian folklore tells the tale of the Ahayuuta brothers, twin gods who use lightning to protect their people. And the Navajo twins, Killer-of-Enemy

Gods, did just that—they killed monsters in ancient times to make Earth safe for human inhabitants.

Hindu mythology speaks of the hero King Rama, one of the most widely worshipped gods who slays the demons Tadaka and Shubahu and frees his people from the demons' evil. The films *Ramayana: The Legend of Prince Rama* (1992) and *Hanuman* (2005) depict the tale of this mighty warrior. And, according to *The Economic Times* (September 6, 2009), an upcoming film titled *Hanuman* will star Keanu Reeves as King Rama. The popular epic *Ramayana* tells the story of King Rama, and the opera *Ayodha*, which premiered in Bangkok in 2006, was the first opera that recounted the Ramayana. And, the Kecak (Ramayana Monkey Chant) is a performance that depicts King Rama's battle against an evil king who kidnapped Rama's wife.

In Eastern Kenya the mythical warrior hero Liongo is revered by the Swahili and Pokomo peoples. Liongo boasted the strength of many and the height of a giant so tall only the tallest of men reached to his knees. Immortal, he could not be harmed unless his enemy somehow managed to thrust a needle into his stomach— quite a difficult feat indeed, and one that was nearly impossible because no one but Liongo and his mother knew of his weakness. Many songs and narratives relating Liongo's life and deeds have been recounted orally from generation to generation. Although his tales are widely told, there are only a few written narratives, including the poems *Ukawafi of Liongo* and *Hadithi yar Liongo*.

The Irish hero Cuchulain (Also Cú Chulainn) used his magical sword and visor to fight the fiercest of enemies, but it was Cuchulain's magical spear that was the most dangerous—for a spear wound meant certain death. Cuchulain defeated the strongest woman in the world, rescued a princess, and single-handedly conquered a great army. Maybe Cuchulain's fourteen fingers, his fourteen toes, or his fourteen pupils had something to do with his success, but we seriously doubt it. The best way to survive an encounter with Cuchulain was to avoid him—not only was he a mighty warrior, but his war cry frightened men to death.

The book *Cuchulain of Muirthemne* (1902) by Lady Augusta Gregory, the play *The Death of Cuchulain* (1939) by William Butler Yeats, and the poem *Cuchulain's Fight with the Sea* (1892), also by Yeats, recount the legend of Cuchulain. A more modern representation is found in the 1989 novel *Red Branch* by Morgan Llewellyn. Cuchulain is also a 6' 3" 430-pound character in Marvel Comics, whose first appearance was in the *Guardians of the Galaxy Annual* #3 (1993). In addition, Cuchulain appears in the video game Final Fantasy XII. In film, Cuchulain single-handedly stops Queen Medb's army (except for one man) in *Touches of Erin* (2005) and appears in the animated film *The King's Wake* (2000). And, in the TV series *Gargoyles*, Cuchulain is a character in the second season episode titled "The Hound of Ulster" (1996).

Although there are many other legendary mythical heroes, it would be impossible to list them all. However, here's just a few more:

Beowulf: A mighty Norse warrior who defeated the mighty Grendel, a fearsome beast that loved to eat men. (See the section Mythic Monsters and How to Fight Them for more details.)

Fionn Mac Cumhaill (also **Finn McCool**): Using supernatural powers and an incredible ability to fight, this Celtic hero fought in many battles and saved the palace Tara from burning to the ground at the hands of the fairy Aillen, an event that occurred every year until Fionn defeated this evil being.

Gesar (also **Gesar Khan**): Tibetan and Mongolian mythology tells of this god who protects warriors and horses and battles demons with the sun, the moon, and the stars as his armament.

Gilgamesh: A Mesopotamian warrior with superhuman strength who protected his people from evil by building the walls of Uruk around the city.

Yi: A Chinese hero who saved the world by destroying nine of the ten suns with arrows. He also killed six monsters, including the Dragon Headed beast and the Nine-Gullet beast.

FOLK HEROES

Folk heroes are similar to mythological heroes in that folk heroes can be mythological. However, mythological heroes are typically

William Adolphe Bouguereau, *Dante and Virgil in Hell*

In Bouguereau's powerful painting—inspired by a scene from Dante Alighieri's *The Divine Comedy*—Dante and the poet Virgil watch as two demented inhabitants of hell endlessly tear each other to pieces. Bouguereau chose to show the damned in hell as naked and therefore "defenseless," particularly since the word naked literally means "unprotected." The painting is considered to be a commentary on the weakness of human flesh and the transience of morality.

gods; folk heroes may be gods or real people. A folk hero is someone who engages in extraordinary deeds involving self-sacrifice; whose physical attributes and exploits become exaggerated over time through the retelling of the story; and whose tale is told in folklore such as songs and stories.

Robin Hood: One of the most famous folk heroes throughout the world is England's Robin Hood who stole from the rich to give to the poor. For those in positions of authority, Robin Hood was a criminal, but to the public he was a hero. The tale of Robin Hood has progressed throughout the years with accounts dating back to the late 1300s when ballads and plays began to tell of this great hero. Throughout the years, the legend grew and changed as new stories were told and old ones were revised, but the hero remained the same.

"Robin Hood and the Potter," found in a collection of poems written around 1500, is one of the first ballads about this legend. Since then, many ballads, including "A True Tale of Robin Hood" and "Robin Hood's Delight," tell Robin Hood's story. Dozens of classic books also feature Robin Hood: *Ivanhoe* (1819) by Sir Walter Scott, *Robin Hood le proscrit* (1872) by Alexandre Dumas, and *The*

Robin Hood Fights Evil

"Robin Hood fights evil through trickery, guile, and mockery. Robin's often a master of disguise—dressing as a potter, butcher, shepherd, old woman, palmer, and others to lure his foes into an ambush. Then, and by targeting forces of corruption like the Sheriff of Nottingham or the Bishop of Hereford, Robin exposes the hypocrisy of high officials. He makes these figures look absurd by having the sheriff dance in his boots. And the fundamental irony of the tales—an outlaw more honest than a sheriff or more religious than an abbot or bishop—is part of the way Robin Hood fights evil." —Allen W. Wright is a Robin Hood expert and author of the Robin Hood Bold Outlaw of Barnsdale and Sherwood website (www.boldoutlaw.com).

Merry Adventures of Robin Hood (Scribners, 1883) by Howard Pyle. Robin Hood made his mark in comics from 1956 to 1958 in *Robin Hood Tales* (published by Quality Comics and later DC Comics who took over the comic, among others, from Quality). DC Comics also published Robin Hood stories in the series *The Brave and the Bold*, which ran from 1955 to 1983.

Robin Hood drew his share of moviegoers to films like Douglas Fairbanks's *Robin Hood* (1922), one of the first films to present this legend and one of the most expensive films of its time to produce, and *The Adventures of Robin Hood* (1938), starring the legendary Errol Flynn as the hero who fights for the poor and courts Maid Marian, played by Olivia de Havilland. According to a movie review in *Entertainment Weekly*, the 1991 film *Robin Hood: Prince of Thieves*, starring Kevin Costner as Robin Hood, lacked the excitement fitting for this legend. The film became fodder (as did the Robin Hood legend in general) for director Mel Brooks's parody *Robin Hood: Men in Tights* (1993). The anticipated 2010 film *Robin Hood*, directed by Ridley Scott and starring Russell Crowe as Robin Hood, is a prequel that ends with the title character being betrayed and forced into the role of outlaw hero.

Robin Hood is also found in video games such as Conquests of the Long Bow: The Legend of Robin Hood (1991) and Shrek Super-Slam (2005). Also, *The Wizard of Id*, the cartoon created by Brant Parker and Johnny Hart, features a character called Robbing Hood, who is shown robbing from the rich to give to the poor in the July 27, 2009, strip.

Geronimo: Geronimo was another great folklore hero. To maintain the rights to Apache land, this Native American led the fight against the United States and Mexico between 1858 and 1886 and became famous for evading thousands of troops and avoiding capture. One of the earliest films depicting this great hero was *Geronimo's Last Raid* (1912). Another film, *Geronimo* (1939), cast Chief Thundercloud, a Native American Indian whose true name was Victor Daniels, as the legendary hero. Later, the story was retold in a 1962 film by the same title. Other films include *The Battle of Apache Pass* (1952) and *Geronimo: An American Legend* (1993).

The cover of the 1950 comic book *Geronimo Indian Fighter #1: Massacre at San Pedro Pass* (published by Avon) depicts Geronimo fighting settlers in covered wagons, and the cover of the 1951 comic book *Geronimo and His Apache Murderers #3* (Avon) depicts a fierce-looking Geronimo wielding an axe and readying to butcher a soldier. An interesting take on the Geronimo legend occurred when World War II U.S. paratroopers shouted "Geronimo" when jumping out of a plane shortly after viewing the 1939 film *Geronimo*. This "war cry" soon took on a life of its own and eventually became part of Lieutenant Colonel Byron Paige's paratrooper song "Down from Heaven," a song that is still heard today. The film *Hot Shots! Part Deux* (1993) spoofs this ritual. We'd tell you what happens in the scene, but we'd hate to ruin the joke.

Although there are many books written about Geronimo, they are mainly nonfiction. One book of note, *Geronimo: His Own Story: The Autobiography of a Great Patriot Warrior* (by Geronimo and told to S. M. Barrett; Plume, 1996) is a revised edition of *Geronimo's Story of His Life* published in 1906.

John Henry: In the late 1800s, man battled machine for the right to work. John Henry, an African American man and a slave who grew into a legend, was a railroad worker from West Virginia in the days when mountains were cleared and tracks were laid by hand. There was no better person to do the job than the strapping John Henry. But the advent of the steam drill worried the workers who drilled the Big Bend Mountains, especially John Henry, who feared the machine would replace the laborers. He challenged the drill to a contest to determine if man or machine could perform better. Although the machine won and John Henry died from his efforts, he became legendary. Not all sources consider John Henry a folk hero, but most agree that John Henry symbolizes the working man and a strong work ethic.

Songs about John Henry have been recorded by dozens of singers, but the most famous recording is the "Ballad of John Henry." The blues musician W. C. Handy penned the first printed score. Others put their own musical twist on this tale giving it a rock, blues, or folk music feel, including Johnny Cash ("The Legend of John

Henry's Hammer"), Woody Guthrie ("John Henry"), Bruce Spring-steen ("John Henry"), and Joe Bonamassa ("The Ballad of John Henry").

Although John Henry is immortalized mostly in song and fable, he does appear on screen in Disney's *John Henry* (2000) and in Shelly Duvall's *Tall Tales and Legends* (1986 episode titled "John Henry"), in which the celebrated actor Danny Glover stars as John Henry. Two recommended novels on this subject are *John Henry* by Roark Bradford (Ayer Co., 1931) and *A Man Ain't Nothin' but a Man* (Little, Brown, 1975) by John O. Killens.

The most powerful, and perhaps the most well known, John Henry character in modern times is the DC comic hero Steel (a.k.a. Dr. John Henry Irons), who first appeared in the *Adventures of Superman #500* in 1993. Steel is an imposing superhero who fights evil with brute strength, a powered armor suit, and a huge hammer. He was spurred to action after a powerful weapon he developed for the military was used to murder innocent civilians.

Spartacus: For a folk hero who has inspired throughout time, ancient and modern cultures need look no further than Spartacus. This gladiator amassed a huge army of slaves and led them in an uprising against the Roman Republic in 73 B.C. But sheer effort and the number of men were not enough to defeat the Roman Repub-lic. Spartacus and many of his men were killed in battle. Although Spartacus didn't survive, the legend of this great man and his heroic deeds did.

Perhaps the best-known book is Howard Fast's novel *Spartacus*, a book Fast couldn't sell to mainstream publishers after he refused to testify in front of the House Un-American Activities Commit-tee. Fast published the book himself in 1951, and it went on to sell millions of copies over time. The release of the 1960 film *Sparta-cus*, directed by Stanley Kubrick and starring the legendary Kirk Douglas as Spartacus, brought additional attention to Fast's book and increased sales. The original score for that film was written by Alex North, who wrote scores for many other films, including *Good Morning Vietnam* (1987) and *Prizzi's Honor* (1985). Fast's novel was adapted again in 2004 for the TV miniseries *Spartacus*.

Arthur Koestler also wrote a book on this subject titled *The Gladiators* (Macmillan 1947). In 2010 audiences saw the airing of *Spartacus: Blood and Sand*. Produced by Sam Raimi, this television series relates a modernized version of the Spartacus story, aimed at the current generation of viewers, and starred Andy Whitfield as Spartacus. Lucy Lawless, who starred in the television series *Xena: Warrior Princess*, is also in the series.

Tomoe Gozen: Another great warrior was Tomoe Gozen, a female Japanese samurai who fought during a time when men led the world and it was rare for women to engage in battle. Tomoe Gozen fought in the Genpei War (1180–85), but the folklore that evolved also has her fighting demons and gods. Sources remain unclear as to whether she was indeed a real person who became a folklore hero or a fictional creation. Regardless of her origins, Tomoe Gozen is considered an exceptionally skilled and brave fighter.

In print, Tomoe Gozen first appeared in *Heike Monogatari*, a medieval Japanese narrative written sometime between 1190 and 1220. More modern accounts of this hero are told in the trilogy *The Tomoe Gozen Saga* (*Tomoe Gozen, The Golden Naginata*, and *Thousand Shrine Warrior*, Ace, 1981–84) by Jessica Amanda Salmonson. Tomoe Gozen is resurrected as the character Saisei in the manga series *Samurai Deeper Kyo* (1999–2006), written and illustrated by Akimine Kamijyo. This series was made into an animated television show in 2002 and into a video game. And, in the 2008 video game Persona 4, the sixth in this role-playing game series (RPG), Tomoe Gozen is Chie Satonaka's persona.

Wong Fei Hung: Chinese lore speaks frequently of the folk hero Wong Fei Hung (Also Huang Fei-hong), a martial arts expert who lived from 1847 to 1924. In an era when battles against evil were fought by hand, when a man's honor was all important, and when dignity and respect were earned and valued, Wong used his martial arts training to help those in need, to defend against bullies, and to bring peace to his people. The retelling of Wong's story and his deeds, and the new stories that evolved from his real-life adventures, particularly those portrayed in film, led to Wong's status as a folk hero.

Known for his martial arts skill and mastery, Wong is featured in many films, most of them produced in Hong Kong and dating back to as early as 1949. Imdb.com lists eighty-eight films, but other sources point somewhere between ninety and a hundred. Regardless of the number of films, it is apparent that Wong Fei Hung is a popular subject and that Tak-Hing Kwan, who played Wong in many of the films, made a career out of portraying this hero. The older films, part of a series, include *Story of Huang Fei-hong* (1949), *Huang Fei-hong's Victory at Fourth Gate* (1955), and *Huang Fei-hong and the Battle of Saddle Hill* (1957). What's interesting about these old flicks is that Wong used his skills as a doctor to treat the wounded once he won the battle.

More recently, Jet Li, the martial arts champion, portrayed the heroic Wong in the 1991 film *Wong Fei Hung*. The film takes place in nineteenth-century Canton and pits Wong against foreign armies. In 1992, the hit movie won four Hong Kong film awards. Soon two other films on the subject followed, both starring Jet Li as Wong—*The Invincible Shaolin* (1993) and *Once Upon a Time in China and America* (1997). The 1993 film *Deadly China Hero* also stars Jet Li as Wong, but this movie, unlike the others, is a comedy.

Wong Fei Hung also appears in the Tiger and Crane comics (Blue Water Productions, 2008). Here Wong prevents the Japanese from winning World War II with the help of a great American spy.

Other folk heroes include:

Benkei: Found frequently in Japanese folklore, Benkei was a mighty warrior hero. Some accounts state he was a god; others believe he was human, but all spoke of Benkei's imposing stature— somewhere between 6'5" and 8' —tall by any standards in Japan during the twelfth century. Armed with a sword and great strength, Benkei defeated ninety-nine men on Gojō Bridge near Kyōto, losing only to the hundredth man, General Minamoto no Yoshitsune, in a duel that took place during the Genpei War—a duel that forged a lasting and loyal relationship between the men. Kabuki theater tended to dramatize the moral conflict of choosing between individual desires and loyalty, with Benkei choosing his loyalty to Yoshitsune. Noh plays, such as *Benkei at the Bridge*, often related the story of the one-hundred-sword duels. And sometimes, films, as in the case of *The Men Who Tread on the Tiger's Tale* (1945), are based on a Noh play (*Ataka*), but the play was inspired by Kabuki (Kanjinchō). While there aren't any rules as to how this folk hero's legacy is told, the story of his courage has been expressed so many times that it is difficult to ascertain truth from legend. Today, Benkei is a revered figure in Japanese culture and is portrayed throughout pop culture, including video games such as Mystical Ninja Starring Goemen (1998), Genji: Dawn of the Samurai (2005), Okami (2008), and Warriors Orochi Z (2009).

Rodrigo Díaz de Vivar (also **El Cid Campeador** or **El Cid**): Spain's national hero who aided Alfonso VI in defeating the Moors around 1090. Ballads, poems, books, and works of art immortalized this legend and turned this military leader into a folk hero. The 1961 film *El Cid*, starring Charlton Heston in the lead role, was nominated for three Academy Awards and won Special Mention for best foreign film in Spain's 1962 Cinema Writers Circle Awards.

Tamanend (also **Tammany**): Throughout American history, settlers and Native Americans fought bloody battles over the right to occupy the land. A clan chief named Tamanend (one of the chiefs of the Lenni-Lenape located in the area now known as Philadelphia) was tired of the fight and decided the battle should end. He met with colonist leaders and other clan chiefs some time in the 1680s and proclaimed that from that day forward the colonists and the Native Americans would live in peace forever. Following his death in the late 1690s, stories and plays about Tamanend made him into a folk hero. So great was his proclamation of peace that he was dubbed King Tammy by those who lived in Philadelphia. His legend took on national significance, however, because of the role Philadelphia played in founding the nation. Tammany societies popped up all over the country and Tammany festivals celebrated this historic occasion. *Tammany* (or *The Indian Chief*), an opera whose libretto was written by Ann Julia Hatton, hit Broadway in 1794 at the John Street Theatre and had a very successful run. Tamanend also appears in James Fennimore Cooper's classic novel *Last of the Mohicans* (1826).

FICTIONAL HEROES

Fictional heroes are easy to create—slap a good guy into a bad situation and make him come out on top—but great fictional heroes are much harder to fashion. Great fictional heroes just don't fight the bad guys, save the weak, or battle for justice. They possess and display human qualities—qualities that show weakness, pride, insecurity, a concern for others, and more. They are heroes that we think about long after we finish reading a book or a comic or watching a movie. They are heroes that we care about—sometimes quite deeply—and who we aspire to emulate, however we can, within the confines of our own worlds. It would take an entire book to cover the great fictional heroes, so we'll focus on some of the most familiar ones.

Lone Ranger: The advent of American radio shows, and later television, brought a slew of great heroes to the airwaves and to the screen. In 1933, the Lone Ranger rode in on his horse to save the day. Fighting injustice alongside his sidekick Tonto, this cowboy became a hero for adults and children alike. Many children ran through their neighborhoods costumed as this mysterious masked man and pretended to save innocent people from evil. The radio show lasted for close to 3,000 episodes, and the television series ran 221 episodes from 1949 to 1957. The first of eighteen Lone Ranger novels, *The Lone Ranger*, was published in 1936. The Lone Ranger has appeared in newspaper comic strips and in comic books since the late 1940s. The most recent, and one of the most popular, is *The Lone Ranger* (Dynamite Entertainment 2007), created by writer Brett Matthews and artists John Cassaday and Sergio Cariello. Although the Lone Ranger departed at the end of his radio and TV episodes with his famous saying "Hi-yo, Silver, away!" we're pretty sure the Lone Ranger will continue to fight evil for many years to come.

James Bond: While the Lone Ranger rode in on his horse to save the day, James Bond rode in on anything he could find. As a British MI6 officer, Bond was a man on a mission to rid the world of evil. He was a simple guy who liked simple pleasures but found them in the most difficult and dangerous ways. Bond fought in perilous and exhilarating action-packed scenes that left the viewer breathless.

Killing was part of Bond's profession but that didn't make the killing easy for him, a quality that made him more likeable as a hero. And Bond always got the girl and the martini. He certainly liked his pleasures, but when it came to women he loved them and left them.

Peter Mihaichuk, *Poison*

"I think the success of this piece of art is due to the nature of the model: an innocent nine-year-old girl with a huge smile. The amount of 'good' is ultimately what made the piece so successfully evil in the end. Perhaps proof that there is evil within us all." —Peter Mihaichuk is a production designer and concept artist within the film industry.

On Identifying with Heroes

"[Heroes] represent the struggles we all go through—but blown up to larger-than-life size. We get to recognize in them our own flaws and shortcomings and see them overcome. Heroes are like us, but better."—Gregg Hurwitz is the author of ten thrillers, including *They're Watching*, and he also writes comics for Marvel, including Wolverine, Punisher, and Moon Knight.

But Bond's a loyal man when it comes to his work, a man bound by duty and honor. A great hero in the truest sense of the word.

Secret agent James Bond was created by Ian Fleming in 1953 and was the hero of *Casino Royale* and eleven other novels. *Casino Royale* didn't make it to the big screen until 2006 when it became the twenty-first James Bond movie, although there was a spoof by the same name released in 1967 starring Peter Sellers. Following Fleming's death, the James Bond novels were penned by several authors and many of the books have been adapted for film. Other than *Casino Royale,* some of the best James Bond films include *Quantum of Solace* (2008), *Die Another Day* (2002), *The Man with the Golden Gun* (1974), *A View to a Kill* (1985), and *Diamonds Are Forever* (1971). James Bond was also a character in daily newspaper strips in the *London Daily Express* (syndicated to other papers)—that ran from the late 1950s to the early 1980s—and in comics published by Marvel, Eclipse Comics, Dark Horse Comics, Topps Comics, DC Comics, and Semic Press (in Sweden). James Bond also appears in video games. It seems that after all these years, the public still considers James Bond a great hero.

Dirk Pitt: Hero might as well be Dirk Pitt's middle name. The protagonist of Clive Cussler's books, Pitt is a man who seems larger than life while at the same time your average Joe. He saves the world from one catastrophe after another, battling evil intent to destroy all, yet he's a humble man with a compassion for others. He has good friends, children he adores, and a tie to his home, which happens to be inside an old airplane hangar, along with his prized collection of classic cars. He'll do whatever is necessary to protect those he loves—and those he doesn't know—and it seems like the world's fate continually lands on his shoulders. But through it all, Pitt emerges victorious, albeit a little banged up. No matter what fate throws Pitt's way, he's always willing to risk his life to thwart evil.

Dirk Pitt first appeared in 1973 in *The Mediterranean Caper* and in nineteen subsequent books at the time of this writing, including *Arctic Drift* (Putnam Adult, 2008), *Black Wind* (Putnam, 2004), *Sahara* (Simon & Schuster, 1992), and *Raise the Titanic* (Viking Adult, 1976). Both *Sahara* and *Raise the Titanic* were made into movies, but neither one scored well with critics and fans—perhaps because Dirk Pitt is such a great hero that it's impossible for any actor to fill his shoes.

Rocky Balboa: Another great hero who arrived on the scene in the mid-1970s was Rocky Balboa, the underdog boxer who only wanted a shot at success, who worked hard to achieve his goals, and who got the title (and the girl) in a tremendous show of determination and perseverance. Rocky, a small-time fighter with little opportunity for success outside of the ring, is given the break many can only dream about—a chance to be the best fighter in the world. When one of the contenders for the World Championship fight is injured, Rocky is fated to take his place. Although Rocky knows he has little chance to defeat his opponent, his goal is to prove himself to everyone by finishing the fight, an accomplishment no one has achieved when faced against the undefeated Apollo Creed. Of course Rocky's hard work and training paid off, and Rocky became the underdog hero who showed the world that anything is possible.

Rocky (1976) was written by Sylvester Stallone, who also starred in the film, a role that thrust Stallone into the spotlight as a movie star. The film was shot on a small budget, achieved huge commercial success, and won three Oscars, including Best Picture. Five Rocky sequels followed (*Rocky II*, 1979; *Rocky III*, 1982; *Rocky IV*, 1985; *Rocky V*, 1990; and *Rocky Balboa*, 2006), and each found success at the box office. Rocky video games were also released (Rocky Super Action Boxing, 1983; Rocky, 2002; Rocky Legend, 2004; and Rocky Balboa, 2007).

Luke Skywalker: The theme of the underdog battling a more powerful enemy is also seen in *Star Wars: Episode IV—A New*

Hope (1977) and *Star Wars: Episode V—The Empire Strikes Back* (1980) where hero Luke Skywalker fights the evil and menacing Darth Vader. Luke is an ordinary man who embarks on the journey of a hero, becomes a Jedi knight, and faces trials that force him to confront his own weaknesses and discover his strengths if he is to emerge victorious and survive. Of course Luke doesn't have to go at it on his own; he has the help of some trusted friends (Han Solo, R2-D2, and C3-PO) and a mentor (Yoda), who will do all they can to help him succeed. What makes Luke Skywalker such a great hero is his humanity, his willingness to acknowledge it, and his fortitude when facing evil.

The original Star Wars film is the number three top-grossing film in the United States of all time. The other films in the saga also achieved great success. Luke Skywalker also battles evil in over three dozen video games, including Star Wars: The Force Unleashed (2008), Star Wars Battlefront II (2005), and LEGO Star Wars: The Complete Saga (2007).

Indiana Jones: Just like we root for Luke to win the fight against evil, we also root for Indiana Jones, an unassuming archaeology professor with a mild-mannered demeanor in the classroom. But throw Indiana Jones into a foreign city with his fedora and bullwhip and the fate of priceless artifacts at risk and he becomes a hero. He's a man determined to win the fight, and he'll do whatever's necessary to accomplish his goals. He battles the Nazis, faces certain death in a multitude of situations, and even manages to overpower supernatural forces. But he never waivers from his convictions or forgets about those who are important to him.

Indiana Jones, played by Harrison Ford, appears in the films *Raiders of the Lost Ark* (1981); *Indiana Jones and the Temple of Doom* (2004); *Indiana Jones and the Last Crusade* (1989); and *Indiana Jones and the Kingdom of the Crystal Skull* (2008), all directed by Steven Spielberg. A fifth Indiana Jones film is in the pitch stage as of this writing, according to IMDb.com. Indiana Jones is also a character in the popular television series *The Young Indiana Jones Chronicles* (1992–1993) and in *The Adventures of Young Indiana Jones* (a series of TV movies and videos) that were produced in the mid to late 1990s. And, there's even Indiana Jones video

On Good vs. Evil

"What's more exciting than watching Evil triumph over Good every once in a while? Not much! . . . if it weren't for evil triumphing over good, we'd never have classics like *The Empire Strikes Back*. There's definitely something eerily rewarding about seeing Freddy get the very last laugh in the first installment of *A Nightmare on Elm Street*. Not to mention the excitement of watching Rob Zombie's crazy family in *House of 1,000 Corpses* run amok. If I had to make a choice though . . . give me a great good triumphs over evil story any day! Without it, we'd never get to see Dracula sent spinning back to hell at the end of *The Monster Squad*."—Scott Neumyer is a writer, photographer, and self-confessed pop culture geek with experience in online marketing and publicity and as a media buyer for a major national film distributor.

games—Indiana Jones and the Staff of Kings (2009), Indiana Jones (2007), Indiana Jones and the Emperor's Tomb (2003), Indiana Jones and the Infernal Machine (1999)—and an Indiana Jones ride at Disneyland (Indiana Jones and the Forbidden Eye).

Ellen Ripley: Great heroes aren't just males. Ellen Ripley, the protagonist in *Alien* (1979), *Aliens* (1986), *Alien*[3] (1992), and *Alien Resurrection* (1997) showed the world that women can fight evil, that they don't need to rely on men to do the job, and that they are strong, resourceful beings who use intelligence, wit, and strength to win the battle. Ellen Ripley doesn't shy away from evil but confronts it with courage, despite knowing the odds are against her. Of course, the evil she faces is not human, but alien, aliens with powers beyond belief, powers that force her to dig deep and fight hard to survive.

Buffy Summers: Another great female hero is Buffy Summers, a slayer of vampires. In 1997, Joss Whedon's television series *Buffy the Vampire Slayer* introduced viewers to a new kind of a hero—a high school student who fought evil. She was a strong and independent young woman who understood the importance of not going at it alone, especially when the fate of the world rested in her hands. She enlisted the help of her friends and used the guidance of a Watcher. The series ran from 1997 to 2003 and was a huge hit, unlike the film of the same name, released five years earlier in 1992, where critics felt Buffy was more comical than heroic. A remake of the film has been optioned with a potential release date of 2012.

What makes Buffy a truly great hero is not that she fights evil—and not just vampires but all kinds of monsters—it's that despite her reluctance to do so, she does it anyway. Sure, she'd rather be a normal teenager but that's not her fate. Her fate is to save the world from evil.

Buffy appears in the comic series *Buffy the Vampire Slayer* published by Dark Horse Comics. This popular comic began in September 1998 and was in its eighth season as of September 2009. There are also dozens of Buffy novels and video games whose titles include Buffy the Vampire Slayer (Electronic Arts, 2002) and Buffy the Vampire Slayer: Chaos Bleeds (Atari, 2003).

Harry Potter: Nearly everyone has heard of another popular teenager who fights evil—the boy wizard named Harry Potter. Harry seems like an unlikely hero at first. His parents were murdered by the dark Lord Voldemort, he is forced to live under a staircase, and he seems to have little power to control his own life, let alone anything else in the world. But that all changes when Harry discovers he is a wizard and begins school at the Hogwarts School for Witchcraft and Wizardry. Armed with his magical wand, the support and assistance of two great friends, the knowledge imparted to him by great teachers (including his mentor Albus Dumbledore), and the backing of the wizarding world, Harry risks his life to save the lives of others and to bring permanent peace from the clutches of evil that threatens all. It is Harry's inner strength that makes him a great hero, for it's certainly not brawn (he's of average build)—rather it's Harry's confidence in his ability to succeed, his intelligence, his acknowledgment of his weaknesses, and his perseverance that enable him to conquer evil.

Harry Potter was created by author J. K. Rowling and first appeared in 1997 in *Harry Potter and the Philosopher's Stone* (published by Bloomsbury Children's Books in the United Kingdom). The same book was released in the United States in 1998 as *Harry*

Potter and the Sorcerer's Stone (Arthur A. Levine / Scholastic Books). Six other Harry Potter books followed, as did eight films, including the two-part *Harry Potter and the Deathly Hallows* (2010 and 2011). Both Rowling's books and the films set records for sales, making Harry Potter one of the most well-known and admired heroes.

Other heroes include the following.

Commander William Adama: A man who in the face of adversity and who, when all hope seemed gone following the annihilation of most of his planet's population in a nuclear attack, led his people in the fight against the Cylons (a race of sentient machines) and helped them start life anew. He is dedicated to his crew, his family, and his people and does his best to exceed everyone's expectations. But he is also flawed, as are all great heroes, for he does allow his emotions to flavor his decisions at times, decisions that could spell disaster. Commander Adama was played by Edward James Olmos in the highly popular television series *Battlestar Glactica* (2004–2009).

Jack Bauer: The clock is running, and federal agent Jack Bauer is always trying to beat a deadline to avert an emergency before it happens. He'll do whatever is necessary to protect the public good, even if it involves breaking the rules, and he'll risk everything to succeed. Jack is the main character in the popular television show *24* and is portrayed by Kiefer Sutherland. The show began in 2001; each episode takes place during a single hour and each season occurs during a single day. The show was nominated for dozens of awards and won numerous Golden Globe and Emmy awards, including Outstanding Drama Series. The TV movie *24: Redemption* was based on the television show. There are also numerous novels, including *24 Declassified: Trinity* (Harper Entertainment 2008), *24 Declassified: Cat's Claw* (2006), and *24 Declassified: Collateral Damage* (2008).

John McClane: This hero of the Die Hard films doesn't want to be a hero. He just wants to live his life without trouble. But trouble finds him in the most unlikely of ways, and he is forced into action to save others. If there were this many real-life terrorist attacks with only one man to stop them, we'd all be in trouble. But John

McClane survives the toughest of situations and gets the job done at great risk to himself. Yet if we were to ask John if he were a hero, we wouldn't be surprised to hear him say "no." John McClane was played by Bruce Willis in *Die Hard* (1988), *Die Hard 2* (1990), *Die Hard: With a Vengeance* (1995) and *Live Free or Die Hard* (2007). Die Hard: Nakatomi Plaza is a first-person shooter video game released in 2002. The game is based on the first Die Hard film and allows gamers to play as John McClane.

REAL-WORLD HEROES

Real-world heroes are everywhere. They are the policemen, firemen, paramedics, doctors, nurses, soldiers, teachers, children, mothers, and fathers. They are unsung heroes who work tirelessly to make a difference in the world. They don't seek glory, and in fact, most shun it when glory comes their way. Their goal is simple—to help others in need. The chore may be big, or little, but these real-world heroes do not shy away from the fight—they embrace it.

Clara Barton: One such hero was Clara Barton whose deeds during the Civil War (1861–65) earned her the respect and admiration of

---

Firemen

Most people don't often think about firemen. After all, we only see or hear of them when someone's in trouble, when fire flames from a building, when the station alarm peals through the quiet night, or when a roaring red truck flies past us in traffic. Fact is, firemen train diligently for a variety of situations and they risk their lives to save ours. We might ask what sane person would rush into a burning building to save a kid, an old lady, or even a pet—it goes against human nature to put ourselves at such great risk. Yet these heroes, these men and women who dedicate their lives to saving ours, put themselves at risk over and over again—not because they want to be heroes but because they believe in helping others in need.

International Federation of Red Cross and Red Crescent Societies

This powerful community of international volunteers works tirelessly to help those in need, especially those whose lives are
threatened by disease, poverty, natural disasters (hurricanes,
floods, earthquake), human-induced disasters (bombings, arson),
and political situations resulting in homelessness. The organization also works to raise awareness regarding the value of human
life and to educate people about disease prevention and treatment, sanitation, disaster preparedness, and more. The International Federation of Red Cross and Red Crescent Societies
provides these services to all in need without discrimination.

many. The United States was in a battle—not against foreign enemies but among its own states with the issues of slavery and
states' rights driving the fight. The war cost many lives; estimates
place the number of dead over 620,000. Clara Barton, the "Angel of
the Battlefield," was a nurse who placed herself in harm's way,
often crossing into enemy territory to provide care for injured
troops. In 1881, Barton established the American Red Cross, an
organization dedicated to providing help to those in need.

Many nonfiction books and articles document Clara Barton's
heroic efforts. In fiction, Mary Pope Osborne's bestselling children's
book *Magic Tree House #21: Civil War on Sunday* (Random House
Books for Young Readers, 2000) takes the protagonists, Jack and
Annie, back in time to help Clara Barton on the battlefield. Ava
Dianne Day's historical thriller *Cut to the Heart* (Doubleday, 2002)
pits Clara Barton against evil while tending to the wounded at
Union Army headquarters. And the graphic novel, *Clara Barton:
Angel of the Battlefield* (Coughlan Publishing, 2006), written by
Allison Lassieur and illustrated by Brian Bascle, is a nonfiction
account of Clara Barton and her heroic deeds.

Emmeline Pankhurst: In 1920, women in the United Kingdom celebrated a huge victory thanks to the work of Emmeline Pankhurst
and the women of the suffragette movement who fought for
women's right to vote. Pankhurst's relentless work on behalf of

Teachers

Some people believe teachers have it easy. They work a regular day and have great benefits, including summers off. But what most people don't realize is how difficult it is to teach and that a teacher's day does not start and end in the classroom. There's papers to grade, tests to prepare, after-school activities, etc. For those who teach in economically disadvantaged areas, teaching takes on a whole new meaning. Here, supplies are needed, library and textbooks are precious commodities, and students don't often see the value in obtaining an education; they feel stuck in a hopeless situation. These teachers must not only inspire their students to learn, but they must instill in them a sense of hope that the future holds promise and that the key to achieving success lies in an education. That's not easy to accomplish, yet thousands of teachers work hard each day to ensure their students have a chance at a fulfilling and educated life, that no one is left behind in the dust. It is thanks to these teachers—and all teachers throughout the world—that children have hope for the future, a future fueled by education and caring.

women enabled the United Kingdom, and the world, to move closer toward a point where all people were considered equal under the law. Pankhurt was named one of the 100 Most Important People of the 20th Century by *Time Magazine* in 1999.

Emmeline Pankhurst is no stranger to popular culture. Her fight for the right to vote appears in the lyrics of "Sister Suffragette," sung in the 1964 Disney hit *Mary Poppins*. In 1974, the famed Welsh actress Sîan Phillips portrayed Emmeline in the BBC miniseries *Shoulder to Shoulder,* a dramatization of Emmeline's heroic fight for the right to vote. The series premiered in the United States in 1975.

Mother Teresa: A little over two decades after Emmeline Pankhurst helped women win the right to vote, Mother Teresa worked to aid the poor in Calcutta, India. During the 1930s and the 1940s extreme poverty caused suffering among many, and Mother Teresa set out to change that in 1948 when she created a school in the slums, provided financial help to the people, and began her own order, the

Missions of Charity, to assist the poor. Soon, people around the world recognized her work and joined the fight to aid those in need. In 1979, Mother Teresa won the Nobel Peace Prize.

The film *Mother Teresa* (1986) was named Best Documentary during the 1987 Boston Society of Film Critics Awards. And, Golden Globe award–winning actress Olivia Hussey portrayed Mother Teresa in the TV movie *Madre Teresa*, first shown on Italian television in 2003. Mother Teresa's story is told in manga— *Mother Teresa* (YoungJin Singapore Pte. Ltd., 2008) by Ykids and *EduManga: Mother Teresa* (Digital Manga Publishing, 2007) by Masahide Kikai and Ren Kishida—but it's the comic book from Marvel titled *Mother Teresa of Calcutta* that really captured kids' attention. According to John Dart in his 1987 *Los Angeles Times* article "Stories of Pope, Mother Teresa Also in Print—[Antonio] Serra to Join Ranks of Comic Book Elite," the 1984 comic sold 350,000 copies.

Jackie Robinson: Changing the world doesn't come easy, and Jackie Robinson was no stranger to the struggle. Playing baseball in the major leagues is a dream for many American children, but during the 1940s it seemed to be a dream attainable only by Caucasian youths. Segregation was the norm and that meant African Americans had to play baseball in the Negro leagues. But Jackie Robinson changed all that when he joined the Brooklyn Dodgers in 1947. Life was difficult for Robinson; he had to deal with many people

World Health Organization (WHO)

The World Health Organization (WHO) was established in 1948 to create a "global health organization." Participation is available to countries who are members of the United Nations; other countries may participate under special approval. At the time of this writing 193 "member states" participate in WHO and work in conjunction with other agencies to provide global health care, education, and preventative measures to those in need, addressing issues related to immunization, drinking water, environmental pollution, HIV/AIDS, food safety, health education, and more.

who believed he didn't belong and who were determined to stop him from playing. But Robinson persevered and proved them wrong. He played in six World Series and was inducted into baseball's Hall of Fame in 1962.

Jackie Robinson's life is told in many nonfiction works, including *I Never Had It Made: An Autobiography* (Ecco, 1985) by Jackie Robinson and Alfred Duckett. Robert B. Parker's *Double Play* (Putnam Adult 2004) fictionalizes the Jackie Robinson story and tells—through the eyes of Robinson's bodyguard—what it was like for Robinson to break baseball's color barrier. In Donald Honig's mystery, *The Plot to Kill Jackie Robinson* (Dutton, 1992), a sportswriter discovers a plot to murder Jackie Robinson during his first major game, an idea that doesn't seem so farfetched given the hatred directed toward Robinson at that time in history.

Numerous films also portrayed this significant historical event. Jackie Robinson played himself in *The Jackie Robinson Story* (1950), but the film was criticized due to poor production quality. The legendary actor Michael Landon directed another Robinson film—*The Jackie Robinson Story* (1974)—and Robert Redford is portraying the Dodgers manager in an untitled film about Jackie Robinson's life, scheduled for release in 2012.

Rosa Parks: Although Jackie Robinson broke the color barrier in baseball, segregation was still prevalent in other areas, including Montgomery, Alabama, where Rosa Parks made history in 1955 when she refused to give up her bus seat to a white passenger, not out of pure defiance but because she was exhausted. Parks' decision led to the desegregation of the South. In 1995, she was awarded the Presidential Medal of Freedom, "America's highest civilian honor," by President Bill Clinton.

Rosa Parks's story appears in several notable television movies. *Boycott* (2001) relates the major incidents of the civil rights movement in the 1950s. According to Phil Gallo in his 2001 *Variety* article "Boycott," the movie was inspired by the book *Daybreak of Freedom: The Montgomery Bus Boycott* (University of North Carolina Press, 1997) edited by Stewart Burns. The movie was also the first in which every scene was digitally hand painted, a technique that enabled the moviemakers to combine current film footage with old news, stock, and other footage to create a "visually seamless" production. In 2002, Angela Bassett starred as Parks in *The Rosa Parks Story*, a movie that was nominated for fourteen awards and won Best Film, Best Actress, Best Screenplay, and Best Supporting Actress in the 2003 Black Reel Awards, and more.

One publication of note that discusses Parks's achievements is a 1956 comic titled *Martin Luther King and the Montgomery Story*, published by the Fellowship of the Reconciliation and distributed throughout the South; a copy now resides in the Smithsonian Institution in Washington, D.C. Another comic book is *Rosa Parks and the Montgomery Bus Boycott* (Capstone Press, 2007), written by Connie Colwell Miller and illustrated by Dan Kalal.

Martin Luther King: Now that we've mentioned Martin Luther King, Jr., we should take a look at this real-world hero who won the Nobel Peace Prize in 1964 for his contributions to desegregation and civil rights. King led the Montgomery bus boycott and delivered his famous "I Have a Dream" speech to 200,000 civil rights marchers in Washington, D.C., in 1963. The words of that

---

Street Cops

Imagine facing the toughest of situations on a continual basis— confronting dangerous weapons, violence, gangs, drug addicts, and the mentally ill and having to diffuse these situations with the greatest calm and minimal use of force. It isn't easy, and it's a task most of us couldn't handle—being a street cop takes dedication, training, attention to detail, an ability to communicate well with others, and a real knowledge of the streets and the situations that occur there. Street cops rise to action when called. They know the risk and that the indirect consequences of their actions could be deadly for them or someone else. Yet, no matter what, street cops strive to protect us from danger. They brave situations that others wouldn't dare face. And they do it with humble pride and fierce dedication. They are our protectors and our friends. And without them, our world would not be the same.

---

speech, which spoke of the dream of freedom and equality for all, continue to inspire people of all races and religions. In 1986, Martin Luther King, Jr. Day became a United States national holiday.

Ho Che Anderson's *King: A Comics Biography of Martin Luther King, Jr.* (Fantagraphics Books, 2005) is a compilation of his trilogy of graphic novels about Martin Luther King, Jr., and the civil rights movement. It is obvious Anderson did his research on this subject, and his work brings history to life for the current generation.

Dozens of films and books exist about Martin Luther King, Jr., although most are nonfiction or documentaries. One of the most recent is the upcoming untitled film scheduled for release in 2011, produced by Steven Spielberg. According to Tatiana Siegel in her May 2009 *Variety* article "Martin Luther King Jr. Bio Set for Big Screen," Steven Spielberg had wanted to make a film about Martin Luther King, Jr., for a long time.

Che Guevara: Around the same time that Parks and King were fighting for civil rights in the United States in the mid-1950s, Ernesto (Che) Guevara, discouraged by the economic inequalities among people and convinced that these inequalities were tied to the current form of government, led and won the fight against dictatorship in Cuba and was hailed as a revolutionary hero who brought equality and justice to many. Murdered in 1967, Guevara remains a legend among young and old alike, and throughout the world.

Two notable films are *Che: Part One* (2008) and *Che: Part Two* (2008). Both were directed by Steven Soderbergh and starred Benicio Del Toro as Che Guevara; Del Toro received the Best Actor award at Cannes in 2008 for his role. The films, told from Guevara's point of view, are mostly in Spanish.

Lech Walesa: Freedom also was a concern for Lech Walesa who helped rid Poland of communism in the 1980s and served as Poland's president from 1990 to 1995. Walesa believed that liberty was a right of the people and that it was the responsibility of all to ensure these rights were guaranteed. Winner of the 1983 Nobel Peace Prize, Walesa also founded the first independent trade union in the Eastern bloc and was awarded the Presidential Medal of Freedom in 1989.

Lech Walesa played himself in the 1981 film *Man of Iron*, a

Golden Palm winner about Solidarity, and in the Polish political satire *Bajland* (2000). News footage of Walesa appears in the 1988 film *Moonwalker* starring Michael Jackson and in Jackson's music video *Man in the Mirror*.

Unknown Rebel: In 1999, the world froze in terror when live television images of a man standing his ground against eighteen tanks and blocking their movement into Tiananmen Square in the People's Republic of China were broadcast. The Unknown Rebel (or Tank Man) became a symbol of courage for billions of people, especially the Chinese people who rallied that fourth day in June to fight for democracy in a country ruled by communism. The protest resulted in the murder of many by government forces; sources conflict regarding the number of people killed and range from several hundred to close to ten thousand, with thousands of others injured. However, Nicholas D. Kristof states in his June 21, 1989, *New York Times* article "A Reassessment of How Many Died in the Military Crackdown in Beijing" that true estimates are more likely between four hundred and eight hundred people. The Unknown Rebel's actions represent each man's ability to stand up to and fight against might in the pursuit of justice and freedom.

Although many songs and movies relate the events at Tiananmen Square, some are specifically about the Unknown Rebel. In 1996, the metal band Nevermore released the song "The Tiananmen Man" (on the album *The Politics of Ecstasy*). And an episode of the hit television show *The Simpsons* ("Goo Goo Gai Pan," 2005) pays tribute to the events of Tiananmen Square and the courage of the Unknown Rebel in a comedic way. In the 1992 film *Rapid Fire*, the actions of Brandon Lee's character are fueled by his anger over his father's death in Tiananmen Square. In addition, *Summer Palace* (2006) reenacts the events at Tiananmen Square, as does the 2010 film *Tiananmen Square*.

Nelson Mandela: Like the Unknown Rebel, Nelson Mandela stood strong against opposing forces in the quest for change. He led the revolution in the fight against apartheid and for a free and democratic South Africa beginning in the early 1960s. Jailed for twenty-seven years for his beliefs (on "terrorist" charges), he never wavered from his convictions and refused to do so in order to obtain his freedom. Mandela was released in 1990 and was elected president of South Africa in 1994, nearly thirty years after he began the fight for equality and freedom for all South Africans. Mandela was awarded the Nobel Peace Prize in 1993.

Nelson Mandela appears in approximately forty films or TV movies, mostly documentaries. Most notable is the Oscar-nominated film *Mandela* (1996) directed by Jonathan Demme. The film chronicles Mandela's life and his struggle to liberate South Africa. Others interesting films are the TV movie *Mandela's Fight for Freedom* (1995) and the feature film *Invictus* (2009).

Other real world heroes include:

Aung San Suu Kyi: The voice of Burmese democracy, Aung San Suu Kyi inspires her country in the fight for freedom from the confines of her home in Myanmar where she is under house arrest by the military, despite being elected Prime Minister in 1990, a position she never assumed. Aung San Suu Kyi was awarded the Nobel Peace Prize in 1991 and the Jawaharlal Nehru Award for International Understanding in 1992. Cartoonist Akazu Mizuha celebrates Aung San Suu Kyi's struggle to obtain democracy for her people in *Aung San Suu Kyi: The Fighting Peacock* (Irrawaddy Publishing Group, 1994). Furthermore, *Letters from Burma* (Penguin, 1997) is a compilation of fifty-two articles Aung San Suu Kyi wrote for a Japanese newspaper. She also was featured in the 1995 movie *Beyond Rangoon* directed by John Boorman. This fascinating film, based on a true story, portrays the fight for democracy during a student uprising. The group U2 also honors Aung San Suu Kyi's spirit and determination with the song "Walk On," which won record of the year at the 2002 Grammy Awards.

Doctors Without Borders (Médecins Sans Frontières [MSF]): An international organization of volunteer medical and nonmedical personnel who provide medical care to those in crisis throughout the world, mostly in areas where medical treatment is unavailable due to poverty or war. Created in 1971, the organization aids people in close to sixty countries. The National Geographic 2003 TV documentary series *Doctors Without Borders: Life in the Field* was narrated by Kiefer Sutherland. The 2008 documentary film *Living in Emergency: Stories of Doctors Without Borders* explores how four volunteers cope with providing care in Liberia and Congo in harsh and dangerous environments.

Erin Brockovich: She took on the Pacific Gas & Electric Company after she discovered the company was intentionally contaminating land with toxic waste, actions that sickened many people. The Academy Award–winning film *Erin Brockovich* (2000) was directed by Steven Soderbergh and starred Julia Roberts as Erin Brockovich. Although movie critic Roger Ebert thought the film lacked "focus and energy," it was nominated for forty-two awards and won twenty-seven, many by Julia Roberts for her portrayal of Brockovich.

Karen Silkwood: Karen Silkwood fought to expose the wrongdoings at an Oklahoma nuclear plant where she worked in the early 1970s, practices that endangered many people's lives. She died in a mysterious accident, which many believe was murder. Her story is portrayed in *Corporate Crimes Comic #1* (Kitchen Sink Press, 1977) and in the Mike Nichols–directed film *Silkwood* (1983). The film starred legendary actress Meryl Streep as Karen Silkwood, costarred Kurt Russell and Cher, and was nominated for five Oscars.

Dr. Muhammad Yunas: Dr. Yunas revolutionized banking and fought poverty by providing millions of poor people the opportunity to begin small businesses and escape from poverty. Without Dr. Yunas's help these people could not secure financing. Dr. Yunas won a Nobel Peace Prize in 2006 and President Barak Obama awarded him the Medal of Freedom in 2009. The film *Banker to the Poor* is scheduled for release in 2010 and tells the story of Dr. Yunas's work to fight despair and provide opportunity for those who once saw none.

Mythic Monsters and How to Fight Them

Ahuizotl: This Aztec monster savors human flesh and loves human eyeballs, fingernails, and teeth. Half-human and half-monkey, the Ahuizotl lures its victims with a cry that resembles a newborn baby. Once the prey is within reach, the Ahuizotl makes the kill by using the hand-shaped appendage at the end of its tail to drown the victim in the water in which it lives. Fishermen have fought

Jennifer Singleton, *Ashes*

"Ashes is a story in art of a ghost returning to the place of her death, the river in which she was drowned. As this once innocent soul reflects on the man who took her life she contemplates a ghostly revenge."—Jennifer Singleton is a gothic artist from Australia.

unsuccessfully against this creature and have even offered portions of their catch to appease the predator. But the Ahuizotl's taste is for human flesh not fish, and it will do whatever is necessary to satisfy this desire.

Akvan: Among the legends of ancient Persia that still echo in the deserts of Iran and Iraq is the tale of the fierce trickster demon Akvan. Like many trickster demons Akvan draws sustenance from the misery and pain that he causes, and he has been known to cause a great deal of that kind of harm. One needs to look no further than the translation of the creature's name—evil mind—to understand the nature of this beast.

The class of Persian demons called div ("evil spirits") exists for no other purpose but to do harm, and Akvan is one of the most powerful among them. His power is vast and inexhaustible; his insights into human misery profound.

Akvan is fearsome to behold as well—tall, powerfully built, a wide-grinning mouth, typical demon face, horns curved up from the brow, spike-like talons at the ends of his fingers and toes. With armament like that it would seem that Akvan preferred to attack and instantly kill his victims, but that is clearly not so. Akvan is far more fixated than that—he derives pleasure from misery, not mere physical pain, and enjoys prolonging the death of his victims.

In the Persian epic poem, *Shah-Nameh* (*The Book of Kings*), penned by the great Firdusai in 1009 at the behest of the Sultan Mahmud of Ghazna,[1] the various atrocities of Akvan are detailed. However, Akvan was foiled by the great folk hero Rustam, who played on one of Akvan's peculiar quirks—the fact that this creature would always do the opposite of whatever was asked of him. In the poem, the demon traps Rustam and demands that Rustam choose his death—to be thrown down a mountain or tossed into the sea. Rustam, wise to the ways of Akvan, demanded to be thrown down the mountain. Thinking that he has tricked the hero, Akvan threw Rustam into the sea instead. Rustam was a strong man and an excellent swimmer, however, and swam to safety.

This ancient poem provided advice for generations of travelers

1. *A Field Guide to Demons*, Carol K. Mack and Dinah Mack, 1998.

who happened to encounter the demon. When trapped and forced to name the manner of their death, the wise and well-informed traveler would use Akvan's penchant for reverse thinking to orchestrate an escape. But there are plenty of folktales in which the victims of Akvan either did not possess this bit of information, or didn't think through their answers carefully enough, and instead of escaping fate they fed the dreadful appetite of this immortal demon.

Anjing Ajak: By day a Anjing Ajak is a normal man. By night he turns into a cannibalistic killer (resembling a wolf-man) and attacks his prey with talons and teeth. Although it may seem difficult to kill this creature, found in the Indonesian nation of Java, the Anjing Ajak can be destroyed with a bullet to the heart or brain. Of course, when that happens, someone's father, brother, cousin, or nephew is not coming home for dinner, unless of course the Anjing Ajak is served as a sumptuous meal.

Ao Ao: When the natives of Paraguay (also some parts of Argentina, Brazil, and Bolivia) hear a howling that sounds like "ao ao ao" it's time to watch out. This carnivore is on the hunt and humans are its prey. Some say Ao Ao resembles a sheep with fangs; others describe him as a piglike mammal. But all agree Ao Ao is a dangerous monster able to pursue for great distances who won't stop hunting until he conquers his prey. The only way to fight this monster is to climb a tree, but not any tree will do. If the tree is anything other than a palm tree, Ao Ao will dig at the roots until the tree falls and the prey is captured.

Asuang (also **Aswang**): These creatures terrorize Filipinos and no one is immune. Although there are numerous theories as to how the Asuang came into existence (reanimated zombies, deceased people who are cursed, witches), there is no debate that these bloodthirsty, corpse-eating monsters are to be feared and avoided at all costs. Asuangs can change their appearance at will and hunt the vulnerable, especially pregnant women—their unborn children make a delectable meal. Some believe a stingray's tail, holy water, and salt can be used to fight off an Asuang, as can metal and garlic. Others state garlic oil is fatal to this monster, but all agree that the Asuang leaves no waste when feasting on humans.

Dawn of the Dead

"My favorite Good vs. Evil film has to be George A. Romero's *Dawn of the Dead*. Romero got it right. 'They are Us.' Good and evil are all a part of us and it is only when we are faced with the fantastic are we able to decide if we are meant for the evil or divine. In *Dawn of the Dead*, we are faced with the question: 'What if our neighbors, family, and friends began returning from the grave?' Would we be able to kill them . . . again? And what if they were using us as a food source? Does that make them evil or the next evolution of mankind? Romero layered this horror classic with so much subtext that it is hard not to be affected by the film. It is at times an allegory for the AIDS pandemic and at other times a biting satire of American consumerism. It is the horror film that cannot only deliver the scares but can also make us wonder and think. . . ." —Brian Patrick O'Toole is a screenwriter and independent producer whose works include *Dog Soldiers* and *Cemetery Gates*. He writes the monthly "Horrorcade" column for *Fangoria* magazine.

Legend states that following World War II a missionary decided to disprove the existence of the Asuang by showing that a human was responsible for the grave robbing in a local cemetery. Armed with a pistol, the missionary camped out for several nights next to a Filipino grave. On the third night a slobbering sound woke him and he saw a creature (with a freshly unearthed half-eaten arm in its mouth[2]) that resembled no other—translucent flesh, green-glowing eyes, bent torso resembling that of an elderly man. Although the missionary fired at the creature, it escaped. Thereafter, the missionary believed in the existence of the asuang.

Baobhan Sith (White Women of the Scottish Highlands): There's really no escaping this vampire that takes on the look and persona of a beautiful woman dressed in green and lures men to their

---

2. Kind of reminds us of those giant turkey legs you buy at amusement parks, but we doubt the arm tasted half as good; however, the Asuang will most certainly disagree.

death. She then drinks her victim's blood through her fingernails. The only way to fight this beauty is on horseback or with cold iron. Of course, like most vampires, the Baobhan Sith despises daylight. It's best to stay out of the way of this creature's clutches . . . once you're in her embrace, there's no escape.

Basilisk: Talk about a deadly stare—a simple look is all it takes for the mighty Basilisk to kill. This European monster is one of the most feared and deadly in the world. Accounts vary as to the physical appearance of Basilisk, but the most common description is of a creature with a snake's head, a tail, and a body that resembles a chicken. There are three types of Basilisk: a golden Basilisk that kills with its glare; an evil-eyed Basilisk that kills its prey with a third eye; and a Basilisk that kills with a mighty sting that removes the flesh of its victims. No one who has come in direct contact with a Basilisk has survived. Amazingly, both weasels and cocks can defeat this monster—the weasel is immune to the Basilisk's power and can kill the creature with its bite; the cock can kill the Basilisk with its crow.

Legend states that a knight was sent to kill the Basilisk but failed when the knight lanced the Basilisk and the Basilisk's poisonous blood killed both the knight and his horse. Later, a farmer killed the Basilisk with a mirror (the monster died when it saw its own reflection). In *Harry Potter and the Chamber of Secrets*, Harry Potter slays a Basilisk with a sword after the creature is deliberately released from the Chamber of Secrets in order to attack students.

Beast of Gevaudan (also **Le Bête de Gevaudan**): This beast is said to have feasted on at least a hundred people from 1764 to 1767 in the Auvergne and South Dordogne regions of France, mainly women and children. Wolflike with a prehensile tail and a fur mane, the Beast of Gevaudan is more the size of a cow than a wolf. This creature is a fierce predator and can leap long distances (up to thirty feet) to capture its prey.

In 1765, King Louis XV sent professional wolf hunters to capture the beast but they failed. The king then sent François Antoine to capture the beast, and in 1765, Antoine killed a creature that appeared to be an unusually large gray wolf. Some claimed it was the Beast of Gevaudan; others disagreed, especially when a new beast began attacking dozens of others. Legend states that the Beast of Gevaudan was killed in 1767 by hunter Jean Chastel. Thereafter, no new killings occurred.

Campe: This fearsome dragon guarded the twin giants after they were imprisoned by the God Cronus. Greek mythology states Campe had a scorpion's tail, dark wings, a scaly body, a thousand snakes for feet, and fifty wild beast heads that emerged from its body at the waist. The image alone is enough to scare most people, but not Zeus, who killed this great monster with a lightning bolt when he rescued Cyclops (the one-eyed giant) during a battle with the Titans.

Centaurs: Raw flesh is the meal of choice for these savage beings. Half-man and half-horse, most Centaurs were violent and refused to abide by the rules of society; however, some centaurs were not savage and abhorred violence. According to Greek mythology, Hercules battled the Centaurs and killed them with poison arrows. Centaurs have appeared often in pop culture: they are one of the eight fairy families in Eoin Colfer's book, *Artemis Fowl*; the Centaur Oreius leads the battle in good versus evil in the 2005 film *Chronicles of Narnia*;[3] and a Centaur is one of the sub bosses in the video game Mortal Kombat.

Cerberus: Cerberus isn't any ordinary guard dog and is far scarier than any dog we've ever encountered. This three-headed dog with a serpent's tail and snake heads on its back guards the Greek underworld and terrorizes souls as they enter, as if it wasn't bad enough to be sent to the underworld for all eternity. Hercules captured Cerberus—some say he wrestled the dog until he submitted and then dragged Cerberus from the underworld; others believe the Cerberus left willingly after Hercules treated him with kindness (the first time anyone had done so). Cerberus appears in numerous works including Dante's *Inferno*, Virgil's *Aeneid*, and J. K. Rowling's *Harry Potter and the Philosopher's Stone*.

---

3. Although several centaurs were mentioned in C. S. Lewis's book, on which the film was based, the centaurs were not named by Lewis.

Chemosit (also **Nandi Bear**): Africa is home to this creature that attacks natives on moonless nights. Chemosits love eating human brains and will kill to fulfill their desire for this delicacy. Accounts of the Chemosit vary—some describe it as a big ape with red or yellow hair; others state the Chemosit has the body of a hyena and the head of an ape. All agree the Chemosit has sharp claws and teeth—perfect killing weapons. Although some natives have tried to hunt the Chemosit, they've failed. It seems the only way to kill the Chemosit is by capturing the creature inside a hut and burning both the hut and the beast.

Chupacabra: This "sucker of goats" drinks the blood and body fluids (and sometimes organs) of livestock through a single or double puncture made with its fanged teeth. The legend of the Chupacabra spans the globe and accounts about its description vary. In 1995, the *San Juan Star* described the Chupacabra as a reptile-like creature with red eyes and fangs. Others state the Chupacabra has powerful claws and fangs and hops like a kangaroo. Attempts to capture and kill the Chupacabra have failed, for this elusive creature quickly disappears once sighted by humans. In the rural community of Calama, Chile, officials turned to the national guard for help in capturing the Chupacabra after the monster slaughtered a significant number of livestock. Hundreds of armed men searched for the Chupacabra but it eluded capture.

Chimera: Armed with the best weaponry found on an assortment of scary beasts, this murderous monster was a fire-breathing predator that attacked humans at whim. The Chimera was said to have a scorpion's tail, a goat's body, and the head of a lion; however, other accounts state the Chimera had two or three heads (lion, goat, and/or dragon). According to Greek legend, the Chimera attacked towns and ate the living. In Lycia, King Iobates enlisted the unconquerable hero Bellerophon to kill the Chimera after the monster terrorized Lycia. With the help of Pegasus, the winged horse, Bellerophon killed the Chimera with a lead-tipped spear. An alternate version of the story states Bellerophon chopped off the Chimera's head(s).

Chimeras are seen in numerous games, including the video game

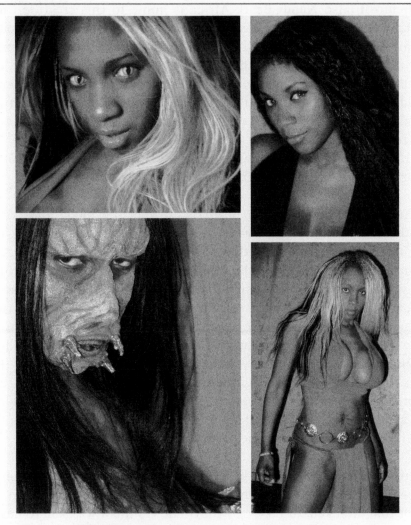

Many faces of scream queen Monique DuPree

"I think the reason why people are so fascinated with this is because of their own struggles of good vs. evil within themselves. We all hold the power to do good and evil. I prefer to play the monster. It's something fulfilling for me to be in the mind space of the bad guy. It's kind of like having the best of both worlds because I'm generally a good person at heart. Playing a monster in a movie helps me to exercise the bad in me."

—Monique Gata DuPree is a scream queen and star of *Shadowhunters 2: Oria* and *Bachelor Party in the Bungalow of the Damned*. Photos by Anthony Saint Thomas.

Final Fantasy Four and the board game Dungeons & Dragons. Chimeras also play an important role in the popular Japanese manga and anime series, *Fullmetal Alchemist*. Here Chimeras are a mix of animals or a fusion of human and animal.

Cuegle: Walking upright on two legs with handless arms, three eyes (two red, one blue), and five rows of teeth so sharp it can kill and devour its prey easily, the Cuegle is a black-skinned monster found in the Cantaberian folklore of Northern Spain. This creature loves to hunt the weak, especially animals and babies. But the only way to defeat the Cuegle is to avoid it. Holy or oak leaves repel this monster, so it's good advice to place leaves around the house or near a baby's cradle . . . that is if you or your loved ones don't want to become the Cuegle's next meal.

Cyclops: It might be easy to feel sorry for Cyclops—they are, after all, somewhat ugly beasts with a single eye in the middle of their heads—but these savage giants from Greek mythology devour humans. In Homer's *Odyssey*, the Cyclops are fearless; however, it was possible to defeat them. The Cyclops Polyphemus was blinded by a hot poker to the eye after Odysseus tricked the monster into drinking so much wine he passed out. Other authors stated Apollo killed the Cyclops with an arrow to avenge Apollo's son's death.

Two giant Cyclops are in the 1958 film *The 7th Voyage of Sinbad*. One attacks Sinbad and the other fights a dragon. In comics, Cyclops is a superhero and leader of the X-men. Created by Stan Lee and Jack Kirby, Cyclops first appeared in 1963 in *X-men #1*. Using his ability to emit powerful blasts from his eyes, blasts capable of tearing through steel and pulverizing rock, Cyclops (and the X-men) wages a battle against evil.

Dobhar-Chu (also **Dobhar-chú, Dobarcu, Doyarchu,** and **Dhuragoo**): Part dog and part otter, the Dobhar-Chu or "water hound" is a lake monster of Irish mythology that is covered in white fur and measures eight feet. This monster kills at will and doesn't discriminate between women, men, or children; it's pure beast and one that loves human flesh. The Dobhar-Chu surprises its victims at the water's edge and then wrests them into the water where they meet a vicious and untimely death. According to legend, the Dobhar-Chu killed a woman in 1722; her husband rushed to her aid and stabbed the creature in the heart, killing it. But a horrific noise came from the beast as it died, and from the waters rose its angry mate. It took two men to kill the second Dobhar-Chu; and since that day no one has reported another sighting of this beast.

Dragon: These massive serpentlike creatures often breathe fire and scorch anything in their paths. Dragons occur in myth throughout the world, yet the description varies from culture to culture. For the Chinese, dragons are gentle and wise creatures; most other cultures view dragons as monsters with magical powers. For years, popular culture portrayed these creatures as something to be feared. Over time, people realized dragons were not necessarily the beasts people imagined them to be, and the resulting attitude became one of awe and acceptance. Of course, only some dragons are likable creatures; the rest are to be feared.

One of the most famous battles with a dragon occurs in the epic *Beowulf* when the dragon leaves its lair and burns everything in sight after someone steals the dragon's golden cup. Beowulf, now king of his people, slays the dragon, but his injuries are fatal.

Dragons appear in over 140 television shows and movies worldwide, including the 1966 Japanese movie *Kairyu daikessen* (*Battle of the Dragons*), *Dragonslayer* (1981), *Dragonheart* (1996), and *The Mummy: Tomb of the Dragon Emperor* (2008), where a Chinese emperor, who is brought back to life, transforms into a three-headed dragon and uses his power to try to enslave the world. Smaug, the antagonist in J.R.R. Tolkien's *The Hobbit* (Allen & Unwin, 1937), is a dragon felled by an archer. In Anne McCaffrey's series *Dragonriders of Pern*, humans and dragons communicate with one another through telepathy. And, in Christopher Paolini's *Eragon* (Knopf, 2003), *Eldest* (2005) and *Brisingr* (2008), a human and a dragon work together to rid the world of evil.

Empusa (also **Mormolykiai**; plural **Empusae**): Devouring human beings, especially travelers, is what Empusa liked to do best. This Greek monster, who served Hecate (the goddess of magic and witchcraft), could assume different forms—a beautiful Phoenician woman, a donkey-faced human, etc.

In one of the most famous accounts of the Empusa, a young man was confronted by the monster. After the dreaded Empusa changed shape several times before the man's eyes and the man realized what he was facing, he attacked the Empusa with harsh words, which was enough to scare the monster away.

Fachan: The sight of a Fachan is enough to make anyone stop in their tracks. But it's not a good idea to hesitate for even a second near this creature that makes its home in the highlands of Scotland. It's said that the glare of the Fachan's single eye can force a man to remain helpless in place, vulnerable to the creature's attack. Once the Fachan grabs hold of its victim there is no escape, for the Fachan has a thick arm that extends from the middle of its chest and a powerful hand with an unbreakable grip. Should one be lucky enough to avoid the glare of the Fachan, the only recourse is to outrun this creature; but even that will be very difficult. The Fachan, taller than the tallest of men, has a single leg and can leap very quickly; however, agility is not this creature's strength, so it's possible to escape with clever maneuvering.

Ga-Gorib: Throwing people into pits was great fun for the Ga-Gorib (or "thrower down"), a demon found among the Khoikhoi tribes of Southwestern Africa and the Xhosa people of South Africa. Ga-Gorib also enjoyed stoning people. Although the stones often bounced off Ga-Gorib's victims and knocked the demon back into the pit, it didn't stop Ga-Gorib from harassing those who came near. In the most famous legend describing Ga-Gorib's death, Heitsi-eibib defeated and killed Ga-Gorib by causing the demon to fall into its own pit after a long and violent wrestling match.

Garkain: It's best to stay far away from the Garkain, a monster that dwells in caves and other unpopulated areas throughout the Northern Territories of Australia. Aboriginal folklore states that the Garkain, described as a hairy hominid, travels to nearby forests and paralyzes unsuspecting humans with its stench before pouncing from a tree and feasting on its victims. More recent myth describes the Garkain as a more supernatural hominid that has huge black wings and the head of a fruit bat. Although normal weapons can kill a Garkain, the difficulty lies with the monster's stench—if a man gets close enough to deliver a kill shot, the stench paralyzes the man and certain death results.

The Goatman: This creature does not discriminate when it comes to prey and chases livestock, house pets, and humans. Sightings have been reported throughout the United States from the East Coast to Texas, but witnesses seem to disagree as to whether this beast has a black goat head on the body of a man or the head and body of a man on goat legs. They do agree, however, that the Goatman is one brutal beast. Some reports state that when humans fled in cars (the only means of escape from this monster) the Goatman chased after the cars and attacked them with an axe until the beast could no longer maintain pace with the vehicles.

Gorgon: Vicious creatures who were fated to guard the entrance to the Greek underworld, Gorgons could turn men into stone with a single glance. There are three female Gorgons—Medusa, Sthenno, and Euryale—but Medusa, the only mortal Gorgon, has become the most famous as a result of her portrayal in film and literature. With hair made from writhing snakes, scales covering the body, and sharp fangs, Gorgons could kill anyone that stood in their way. Some state these creatures have rattles on their tails, the power to steal power from the Greek gods, brass hands, fangs, and/or a beard; others believe Gorgons shoot fire from their fingertips. Legend states that Perseus—with the help of a helmet that made him invisible, winged boots, a reflective shield, and an unbreakable sword—brought back Medusa's head to King Polydectes as a wedding present.

Throughout history, Gorgons have been portrayed in a variety of ways. In *A Tale of Two Cities* (1859) by Charles Dickens, Dickens uses the Gorgon to foreshadow death for one of his characters; the chapter is aptly named "Gorgon's Head." In the 1981 film, *Clash of the Titans*, Medusa's blood turned into giant scorpions, and, in the popular game Dungeons & Dragons, a monster named Medusa has writhing snakes for hair.

Grendel: For twelve years, Grendel attacked King Hrothgrar's men at their nightly gatherings in the mead hall and took them back to his lair where the monster ate the man and enjoyed a tasty meal.

Beowulf, the world's oldest poem, recounts the legend of Grendel. Here, Beowulf, the only person who does not fear this hairy monster, battles Grendel and tears off the monster's arm, leaving Grendel to die.

Grendel appears in numerous films and television shows such as the 2005 film *Beowulf and Grendel* and the 2007 animated film *Beowulf*, in which Crispin Glover portrays Grendel and Angelina Jolie portrays Grendel's mother. An interesting take on Grendel is presented in the animated film *Grendel* (based on John Gardner's 1971 novel *Grendel*). Here, the monster's point of view is used to relate the story to the audience. Grendel also appears in comics (*Beowulf, Dragon Slayer* by DC Comics, 1975–76) and in video games such as Final Fantasy VIII and Beowulf the Game. And, in James Rollins's thriller *Ice Hunt*, an ice station named Grendel is inhabited by huge and powerful creatures that are left over from ancient times.

Haugbui: This monster from Scandinavian legend was a ferocious beast. In addition to murdering, the haugbui used trollskap, a powerful sorcery, to inflict illness and bad luck on its victims. Those subjected to the Haugbui's wrath (and their families) suffered for generations. Although the Haugbui, whose name means "mound dweller," could be killed by a tremendous show of force or fire, villagers preferred to appease this monster with calves milk or freshly brewed ale. If the Haugbui seemed especially ferocious and uneasy, villagers would sacrifice a cow to maintain the peace. When it became apparent that the Haugbui preferred the offerings over humans, along with the treasure it hoarded in its lair, villagers made offerings to the Haugbui on a regular basis, a practice that continues to this day.

Hellhounds (also **Devil's Dandy Dogs**, **Gabriel Hounds**, **Night Hounds**, **Yeth Hounds**, and **Wish Hounds**): When on the hunt, hellhounds seek more than a hot meal of human blood and flesh; they seek an immortal soul to take back to the their master—the devil. These massive black hounds, prevalent in European folklore, hunt at night. They have fiery eyes and scorching breath and the stamina to chase their prey until the prey is exhausted. Then the Hellhound makes its kill. The only way to survive an attack is to outrun the

Shelley Walker, *The Dark Lady*

"I think most people like to believe in the inherent good within themselves and others, so in such stories they can imagine themselves in the hero's place and get some gratification out of that. It also offers hope in a way, when good wins. The world can be a cruel place, everyone has dark times, and reading a tale where good wins reminds people that things will get better."

—Shelley Walker is a painter of eclectic fantasy and gothic art, whose work has been featured in several publications and online galleries.

Hellhound until early morning. No one really knows if it's the first cock's crow of the day or impending daylight that scares the Hellhound, but the instant the beast hears the crow, it abandons its prey and heads for home without a kill . . . that is, until the Hellhound goes on the hunt again.

Hydra: This nine-headed dragon was feared by all. Perhaps it was because the Hydra was vicious, or maybe it was because Greek mythology states that this monster was nearly impossible to kill. One of the Hydra's heads was immortal, and if one of the mortal heads was chopped off two grew instantly in its place. Hercules killed Hydra as one of his twelve labors, but it was a daunting task. First, Hercules cut off each of the Hydra's mortal heads and quickly sealed the wounds to prevent regrowth. Then Hercules used a boulder to trap the immortal head and conquer the beast.

Jiangshi (also **Chiang-shih, Kiang-sh,** or **Chinese vampires**): In Japanese and Chinese mythology, the Jiangshi or "hopping vampire" fed upon the life force of unsuspecting travelers. This reanimated corpse was blind, had a dangling tongue and long fingernails, and was "born" when a person committed suicide and the soul refused to leave the body. It's possible to avoid confrontation with the Jiangshi by holding one's breath. Loud noises drive the creature away and garlic, salt, red peas, and white iron protect against an attack. In the Chinese practice of feng shui, a six-inch piece of wood is installed across the doorway to keep the vampire from entering the home. If the Jiangshi lives long enough to achieve the ability to fly, only a bullet or thunder will kill this monster.

Jormungandr (also **Jormungand, Midgard,** or **World Serpent**): In Norse mythology, the Jormungandr was a sea creature so large it could reach across Earth and hold its own tail. Thor and the Jormungandr were enemies, and they were fated to fight until the end of time. When they first met, the Jormungandr was disguised as a massive cat, and although Thor only managed to lift the cat so that one of its paws no longer touched the ground, Thor's feat was considered impressive. The second time they met, Thor caught Jormungandr on a fishing line and pulled the massive sea monster from the water; however, Jormungandr escaped when Thor's fishing partner (the giant Hymir) cut the line. It is predicted that Thor will kill Jormungandr the next time they meet, which will occur at Ragnarok (the end of days). But it will also mean death for Thor, who will die from the monster's venom.

In the Marvel Comics the Mighty Thor series, Thor kills a Jormungand (known as the Midgard Serpent); unlike the myth Thor doesn't die but is cursed to live forever. Thor also battles Jormungand in the computer game God of Thunder.

Kongamato: We typically think of dinosaurs as creatures that existed hundreds of millions of years ago. But, in fact, there is a creature resembling a pterodactyl in existence today. This reddish monster hunts humans at night throughout the sub-Saharan region of Africa. If the creature can't score fresh meat, it will settle for a meal of decomposing flesh taken from shallow graves—it seems the Kongamato knows how to dig with its long beak and sharp claws. Legend states that the Kongamato also brings floods and famine. The best way to deal with the fierce and deadly Kongamatos is to avoid the creatures all together. But if that's not possible and the beast comes hunting for some fresh meat . . . yours . . . chant the protective spell "Muchi wa kongamata!" and you'll drive away the Kongamato.

Mamlambo (also **Brain Sucker**): The name of this beast is enough to cause fear in any rational-minded man—just the thought of sharp fangs piercing a skull and sucking out brain matter is more terrifying than any of the scariest horror films. After all, this monstrous water snake is real according to South African legend. Some state the beast is sixty-seven feet long with the body of a crocodile, the head of a snake, and short legs; others describe it as having the hindquarters of a snake and the head and torso of a horse. Either way, it's best to avoid the Mamlambo, especially since it has the ability to attack on land or in water.

After nine people were killed near the Mzintlava River Bridge in the Eastern Cape region of South Africa, hunters were sent to kill the Mamlambo. But the feared Mamlambo outwitted the hunters, or perhaps just knew to avoid them, and the men returned from the hunt without their prey.

Minotaur: A great monster with the head of a bull and the body of a man, the Minotaur was confined to a labyrinth built to prevent the creature from harming others. To satisfy this bloodthirsty beast, fourteen Athenians were forced into the maze every nine years. Then the hunt began. The men and women navigated the labyrinth desperate to escape the Minotaur and discover a way out of the maze. But the Minotaur always succeeded in its quest and enjoyed fourteen sumptuous meals of blood and flesh. According to legend, the Athenian hero Theseus engaged in a horrific battle with the Minotaur inside the labyrinth and slew the monster with his sword.

Mokele-Mbeme (also **N'yamala**, **Guanérou**, and **Diba**): A fearsome monster dwells in Likouala swamps and Lake Tele in the Republic of Congo. This predator, whose name means "one who stops the flow of rivers," is said to resemble a dinosaur with a massive body, long tail and neck, small head, and four thick legs. The Mokele-mbeme kills humans to defend its territory; otherwise, the creature prefers to eat grass and plants. Sightings date back for centuries, and accounts of the mokele-mbeme are entrenched in the folklore and history of this region. In 1920, four members of a team sent by the Smithsonian Institution to study and obtain plant and animal specimens and document life in Africa met an ill-fated death in the area where the mokele-mbeme was said to live. One account states warriors killed a mokele-mbeme with spears and rocks after the beast attacked a defensive barrier the villagers had erected across the river. The villagers cooked the beast and enjoyed a celebratory meal, but they all became ill and died shortly thereafter.

The Nemean Lion: According to Greek mythology, nothing could stop the Nemean lion from devouring people and animals in Argolis, an area located in the Nemean region. Nothing that is, except for Hercules, who killed this ferocious beast. Armed only with a bow, arrows, and a club, Hercules hunted the forest for the Nemean lion's lair. The beast, a clever creature, surprised Hercules from behind and rushed him with a mighty roar. Without hesitation, Hercules turned and fired his bronze-tipped arrows, but the arrows failed to damage the Neamean lion's impenetrable hide. When the beast pounced on Hercules, Hercules stunned it with a blow to the head, strangled it with his bare hands, then skinned the lion and wore the pelt as an armored cloak. The lion's jaws formed a helmet, and the paws, tied across Hercules's chest, held the pelt to his body.

Ogre: Strong bodies and incredible strength give this beast the perfect attributes to prey and feed on humans, although if it weren't for their massive size, huge heads, and eating habits, they might be mistaken for an extremely overdeveloped man with a strange and horrific appearance. Ogres are often depicted as cruel and ugly beings with a lack of intelligence and an insatiable appetite. Although Ogres appear threatening, it is easy to outwit them. But if an Ogre catches its prey off guard, it will down a tasty meal of human flesh.

Ogres in comics are often mutant creatures created through genetic engineering. In Marvel Comics, the Ogre first appeared in *Uncanny X-men #28* (1967). And in 1996, DC comics introduced an ogre in *Batman #535* (*The Ogre and the Ape*). In the film *Shrek* (2001), the king and his soldiers post wanted signs and rewards for the capture of mythical creatures, including Shrek, the ogre who eludes capture by scaring off the hunters. In *Shrek 2* (2004), the king hires Puss in Boots to kill Shrek, but Shrek escapes death by befriending Puss in Boots.

Redcap (also **Powrie**): Travelers unfortunate enough to encounter the Redcap become prey for this evil sprite that murders with a wooden scythe or an iron pike. The Redcap then stains its hat, made from dried human skin, with the blood of its victims—it's not difficult to imagine how this monster got its name. Because the Recap perishes if the blood on his cap dries, this murderous creature must continue to kill; no one is safe near the castles and villages that this sprite haunts.

Found in British, Irish, and Scottish folklore, the Redcap is described as a thin, goblin-type creature with leathery skin and minimal hair. Travelers shouldn't be fooled by the Redcap's diminutive appearance—this sprite is quick on its feet, despite the iron shoes it wears, and will not hesitate to murder anyone that crosses its path. And, it's impossible to outrun the Redcap; the only way to survive an encounter with this murderous creature is to quote a passage from the Bible, which will cause the Redcap to lose a tooth and run away.

In Mike Mignola's short story "Iron Shoes," an iron-shoed goblin throws spears at Hellboy when Hellboy encounters the goblin during an investigation of an abandoned castle in Scotland. Redcaps also appear in the graphic novel *The Hero Discovered* by Matt Wagner.

Trolls: These creatures avoid prying eyes (and thieves and treasure hunters) by making their homes in dark, sheltered places like caves and dungeons where they can hoard the gold, jewels, and gems that they've stolen. Physically, Trolls are similar to Ogres, although Trolls possess a greater intelligence, one that enables them to outwit humans to steal and amass a wealth of treasure. The only way to defeat a troll is to outsmart it, for these creatures are physically strong and capable of conquering the strongest of humans. Trolls appear in J.R.R. Tolkien's *The Hobbit* (Allen & Unwin, 1937) and the *Lord of the Rings* (1954).

Werewolves: It's difficult to imagine transforming into a wolflike form and hunting humans at night with incredible speed, murdering people with brute strength, claws, and fierce teeth. But according to European mythology, that's exactly what happened to some individuals, albeit in a variety of ways. Some transformed completely,

---

Categorizing Good and Evil

"People need to label and categorize things as either 'good' or 'evil' in order to feel secure, superior even. Good was something noble to aspire to; and evil made you ugly and stupid, and doing bad things would ultimately destroy you . . . but it's all so unrealistic. It's just not that simple. The evolution of Luke Skywalker and Darth Vader through movies, novels, and comic books is an excellent example of how the battle between good and evil has become more complex. Each side has an equally legitimate point of view and motivation to succeed at all costs."

—Kelly J. Compeau is creator, head writer, and art director of *The Black Tower*, a dark webcomic series.

---

walked on four legs, and hunted just like a wolf while maintaining their intellectual ability, an attribute that enhanced their hunting capabilities. Others partially transformed and kept their ability to walk upright. Still others didn't transform at all but were possessed by a werewolf spirit.

In fiction, transformation into a werewolf is dependent on the cycles of the moon; however, that is not the case in real life. Werewolves can transform at will, making them the perfect hunting beast capable of eluding capture. All the werewolf must do is outrun its pursuers and transform back into human form without being seen—no one would know what happened and the beast could continue to kill at whim.

Cultures vary in their beliefs as to how to defend against a werewolf attack—wolfsbane, mountain ash, rye, or mistletoe—but all agree it's best to avoid this creature. Should a loved one become a werewolf, there are cures, including exorcism, physical exhaustion, scolding, striking the werewolf with a knife, etc. Again, these methods differ among the folklore and are dependent on the country of origin.

Dozens of films center around werewolves. One of the classics is *Werewolf of London* (1935) where two werewolves are on the loose and it's up to a botanist to stop them with a rare plant. Another great film is *The Wolf Man* (1941); Lon Chaney, Jr. stars and draws

---

On Fighting Evil

"The Vampire Huntress Legend series takes a look at how one family takes a stand against vampires, werewolves, demons, and everything else that goes bump in the night. Each member of the family has a spiritual gift, which they use to sense danger and kick-ass!

"Damali Richards is 'The Neteru'—a super heroine—who can hear demons, smell them, see them with her third-eye second sight . . . her body is a lean, mean, fighting machine, and she takes heads off with her mystical 'Madame Isis' blade."

—L. A. Banks is the *New York Times* bestselling author of the Vampire Huntress and Crimson Moon series.

On Creating Werewolves

"I researched real wolves for my werewolves. . . . When I felt I had a handle on real wolves, then I wanted to work on were-wolf society. How would it change wolves to think like people, at least part of the time? I turned to Norse and Greek myth for my two main branches of werewolf society . . . I also spoke to people who study wolves for a living, or for a very dedicated hobby. When I had all my information in hand, and head, I mixed it all together in that alchemy that is my imagination and out came my werewolves." —Laurell K. Hamilton, *New York Times* bestselling author of the Anita Blake series.

---

the audience's sympathy for the creature. The film also features legendary actors Claude Rains and Bela Lugosi. Other notable films include *An American Werewolf in London* (1981), directed by John Landis; and *The Wolfman* (2010), starring Benicio del Toro as this fearsome beast.[4]

Whowie: This Australian monster had a strange combination of body parts, each very large—ant's body, lizard's head, and snake's tail—that when joined together created a formidable and vicious being that hunted and murdered humans, a meal that was the Whowie's favorite. Legend states that warriors trapped and killed the Whowie after the beast ate an entire Aborigine village; except for a young boy who somehow escaped the monster's clutches. The Whowie's spirit lives on in the cave where it had made its lair, and at times locals can hear it roar.

4. Jonathan Maberry wrote the novelization of the movie for Tor Books, 2010.

7 DID YOU USE PROTECTION?

Sam Flegal, *Knight Magic*

"My piece *Knight Magic* shows a knight calling on his totem raven spirit to bless his armor. It shows a knight, commonly represented as good, preparing for battle. However, this piece is different from most of my work as I have a tendency to lean toward the sinister, and I tend to like stories where evil is triumphant." —Sam Flegal has a BFA, and is a professional illustrator and an "erosion artist"—doing portraits of people as they would appear if they were zombies.

CHARMED, I'M SURE

Throughout history—and popular culture—holy weapons, charms (or amulets), and talismans have aided heroes in the fight against evil; and because evil is very powerful and takes many forms—both supernatural and human—it was necessary to have a huge cache of weapons beyond the standard sword, gun, knife, etc. Some holy weapons, charms, and talismans protect against evil; others drive away evil once it arrives. If good is to prevail, it's important to be armed with the proper weapon.

Talismans and amulets are often mistaken for the same thing, but they are, in fact, different. Amulets protect a person from evil or bring good luck. Talismans, however, have magical or supernatural powers of protection that are transferred to the possessor of the item. Excalibur, King Arthur's legendary sword, is a perfect example of a talisman. The magical sword was unbreakable, and as long as the sword was in King Arthur's possession he defeated all and couldn't be harmed. Another example is the Holy Grail, a vessel that was said to heal all wounds; those who possessed the Holy Grail could achieve immortality. And then there's the Philosopher's Stone, an elusive and sought-after talisman that was said to turn base metals into gold and to give the possessor physical health and therefore the possibility of immortality.

References to holy weapons, charms, and talismans are abundant in popular culture. One of the most famous is found in Bram Stoker's 1897 book, *Dracula*, where the highly recognized holy weapon, the crucifix, is used to repel vampires. In the 1931 film by the same name (starring Bela Lugosi as Dracula) and in the 2004 film *Van Helsing*, crucifixes and holy water are used to defend against Dracula.

In the 1906 children's novel *The Story of the Amulet* by E. Nesbit, an ancient amulet is supposed to grant the children everything they want. But because they only possess half the amulet, the amulet transports them through time so they can search for, and hopefully find, the other half.

Beginning in the 1930s there was surge in the use of holy weapons, charms, and talismans in popular culture, particularly in comic books where heroes used these items to fight the battle against evil. According to comic book reviewer Glenn Walker, Dr. Occult (first appeared in 1935) wields a magical disc called the Symbol of Seven; Dr. Fate (1940) uses the Cloak of Destiny, the Amulet of Anubis, and the Helm of Nabu; Green Lantern (1940) uses a magical ring and a lantern; Wonder Woman (1941) uses her Lasso of Truth, magical bracelets, and a magical tiara; Sargon the Sorcerer (1941) uses the Ruby of Life, which enables him to control whatever he touches; Thor (1962) uses Mjolnir, a mystic hammer; Dr. Strange (1963) uses the Orb of Agamotto, the Cloak of Levitation, the book of Vishanti, and an amulet called the Eye of Agamotto; Nightmaster (1969) wields Night Sword, a magical sword that warns of danger and protects; and Hector Ayala (1975) uses the Sons of the Tiger, mythic pendants that transform him into the White Tiger, a superhuman being with incredible strength and skill.

The year 1975 also saw the release of the film *Monty Python and the Holy Grail*, a humorous take on the search for the Holy Grail. And in 1981, *Raiders of the Lost Ark*, the first of the Indiana Jones films, was released. In this film, another holy weapon, the Ark of the Covenant, plays an tremendous role. Here, the Nazis search for the Ark, a holy weapon so powerful it would make their army invincible. In a twist of fate, the Ark, when opened, unleashes a powerful energy that kills all the Nazis. Another film, *Omen III: The Final Conflict* (1981), uses holy weapons to fight evil. Priests armed with ancient holy daggers battle the Anti-Christ, who seeks control of the world.

Aptly named, the comic character Talisman made her first appearance in 1983. This Marvel superhero gains supernatural powers from the Coronet of Enchantment, the talisman she wears on her forehead. In the film *Nightmare on Elm Street* (1984) and the subsequent films in that series, victims of the supernatural serial killer Freddy Krueger hear a twisted version of the nursery rhyme "One, Two, Buckle My Shoe." The words warn the victims to arm themselves with a crucifix as protection against Freddy. Of course, Freddy always finds his victims.

Published in 1984, *The Talisman* by Stephen King and Peter Straub tells the story of a young boy who must find an enchanted crystal called the Talisman to save his dying mother. This popular

Power Talismans

"Superheroes require more power because they face uglies that make the standard Joe Van Helsing wet their pants and run. In dealing with these other dimensional nasties, more than just a strong chin, a flashy costume, and a holy symbol are needed. Everyone has their own tools . . . These talismans are not just their protection against evil, they are also their sources of power . . . Without them, the superheroes would be mere mortals like us." —Glenn Walker is a professional writer and founder of the Writers Chatroom.

book is the basis for the Talisman graphic novel series released in the fall of 2009 by Del Ray Books.

Soon, two other heroes who use talismans and amulets came onto the scene. Neil Gaiman introduced the world to the popular superhero Morpheus, a.k.a. the Sandman, in 1989, a comic character who uses a ruby, sand, and a helm. And, Sailor Moon, the hero of the 1995 television cartoon series, uses jewels in her tiara, hair, and broach to fight evil.

In 2000 *Static Shock* was released, a Kid's WB animated series. One of the characters, Anashi the Spider, is a West African superhero who obtains his powers from an ancient golden spider amulet. Then there's the hit film *Lord of the Rings: The Fellowship of the Rings*, released in 2001—Galadriel, the Queen of Lothlorien, uses a basin of water as a mirror to reveal the future; the discovered knowledge is then used to fight evil.

The seventh season of Joss Whedon's popular television series *Buffy the Vampire Slayer* (2002–2003) shows Spike using an amulet to pulverize the Turok-Hans (super powerful vampires) with light harnessed from the sun. Around the same time, several films showed viewers the power of amulets, holy weapons, or talismans. In *Hellboy* (2004), the titular character wears a rosary adorned with crosses around his wrist. In *Venom* (2005), Miss Emmie surrounds her house with crosses and fetishes, and wears a rattlesnake skull amulet. And in *Amityville Horror* (2005)—a film that scared thousands and thousands of moviegoers and made them afraid to go home after the film ended—a crucifix and holly were used to drive away evil spirits.

Protection from evil spirits is also the theme of *Wendy Wu: Homecoming Warrior,* a 2006 Disney Channel movie. Wendy is the reincarnation of a powerful warrior, but she lacks the martial arts skills she needs to defeat an evil spirit intent on destroying the world. Unfortunately, Wendy is the only one capable of conquering the spirit, so a Buddhist monk gives Wendy a powerful amulet to protect her while she learns the necessary skills.

Two video games popped onto the scene in 2006 and 2007 that use amulets and talismans. The first, the Elder Scrolls IV: Oblivion, pits the player against evil creatures from another dimension called Oblivion. The player must find the king's amulet, and other items to save Earth. In the second game, Twilight Heroes, powerful talismans give superpowers to the player and these powers are used to fight villains, robots, and monsters.

Finally, in the film *The Haunting in Connecticut* (2009) and in the book *Cirque Du Freak: The Vampire's Assistant* (Little, Brown, 2001), crosses are used to fight evil. In the film, a reverend brings a magnetic iron cross to banish evil spirits haunting a house. And in the book, the main character tries to kill a vampire with a cross and holy water.

As we can see, holy weapons, charms, and talismans play a significant role in pop culture—as they do in real life—and these items have done so for hundreds, thousands, of years. It's not enough for us mortals (or superheroes) to rely on our own powers when fighting evil. We need help—a guarantee, or at least reassurance, that we have the ability to win and that good will conquer evil. Holy weapons, charms, and talismans give us that edge, enable us to do things we might not ordinarily be able to do; and they help instill the belief that when good is pitted against evil, good will win.

TOOLS OF THE TRADE

There are many different holy weapons, charms, and talismans found in cultures throughout the world and throughout history.

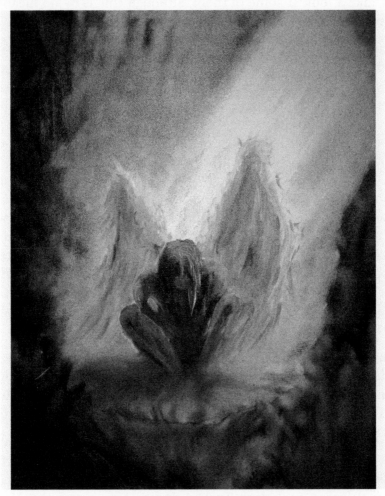

Doug Schooner, *First Angel*

"*First Angel* is a portrait of Lucifer, a.k.a. Scratch, Beelzebub, the Devil, Satan, as he is first placed in hell. It is a new place, he is alone, an angel imprisoned against the cold rocks. His fury has yet to awaken and begin an eternal fire. Having lost his battle and been cast out, light still bears down on him to consummate the judgment upon him. As with any leader who has lost, he is still certain that he is right. Very few try to be evil, they are merely trying to make things better from their own perspectives. Sometimes those perspectives conflict with our own and that is what divides them from us."—Doug Schooner is an artist.

Let's take a look at some of them, although this is by no means an exhaustive list.

Abracadabra: In ancient times, Magi holy men created the Abracadabra, one of the most well-known talismans, to protect against everything bad, including illness and death. This talisman consists of an upside down triangle that contains the word "abracadabra." Each subsequent line inside the triangle begins with the letter "A" and continues until the edge of the triangle, with each line containing as many letters of the word abracadabra as possible. So, the first line spells out abracadabra, the second abracadabr, the third abracadab, and so forth until the final line at the point of the triangle only has the letter "A." Initially, abracadabra talismans were written on paper, folded into a cross shape, and worn around the necks of those seeking protection; later this talisman was engraved onto assorted metals and worn as a charm. Most people today, at least those who have seen a magic show, are familiar with the word abracadabra; it's the "magic" word magicians use when revealing a trick.

Abraxas: The word "abraxas" was engraved on ancient stones and used for protection against illness by those in the Gnostic religion; often pictures of mythical creatures accompanied the word. Historians state that Abraxas was a god that was both good and evil.

All-seeing eye: If you've ever handled U. S. paper currency, particularly a one-dollar bill, then you've seen the all-seeing eye, which is contained within the Great Seal of the United States. Found in many cultures (including Turkey, India, Africa, and the Middle East), the all-seeing eye is a single human eye surrounded by beams of light, and it is said to provide the protective power of God against evil.

Amoghshiddhi Buddha: Worn as an amulet, the image of the Lord Buddha is used by Thai Buddhists to protect against evil and fear.

Amulet: An object that uses charged energies to protect against evil.

Angel statue: There are many types of angel statues—created from a variety of materials and posed in different manners—and each serves a different purpose, i.e., to provide peace, protect against illness, or bring love. Angel statues can be found in homes, offices, and museums throughout the word. Because angel statues bring peace and serenity they are considered a protection against evil and a means to bring us closer to God.

Ankh: In ancient Egypt, the ankh represented eternal life, both physically and spiritually. Based on the hieroglyphic that meant eternal life, the ankh was shaped like a cross with an oval at the top. Many depictions of the ancient gods show them carrying an ankh; the ankh also appeared on numerous coins from ancient Cyprus. Wearing an ankh is said to protect a person from evil, particularly illness.

Archangel Michael: For Muslims, Archangel Michael obtains mercy for sinners from Allah. For those who practice the Jewish faith, Michael (whose name means "Like Unto God") controls natural phenomena. Michael also protects heaven and those engaged in battle. Many wear jewelry or carry other objects with a picture of Archangel Michael to safeguard them from harm. In fact, Michael is the patron saint of policemen, many of whom wear St. Michael medals for protection.

Aspand (also **espand, esphand**, and **esfand**): Muslim nations rely on the surviving Zoroastrian rite of burning the aspand seed over charcoal and chanting a spell to protect children from evil, particularly that of the evil eye.

Ba Gua mirrors: The practice of feng shui (Chinese geomancy) uses Ba Gua mirrors to protect improperly situated houses from evil. A concave, octagon-shaped mirror—with painted black, red, and yellow Ba Gua symbols that ring the center—is placed on the side of the house to absorb negative energy and prevent it from entering the house. A convex, octagon-shaped mirror painted the same repels harmful energies and is placed above the front door. This practice originated thousands of years ago.

Bluestone: Protects those who practice voodoo from evil.

Cat's-eye shell: These shells, resembling eyes, are used widely in the Middle East and Europe to create protective charms that ward off the evil eye. Cat's-eye shells are also found in African American mojo bags.

Circle of Protection: This Wiccan talisman protects the wearer from harm.

Cord amulet: Newborn babies in India are given a cord amulet to ward off the evil eye. The cord, made from string, is placed on the baby's neck or wrist; beads may be used for decoration. When the cord breaks, it is believed the baby is old enough to resist evil. In Brazil, cord amulets also provide protection, although these bracelets are made from paper instead of string. And, in Israel, red string bracelets are given to those who visit Sarah's shrine (Sarah was the wife of Abraham, the founder of Judaism)—when the cord breaks a blessing occurs.

Corno: (also **cornuto**, **cornicello**, or **Italian horn amulet**): In Italy, these amulets, shaped like twisted horns, are usually made from gold, silver, or red coral and protect against the evil eye. Because

---

Potato Magic: This Spud's for You

"We've all read the myths and tales pertaining to herbs and plants that had magical properties in the hands that knew how to use them. A popular example is mandrake, a prized member of the beautiful, yet potentially deadly nightshade family; perhaps brought into magical practice because the root resembles the human form. There are those who speculate that mandrake was used like a do-it-yourself voodoo doll, and the roots have been a sought-after magical treasure since biblical times.

"The cultures of Asia have ginseng—a somewhat more people-friendly root that has been used for centuries as a refreshing tonic, an aphrodisiac, and is a popular addition to the recent wave of 'energy drinks'—whose ephemeral buzz comes more from caffeine and sugar. In these forms the amount of the root is practically nil. The curious, however, need only travel as far as an Asian grocer or if you're lucky enough to have a Chinatown of any capacity nearby—great food—to snatch up a bottle of the stuff for yourself. As we've mentioned, there's really no way to 'own' the rights to ginseng so there's no rush to these claims for their validity. However, thousands of years of steady business has to at least mean something.

"But consider the humble potato. The fourth largest crop in the world, tubers can be grown over most of the world, but the 'wild potato' rode along the dusty streets of Peru and made himself known to Europe in 1536. And well, let's face it—if you know any one singular fact about the history of Ireland, it's probably that a long time ago there was an Irish potato famine (1845), which was caused by an icky fungus that goes by the much cooler moniker 'late blight.'

"From a love spell circa 1920: Take a potato and wash it thoroughly. While you do so you must concentrate on the two people you wish to bring together, or pick someone for yourself. Then, carve the names and birthdates of the two folks in question and encircle them with a heart—probably the most challenging part of the spell one would think.

"Provided there's any room left on the damn thing, you can add words or phrases pertaining to the hopeful couple. Next, sprinkle the potato with basil and rub it in to get the mojo working. Now, bury the potato in a safe and close location by the light of the full moon. Technically, the moon should be shining down on the burial spot if you can swing it. Then, just water regularly and wait for things to green, which will be a sign of the couple's growing love—should flowers also bloom, then there's family matters in the near future.

"Native American ritual for rain circa 1829: Take a potato that has already begun to sprout beside a riverbank that's beginning to run dry. Sprinkle the potato with echinacea, a spiny-looking flower common to North America that has many uses in herbal medicine. The Native Americans used the echinacea as an offering to the spirits and as a catalyst for the spell. If all is done properly, before the plant flowers there will be rain.

"In the folklore of the English, it was believed that potatoes could cure rheumatism if they were carried in one's pocket. It was believed that the potatoes were removing the uric acid from the body. Potatoes also have been purported to cure acne, act as a salve in curing boils, cure constipation, and soothe sunburn. They'll take away the lines from under your eyes, and they're still delicious deep-fried and smothered in ketchup!"
—David F. Kramer is a Bram Stoker Award winner.

the evil eye attacks men's reproductive systems, men wear the corno to protect their ability to procreate. Mothers and babies wear them, too. The mano curato, a variation of the corno, is also used to ward off the evil eye but is shaped like a horned hand.

Crucifix: For Christians, this holy weapon protects against demons and represents Christ's triumph over evil.

Devil pod (also **bat nut**, **goat head**, **bull nut**, or **buffalo nut**): A devil pod is placed above the door or included in a mojo bag to ward off evil. This black seed pod comes from the Asian plant *Trapa bicornis* and is approximately three inches in length. Interestingly, the pod's shape often resembles a devil, a demon, or other evil entities.

Eye in Hand: This protective amulet looks exactly like it sounds— it's a hand with an eye in the middle. The amulet can be worn as jewelry or hung on the wall to protect against the evil eye. In Turkey, the eye is created with a blue stone because it is believed the evil eye is blue. Other areas of the world (India, Arab countries, and Israel, for example) use different colored stones or ivory to create the amulet, but the result is the same—the eye in hand protects against evil.

Eye of Horus: This powerful ancient Egyptian symbol was used to protect against evil. The symbol consists of a right eye similar to Horus's, the sky god who took the form of a falcon.

Fourth Pentacle of Mars: Success in war is all important if a person wishes to survive evil. The Fourth Pentacle of Mars amulet is worn by Wiccans in battles of all kinds to ensure victory.

Gau (also **Ghau** or **Gao**): In ancient times, the Tibetan prayer box, worn as jewelry, was crafted from metal and contained a prayer that had been blessed and handwritten by a priest to protect against evil. Today, the Gau still protects against evil; however, amulets, plants, and other symbolic objects are placed inside.

Guan Yin (also **Kwan Yin** and **Quan Yin**): To ensure the sea did not wrought evil on fishermen in China, the men prayed to this compassionate goddess for protection, particularly the thousand-armed version of her. Farmers and travelers also prayed to this goddess. Also, she is said to help souls in the underworld.

Guardian masks: These fierce protectors against evil are used in Nepal and are placed on walls and next to doors and windows. The masks often depict a ferocious warrior or a mythological figure who has an open third eye and wears a pointed crown.

Hanuman pendant: For the courage to fight evil and protection from it look no further than the Hanuman pendant. This amulet is named after Hanuman, the Hindus' greatest mythological hero.

Horseshoe: Across the globe horseshoes serve as protective charms against demons, devils, and other evil, although their use varies. In North America, horseshoes are hung pointing up next to or above doorways to protect structures such as homes, business, and barns, from evil and to bring good luck. In most of Europe and Latin America, the horseshoe is hung facing down. Whether the horseshoe is pointed up or hung upside down, this protective charm is one of the most embraced in the world.

Mojo bag: This Wiccan pouch is an essential prayer bag used for a variety of purposes, mainly to ward off evil or bring good luck. The bag—crafted from flannel, silk, or leather—is filled with charms, stones, herbs, fetishes, and other objects and is worn against the body, either around the neck or in a pocket. It's important that the mojo bag remain hidden from the sight of others.

Naga effigy doll: A remote tribe of hunters, called the Naga or Snake people, live in eastern India and use a Naga effigy doll to perform magic against their enemies. Bits of hair, nail, skin, or other body parts of the enemy are placed inside the effigy doll, which is then used to place a curse on the enemy.

Ojo de venado (also **deer's-eye charm**): Made from the seed of the *Mucuna pruriens* (or velvet bean) plant, this Mexican charm protects newborns against the evil eye, although others may use the charm as well. The charm is either worn as a necklace or a bracelet, carried in a pocket, or hung from the rearview mirror of a car. Each charm has the image of a holy saint.

Pentagram of Solomon: This amulet dates back to biblical times when King Solomon wore a magical ring decorated with a pentagram and other symbols and used it to trap demons and evil spirits. Today, the Pentagram of Solomon amulet protects the wearer from these evil beings. The amulet is a round medallion with a pentagon in the middle; other symbols surround the pentagon.

Powerful hand (also **hand of power** or **Spanish mano ponderosa**): This talisman, originally used over eight hundred years ago to guard against enchantment, points upward and provides magical protection to those who use it, mainly Roman Catholics. Some Wiccans use life-size replicas of the powerful hand as a protection against evil. Other versions of the powerful hand include:

- *African American helping hand*—turned sideways with the hand open.
- *Arabic and Jewish hamsa hand*—fingers face downward; sometimes has one thumb, sometimes two, but always five digits.
- *Mexican milagro hand*—shows the back of the hand ending at the wrist with the fingers extended.

Scarab: To defend against evil on the journey to the afterlife, ancient Egyptian bodies were buried with heart-shaped scarabs. These beetle-shaped symbols, typically cut from stone or hand-crafted into jewelry, are now worn as decorative objects and are believed to give the wearer the sun's protection.

Skulls: In Nepal, 108 skull beads carved from bone or wood, forged from metal, or molded with plastic are strung together to create a mala (a set of prayer beads). Each of the skulls represents one of the 108 gods, and when worn as a necklace the skulls are a powerful protection against evil.

Star of David: The six-pointed Star of David, named after King David, the ancient military hero who supposedly wore the symbol on his shield in battle, is now considered a Jewish protective symbol. The Star of David, comprising two "intertwined equilateral triangles" that protect the wearer from harm, represents God's ability to rule over and protect the universe. In Kabbalah tradition, the symbol protects against evil spirits and represents the opposing sides of man (good vs. evil, etc.). And, in the Middle East and North Africa, the Star of David is worn to bring good luck.

Stones: Cut from the earth and found in jewelry, amulets, and decorative objects, stones are used for a variety of purposes, including as a protection against evil. Some stones, such as those corresponding with each sign of the Zodiac, protect individuals born during a specific time of year from illness. Other stones protect everyone. Here's a few examples and their protective purposes:

- ► *Agate*—protects against evil.
- ► *Amber*—protects against the evil eye.
- ► *Amethyst*—protects against evil sorcery.
- ► *Black amber* (also *jet*)—protects against psychic attacks and other evil.
- ► *Carnelian*—protects against the evil eye.
- ► *Cat's-eye*—protects against witchcraft.
- ► *Crystal quartz*—protects against the evil eye. Also enhances other stones' power when used in conjunction with them.
- ► *Diamond*—known as a symbol of love, these stones also repel evil.
- ► *Emerald*—prevents evil spirits from possessing a person.
- ► *Garnet*—protects against the evil eye.
- ► *Hag stone*—repels evil spirits of the dead.
- ► *Jasper*—repels evil spirits.
- ► *Lapis lazuli*—protects against evil spirits called upon to do harm through the occult forces of black magic.
- ► *Malachite*—repels evil spirits.
- ► *Onyx*—protects against black magic and evil spirits.
- ► *Ruby*—protects against witchcraft, psychic attacks, and the evil eye.
- ► *Snowflake obsidian*—repels negative influences.
- ► *Red tigereye*—repels the evil eye.

Symbols: Some symbols, such as an arrowhead or a beetle, are used to protect against evil. Stone-formed shapes work best—the older the stone the better—but in a pinch symbols derived from other materials will work.

Talisman: These man-made magical objects, symbols, or designs protect against evil and bring good fortune to those who possess them. The use of talismans as a means of protection was recorded throughout history, including the use by the ancient Egyptians and Babylonians and those who lived in the Middle Ages. Talismans are still used today and are often carried or worn.

Tattoos: Tattoos as protective amulets are used among some aborigine tribes, Buddhists, and monks.

Thor's hammer: The invincible hammer of the Viking god Thor is used as a protection from thieves, and as a general means of personal protection.

Worry dolls: Although worry is not necessarily an evil, it can be evil for children, especially those who are trying to sleep. Among the Mayans of Guatemala, the worry dolls are used to rid children of this evil. Created from scraps of wood, leftover fabric, and string, six tiny dolls are placed inside a small cloth bag. The child relates his concern to a doll, then sets it under his pillow before bed. In the morning, the doll is gone and so is the worry. Of course, should another issue arise, there are five additional dolls.

Sara Jo West, *Garden Angel*

Although in most organized belief systems angels have been portrayed as divine messengers, it has become common worldwide to view them as protector entities. Angelic statues and icons can be found almost anywhere, even in the possession of people who don't otherwise subscribe to organized religion. In the secular view, angels are often considered "spiritual beings" or "forces of positive energy" apart from any specific religious connection.

FIGHTING EVIL WITH GOD ON YOUR SIDE

Evil is everywhere, and we've fought it for as long as we've existed. The evil that was present thousands of years ago is similar to today's evil—humans warred over land, religion, or resources; jealous men or women fought for the affection of others; disease, famine, and disaster took their toll on lives. But today's evil also battles against good in the guise of righteousness, that the crimes we perpetrate against one another are justified somehow, whether we kill for the sake of religious beliefs, pollute the planet without regard to the consequences, embezzle, cheat, physically abuse, or a myriad of other evils.

It's easy to fight evil with evil, to follow the old adage of "an eye for an eye" without a thought to the consequences. When our emotions get the best of us—or even when they get a small piece of us—the normal human reaction is to fight evil with evil, to seek vengeance for those who have been harmed. Many would argue this is not the way to fight evil; others believe in this method. And while we are not here to dispute people's belief systems, it's important to recognize the differences. After all, who and what defines evil? The answer to that question will remain unanswered forever because the definition varies depending on who you ask. So, let's assume for the sake of this discussion that evil is deliberate harm to others, something that occurs as a result of free will and choice rather than harm that results from an accident or ignorance (although we don't advocate that ignorance is an excuse for evil).

Powerful militaries, governments, police, and others fight a constant battle against evil on global and local levels. Evil isn't difficult to find—it's in our neighborhoods, cities, countries, the world—but it can be difficult to fight. And that's why a lot of people turn to God to fight evil. With God on their sides, evil is something that can be overcome, something that can be conquered, squashed, destroyed. And although some people believe their God has commanded them to fight evil by creating more evil, the majority do not. Most people believe that God is responsible for bringing evil into the world and it's up to us to decide how to address it.

For the Hindus, good and evil are in a constant battle. When

Ignoble Savages

"We are raised in a Manichean world. Our Judeo-Christian religions taught us to fear evil and to obey the Ten Commandments; the movies always showed the good white cowboys overcoming the wild Indians. But we are savages, the worst predators that this planet Earth ever knew and we need to feel justified to commit our brutalities against life. This good vs. evil struggle gives us an alibi and as soon as we demonize our enemy, it allows us to destroy him without the slightest remorse. With storytelling this struggle becomes an exceptional way to blow off steam both for the writer and his readers and you probably know that without problem and struggle you can't really attract attention and emotion."—Hervé Scott Flament is an internationally renowned artist.

necessary, the Hindu god Vishnu comes to Earth to fight evil. In the Christian faith, fighting evil with God on your side means fighting evil with good. It's the idea that human beings have free will and that God (Jesus) is all powerful. Through our good deeds, our love of ourselves and one another, including those who perform evil deeds, the battle against evil will be won—it may not be today or tomorrow, but it will happen. Evil cannot be defeated with more evil. In order for good to win, we must look beyond the external evil and also address the evil we discover inside ourselves.

Similarly, others, like those in the Jewish faith, believe the best way to fight evil with God on your side is to ignore it, to trample darkness (evil) with light (good) by finding an inner strength and rising above the evil until a place is reached where evil can no longer touch us. Addressing evil makes it more powerful. There are times, however, when avoiding evil is not possible, when war or other evil reaches us despite our best efforts. It is during those times that we must quash evil without joining it, without perpetuating the same evil deeds. We must rid the world of evil while reaching for the good, aiming to find a place that has no room for evil.

Fighting evil with God on your side is a theme in the song "Fighting Evil" by Mystic Ruins (on the album *In the Dark*). The lyrics discuss the importance of believing in God and using that belief to shun violence to create happiness and peace. Also, Bob Dylan's song "With God on Our Side" (1963) examines why wars occur if there is a God and God's on our side. And the narrator at the beginning of the film *The Chronicles of Riddick* (2004) states that in normal times good can and should fight evil, but extreme times call for extreme measures; and sometimes that means fighting evil with evil. Although God is not specifically mentioned here, we can infer that this comment refers to the Christian view discussed above where fighting evil with God on your side means fighting evil with good.

In the films *The Ten Commandments* (1956) and *The Prince of Egypt* (1998), God parts the Red Sea so that Moses can help his people escape from the evil of slavery. And, *The 99*, a comic book series launched in 2006 and published in the United Arab Emirates by Teshkeel Media, is aimed at Muslim youths and features ninety-nine superheroes. Each superhero embodies one of Allah's ninety-nine attributes, and the superheroes combine their powers and work together to fight evil. Talk about battling evil with God on your side—these guys have got it made.

DEMONIC POSSESSION

We've all heard the phrase "the Devil made me do it." It's almost become a part of our culture. Sometimes the phrase simply means that someone committed an act that they perceived to be bad, something they might not ordinarily do but that is not necessarily "evil," an act that was indeed within their control but for which they desired to divert the blame. But sometimes the saying refers to true evil, evil that invades the soul and takes over one's action. Evil that is so far away from good that we can't begin to fathom the distance. When a demon or the Devil or Satan (or any one of the other dozens of names for this evil force) gets into the mix it's just plain downright bad news, and the consequences aren't pretty.

So, what is this evil? Evil so vile that people talk about it in hushed whispers behind closed doors. Evil that scares people so much that they'll do anything to avoid it and get rid of it. Evil that sends people screaming in fear.

The Omen

"What is frightening about the movie *The Omen* is the image of this innocent looking little boy who is really the face of the Beast, a monster with divine omnipotence, omnipresence, and omniscience. A force who knows who you are, where you have been, and where you will go. Those are the things that made it scary—just the mere thought of this Beast having the power to rape your mind, and to control your destiny." —Richard Myles is a filmmaker whose classic horror movie *Mental Scars* was released in 2009.

Demonic possession is when an evil entity completely takes over one's body—and it's not for anything good. Who ever heard of a possessed person inventing a new type of medicine or bringing peace to the world? No . . . these evil entities take over behavior to create havoc and destroy lives.

Although there has been debate as to whether demons actually exist, nearly every religion and culture refers to demonic possession in some way. Some believe demons seek those who are infirm (spiritually, psychologically, or physically) and gain entrance to that person's body and soul through the weakness. Others believe demon possession occurs through the cooperation of a witch or wizard. Still others don't know how demonic possession occurs, only that it exists and that it's evil.

In 2007, a woman blamed Satan for attacking her husband and compelling him to burn their baby in the microwave. Was her husband possessed? Who knows? Maybe he was just psychologically ill. If we were to abide by Christian theology in the Middle Ages, we would believe he was possessed by the Devil. During this time period, people were either influenced by God or the Devil. But maybe God permitted the Devil to test this father's fortitude by creating hardship in his life and that of his child—that's the theory they believed in medieval times.

Two great scholars, Socrates and Plato, also spoke about demons and believed in demon possession. And in 1987, Pope John Paul II expressed his belief that the Devil continued to do his work—How else could the Nazis have perpetrated such evil during World War II?[1] While the pope may not have been referring to what we consider a true demonic possession, his words reinforce the belief that the Devil is considered an evil entity that can influence people and cause them to perpetuate evil.

Modern culture continues to believe in demonic possession, and those beliefs vary among cultures and religions; however, many now believe that demonic possession is not responsible for mental or physical illness, as it was thought in the past. But one thing is clear—demonic possession is typically evil.

In the next section we'll discuss demonic possession in a variety of cultures and religions along with the means to exorcise the demons. For now, let's take a look at demonic possession in popular culture.

SILVER SCREAMS

There are over a hundred films and television shows that address demonic possession and exorcism in some form dating back to the 1915 black-and-white short feature *The Bridge of Time* where a demon possesses his relative. The silent film *The King of Kings* (1927) by legendary director Cecil B. DeMille shows Jesus ridding Mary Magdalene of the seven deadly sins via a form of exorcism. And in the 1936 film *Dracula's Daughter*, a countess is possessed

---

On the Word "Exorcism"

"The word 'exorcism' is derived from the Greek word exousia, meaning 'oath,' and refers to 'placing the demon on oath,' or invoking a higher authority to bind the entity and compel it to act in a way contrary to its wishes."—Dr. Jerry Alan Johnson is ordained as a senior priest in Zheng Yi Daoism and is trained in esoteric alchemy and mysticism from both the Shang Qing (Mao Shan) and Tian Shi (Lung Hu Shan) Daoist sects.

---

1. *Vatican Issues First New Exorcism Ritual Since 1614*—Cnn.com January 26, 1999.

by Count Dracula after Dracula is killed by a stake through the heart. She then embarks on a killing spree in order to drink the blood of her victims.

A surge in interest in demonic possession and exorcism occurred in the late 1960s and 1970s with films and television movies like *Rosemary's Baby* (1968), *The Devils* (1971), *The Possession of Joel Delaney* (1972), *The Exorcist*[2] (1973), *Abby* (1974), *L'ossessa* (1974), *Un urlo nelle tenebre* (1975), *Exorcismo* (1975), *The Omen* (1976), *Khake Sar Beh Morh* (1977), *The Possessed* (1977), *Exorcist II: The Heretic* (1977), and *Good Against Evil* (1977). The interest continued throughout the 1980s, 1990s, and into the present day. Films such as *The Exorcism of Emily Rose* (2005), *Amityville II: The Possession* (1982), and *The Unborn* (2009) continued to satisfy our desire to feel like we can exert control over evil and emerge victorious in the fight.

Of course, comedians parodied the classic demonic possession films by presenting new and exciting twists on the subject. In Tim Burton's *Beetlejuice* (1988), a pair of ghosts hire a "bio-exorcist"

The Exorcism of Emily Rose

This 2005 film was inspired by the true story of a German girl named Anneliese Michel, who claimed she was possessed by six demons (some accounts list more). She died in 1976 from starvation and dehydration following an exorcism that was conducted several times a week over a ten month period. In the film, the priest who performed the exorcism was put on trial and held accountable for Anneliese's death. In real life Anneliese's parents and the two clergy who performed the exorcism were convicted of manslaughter." Felicitas D. Goodman's book, *The Exorcism of Anneliese Michel* (Doubleday, 1981), provides an in-depth look at what happened to Anneliese Michel. And the 2006 German film *Requiem* presents another take on this topic.

---

2. Based on the book *The Exorcist* by William Peter Blatty. Blatty was inspired by a 1949 exorcism of a teenage boy. Thomas B. Allen's book *Possessed: The True Story of An Exorcism* (Doubleday, 1993) details this event.

to scare away the human inhabitants of their home, but Beetle-juice is no normal bio-exorcist and his antics serve up a ton of laughs. The 1990 film *Repossessed*, starring Linda Blair and Leslie Nielsen, is a spoof of the film *The Exorcist*[3]. And, Penn & Teller win the fight against Satan through the exorcism process in their 2003 TV series *Bullshit*.

Demonic possession and exorcism are also found in animated works such as *The Duxorcist* (1987), where Daffy Duck opens an exorcism business, and in *The Boondocks* (2005), where a character makes a deal with the Devil and possesses someone in order to get revenge. Popular video games such as Diablo II, Paper Mario: The Thousand Year Door, and The Legend of Zelda: Majora's Mask contain demonic possession. In Paper Mario, the Shadow Queen possesses Princess Peach; and in The Legend of Zelda, Majora possesses the Skullkid when the Skullkid wears Majora's Mask. Demonic possession is also found in Metroid Prime II. In this game, the Ing must possess the bodies of others in order to survive.

Pumpkinhead

In a twisted take on the classic form of demonic possession, Stan Winston's *Pumpkinhead*[4] portrays a human possessing the demon as opposed to the other way around. While this film is not a possession in the true sense of the word, it can be inferred as such because the man, who conjured up the demon to exact revenge for his son's death, is able to witness the demon's horrific deeds through the demon's eyes. In addition, Pumpkinhead becomes one with a character and they both must die in order to end Pumpkinhead's reign of terror. Dark Horse comics published a series titled *Pumpkinhead: The Rites of Exorcism* in 1993 but only published two of the four planned issues.

---

3. Blair played a possessed twelve-year-old in *The Exorcist*. In *Repossessed* she played a mother.

4. The original title was *Vengeance: The Demon*. Winston is best known for his makeup and special effects on dozens of films, including *Aliens* (1986), *Predator* (1987), *Edward Scissorhands* (1990), *Pearl Harbor* (2001), *Artificial Intelligence: AI* (2001), *Iron Man* (2008), and *Terminator Salvation* (2009).

David Leri, *The Exterminators*

"*The Exterminators* is one of only a handful of pieces that I've done over the last twelve years that wasn't for a company or a particular product. I have a story in my mind that involves the human character being hunted down by the evil lizard creatures through a war-torn city, and that is the scene that ended up inspiring that painting."

Dave Leri is a freelance illustrator whose artwork has appeared on many book covers, in magazines, and on gaming-related materials.

Hervé Scott Flament, *St. George*

"St. George is one of the most compelling figures in religious history. There is no real proof that he ever performed the heroic feats ascribed to him, and yet we take cues from him for noble, benevolent, and heroic behavior."

Hervé Scott Flament is a French fantasy fine artist.

Marvel Horror Comics

Marvel Comics have a long tradition of presenting intelligent, complex stories that are both frightening and well told. Among the favorites (*clockwise from top left*): Man Thing, Zombie Wolverine (from Marvel *Zombie Return* #3), Werewolf by Night, The Terror, Ghost Riders, and the landmark *Tomb of Dracula* #1.

Jason Beam, *Andromeda*

"This piece is based on a classic tale of beauty, heroism, and monsters from Greek myth. The characters of myth may have been gods and monsters, but they were as emotionally and psychologically complex as human beings, with all of the flaws that go with it. There is no real 'black' or 'white'—it's always about the infinite colors in between."

Jason Beam's digital work has appeared in many magazines and books, on CD covers, and elsewhere. Model: Joey Decker.

Patrick Don Maitz, *The Vampire Hunters*

Don Maitz comments: "Comic relief has been a major part of the 'scare me' genre. The *Abbott and Costello Meet* . . . (the monster of your choice) type of movies must have been rattling around in my subconscious as this small painting was being created. I believe that humor is an important part of both good and evil. Laughter illuminates our perception of where one stands on the good-to-evil meter."

Art © Don Maitz

Peter Mihaichuk, *Devilfire*

"This piece, commissioned for a friend in return for some awesome tattoo work he did for me, screams with malevolence. Sometimes evil is quiet, sometimes it's subtle; other times it shouts with a towering voice and will not be ignored."

Peter Mihaichuk is a production designer and concept artist within the film industry.

Scott Grimando, *Goddess*

"*Goddess* represents the Earth Mother, the spirit from which all things flow. Nature is neither good nor evil. It simply is. It does what it must. Man created the concept of good and evil."

Scott Grimando is a professional illustrator and conceptual artist whose work has appeared in a wide variety of books and magazines. Some of his most compelling pieces have been collected into *The Art of the Mythical Woman* (SQ Productions, 2009)

Vince Proce, *Ghost*

"This painting tells a story about the struggle against darkness. She cries out
the Lord's Prayer as some evil darkness attempts to consume her. Will the Divine
save her or will she succumb to darkness? It's a classic struggle."

Vincent Proce has been an illustrator for over twenty years.

In comics, characters such as the Deadman and Billy Kincaid have the ability to possess others, as do Emma Frost and Professor X (who takes possession of other people's minds) from the Marvel Comics X-Men series. The Talisman, another Marvel Comics character, has the ability to exorcise demons. Perhaps someone should pit The Talisman against the other characters mentioned above—now that would be a match to behold.

SCARY STORIES

Fiction is no stranger to possession, especially for master storyteller Stephen King, who puts a twisted take on demonic possession with an evil car that kills people in *Christine* (Viking, 1983). In the hands of any other writer we would have our doubts about this possession, but King's readers found themselves hesitating before getting behind the wheel and hitting the road, especially if they happened to drive a red and white 1958 Plymouth Fury[5]. As if King hadn't scared his readers enough, he again tackles demons in *Song of Susannah* (Donald M. Grant/Scribner, 2004) where a demon from a parallel world inhabits a woman.

In *Harry Potter and the Chamber of Secrets* by J. K. Rowling (Arthur A. Levine Books, 1999), Ginny Weasley is possessed by Tom Riddle (the young Lord Voldemort and the feared Dark Lord of evil) and is forced to open the Chamber of Secrets and release the Basilisk, the monster of Slytherin. In this series, Voldemort also possesses Harry Potter and Quirrel (teacher of the Defense Against the Dark Arts class). Demonic possession is also found in W. G. Griffiths' *Driven* (Faithwords, 2002) where an ancient demon inhabits a modern-day lobster fisherman in order to commit murder and in *Takedown* (FaithWords, 2003) where the same demon now possesses a professional wrestler. And in Sara Gran's *Come Closer: A Novel* (Soho Press, 2003) a woman is possessed by a demon, attempts murder, and engages in other horrific acts.

The struggle of good versus evil is a difficult one, one that has existed for as long as recorded history and one that continues to

---

5. The film version was released the same year and was directed by John Carpenter.

occupy our thoughts. After all, no one[6] aspires to be possessed by a demon and to commit acts beyond one's control. So, the next time someone says "the Devil made me do it" watch out because they might really mean it.

THE EXORCISM

It's nearly impossible to talk about demonic possession without discussing exorcism. The word exorcism is derived from the Greek word exorkizein and the Latin word exorcismus and means the driving out of evil spirits or demons. Typically demons possess a person, but they can take over a place or a thing.

Exorcisms have been practiced for many years throughout the world in the struggle of good versus evil. Although techniques vary among groups of people, the result is the same—to drive out evil so that good can triumph.

Africa: Though religious practices vary among the African people, it is not uncommon for pastors to perform exorcisms in African societies. Pastors and elders place their hands on those who are possessed and whisper prayers into the possessed person's ear to drive out the evil. Other ways to exorcise the evil is through Baptism or the use of oil and prayer. Some Africans believe in witchcraft (mainly in south and central Africa) and that the witch Ndoki possesses people, particularly children. Others blame possession on the evil spirit kindoki. In these instances, extreme physical pain is sometimes believed to be the best method to drive away evil spirits.

Baha'i: For the Baha'i faith, the term demon is simply a symbolic way of referring to a human's state of imperfection, a turning away from good. Because demons do not exist as entities with powers of their own they cannot possess an individual. Therefore, there is no need to perform an exorcism.

---

6. Well . . . probably almost no one. There might be those who think it would be neat, but we wouldn't want to venture into that territory. You never know what might happen, especially when dealing with that kind of evil.

Mesmerism

In the 1770s, Viennese physician Anton Mesmer attempted to discount the theory of exorcism by showing that symptoms of demonic possession were the result of a misalignment in an individual's magnetic flow, which he referred to as animal magnetism. First using magnets, and later only his hands, to correct the flow of magnetism, Mesmer cured the "possessed" individual.

Baptist: According to the Reverend Andrew Hudson, the Baptist view of demonic possession is not very different than the Christian view, although the Christian view follows the Bible in totality whereas the Baptist view holds to more defined doctrines. In the Baptist viewpoint, a person can become possessed by inviting a demon to be a part of their lives by calling on spirits, by engaging in the practice of witchcraft, or by getting involved with spirits of the dead.

In a Baptist exorcism, the exorcist does not slap a person, wrestle him to the ground, or recite a special formula. Instead, church leaders are called together to lay hands on a possessed person and pray for the person to be healed and released from bondage. Baptist exorcisms are not a common practice in the United States.

Demonic Activity in the Third World

"In the third world, particularly in Africa, there are a lot more outward and visible demonstrations of demonic activity. There are a whole lot more Satan worship and sacrifices to the Devil and calling to spirits, and I've seen those who were possessed and who have invited demons into their lives. I've participated in the laying of hands on them and watching them be released from the power of darkness . . . The exorcism starts off antagonistic, argumentative, rageful, and by the end the person is melted and weeping in our arms thanking us for rescuing them . . ."

—Rev. Andrew Hudson taught at Kijabe Boys High School in Kenya, East Africa, and now serves as lead pastor at Chelten Baptist Church.

Buddhist: Buddhism does not believe in demonic possession as we typically think of it but rather the idea that evil is a result of one's own actions. If we take that philosophy further, one can conclude that there is no need for exorcisms in the practice of Buddhism. However, some Buddhist priests in Japan scare away evil spirits with a sacred stick, called a shakujo, or by wearing masks and dancing to fool the demons.

Catholic Church: When the Devil attacks a person it's not a pretty sight. Demonic possession can occur when a person turns away from God, invites an evil spirit into their lives through the occult, engages in repeated sin, or participates in satanic rituals. Demonic possession can also occur as the result of a curse.

According to Matt Baglio, author of *The Rite: The Making of a Modern Exorcist* (Doubleday, 2009), "There are three signs that may indicate the presence of a demon: abnormal strength, the ability to understand and speak previously unknown languages, and knowledge of hidden things. However, since these things could also have a natural explanation exorcists usually also look for an aversion to the sacred, that is the inability of the person to pray, enter a church, or say the name of Jesus or Mary. All of these things are

On the Depiction of Exorcisms

"The popular depiction of exorcisms, from the legendary 1973 film, *The Exorcist*, to *The Exorcism of Emily Rose*, includes dramatic events such as poltergeist, physical transformation of the possessed, cursing in ancient Semitic languages, stigmata, and side effects designed to heighten the cinematographic impact of the ritual. In reality, most exorcisms do not contain that kind of Hollywood drama. They are serious affairs that may last for days, weeks, or even months. They are designed to give peace and freedom to the possessed person by binding the evil spirit under an oath ... Television and films tend to highlight the dramatic aspects of the ritual rather than these more common, religious elements."—Robert Brancatelli, Ph.D., is the assistant executive director of the Department of Religious Education at the National Catholic Educational Association.

usually working in concert, so it isn't just the presence of one of them."

Although Catholics use exorcism as a last resort, the ritual is practiced when necessary and only with the permission of a bishop. And it is important to rule out medical and psychological causes for the symptoms of demonic possession. Because different demons respond to different prayers, the exorcism ritual varies; however, the exorcist performs the exorcism within the confines of the overall ritual. This process can take anywhere from fifteen to forty-five minutes, depending on the prayers used.

China: The Chinese don't take any chances. Not when it comes to demons and evil spirits. They've been driving out demons and evil spirits from their villages for centuries. The ancient Wutu[7] ritual is still performed each winter in the village of Nianduhu, located in Qinghai Province, to rid the village of evil and prevent it from returning. Once widely practiced, this ritual varied slightly from village to village.

Young men dress up like tigers by painting their skin—stripes on the body and a tiger face. At the temple, the men chant prayers and drink alcohol, then perform an exorcism dance while brandishing swords carved from branches. In some villages, the men place strips of meat into their mouths to entice evil out of the village; others place buns atop the swords, which each member of the

---

Testing for Demonic Possession

"One of the many tests used in Christian exorcism to determine if an individual is possessed by a demonic being is to discreetly place a crucifix behind his or her head. The individual in question is instructed to close their eyes and slowly count to twenty. An assistant standing behind the individual will then place a cross six inches behind their head. If a demonic entity is possessing the individual's body, it will immediately begin to scream wildly."—Professor Jerry Alan Johnson, Ph.D., D.T.C.M., is a Taoist priest.

---

7. Ancient Chinese name for tiger.

village must touch. The men move from house to house by climbing up the walls of one house and jumping across the roofs of the others; superstition dictates that evil spirits may enter the village if the men access the houses through gates or courtyards. Once finished, the men jump over burning straw placed at the village entrance.

Confuciansim: Attending to the spirits of the dead prevents the existence of demons. Exorcisms are not needed because it is up to man, not spirits or demons, to determine his behavior.

Ethiopia and the Sudan: Many in this area of the world believe in the Zar (or sar) spirit, a spirit that possesses women experiencing marital problems. Descriptions of the Zar ceremony vary as does the belief that the Zar is either exorcised or simply just becomes pleased (and no longer wishes to cause harm). The Zar ceremony often takes place in a large room containing an altar covered with nuts and dried fruit. Incense is lit and the possessed individual may decorate her eyes with kohl. She also wears heavy perfume—the scent is said to purify the soul. Music is played, and the possessed individual dances around the altar. The ceremony leader (always a woman) watches to determine which spirit is doing the possessing. Then the spirit is engaged in a dialogue, an animal is sacrificed, and a sacrificial meal is eaten, signifying the completion of the ritual. Some people also offer gifts to the spirit.

Walpurgis Night (also Walpurgisnacht or Witch's Night)

Bonfires, loud noises, holy water, and incense are used to exorcise demons and witches from towns throughout northern Europe and Scandinavia (Germany, Sweden, Finland, etc.) on the last night in April each year. Some countries, such as Finland, hold carnivals; in other countries people dress in costumes and play pranks on one another. This holiday/festival is named after Saint Walpurga, however the reason is unknown. In Goethe's *Faust* there is a well-known Walpurgisnacht scene.

Haiti: The majority of people in Haiti practice voodoo (Also vaudou). Possessions typically occur during voodoo religious ceremonies and last for finite amounts of time during which the spirit (or loa) takes over the person's soul. These spirits are a part of the culture and are not feared. Sources conflict as to whether demon possessions are sought after or merely accepted as part of voodoo. Some reports state that individuals will sacrifice an animal and drink the blood to attract demons. In other instances, polished stones, herbs, and trance states are used to attract spirits. Some simply rely on ritualistic chanting and dancing to call the spirits.

Demonic possession begins with an inability to move, followed by frenzied trembling, after which the personality of the possessing spirit takes over the individual's body. Though not generally harmful, on rare occasion these spirits attempt to cause harm, and the possessed person must be restrained until the demon spirit leaves his body. Exorcism does not occur in voodoo because it is believed that the spirit leaves the body of its own will and remains for a limited amount of time.

Hindu: There are many demons in Hindu mythology, demons capable of possessing people. Although Hindu exorcism rituals are written in the Veda (sacred texts), exorcisms are rare. When they do occur, Hindu exorcists perform rituals to scare and drive out the demons. These rituals include burning cow or pig excrement,[8]

The Serpent and the Rainbow

In the 1988 film *The Serpent and the Rainbow*, directed by Wes Craven, a researcher travels to Haiti to investigate voodoo and a powerful drug that is used for "zombification." The movie was inspired by Wade Davis's book, *The Serpent and the Rainbow: A Harvard Scientist's Astonishing Journey into the Secret Societies of Haitian Voodoo, Zombis, and Magic* (HarperCollins, 1986).

---

8. The smell's got to be awful, but if it gets rid of the demons who can refuse?

Casting Out the Demon

"The reality of exorcism is far from how Hollywood portrays it. . . . Exorcism is more of a journey and not a one-shot deal where if the exorcist fails to cast out the demon then evil has somehow won the day. . . . Sometimes it's said that people can become liberated right away, but for the most part when you are dealing with what exorcists call a full demonic possession, then it can talk a long time, sometimes years."—Matt Baglio is a reporter and author of *The Rite: The Making of a Modern Exorcist* (Doubleday, 2009).

reciting prayers, burning incense, dancing while wearing scary masks, sprinkling holy water, and offering sweets to God.

Islam: The jinn can be good spirits or evil demons with supernatural powers. The demonic jinn—the most powerful is the devil called Iblis—can be summoned and can transfer their powers to the person who summoned them. Iblis also influences behavior through evil thoughts.

Just as there are many reasons a person can be possessed—including severe anger, jealousy, and fear—there are a variety of ways to conduct an exorcism and rid a possessed person of an evil jinn. Some believe it is best to command the jinn to leave; if it doesn't respond, then cursing is next on the agenda. If that fails, reciting passages from the Qur'an should be tried, followed by a threat to physically harm the jinn. This process can occur twice a day for up to six days before it can become effective. Some believe in beating out the jinn, but only in severe cases where all else fails. Another means to exorcise the jinn is for the possessed person to drink three mouthfuls of water mixed with ground lotus leaves. If a jinn leaves in the presence of an exorcist only to return once the possessed person is out of sight, tying the toes and fingers of the possessed will catch the jinn. Real possessions are rare, and Islamic clergy caution that the symptoms of possession are often similar to those of other illness.

Jainism: Originating in India, Jainism teaches that every living thing consists of two souls—a living soul and an eternal soul—and

Ganesha

The Hindu deity Ganesha is widely revered as the Remover of Obstacles, and has a devoted following even among non-Hindus.

each soul is responsible for its own actions. If a person is believed to be possessed by an evil spirit, a priest may use holy water, ash, or a birch leaf to rid the person of a spirit. If those methods fail, a goat or other animal may be sacrificed. There are also sacred pools, animals, and trees that scare away the evil spirits. These methods are not used much today, except perhaps in remote villages.

Judaism: Both benevolent and malevolent spirits can possess the living. The dybbuk, according to Rabbi Geoffrey Dennis, "is the soul of a sinner who, by reason of his or her offenses while alive is unable to make the proper transition to the afterlife." This spirit then inhabits a vulnerable living body. Although reports of demonic attacks date back many years, the beliefs regarding the cause varied. Exorcism rituals are rare today—most reports date back to the sixteenth through eighteenth centuries—but when they do occur, they are similar to exorcism in other cultures. The rituals include identifying the spirit, understanding the reason for possession, and expelling the demon, "often with the employment of ritual objects (shofar, tefillin, Torah scrolls, even amulets) and rites (candle lighting, fumigation with noxious substances). Most exorcism accounts report a lot of talking, seemingly trying to just annoy the spirit enough that it will leave."

Protestant: Beliefs on exorcism vary among Protestants. Regular exorcisms are the norm for some denominations; others perform exorcisms only in rare instances. In most cases, the ritual is not structured as strictly as the Catholic Church ritual.

Scientology: Exorcising alien spirits (called thetans) is accomplished through a process called auditing. Sometimes thousands of

---

Healing the Victim and the Ghost

"Most distinctive of the Jewish approach [to exorcism] is its philosophic underpinning: that the dead can possess, rather than just haunt, the living. Because of this, unlike Christian rites, the exorcism is seen as doubly therapeutic; ideally both the victim and the ghostly assailant should be healed. Since we are dealing with a 'soul' here, the goal is in effect a tikkun, a rectification for the malevolent dead, allowing it to continue its soul migration."—Geoffrey Dennis is a congregational rabbi, university instructor, and author of *The Encyclopedia of Jewish Myth, Magic, and Mysticism*. (Llewellyn, 2007).

thetans reside in each person, and a person is only believed to be rid of thetans through the completion of a lengthy auditing process. Once a person is rid of thetans, it is believed he can move throughout the universe without the use of a body.

Shamans: The use of Shamans as a channel between demons/spirits and the living dates back many years to the Amazonian Indians and the Australian aboriginals. Shamans are also an integral part of the Native American culture. Shamanism is not a religion nor is it affiliated with a particular part of the world, but rather a technique that is still used today throughout the world. Shamans believe that good spirits help them in their quest to banish the evil ones. Some shamans wear headdresses decorated with eagle and owl feathers, carry carved staffs, and/or decorate their clothing to help protect them against the evil spirits. By communicating with these evil spirits, shaman are able to banish them.

Shinto: Demons and evil spirits take advantage of vulnerable people and use these weaknesses as a means to possess the individual. Exorcism rituals consist of a variety of methods including scaring off the demon with a sword and throwing soybeans while commanding the demon to depart.

Shoki: In Japan and China, Shoki, the god of exorcism, is said to fight demons (or *oni*). During exorcism rituals, Shoki is called upon to expel demons. At times, the expelled demons unite with Shoki to fight evil.

Sikhism: Those who practice Sikhism do not believe in demonic possession. Therefore, there is no need for an exorcism. In fact, an

---

Possession vs. Oppression

When a person is possessed by a demon, the demon controls the individual internally. Oppression, on the other hand, occurs when a person is in control of themselves but demonic forces work against the person. The demon cannot get inside the body but can make life miserable for the individual.

---

exorcism is considered a violation of the *Sikh Rehat Maryada*, the Sikh Code of Conduct and Conventions.

Taoism (also **Daoism**): For Taoists—who have believed in ghosts, demons, and spirits since ancient Chinese times—Earth is inhabited by unseen entities that exist in a place of their own. Some believe demonic possession occurs in stages beginning with a deliberate interaction with the spirit world and ending in the death of the possessed individual.

Prior to an exorcism, Taoist priests may go into seclusion for three days to fast and pray. Exorcism rituals usually occur in the morning when demons are not at their most powerful and can consist of prayer, lighting candles and incense, burning oil, and other means to drive away the evil spirit. Sometimes, talismans, such as strips of paper or paper money, are burned during the ritual and placed into a bowl of water, which the possessed individual then

---

Taoist Demonic Possession

Dr. Wilson Yong outlines the factors that may cause a Taoist to become possessed:

▸ **By visiting places deemed to be inhabited by entities, i.e., wilderness, a location where there is a mass suicide, death, or sadness whereby residue of negative energies are still present.**

▸ **By possessing artifacts, i.e., antiques or heirlooms that had been cursed or had entities entangled in it.**

▸ **Witnessing a certain gruesome event or circumstances, i.e., someone committing suicide by leaping from a building, or fatal accidents.**

▸ **Being disrespectful in a sacred place of worship or offending certain deities in a shrine, holy place, or during worship.**

▸ **Depression can also cause one to be disoriented and increase the chances of getting possessed.**

▸ **Loss of faith in god, a nonbeliever or atheist—provokes or tries to challenge an entity by denying their existence.**

—Born in Malaysia, Dr. Wilson Yong is founder of www.taoistsecret.com

---

Fighting Evil

"The energetic and spiritual connection that exists between a Daoist priest and his or her god is extremely important, especially during an exorcism. It is the true source of his or her divine power and represents the only true authority that the exorcist has over a demonic entity. This divine energetic and spiritual union is so vital to the Daoist priest's survival that without this spiritual connection the exorcist will literally be risking his or her life."—Professor Jerry Alan Johnson, Ph.D., D.T.C.M., is a Taoist priest and mystic.

drinks. Other sacred objects also can be used to exorcise a demon, including a fly whisk or whip.

Zoroastrianism: No one really knows where the idea of demonic possession began, but it is believed to have come from Zoroastrianism, a religion that found its start in Iran and India and is not practiced much today. Zoroastrianism states that there are many demons; some put the numbers in the thousands, others millions. These demons can possess a person when evil wins the battle against good, but it's up to the individual to get rid of his own demons.

Ask the Expert

David F. Kramer, coauthor (with Jonathan Maberry) of the Bram Stoker Award–winning book, *The Cryptopedia: A Dictionary of the Strange, Weird and Downright Bizarre* (Citadel, 2007) and *They Bite: Endless Cravings of Supernatural Predators* (2009) is an expert on the occult and paranormal, and particularly on demons and demonology. He shares his insights on the impact of the film *The Exorcist* and its implications in real-world belief systems.

As the Head Turns: The Exorcist and Its Ilk

In 1973, the closely guarded secret rites of Christian exorcism and pop culture clashed in a big way—in the form of the film *The*

Exorcist, directed by William Friedkin and based on the William Peter Blatty novel. Blatty also wrote the screenplay, which won an Oscar that year along with audio gurus Robert Knudson and Christopher Newman for Best Sound.

The duo deserve a special spot in the Horror Film Hall of Fame for fully harnessing the haunting effect of English composer-musician Mike Oldfield's "Tubular Bells" as the film's main score. Oldfield has been cranking out records at a steady pace since then, most recently with *Music of the Spheres* (2008), but Bells was indeed his biggest commercial success.

It's impossible to hear this seemingly innocuous new-agey tune and not develop the worst case of goose bumps you've ever had. And there's hardly a $2.99 Halloween adventure bargain bin CD that doesn't have a version included along with "Night on Bald Mountain" and "The Monster Mash."

The film had a stellar cast, with Ellen Burstyn as the understandably frazzled mother of a daughter possessed by the Devil. It was also a breakout role for fourteen-year-old Linda Blair as Regan MacNeil. There was talk of an Oscar nod for the young actress until it was leaked that her demonic voice was provided by then fifty-seven-year-old actress Mercedes McCambridge—who was uncredited and eventually had to take Warner Bros. to court for her much deserved recognition. Indeed, many of the most brilliant moments in Friedkin's screenplay were the psychologically charged verbal tennis match between the demon Pazuzu and Father Karras, so the decision was understandable.

The tag team of cassock-clad, rosary-packing exorcists were played by Max Von Sydow and Jason Miller. Von Sydow appears elsewhere in these pages in the guise of planet Mongol's evil overlord Ming the Merciless. The now eighty-year-old has a filmography you could cover an Olympic-sized swimming pool with and appeared in the 2009 film *Shutter Island*. For the talented Miller it was a busy year as he also received the Pulitzer Prize for his play *That Championship Season*. He died in 2001.

The film was released to packed houses—and not only were people dying to get into the theater, they were dying to get out. Television news reports circulated of moviegoers passing out from shock, and being helped out of the theater on wobbly legs, breathing into paper bags in utter revulsion of it all. Yes—the press doesn't get any better than that!

The Exorcist was the fifth-largest grossing film that year. Ushers all packed smelling salts in case anyone fainted—and they often did. Those not strong enough to face the music were carried out like so much luggage, leaving the remaining audience to their inevitable fate.

And for seemingly the first time in movie history, audiences were given a truly new and terrifying Devil. Not a man in a satin cape and wooden mask; not a fey Puck wannabe with a manicured goatee and a sharp suit; and something far more fear inspiring than any multimillion CGI behemoth of today could ever hope to be.

This eclectic mix of prosthetics, foam rubber, machinery, and good old-fashioned Campbell's split pea original was crafted by makeup and special effects legend Dick Smith, responsible for Dustin Hoffman's transformation in *Little Big Man* (1970) and providing the red stuff for some of the bloodiest gun battles ever put to celluloid in *The Godfather* (1972) and *Taxi Driver* (1976). And if it's gore you're looking for, then there's also 1981's mind-blowing *Scanners*—a film that doesn't skimp on the cerebellum.

Indeed, what Ray Harryhausen was to stop-motion effects, Smith was to the fields of foam latex, prosthetics, and plain old Karo syrup, flour, water, and food dye (an easy and tasty way to mix up a batch of theatrical blood). There certainly would be no Tom Savinis, Rick Bakers, Screaming Mad Georges, or Bob Bottins in horror cinema, delighting us with hideous creatures great and small, were it not for the foundation Smith laid down.

Like any successful franchise, however diabolic, the story is all the same—when one film mimics your style, it's homage—when several dozen do, it's fromage. The word was out, Old Scratch was back, kicking ass and taking names—but most of all, he was making money hand over fist. That year, a fledgling comedy show called *Saturday Night Live* lampooned *The Exorcist* in a skit featuring Richard Pryor (who sadly passed away in 2005) as Father Karras and Not Ready for Prime Time Player original Laraine Newman as Regan. In fact, it's safe to say that the last time the dark lord was this commercially viable—well, that had to be back in the Middle Ages. Exorcist clones popped up in pretty much every film market that you would expect, and at least one that you probably wouldn't in a million years.

It would be wrong to say that every exorcist imitator that came down the proverbial pike was haphazardly slapped together by money-hungry, third-rate schlockmeisters—but that camp was certainly duly represented. To catalog all of these examples would probably take another volume of this book, and we'd still end up missing a handful of indie productions, stage plays, and Soho back-alley drag burlesque acts that probably copped the memes and themes of the film, even if just for a laugh.

Hot off the heels of *The Exorcist* came the Italian film *The Tempter* a.k.a. *The Antichrist* (1974), directed by Alberto De Martino and starring Carla Gravina and Mel Ferrer. This film is entirely watchable and has the added element of Gravina's character's past life as a persecuted witch to make things interesting—but it isn't long until tongues are being waggled at holy men and bodily fluids begin to flow that things start to unravel. Throw in your run-of-the-mill goat orgy, and you have yourself a tidy horror film that's worth a rental or a DVD bargain bin grab should a copy cross your path.

The multiple release award goes to *Beyond the Door* a.k.a. *Behind the Door* a.k.a. *Beyond Obsession* a.k.a. *The Devil Within Her* a.k.a. *Who Are You?* a.k.a. *Chi Se* (1974). Directed by Ovidio G. Assonitis and starring Juliet Mills, Gabriele Lavia, and Richard Johnson, this film features 360-degree headspins, surreptitious spewing, and naughty words uttered in death metal tones; it even managed to throw in a little *Rosemary's Baby* to cover all of the bases. In the incestuous department, Assonitis is also responsible for the truly awful *Jaws* knock-off *Tentacles* (1977), so this guy knows his fromage—this is a film that couldn't be saved even by the combined efforts of Henry Fonda, John Huston, Shelley Winters, and Bo Hopkins—and you should avoid it like anal fissures.

The mid-1970s were the heyday for "Blaxploitation" film franchises like *Dolemite*, *The Human Tornado*, *Friday Foster*, and *Cleopatra Jones*, as well as horror films like *Blackula* and *Scream Blackula Scream* (1972 and 1973, respectively). The success of *The Exorcist* inevitably led to the film *Abby* a.k.a. *Possess My Soul* (1974), written and directed by William Girdler. In this film, an ill-timed archaeological dig in Nigeria unleashes a demon that is quick to inhabit the soul of the diminutive but vivacious Carol Speed in the titular role.

The trailer for this film laid it out in classic '70s style: "She took the Devil for a lover and he possessed her, body and soul. *Abby*, a story of terror, lust, and exorcism. *Abby*, the story of a woman possessed!" The role of the exorcist is played by none other than Blacula himself, William Marshall, who more observant and younger (at heart) readers of this book might remember as the "King of Cartoons" from *Pee Wee's Playhouse* (1986–1991).

In this case, the demon in question is an incarnation of the Yoruba god Eshu. While known as a trickster figure to the people of Nigeria and Benin, Eshu was far from diabolic in nature, and probably wouldn't be caught mortal perpetrating even a hint of the kind of supernatural destruction going on here. Interested readers can learn more about Eshu in our previous book, *They Bite: Endless Cravings of Supernatural Predators* (Citadel 2009)[9].

Unlike other *Exorcist* imitators, the producers of *Abby* had the unique experience of actually being sued by Warner Bros. In some ways, this could be seen as an exploitation badge of honor. If there are so many infringing interpretations out there, why go after one in particular? Admittedly, the film is pretty much a straight-up gangster story, with the occult elements almost thrown in as an afterthought. Instead of utilizing those pesky and often expensive special effects, *Abby* relies on a singular image of some creepy face cut into a scene seemingly at random to denote the moments you need to drop your popcorn and grab your boyfriend (or girlfriend).

The rest of the time our heroine is possessed, she merely speaks like James Earl Jones on a bender, contorts her face, and tosses around an endless supply of tough guys like rag dolls. Even the exorcism itself is a pretty secular affair, with nary a mention of Jesus Christ, and a priest wearing a cross that's more Tony Iommi than Pope John Paul. You can find the whole she-bang on YouTube if you're so inclined—and you know you are!

Perhaps the most egregious offender in this department was a

---

9. Written by Jonathan Maberry and David F. Kramer.

real turkey. Rather it was really from Turkey (as in the country), the 1974 film *Seytan* (you're just going to have to guess the English translation). It's kind of difficult to pin down the "wrong" in this film as it's coming hard and fast from all directions—but there are a few red flags that are worth exploration.

First off, the residents of Turkey are pretty much anywhere from 70 to 99 percent Muslim (depending upon if you ask the CIA or a more reliable source about it)—so the whole "Christian rites of exorcism" angle falls a little flat. Otherwise, it's a practically frame-by-frame remake of *The Exorcist*, and as one might expect, it's freaking hysterical.

There's no mention of Satan or Jesus in this "antiseptically free of white collar" exorcism—even the vestments are replaced by a simple scarf worn by the actor who happened to have had the longest beard. Sure there's projectile vomiting, levitation, swiftly moving furniture, and head spinning, but at the end of the day, is it all really worth coming home to? Web surfers can check out YouTube for the film in its entirety. However, just add the term "vs." to your search if you really want to have your occult bone tickled. Some gentle soul out there in webdom with way too much time on his hands has gone to the trouble of editing scenes from *The Exorcist* right up against the mimics in *Seytan*.

Vampire Exorcism

Back in the Middle Ages, plague victims were wrapped in shrouds and buried in mass graves. The decomposition process forced fluid from the nose and mouth. Sometimes, the fluid disintegrated the shrouds covering the bodies. When grave diggers added more bodies to the graves and discovered the conditions of the bodies, they feared that vampires had possessed the plague victims. The solution was to jam bricks or stones into the mouths to exorcise the vampires and prevent the spread of the plague.[10]

---

10. *"Vampire" Picture: Exorcism Skull Found in Italy* by Christine Dell'Amore (National Geographic.com, March 10, 2009).

HOLY WARRIORS

Fighting demons and monsters is a tricky business and requires a special kind of person. Or, in some cultures, a special kind of priest, witch doctor, sorcerer, benign deity, or friendly patron

Peter Mihaichuk, *The Bite*

"In this picture . . . evil obviously won this bloody battle. I believe that evil impulses can never be satisfied, evident in this subject's obvious thirst for more."—Peter Mihaichuk is a professional artist.

demon. Here's a pretty diverse lineup of beings—human and supernatural—who take a powerful stand against evil.

Albularyo: In the Philippines, there are a variety of magic users, and one, the Mangkukulam, serves as a strange kind of supernatural hitman. The Mangkukulam is a sorceress of the darkest arts and she makes a study of revenge and how to exact it through magic. When hired to exact a revenge, the Mangkukulam have been known to magically insert all sorts of deadly items into the victim's body, ranging from poisonous bugs to sharp needles and even broken glass.

When a person is very ill and the curse of a Mangkukulam is suspected, a tough priest is brought in to counteract the curse. This priest, known as an Albularyo, uses very rough tactics to break the Mangkukulam's spell, and apparently violence is the only real way to accomplish this. The Albularyo cuffs and slaps the victim, sometimes beating him, and even at times pouring boiling water over him. Once the link between the victim and the Mangkukulam is severed, the Albularyo draws forth the offending item—pin, glass, broken knife blade, etc.—from the victim. Aside from the bruises and burns left by the "treatment," the victim is otherwise unharmed and is quickly restored to health.

Rough treatment is used in a variety of cures and exorcisms around the world, and it has been suggested that the corporal punishment is designed to get the body to send pain signals in such number and force as to "remind" the body that it is human, which in turns attracts the overwhelmed human spirit and reconnects the body between spirit and flesh. This in turn helps the human—whole now—to have the strength necessary to evict the invading possessive spirit. It is a far more extreme version of slapping an hysterical person to bring them to their senses.

Amagqirha: These "witch-sniffers" from South Africa can sense all evil, especially the evil monsters Uthikoloshe, who sickens and kills villagers by invading their dreams and turning the dreams into the most horrifying and grotesque nightmares. The nightmares are so intense that only the strongest can survive the experience; those who do turn to the Amagqirha for help. Ironically, the only cure is to drink the clarified oil made from the Uthikoloshe's body fat. It's a good thing the Amagqirha can kill this monster with a handful of salt . . . that is if the Amagqirha is lucky enough (or unfortunate enough depending on how you look at it) to confront this monster directly.

Bissat: The hero of a Tartar story. He once faced a one-eyed, man-eating giant and burned out the monster's eye with a red-hot knife.

Boloi: A term often mistakenly used to describe "vampires" or other similar evil predators in Botswana, Africa. The Boloi are a caste of witch doctors, or tribal healers and clerics who practice religious sorcery to protect the people of their village.

Like all people, however, the Boloi are themselves merely human and as some people aspire to higher ideals and a purity of soul and purpose, so too some descend to baser pursuits and goals. Corrupt Boloi can be hired to create hexes and lay spells of misfortune and sickness on people at the behest of paying customers.

Often it requires a Boloi of truer heart and deeper positive faith to counteract these evil spells.

Chung K'Uei (Demon Queller): Just as China has some of the fiercest monsters in the world of the occult, it also has one of the most powerful monster hunters in the form of Chung K'Uei, the Demon Queller.

Chung K'Uei is a big, burly man with a beard and a huge sword and tremendous courage; and yet his origins speak of a man filled with failure and despair. In the eighth century, during the T'ang Dynasty, Chung K'Uei had been a student of the classics and was very devoted to learning, but he failed his examinations and was disgraced. Unable to live with the loss of face he smashed his own brains out on the palace steps. The reigning emperor, Kao-tsu, took pity on him and ordered that the young scholar be given an official and honorable burial. The spirit of Chung K'Uei was so moved by this kindness that he swore eternal fealty to good men everywhere and vowed to linger on Earth as a spirit in human form, battling evil wherever he found it.

A century and a half later Chung K'Uei rescued Emperor Ming-huang from a goblin who was tormenting him and his consorts. Chung K'Uei appeared in the emperor's dreams and ate the goblin.

Upon waking, the emperor had no recollection of the event until he saw a painting by the great artist Wu Tao-tzu, and suddenly it came back to him. Wu could not have known about the goblin or about the emperor's dream, but he had seen it all in a vision.

To this day Chung K'Uei is celebrated in story, song, film, and festival; though over the last century or so artists have taken to making him out to be more of a buffoon than a hero, often depicting him in losing battle with demons, or being subjugated by supernatural temptresses.

Even so, his legend remains, and there are many in China—and also in Japan, where he is known as Shoki—who still revere Chung K'Uei as a great hero and a protector of the innocent against the forces of darkness.

Curupira: Although the Curupira can take on many forms, it often appears as a redheaded boy riding a hedgehog. However, the feet face backward to disorient those who encounter this fierce creature. The Curupira is the protector of the jungle—particularly the Amazon—so it's best to avoid him, especially if your intentions are to harm the environment. For the Curupira will feast on your body for a tasty meal. Lost hunters and hikers can escape the Curupira, but only if they ask permission to use the natural resources prior to doing so and only if the resources are necessary for survival.

Dervish: Iranian Sufi mystics who use dance-induced trances to drive evil spirits out of rural villages.

Gluskab: According to the Wabanaki (a Native American tribe), Gluskab was created to ensure a healthy and lasting world. His task was to protect nature—but that was no easy task for he knew that hunters and fishermen would deplete the world's supplies if they weren't taught how to protect the ecosystem. At first Gluskab sought to protect all the animals by placing them in a magical bag, but when he realized humans would die without the animals, he released them. Similarly, Gluskab sought to control the bad weather by controlling the bird that generated the weather with the flapping of its wings. But that attempt failed, too, for the air became too hot. Armed with the realization that he couldn't control the world in order to protect nature, Gluskab taught the hunters and fishermen how to obtain the resources they needed to survive without destroying the environment.

Hino: The "thunderer" of Iroquois legend who rides the sky with his bow and arrows eternally seeking evil to combat.

Houngan/Mambo: Throughout the world there are many enemies of evil, and just as evil itself manifests in many ways and in many forms so do its enemies. In the case of the religion of Vodoun in Benin and Haiti, the enemies of evil are the Houngan (male priest) or Mambo (female priestess). Their temple, the hounfour (or humfort), is both the center of their religious practices but also the most sacred and protected place, and the workshop where these priests prepare their rituals, charms, and magicks for their ongoing battle with the various demons, spirits, and monsters who plague the native peoples of that African nation.

Kintaro: A Japanese hero, whose name means "Golden Boy." He is the son of Princess Yaegiri. Kintaro lived alone in the woods where he talked to the animals. He was so strong he could bend trees like twigs. In one of his adventures he confronted a demon in the form of a gigantic poisonous spider. He uprooted a tree and used it to crush the monster. Later he joined the suite of the hero Raiko (Minamoto Yorimitsu) and became a famous warrior himself, called Sakata Kintoki.

Kishimo-Jin (also **Karitei-mo**): It's possible for the evil to become good—that's what happened to Kishimo-Jin. Apparently, stealing and eating children wasn't such a good thing to do, at least not according to the great Buddha, who helped Kishimo-Jin change her ways. Today, this Japanese goddess protects children and the weak.

Machi: Few cultures in South America have survived unchanged since pre-Columbian days, but the Mapuche Indians managed it, partly by living in such remote and inaccessible areas and partly through a powerful cultural structure that fiercely resisted change. Their culture has lasted for twelve thousand years and at the center of their society is the Machi: female spiritual leaders and

healers who train for most of their lifetimes to become both healers and monster hunters.

The Machi use animal familiars as allies in their ongoing battle
against a species of vulture-headed witch-vampires called the
Chonchon. These monsters are part of a larger groups of evil spirits called the Wekufe, and they are called into being by malicious
witches called the Kalku, who are the diametric counterparts of the
Machi.

The Chonchon swoops down on people as they walk through
the jungles at night, knocks them to the ground, and savages their
throats with wicked teeth in order to feed on human blood.

The Machi use their potent magic to bless spears and knives in
order to make them effective against the Chonchon, but even so
the best a warrior can do is drive one away temporarily. To kill
one, however, involves the Machi imbuing her familiar with special magical powers, transforming it into a jungle snake or a great
hunting bird, and in those forms the familiars can slaughter the
Chonchon.

Monster Slayer and Born for Water: Among the Diné (or Navajo) of
the American Southwest the name Anaye is used to describe a
group of unnatural spiritual beings who, though born of virgins,
were impure beings and engaged in unnatural practices. These
beings—giants of immense power and cruelty—savaged the land
and tormented the people until the gods themselves took a hand.
However, even the legendary Hero Twins, Nayenezgani (whose
name means "Monster Slayer") and To'baadsistini ("Born for
Water") were unable to overcome them all. The heroic brothers
appealed to their father, Tsohanoai, the Sun-Bearer, who presented
them powerful weapons in the form of four magical hoops. The
Twins' mother, Estanatlehi, the Sky Goddess, created a dreadful
storm which the Twins focused through the hoops and used this
vast power to destroy all but four of the Anaye. This battle was
so fierce that it reshaped the whole of the landscape of Earth
as well.

The four Anaye who remained here on Earth manifest themselves as Cold, Hunger, Poverty, and Old Age. Though still cruel
and eager to do harm, they survived by appealing to Estanatlehi

with the argument that if they were killed, then mankind would live forever in bliss and health and would grow to take advantage of immortality to the point that they would no longer prize the good things of life, or even life itself. This argument touched a chord in the Sky Goddess and she bade her sons relent in their attack.

Moshanyana: A mythic hero from the Sotho people of South Africa who saved all of mankind from a world-devouring monster called Kholumolumo.

Pundit: Any pregnant Indian woman who is unlucky enough to die during the festival of Divali[11] is in even greater danger of returning to life as a Churel—a soulless blood-sucking Revenant. These Churel are repulsive vampires with lolling black tongues, coarse lips caked with rouge, and wild tangles of greasy hair. They have heavy pendulous breasts, and their feet are twisted around backward.

Because they have died so unjustly—carrying new life—they are resentful and return to take out their antipathy on the living. The Churel primarily attacks young families—stalking children, pregnant women, and sometimes handsome young men. Their chosen prey represents those things they have lost, and it is there that their rage is directed. Ideally, though, they prey on their own families, hating their living relatives for having let them die during pregnancy and a holy festival.

The rage of a Churel can never be satisfied, so the best method of defeating one is to prevent it from coming into existence, which is why such care is given to pregnant mothers. If the pregnant mother should die, the last recourse is to bury her with the utmost attention given to every detail of the burial ritual. One slip, one missed element of the complex death rituals, will ignite the anger of the departing soul and a new Churel will be born into the world.

Should this calamity occur, only a Hindu Pundit[12] can drive it out, using complex and often-repeated prayers, special incense, and offerings. This method is difficult and time consuming, and it

11. The Hindu Festival of Light.
12. Priest.

does not destroy the Churel. At most it drives it away for a period of time, but the indestructible creature will generally return.

Shoki, the Demon Queller: The great Chinese supernatural folk hero, Chung K'Uei was not content to slay monsters only in China. He made his way to Japan where he took the name Shoki, and there he made it his business to confront demons, goblins, and all manner of monsters who wanted to prey on the helpless and innocent.

To this day Shoki is celebrated in story, song, film, art,[13] and festival, particularly the Boy's Festival, which takes places on the fifth day of the fifth month of the lunar year (May 5) and is celebrated by every family that has a male child under the age of seven. As the Boy's Festival somehow has become a beacon for evil, disease, and supernatural predators, Shoki has become the festival's hero, and offerings are made to him to keep the children safe.

Sun Wu-King (also **Handsome Monkey King**): Immortality, martial arts skills, and tremendous powers—including the ability to transform into any creature at will and cloning himself to create an army—made Sun Wu-King a creature to be feared. It was his job to guard a holy monk during the monk's journey to the Western Heaven from China. This wasn't an easy task because the monsters of the world hunted the monk for his flesh; eating it would make them immortal. But Sun Wu-King embraced his job—it was a hell of a lot better than the torture he had endured when trapped under a mountain for the past five hundred years. But he didn't go at it alone; he had the help of his Compliant Rod—a massive battle staff that when not in use transformed into a toothpick—and an armor suit.

Vodoun (also **Vodun**, **Voudou**, or **Sevi Lwa**): Vodoun is a religion buried under centuries of misunderstanding, propaganda, and slander by nonpractitioners. Most popularly known as Voodoo by the general public, this faith has earned a very bad and undeserved reputation, mostly by Christian communities who had labeled it as

---

13. Stephen Addiss, *Japanese Ghosts and Demons: Art of the Supernatural*, George Braziller, 2001.

devil worship. Pop culture—films, novels, etc.—have done a great deal of damage to the reputation of what is, quite truthfully, an organized religion, and a positive one at that.

The name "Vodoun" is traceable to an ancient African word for "spirit" in the language of the Yoruba people of West Africa who lived in eighteenth and nineteenth-century Dahomey, but the religion itself has roots going back hundreds, if not thousands, of years. At one time Dahomey was a vast kingdom that occupied parts of today's Togo, Benin, and Nigeria.

When the white slavers plundered Africa for their human cargoes, the slaves brought Vodoun with them to Haiti and other islands in the West Indies, and even to the United States. The religion was, of course, changed by the clash of cultures and the frequent deaths of those Houngans who died as slaves before passing on the complete set of rites and practices, but it survived nonetheless, and is still active in Haiti and even in modern United States. Worldwide there are about sixty million followers of Vodoun.

When Christians from Europe and America tried to forcibly stamp out Vodoun, the priests went underground, hiding their religion by using the names of Christian saints to disguise their own spirits (called Loa).

Vodoun was again attacked and suppressed during the time of Marxist regimes in Africa, but when Benin established a democratic government in 1989 the religion emerged from hiding, and in 1996 it became that country's official religion.

Religions similar to Vodoun, and certainly either spun off from it or influenced by it, have emerged in various places around the world, particularly in South America under the names Umbanda, Quimbanda, or Candomble.

The Vodoun practiced in Benin, Dominican Republic, Ghana, Haiti, Togo, and in the southern United States is the true religion, and it is certainly neither dark nor dedicated to evil, but is instead a positive religion that supports the spiritual well-being as well as the cultural and physical health of the people.

The darker "Voodoo" of movies, fiction, and church propaganda bears little or no resemblance to true Vodoun beyond a purely superficial similarity. Anyone taking a moment to look an inch deeper than the fiction will see the true religion.

However, within Vodoun—as within all religions—there is a constant battle of good and evil. Indeed one of the truest marks of a religion is an acceptance of the duality of universal forces: one that seeks to harm or corrupt humanity, and one that seeks to protect and redeem.

When confronted by the evil Baka[14] it is only a Houngan or Mambo who can stop the evil because ordinary persons do not possess the power to overcome this dreadful evil. Houngans are required to make the complex and powerful charms needed to thwart the Baka or even destroy them.

One of the great tasks facing the Houngan is the balancing of appeal and appeasement that entices the great Loa spirits to help mankind and at the same time discourages them from doing a mischief. The Loa often take sides against one another, often at the behest of someone who has made a particularly powerful prayer and offering. If this appeal leads to the kind of imbalance that results in harm, sickness, or other ill, then a different Houngan is called in to cajole the Loa to relent; or to bring a second Loa in to protect the oppressed person and restore him to health. It is delicate work and every detail of each ritual must be followed with strict reverence, respect for all of the Loas—no matter which side they are taking—and a deep, abiding faith.

The cosmology of Vodoun is very complex, with hundreds of gods and spirits, playing a variety of roles in affairs both great and ordinary. The chief god is Olorun, but he is very remote and seldom bothers with human affairs. Olorun appointed a somewhat lesser god, Obatala, to create Earth and all life forms, though after this was done there was a conflict between the two gods and the lesser god was temporarily banished.

Among the lesser spirits there are those originated from Dahomey (called the Rada) and those who came later (the Petro), sometimes coming into being from the spirit of a notable human who has died.

In Vodoun it is believed that each person has a soul that is composed of two separate spiritual entities. There is the ti bon ange or

---

14. A shape-shifting reanimated spirit of a Bokor, or dark priest of Vodoun.

"little guardian angel" and the gros bon ange or "big guardian angel." It is the little spirit that is the conscious and active part of the soul, and the part that leaves the body during sleep and when a Loa possesses a person during a ritual. While the ti bon ange is absent from the body it is vulnerable, and evil spirits love to attack it, again requiring that the Houngan prepare every charm and follow every aspect of each ritual with maximum precision.

9 WHO YOU GONNA CALL?

Woodrow Hinton III,
Alone in the Dark

"True evil or darkness lies within us. It is buried in our fears, doubt, and anger at our fellow men and ourselves. It convinces us we are weak and alone. We need only recognize this as a lie for good to triumph and accept the darkness as a necessary part of the whole. I think a wise person understands that good can only exist in a world with bad, which negates negative or positive connotations to either term."
—Woodrow J. Hinton III is an award-winning illustrator best known for his horror sci-fi genre–related work in the gaming and comic industry.

WHISTLING PAST THE GRAVEYARD

They scare us and they spook us. They show up out of nowhere and disappear just as fast. Sometimes they linger or brush us with a quick cold wisp; other times they create havoc. Strange things happen when we're around ghosts and some of these are just downright scary.

Ghosts have fascinated people for centuries. Perhaps it's because we don't really know if they exist. It's the unknown that keeps us glued to the possibility. And while some are firm believers in ghosts, others insist it's not possible to exist in any form beyond death.

For many cultures, ghosts are something to be feared and are a presence that signifies doom. According to Beth Conklin in her book, *Consuming Grief: Compassionate Cannibalism in Amazonian Society* (University of Texas Press, 2001), the Wari' have an intense fear of the ghost they call Jima. With incredible strength Jima restrains its victims and then attempts to steal their spirits.

For the Hopi Indians it's the spirit called Masaw that rules the underworld. In Jewish folklore spirits called dybbuk wander Earth until they find a new body to inhabit and control. And, for the Japanese, ghosts are spirits who are caught between two worlds because of their sins.

Psychologists might say that the fascination with ghosts is a

---

Bloody Mary

The legend of Bloody Mary states that if you stand in front of a mirror in a dark room and say Bloody Mary's name three times— some believe it's thirteen times—her ghost will come through the mirror and scratch out your eyes or rip off your face. Some people say it's best to summon Bloody Mary at the stroke of midnight and others believe you must hold a lit candle in front of the mirror. Although we have tried this numerous times in our youth, all we've ever summoned was a fear of this ghost, said to be that of an executed witch. Some people believe Bloody Mary's name is not named after the witch but after either Queen Mary I or Mary Tudor.

---

direct result of the fear of death, a way to overcome that fear and find a means to control it. The belief in ghosts also can ease the transition from life to death by allowing us to achieve immortality. Or maybe people just find ghosts interesting.

There are many types of ghosts—some are happy, some angry, some vengeful, some mischievous. And ghosts can take on many forms depending on the society and the time in history in which they are discussed (and experienced).

In film, ghosts play a pivotal role. Take a look at these terrifying tales: *A-Haunting We Will Go* (1942), *The Uninvited* (1944), *Ghost Ship* (1952), *The House on Haunted Hill* (1959), *Amityville Horror* (1979), *Watcher in the Woods* (1980), *The Fog* (1980), *Poltergeist* (1982), *The Frighteners* (1996), *The Sixth Sense* (1999), *What Lies Beneath* (2000), and *The Others* (2001). Several ghost movies are based on books: *The Shining* (1980), written by Stanley Kubrick and Diane Johnson, was based on the book by Stephen King; *Ghost Story* (1981) was based on the book by Peter Straub; and *The Haunting* (1963) was inspired by Shirley Jackson's *The Haunting of Hill House*. After watching these movies it's difficult not to suffer from phasmophobia.[1]

Not everyone likes scary ghosts; some prefer lovable ghosts. Films like *The Ghost and Mrs. Muir* (1947), *Dona Flor and Her Two Husbands* (1977), and *Ghost* (1990) are sure to warm the heart. And for those who enjoy a dose of comedy, ghost films such as *Topper* (1937), *Lucky Ghost* (1942), *The Canterville Ghost* (1944), *Blackbeard's Ghost* (1968), *Ghostbusters* (1984), and *Beetlejuice* (1988) provide lots of laughs.

In the film *Field of Dreams* (1989), a farmer brings back the ghosts of eight 1919 Chicago White Sox players after he builds a baseball field in their honor. Tim Burton's 1993 animated film *The Nightmare Before Christmas* features a ghost dog named Zero. And then there's Casper the Friendly Ghost, who appeared in both film and television and befriends people rather than frightens them.

Of course, ghosts abound in literature. There's the underworld ghost in Homer's *The Odyssey*; the headless horseman in Washington Irving's *The Legend of Sleepy Hollow* (1819); the ghosts of

1. From the Greek word phasma; means an extreme fear of ghosts.

Hauntings

"I created the Harrow series with the idea of a cubist haunted house story: one house seen from a hundred different perspectives, drawing on my love of supernatural and horror fiction, from the quiet mysterious hauntings of the early twentieth century (with *Nightmare House*) to the all-out chaos of a more cinematic sensibility (with *The Abandoned*). . . . Harrow is one haunted house, created for an infinite number of hauntings."
—Douglas Clegg is the award-winning author of more than twenty novels, including *Isis* (Vanguard, 2009), *Neverland* (Bloodletting Press, 2003), *The Priest of Blood* (Ace, 2006) and others.

Christmas past, present, and future in Charles Dickens's *A Christmas Carol* (1843); the ghost of King Hamlet in Shakespeare's *Hamlet* (1603); and Heathcliff's ghost Cathy in Bronte's *Wuthering Heights* (1847). In Mark Twain's *The Adventures of Tom Sawyer* (1876), Tom and Huck Finn visit a haunted house. A haunted house is also at the center of Shirley Jackson's *The Haunting of Hill House* (1959). And in a twist on the classic ghost story, Oscar Wilde's *The Canterville Ghost* (1891) examines what happens when it's the living who torment a ghost.

Television also has its share of ghosts. The Syfy show *Ghosthunters* follows real-life paranormal investigators as they looks for ghosts; *Ghost Whisperer* focuses on Melinda Gordon's ability to see ghosts and help them move into the light; the Travel Channel's *Ghost Adventures* visits haunted sites; the Biography Channel's *Deadly Famous Ghostly Encounters* seeks famous ghosts; and the Discovery Channel's *A Haunting* explores true hauntings.

Modern literature is full of spooks,[2] including the bitter ghost in Toni Morrison's Pulitzer Prize–winning *Beloved* (Alfred A. Knopf, 1987) and Nearly Headless Nick, Moaning Myrtle, and the Grey Lady in J. K. Rowling's Harry Potter series. In Dean Koontz's *Brother Odd* (Bantam Books, 2006), the main character sees ghosts; in Ann Sebold's *The Lovely Bones* (Little, Brown, 2002) a dead girl is caught between the land of the living and the dead; in Peter

Straub's *Ghost Story* (Coward, McCann & Geoghegan, 1979) ghosts seek revenge; and in Tom Piccirilli's *Headstone City* (Bantam, 2006) the dead visit the living.

We also encounter ghosts in comic books where ghosts fight for justice (Spectre, Deadman, and Danny Phantom), in songs ("Thriller," "The Ghost in You," and "Fear of Ghosts"), and in computer/video games (Ghost Master and Casper's Scare School).

I AIN'T AFRAID OF NO GHOSTS

We've all seen the movie *Ghostbusters* (1984) starring Dan Aykroyd, Bill Murray, and Harold Ramis as the quirky and lovable paranormal investigators who blow through New York City in their Ectomobile with their proton packs, gadgets, and gizmos and chase after ghosts. Amid blunders and successes, the ghost-busters chase demonic spirits (Zuul and Vinz Clortho); unleash a group of ghosts onto the city, and encounter another demon (Gozer the Gozerian) who has assumed the form of a woman and then the form of a giant Stay Puft Marshmallow Man.

Though the characters in the film took their jobs seriously, real-life ghost hunters (or paranormal investigators) don't investigate ghosts this way, nor do they capture them. In order to understand today's ghost hunters, let's take a brief look back in time.

On Investigating Hauntings

"There is a great variety of approaches which paranormal investigators may take in the field. . . . Most investigators are either looking for a haunting, looking for scientific proof of a haunting, or trying to disprove a haunting. . . . A scientific approach is the only way an investigator can produce results that give credibility to the existence of paranormal phenomena. One must be able to quantify, qualify, and reproduce an anomaly to present it as valid evidence."—Chris Gay is the founder and team leader of the NJ Ghostbusters.

---

2. Another name for ghost.

Jennifer Singleton, *How Beautifully She Fades*

"This artwork depicts the ghost of a woman long dead, but who still haunts the empty halls of her manor, clinging to memories of life and refusing to move on. Her deep regrets, bitterness and broken heart keep her a willing captive within the shadows of once was."—Jennifer Singleton is a gothic artist from Australia.

Throughout history, people have reported seeing ghosts. They've been intrigued by ghosts, feared them, embraced them—even created stories about them. Often, as was the case with Victorian ghost hunters, the presence of ghosts was validated through the repetitive patterns seen among those who experienced the phenomenon, patterns with a statistical significance that could not be chalked up to chance.

In the formative years of ghost hunting, mediums contacted ghosts through séances, which enabled them to communicate with the spirits. In the late 1880s, the fascination with paranormal phenomena increased and people began to seek scientific evidence and employ the use of cameras to prove the existence of ghosts and other phenomena. Inventor Thomas Edison was convinced it was possible to design an apparatus to communicate with the spirits. Although he never created the device, Edison gave credence to the reality of ghosts.

One of the first formal groups to investigate paranormal phenomena was the Ghost Club Society, founded in 1862 in Cambridge, UK, and still in existence today. Since then, the number of societies that investigate the paranormal has increased tremendously, and today they are located across the globe.

The process of ghost hunting varies depending on the investigator and the situation; however, the basics are mostly the same. First, the ghost hunter will gather preliminary information about the haunting—where, when, what, how—as well as any background information about the location of the haunting such as significant events and former residents (gathered through interviews and written documents).

Next, a site investigation occurs. The investigation can take place with a few people or as many as thirty or more (when investigating a haunted battlefield, for example). Photographs, video footage, sound recordings, and other evaluations of the environment occur—using a variety of equipment—in order to prove or disprove the presence of a paranormal phenomenon. The investigation can take a few hours or last several days. Some ghost hunters prefer to conduct their investigations between 9 p.m. and 6 a.m.—that's when the ghosts' energies are strongest and most prevalent.

Ghosts are unreliable—they can't be counted on to show up in the same place and at the same time on numerous occasions, although sometimes they will. If someone claims a ghost can be commanded to appear at will, then it's most likely a hoax.

Upon completion of the on-site investigation, the ghost hunter must evaluate the collected data. This process can take days or weeks, depending on the amount of data. The investigation may reveal who is haunting a location and why, but it does not get rid of the ghosts. Unlike the film *Ghostbusters*, ghost hunters do not have proton packs and ghost traps at their disposal. They do have, however, a means to better understand paranormal phenomena.

TYPES OF HAUNTINGS

The cold prickle of your skin, strange and eerie noises that appear out of nowhere, doors that open or close on their own, the feeling that someone is nearby when no one is in fact there, the smell of perfume, or an untouchable aura that seems so real. These are the things that can characterize hauntings. Some involve ghosts or other sights that people believe to be connected to the dead; however,

---

Perfect Horror

"*The Haunting* (1963) . . . is a perfect horror film without a doubt. The film nicely adapts Shirley Jackson's novel, *The Haunting of Hill House*, and spins it in a few new directions so that the viewer will be surprised even if they've read the book. The reason this flick works so well is that it coaxes the viewer into becoming an active participant in the development of the story and the revelation of the horrific elements. We see no monsters, no blood. Nothing jumps out at us. Virtually everything frightening that happens occurs in the mind, or perhaps the perceptions, of the four central characters. The mood is at times so claustrophobic that we can feel the chill in the air and the icy movement of the breeze. This works so well because it respects the imagination of the viewer, just as the book respects the reader. . . ."—Adam G. Palmer is a film critic.

---

hauntings can occur in a variety of ways and each person's response is unique. Some people become frightened and believe a haunting is something evil while others welcome the experience. All seem to agree that a haunting can make your hair raise on end, make you question your sanity, or provide comfort in a strange way.

Hauntings occur in a variety of ways, and experts differ in their opinion about the types of hauntings. Some say there are three types, others four, some six. For our purposes, we explore all types. So sit back and take a look into these strange occurrences.

Demonic (or **inhuman**) **haunting:** Fear feeds demonic ghosts, the evil that lurks and preys on the living. Demons never had a human form and are often described as a black mist or fog; sometimes they appear as terrifying creatures. Demons revel in destruction and love to create havoc. They can be sneaky and can manipulate the living by convincing them to engage in harmful activities that can even result in death.

The classic 1973 movie *The Exorcist* is perhaps one of the most noted films depicting demonic possession. Here a demon possesses a twelve-year-old girl and forces her to engage in horrific acts of violence to both herself and others. If you've ever seen the movie you'll never forget the main character Regan, especially after you watch her head spin backward and hear the ominous male voice

---

The Other Shape

The other shape,
If shape it might be call'd that shape had none
Distinguishable in member, joynt, or limb,
Or substance might be call'd that shadow seem'd,
For each seem'd either; black it stood as Night,
Fierce as ten Furies, terrible as Hell,
And shook a dreadful Dart; what seem'd his head
The likeness of a Kingly Crown had on.
Satan was now at hand, and from his seat
The Monster moving onward came as fast,
With horrid strides, Hell trembled as he strode.
—John Milton, *Paradise Lost*

---

that emanates from her mouth. With nowhere else to turn, the family performs an exorcism in the hopes of regaining their daughter's soul.

Some people believe demons have existed for thousands of years and will inhabit this world forever. And although cultures differ on their opinion about how demonic hauntings manifest themselves, most agree that it's definitely evil.

Doppelganger haunting: Considered extremely rare, Doppelganger hauntings are considered a foreshadowing of something evil, often of impending death. The person haunted by a doppelganger sees someone who could be their clone and who wears the same clothes and has the same haircut and facial expressions.

Intelligent (or **traditional**) **haunting:** Mention the word ghost and most people think of intelligent hauntings. An intelligent haunting occurs when a ghost creates sounds, moves objects, or produces some other physical activity in an effort to communicate and interact with the living. Typically these ghosts are aware of their surroundings and the living people who occupy that space.

Intelligent hauntings are not always the stuff we see in movies like the *Amityville Horror* (1979) where evil ghosts—that are downright nasty—terrorize and physically harm people until they cower in fear. Some ghosts are earthbound because they are connected to a loved one, don't realize they are dead, or fear the unknown. These ghosts tend to be harmless, an annoyance more than anything else, or even a comfort in the case of the ghost of a deceased loved one. Although intelligent hauntings are thought of as the traditional type of haunting, they are in fact uncommon.

Poltergeist haunting: Some believe poltergeist haunting is a subcategory of the demonic haunting; others place it in a category of its own. Mischief is what most poltergeists are all about; however, some are evil. These ghosts like to play by creating noise or by moving objects. Some people theorize that poltergeists are the result of an unconscious manipulation of objects via psychic energy emitted by the person who is present at the time of the haunting, but others disagree. Although poltergeist hauntings can occur over a long period of time, most seem to stop after a few days or weeks.

Crisis Apparitions (or Death Visitants)

"They're one of the most common paranormal experiences, as the statistics illustrate so well, and they're surprisingly consistent. That is, the kinds of accounts gathered by my Victorian ghost hunters[3] sound exactly like the kinds of accounts given by people today. I gave a talk on this subject for the National Academy of Sciences and asked everyone in the audience who'd either had such an experience or knew someone who had to raise their hands. A good third of the five hundred or so people in the room put up their hands. Just incredible."—Deborah Blum is a Pulitzer Prize–winning science writer and the author of five books, including *Ghost Hunters: William James and the Scientific Search for Proof of Life After Death* (Penguin, 2006) and *The Poisoner's Handbook: Murder and the Birth of Forensic Medicine in Jazz Age New York* (Penguin, 2010).

Steven Spielberg's popular film *Poltergeist* (1982), with its famous line "they're here," explores the world of poltergeist hauntings. Silverware bends on its own, glasses break without anyone touching them, chairs are stacked by themselves. Then the intensity increases and the poltergeist takes a child into its world through a closet, a world that contains evil. *Poltergeist II* (1986) and *Poltergeist III* (1988) soon followed. And in 1996, the Syfy Channel explored the world of evil poltergeists in its series *Poltergeist: Legacy*.

The poltergeist character of Michael "Mickey" Silk first appeared in a 1983 issue of the Marvel Comics *Spider-Woman I #49* and made an appearance in other comics, including Avengers and Beauty and the Beast. Silk possessed uncontrollable psychokinetic powers that caused strange things to occur.

Portal Haunting: These hauntings occur when energies or spirits cross from one dimension into the other through a portal, often found in cemeteries.

---

3. The investigation included tens of thousands of people and "found that such experiences occur at over 400 times chance."

Residual haunting: Those things that go bump in the night (or the day) and scare the bejesus out of you can be the work of a residual haunting. Residual hauntings are typically the result of some traumatic environmental event such as murder that left behind the "energy" of the event. A re-creation of the event through noises (screaming, crying, footsteps) or ongoing smells (they also can be sporadic) occurs until the energy is depleted. That laugh you heard when no one was home, the creaking of the floorboards in an otherwise empty house, or the recurring coppery smell of blood are all examples of residual hauntings. People often confuse residual hauntings with intelligent hauntings; however, residual hauntings are believed to be caused by traumatic energy rather than a ghost, and there is no interaction between the living and the ghosts.

Shadow people haunting: These shapeless black masses (sometimes smoke or steam) have no discernible features and possess the ability to move through solid matter at will. Most who encounter shadow people experience a dreadful feeling and describe the mass as wearing a wide-brim hat or a hood.

THE TOOLS OF THE GOST-HUNTING TRADE

Just like each carpenter or painter has his own tools of the trade, so do ghost hunters. Equipment ranges from the basic (compass) to the high-tech (thermal laser thermometers), and the equipment used is dependent on the type of haunting. Good ghost hunters know to avoid the rain, snow, or cold weather—the moisture in the air may distort the results and indicate the presence of a ghost when one is not present. The same goes for smoking or eating. Many of the tools listed below are extremely sensitive and can perceive the smallest of changes in the environment. Last thing a ghost hunter wants is to think a ghost is present when in fact the audio recorded is someone sneaking a snack in the next room.

Artist's pad and colored pencils: Used to diagram the environment and color-code movement positions or sounds.

Audio ENF translater: Translates electromagnetic field (EMF) readings into audio that can be analyzed.

Batteries: It's always a good idea to have extra batteries—you don't want to miss recording anything.

Compass: One of the most rudimentary of ghost-hunting tools. A substantial deviation from magnetic north may indicate the presence of a ghost.

Digital still camera: When a ghost decides to move the furniture or open the door or bend the silverware it doesn't take high-tech equipment to record the change. Sometimes a digital camera will do just fine. And, a film camera may record images invisible to the naked eye.

Digital video camera: A lot of people are skeptics when it comes to ghosts. But there's no way to argue with technology . . . well, there is digital manipulation, but let's assume we're talking about honest ghost hunters. With a digital video camera the proof of a presence is recorded for all to see.

Digital voice recorder: Sometimes digital voice recorders can capture ghost voices imperceptible to the human ear. This process is called EVP or electronic voice phenomenon.

Scott Morrow's Rules for Ghost Hunting

▸ Don't go alone on any investigation. It is for your safety as well as the person you're going to visit. This is the most important rule and it should never be broken. You never know what you're dealing with.

▸ Never invite anything to stay with you, come with you, or be around you.

▸ Never provoke anything even if you think it's going to get a reaction. Sometimes provoking can cause harm to you or the person you're trying to help or your team.

—Scott Morrow is co-host of the reality-television show *Haunted Destinations* and host of *The Fearless Ghost Hunter Show* on Blog talk radio.

Dowsing rods: Typically used to detect water, dowsing rods can also be used in ghost hunting to detect an energy field.

Electromagnetic field strength meter (EMF meter): Some people believe ghosts change the electromagnetic field, and this meter detects that change.

Flashlight: When you're wandering around in the dark looking for ghosts, it's good to have a trusted flashlight on hand.

Forensic evidence collection kit: You never know when a ghost will leave behind something useful. This kit enables the ghost hunter to collect the evidence for later analysis.

Infrared camera: Unlike a traditional camera that relies on visible light to form an image, infrared cameras work even in total darkness. These cameras emit light at a wavelength invisible to the human eye and allow the camera to record images that it otherwise would not be able to see.

Infrared illuminator: When it's so dark that you just know evil surrounds you and your infrared digital camera needs a boost, infrared illuminators can come in handy to improve the function of infrared equipment.

Ion counter: This device detects changes in positive and negative ions in the air, said to be affected by the presence of a ghost.

Microphones (parabolic or amplified): There's no sense in attempting to record ghosts without the proper equipment. Microphones capable of picking up sounds beyond those directly in front of the device are useful when covering a large area.

Motion sensor: It's important to know where your ghost is, especially when hunting one. Motion sensors enable ghost hunters to track ghosts even when they can't see them.

Night vision scope: This device enables the ghost hunter to see his environment in total darkness.

Paper and pencil: It's crucial to take notes during a ghost hunting. Something that may seem insignificant may later prove to be

Bill Sharpe's Rules for Ghost Hunting II

▸ Have two separate interviews of the inviting person by two separate people. Compare notes.

▸ Do homework on the location.

▸ Evaluate the location to determine the size of the investigation team that will be most effective.

▸ Always wear soft shoes for quiet.

▸ Make sure that only one or two people know anything about the location before the investigation.

▸ Ask a person at the location as to any limits of where you can or cannot investigate.

▸ Compare notes immediately after the investigation and then again at an agreed later date.

> —Bill Sharpe is the lead investigator and organizer for Tampa Ghost Watchers.

important. Noted sights or noises can be correlated with recordings at a later time.

Radiation monitor: This device detects gamma rays in addition to Alpha, Beta, and X-rays. It is believed that a fluctuation in radiation occurs when a ghost is present.

Surveillance cameras and computers equipped with digital videos recorders (DVRs): When it comes to ghosts, it's important to have adequate coverage. Hook multiple surveillance cameras up to a computer and a DVR and track the ghost's movements throughout the environment. No blind spots here or missed opportunities.

Thermal laser thermometer: That chill you feel in the air that comes out of nowhere and raises your hair on end before disappearing just as quickly . . . could be a ghost. These temperature changes can be measured using thermal laser thermometers.

FAMOUS HAUNTINGS

While this is no means a complete list of famous hauntings, we've attempted to cover the major ones across the globe.

Alcatraz Island: Otherwise known as "The Rock," Alcatraz Island is famous for housing hardened criminals such as Al Capone (Scarface) and Robert Stroud (the Birdman of Alcatraz). This prison, located on the San Francisco Bay in California, was converted to a tourist attraction and opened to the public in 1973. Throughout its history, guards and prisoners have experienced strange happenings (hearing men walking, screaming, and sobbing) when no one else was present. Strange smells also occurred without explanation, as did drops in temperature. The 1962 film *Alcatraz* starred Burt Lancaster as Robert Stroud.

Amidaji: A samurai ghost haunted and visited this temple in Japan each night. The legend was retold in a 1904 book, *Kwaidan: Stories and Studies of Strange Things*, written by Lafcadio Hearn.

Bell Witch: Between 1817 and 1821, the Bell Witch haunted the Bell family, a group of pioneers in Tennessee, who heard her voice and experienced her violence. No one really knows why the Bell Witch set out to terrorize and harm this family, but it is believed she was responsible for John Bell's death. Throughout the years, many claimed to have seen or experienced the Bell Witch and documented these instances extensively. The legend of the Bell Witch became so widespread and so popular that General Andrew Jackson traveled to Tennessee to experience the witch firsthand. The 2006 film *An American Haunting* (based on the book *The Bell Witch: An American Haunting* by Brent Monahan) and the 2004 film *The Bell Witch Haunting* were products of this legend, as were many books on the subject.

Mary Brogovy: Mom always warned you not to pick up hitchhikers. In Chicago, Illinois, you'd better heed this advice. Many motorists have picked up a blond hitchhiker dressed in a white dress and dancing shoes (the ghost of Mary Brogovy) and taken her home . . . to Resurrection Cemetery where she promptly disappears into the air.

Lizzie Borden: August 11, 1892, is the date Lizzie Borden was arrested for the murder of her parents. She supposedly killed them with a hatchet but was acquitted of the crimes. Those who work (and stay) in the Lizzie Borden house in Fall River, Massachusetts (now a bed-and-breakfast), report that they hear women argue and cry when no one is there, that doors open and close on their own, and that shoes move by themselves across the floor.

Boston Commons: Public hangings and executions were common at this Massachusetts spot until 1817. Apparently, those who were hanged were not happy about it. Numerous ghosts have been sighted in Boston Commons over the years, but the most frequent sighting is that of two women wearing dresses from the 1800s.

Disney's Haunted Mansion: Who would have ever thought that an amusement park haunted mansion would be home to a real haunting. Certainly not those who envisioned the Haunted Mansion ride located in California. Disneyland employees report numerous sightings of a man with a cane and another man wearing a tuxedo. Talk about a scary ride—this one is for real.

Dragsholm Slot: Home to three ghosts (the White Lady, the Gray Lady, and the Earl of Bothwell), Dragsholm Slot in Denmark receives a nightly visit from the ghost of Earl of Bothwell when the earl rides his carriage through the castle courtyard. The earl died in the castle's prison in the 1500s.

Edinburgh Castle: David I built Edinburgh Castle around the year 1130 atop a volcanic rock that had long been used as a military

---

Lizzie Borden Nursery Rhyme

Lizzie Borden took an axe,
And gave her mother forty whacks;
When she saw what she had done,
She gave her father forty-one.
—from *Mother Goose's Melodies* (facsimile edition of the Munroe and Francis "Copyright 1833" version).

---

outpost. Now considered one of the most haunted places in Scotland, Edinburgh Castle is famous for its hauntings.

Talk about a great security system—the drummer boy is a headless ghost who appears when the castle is about to come under attack. Of course, that hasn't happened in many years—perhaps the drummer boy went into retirement when the Scottish government opened the castle to tourism.

Tourism hasn't scared away the rest of the ghosts. The lone piper (or ghostly piper) travels the tunnel beneath the castle where it is said he disappeared. At times his music can be heard inside the castle. Lady Glamis, who was burned at the stake by King James V in 1537, also haunts the castle, as do the spirits of those who perished in dungeons.

Flying Dutchman: Anyone who has heard of the Pirates of the Caribbean movies knows about the Flying Dutchman, a fictional ghost ship that escorts lost souls to their final destination. For years, this ghost ship has haunted the seas; reports date back to 1881 when a royal navy ship encountered the apparition near Africa.

Gallows Hill: Witches burned at the stake in Salem, Massachusetts, haunt Gallows Hill. Just goes to show burning witches did more harm than good—now they're around forever instead of a mere lifetime.

Gettysburg battlefield: Gettysburg, Pennsylvania, was the place many men took their last breath on Earth during the famous Civil War battle that occurred there. However, ghosts dressed in military uniforms haunt these grounds.

Jacob Schnell mansion: Strange noises and temperature fluctuations haunt this property in Nashville, Tennessee. Many believe Jacob Schnell haunts his former mansion in an attempt to reclaim it.

Kehoe House: This famous bed-and-breakfast in Savannah, Georgia, serves up something besides breakfast—haunted rooms.

Lemp mansion: Located in St. Louis, Missouri, this mansion is haunted by the ghosts of several deceased members of the Lemp family, mainly Charles Lemp. Doors open and close by themselves,

---

Ghosts

A house is never silent in darkness to those who listen intently; there is a whispering in distant chambers, an unearthly hand presses the snib of the window, the latch rises. Ghosts were created when the first man woke in the night.
—from *The Little Minister*, by James Matthew Barrie

---

objects move on their own, music comes from nowhere, cold spots mark the site of suicides that occurred at the mansion, and some claim to have seen ghosts.

Lowcountry Ghost Walk: Ghosts are a plenty in Charleston, South Carolina, particularly along the Lowcountry Ghost Walk where ghosts travel the streets and a ghost called the Gray Man warns beach visitors about impending and dangerous storms.

Mammoth Cave National Park: It's no surprise that ghosts dwell in the labyrinths that are part of "the world's longest known cave." In Mammoth Cave, located in Kentucky, the ghosts of a black slave and a southern lady haunt visitors.

Old Bernardsville Public Library: Imagine issuing a library card to a ghost—that's exactly what the librarians did at the Old Bernardsville Public Library in New Jersey. The ghost of Phyllis Parker has haunted the library since 1877. When the body of Parker's lover was delivered to the building in a pine box after he was hung for being a British spy, Parker opened the box unaware he was inside, went crazy, and killed herself. Her ghost has haunted the building ever since.

Philippine Military Academy: Someone should have told these soldiers that their services are no longer needed and that their ghost platoon can stop marching the parade ground of this military academy located in Baguio City.

Port Arthur: This town in Tasmania was a former prison settlement that housed up to 1,600 convicts from 1830 to 1877. Workers and visitors wonder if the deceased convicts stuck around—ghosts are often seen, unexplained strange noises occur, and objects move on their own.

Elvis Presley: Many have claimed to see Elvis's ghost in a variety of places across the globe, including Graceland. Each year in Memphis, Tennessee, on the anniversary of Elvis's death, thousands of Elvis fans attend a candlelight vigil at Elvis's grave. Some participate in a séance in an attempt to conjure up Elvis's ghost.

Provincial Hotel: Once a hospital for confederate soldiers, the Provincial Hotel in New Orleans is no stranger to the ghosts of soldiers or surgeons.

San Antonio: Famous for the Alamo, San Antonio, Texas, is a hotspot for ghosts. Locals claim ghosts of those killed in this battle wander the streets of the town.

Screaming Tunnel: Legend states that if you light a match at midnight inside this tunnel—located in Niagara Falls under the railroad tracks that connect Niagara Falls to New York and Toronto—a scream will be heard and the match will be extinguished. David Cronenberg used the tunnel in his 1983 movie *The Dead Zone*, based on Stephen King's book.

Spy House: Built in 1663, the Spy House Museum in Port Monmouth, New Jersey, is home to . . . you guessed it . . . ghosts. A sea captain looks through a telescope, a colonial woman tends to her chores, a mother dressed in white leans over a crib, and young girls play in the yard—and they're all ghosts.

Tower of London: Construction began on this castle in 1078, also the site of a prison and torture chambers. Hundreds of prisoners faced their death here, and it's no wonder the place is haunted. Queen Ann Boleyn's ghost has made her presence known since Henry VIII had her beheaded in 1536. Occasionally, Sir Walter Raleigh's ghost makes an appearance, as do Lady Salisbury and Lady Jane Grey, usually on the anniversary of their deaths. The 1963 film, *The Tower of London*, stars Vincent Price as Richard III, a man haunted by the ghosts of those he had killed.

Toys "R" Us: The 1980s jingle for this toy store talks about remaining a kid in order to play with toys forever. We figure the ghosts haunting this store in Sunnyvale, California, took the jingle to heart. Toys and books are often scattered throughout the store when the employees come into work in the morning, items that were put away the previous evening. It looks like these ghosts are having a lot of fun. Who said you can't stay a kid forever?

Waverley Hills Sanatorium: This former clinic in Louisville, Kentucky, saw its share of death in the early 1900s when patients were sent to receive treatment from tuberculosis. Unfortunately many died on a daily basis. Voices and apparitions have been recorded at the site, and the Sanatorium has been featured on the Syfy series *Ghost Hunters*.

White House: The ghosts that haunt this 132-room property in Washington, D.C., might be enough to scare anyone from seeking the presidency. After all, who would want to share a home and an office with the ghosts of Abraham Lincoln, Abigail Adams, and Dolly Madison?

Windsor Castle: Home to the Queen of England, Windsor Castle is known for its hauntings. The ghost of Elizabeth I roams the halls along with George III, King Henry VIII, and King Charles I. Fortunately for the queen, these ghosts don't seem to intend any harm.

Scott Grimando, *Jack Be Nimble*

"*Jack Be Nimble,* written by psychiatrist Donald A. Moses, tells the tale of a man chasing his own demons. Deep within the dream realm he must ask himself, is he a cop or a killer. It has a strong pulp/noir element to it."—Scott Grimando is an illustrator and conceptual artist.

GETTING PULPED

In the dime novels of the late nineteenth century, good guys tended to be almost comically moral and decent and bad guys were cartoonishly bad. They were the proverbial white and black hats that were hugely popular in their day but whose luster faded with the troubled twentieth century. In the decades spanning World War I, the Great Depression, and World War II, adventure fiction underwent a major thematic change: life became darker and more real, and the increases in communication via the radio brought the world's woes into our living rooms every night. The writing of the first half of the twentieth century reflected this as stories focused less on clear cut good vs. evil and crime and punishment, and began to explore justice and injustice. Writers began to shade characters so that they were "sort of good" and "kind of evil"; or, more often, "tarnished good" and "corrupt but not actually evil." The dividing line between the moral polar opposites of good and evil became fuzzy.

The Pulp Fiction era chronicled it all. At the outset of the pulps there were still those white hats, but by the end of the era, as the world recovered from World War II and stories about the realities of war filtered through our society, those white hats got pretty well battered. Even the villains became multidimensional and less completely black as writers began to explore the "why" behind their villainy.

The pulps were potboiler magazines inexpensively produced and printed on rough "pulp" paper. The stories were written very quickly by writers who were paid by the word and trying to make rent; plots were generally high concept, and the magazines were sold at affordable prices so that kids and adults could buy a lot of them. Story quality varied wildly from almost execrable claptrap to truly deathless prose. These pulp tales were often fantastic, the characters typically larger than life, the stakes always high, and the threats insanely dire. In short, they were absolutely wonderful. Without the pulps the comic book superhero would certainly never have come about, and many of the most enduring heroes were inspired in whole or part by pulp characters. Aspects of Doc Savage (including his Fortress of Solitude) can be found in Superman; and

moody antiheroes like the Shadow and the Spider were clear influences on Batman.

The pulps also had a certain look about them that attracted the
demographic for whom they were intended: boys and young men.
The brightly colored covers featured a mix of horrific images (monsters, ghouls, Nazis, fiends, etc.), scantily clad women with heaving
bosoms, and heroes with big muscles, lantern jaws, and guns. Here
were heroes the readers wanted to be, and here were the kinds of
women they wanted to rescue (for whatever rewards went with
that). Plus there were vile enemies they wanted to trounce. It was
escapism that allowed (and even invited) the reader to regard the
hero as his proxy.

Throughout the pulp era there were hundreds of titles, some
very successful and others lasting little more than an issue or two.
The cream of the crop included *Adventure, Amazing Stories, Black
Mask, Dime Detective, Flying Aces, Horror Stories, Marvel Tales,
Oriental Stories, Planet Stories, Spicy Detective, Startling Stories,
Thrilling Wonder Stories, Unknown,* and *Weird Tales.* As you can
tell from the titles, the magazines all featured some aspect of the
struggle between good and evil, or right and wrong. Dozens of magazines, thousands of issues, tens of thousands of stories, and each
one of them with a bad guy. Not all of them, however, had a good
guy. There were quite a few pulp stories that were early attempts
at what became the Noir genre—antiheroes who were sometimes
criminals themselves, but not as evil as the other criminals with
whom they associated. In later years, mainstream authors like
Elmore Leonard, Carl Hiassan, John D. MacDonald, Tim Dorsey,
George Pelecanos, Walter Mosely, and others would continue to
explore the storytelling potential of the antihero.

In fact a lot of mainstream writers either got their start writing
pulps, or wrote stories for the pulps as a way of reaching a new
readership. Some were probably lured there for the sheer fun of it.
Notable authors who also wrote pulps include Poul Anderson, Isaac
Asimov, Robert Bloch, Ray Bradbury, Max Brand, Edgar Rice Bur-
roughs, William S. Burroughs, Raymond Chandler, Arthur C. Clarke,
Joseph Conrad, Philip K. Dick, Arthur Conan Doyle, C. S. Forester,
Erle Stanley Gardner, Zane Grey, Dashiell Hammett, Robert A.
Heinlein, O. Henry, Frank Herbert, Robert E. Howard, Rudyard

On Heroes in Pulp Friction

"In the pulp magazines you did occasionally have the pure, square-jawed heroes, combating evil with nary a gray area troubling their psychic makeup. But the conflicted or troubled characters are generally the more interesting ones. You want your heroes leavened (or whatever the opposite of 'leavened' is—deflated?) by a bit of dirt in their background, a bit of darkness to add texture and complexity."—Charles Ardai is the founder and editor of Hard Case Crime, a line of pulp-style paperback crime novels.

Kipling, Louis L'Amour, H. P. Lovecraft, John D. MacDonald, Robert Silverberg, Upton Sinclair, Jim Thompson, Mark Twain, H. G. Wells, Tennessee Williams, and Cornell Woolrich. And that list is by no means complete.

Sub-genres within pulps were many: sword and sorcery, fantasy, horror, westerns, romance, sports, war, railroad, and detectives—along with dozens of other twists and turns on these models. Naturally most of these sub-genres lent themselves easily to the "good vs. evil" theme. Good guys vs. bad; heroes vs. monsters; cops vs. robbers. Of course, some stories within the genre veered away from the direct good and evil conflict to explore themes of moral ambiguity, temptation, and personal redemption. Pulp tales were mostly, but not always, about a fight against the Big Bad.

In the adventure, horror, and fantasy books, however, good and evil were central themes. The villains were usually very, very bad. The heroes, on the other hand, varied between being good to the point of appearing spotless (as with Doc Savage) or were murky and nearer to being a lesser of evils rather than a true hero (as with Conan the Cimmerian).

Some of the characters and stories that came out of the pulp era proved so popular and crucial to the pop culture of the last century that they've become legendary even to modern readers who may not have actually read the original stories. Millions know that Arnold Schwarzenegger broke into the popular mainstream with his role as Conan the Barbarian, but (sadly) not as many know that Conan's adventures were first published in the pages of *Weird Tales* in 1932. Likewise, who doesn't know about Tarzan—and how many folks know that he first appeared in the pulp *All-Story Magazine* in 1912?

The pulp formula—short chapters ending in narrative hooks, lots

Lloyd Kaufman of Troma Entertainment

"A book that influenced me while at Yale was C. S. Lewis's *Mere Christianity*. It proves the existence of God by showing that in every society on Earth from the most primitive to the most sophisticated, ingrained in all of them is an innate sense of goodness. It is more satisfying in all cultures to have good triumph over evil, but in reality (and in Tromaville) it is never that simple."

—Lloyd Kaufman is the president of Troma Entertainment, and creator of cult classics like the *Toxic Avenger, Sgt. Kabuki-Man NYPD,* and *Poultrygeist: Night of the Chicken Dead.*

of action, bizarre villains, and larger-than-life heroes has influenced everything from comic books to TV shoes like *Heroes* to mega-bestsellers like Dan Brown's *The Da Vinci Code*. Although influenced by the Penny Dreadfuls of nineteenth-century England, the pulp is regarded as a uniquely American form of storytelling.

BEATING THE PULP OUT OF THE BAD GUYS

Arch enemies and supervillains were not introduced in the pulps, but they were refined there. Much of the groundwork for the super criminal and the superhero was laid in the second half of the nineteenth century, mostly with French and English writers. Though there were some important American novels published in the same era, it's fair to say that it was in the twentieth century that American writers took the thematic ball and ran with it.

The villains of these overlapping eras came in a variety of unsavory flavors. The early pulp stories tended to feature villains who were evil for evil's sake, contributing to new stereotypes like the Criminal Mastermind and the Supervillain. Over time pulp writers brought in a variety of kinds of villains, including some who existed simply to play "foil" rather than being true adversaries of any complexity, existing to demonstrate qualities that are diametrically opposed to those virtues that define a hero as such. Pulp writers began to explore motivations, to crawl inside the head and the back-story of the villain to determine why they are bent on doing harm or committing crimes. Here are some classic archetypes:

The Alien Threat: We can look back to nineteenth-century science fiction for the foundation of this genre: H. G. Wells's *War of the Worlds*. Pulp writers spun thousands of variations on the alien invasion premise, exploring both the plausible and implausible, and only occasionally hardwiring any real science into the tale. People didn't read the pulps for a dose of reality anyway.

The alien invasion has become a staple of science fiction stories. The motivation for the invasion varies: conquest, food, breeding stock, making way for an interspatial bypass, the search for slave labor, kicks. These stories are often allegories for our fears of international threats such as those posed by the Nazis, the

Communists, terrorists, military juntas, and even corporate takeovers. In pulp stories these invasions ranged from tentative probes by spies who looked like (or appeared to look like) humans; attacks in remote areas; insidious takeovers using mind control, pods, or some other "infection" or wholesale military invasion. Some of the smaller scale stories were built around aliens who were here to observe and prepare for the coming invasion. One of the earliest pulps, Hugo Gernsback's *Amazing Stories*, frequently reprinted the nineteenth-century cautionary science fiction writings of Jules Verne and H. G. Wells, and many of the pulp writers who contributed to that and other magazines mined their alien/human clash of culture tropes for fresh stories.

The Archenemy: Writers who wrote ongoing series featuring the same character ran into trouble when they tried to come up with a completely new and interesting villain each time. Some managed it—such as in the Doc Savage series, where only one villain—the brilliant John Sunlight—ever makes a second appearance in a total of 181 adventures. Most series heroes encountered one or more villains over and over again—sometimes interspersed with some newcomers. This "rogue's gallery" was endorsed by readers who came to love certain villains and wanted them back again.

The Brilliant Terrorist: This kind of villain isn't always actually evil. Jules Verne explored the "bad for a good purpose" kind of genius, like Robur the Conqueror and Captain Nemo, who in retrospect are somewhat like modern ecoterrorists. They are willing to destroy in order to prove a point or protect something they consider more valuable than ordinary human life. Elements of this can be found throughout the pulps, such as in Edmund H. North's short story "Farewell to the Master," published in *Astounding*, upon which the 1951 film *The Day the Earth Stood Still* was based. In it an alien comes to Earth to warn us to shape up or face punishment in the form of extinction. Often in these tales, the ignorance of humans (frequently the paranoid military or the panic-like-sheep general population) serve as the antagonists by continuing to do whatever it is that they're being told not to do; and they often try to kill the person who is trying to share this cautionary warning.

Gort Klaatu Barada Nikto

In the short story, "Farewell to the Master," the alien Klaatu was accompanied by a giant alien robot named Gnut (changed to Gort for the film *The Day the Earth Stood Still*). The story ends with a twist when Gnut informs the confused humans: "You misunderstand, . . . I am the master." Not only were these the first non-hostile aliens in modern fiction, both the humanoid and the robot were more or less concerned with achieving a peaceful resolution. This was exceedingly rare in the xenophobic days of the pulps.

The Criminal Mastermind: Author Paul Henri Corentin Féval is credited with creating the first of the many literary criminal masterminds with his 1862 novel *Jean Diable* (a.k.a. *John Devil*). The villain is a devious and calculating evildoer who manipulates a criminal empire, much to the chagrin of the heroic Scotland Yard Chief Superintendent Gregory Temple. The following year Féval began a series of novels about a complex criminal empire. He retrofitted Jean Diable (and a few other previous novels) into the series. That series laid the groundwork for all fictional criminal empires to come, and some scholars believe that the concept of a gangland code of honor embraced by the Mafia was to a fair degree influenced by these popular novels. What marks this kind of story, however, is the presence of a genius criminal who sits like a spider at the center of a vast and tangled web of plots and crimes. His agents

Good from Bad

In 1862, Féval founded the magazine *Jean Diable,* named after his novel. One of the editor-writers for the magazine was Emile Gaboriau, who would later create the character of police detective Monsieur Lecoq, a brilliant investigator who influenced Sir Arthur Conan Doyle's creation of Sherlock Holmes. Just as every hero needs a good villain, every truly legendary villain needs a hero worthy of him.

occasionally fall at the hands of the inspector or detective hero, but often the master criminal eludes capture. Sherlock Holmes's foil, Professor Moriarity, is perhaps the best known of these criminal masterminds. Another classic criminal mastermind was the insidious Dr. Fu Manchu of Sax Rohmer's pulp thrillers, a genius of frightening dimension who was bent on global conquest.

The Gang Leader: Not all master criminals are criminal masterminds. Some are merely smarter, more charismatic, or better positioned than the other thugs and are the ones calling the shots. These kinds of criminals seldom posed huge threats for the heroes, but they were more realistic in that they represented the kind of predators who fed on folks in the real world. In pulps, this could mean anything from a gang doing a smash-and-grab in a jewelry store to a kidnap ring to white slavers. The leader of the gang was typically ruthless, willing to spill blood, take lives, break hearts, and ignore all laws. We are supposed to dislike them, even hate them, because they represent the kinds of threats that pollute our lives—pick up any newspaper and you'll see—and we are supposed to root for the hero when he smashes into the gang, whether with flying fists or hot lead.

The Great Unknown: These stories allowed for a lot of truly creepy storytelling that includes the entire Cthulhu story cycle begun by H. P. Lovecraft and the countless "indescribable horror" tales that sprang up thereafter. The premise here is that there is something supernatural that is so alien that human language is inadequate to the task of describing it. Lovecraft's detractors criticized him for copping out and not describing the monsters who plagued the protagonists; but to be fair to the author's intention, these were creatures whose appearance was so grossly outside of human understanding that the sight of them was enough to unhinge the mind. They were literally indescribable. Other "great unknowns" are monsters whose nature is not understood until late in the story (if at all), and part of the plot is the attempt to quantify these creatures.

The Mad Scientist: There's a very long tradition of the mad scientist as the antagonist for a story, though one of the very first—Victor

Frankenstein—was actually the protagonist of Mary Shelley's novel and the terrible things he did were intended to be for the betterment of mankind. A lot of mad scientists are just that: mad. They are obsessive people who have crossed the line from being a genius with a goal to being a dangerously obsessed psychopath. In the pulp era, the subtleties of "I did it for the common good" (which explained the motives of Frankenstein and has been since used many times over) was often replaced by someone who was mad and evil. A variation of this is the scientist who is devoted to the results-based obsession of pure research and doesn't care about the effect his invention may have on the rest of the world. Such characters were often exploited by criminals of various stripes who manipulated, begged, borrowed, or stole these inventions and used them as weapons.

The Masked Villain: The pulps loved their villains to be masked and mysterious. Usually there was a big reveal in the last couple of chapters, though most readers of the pulps figured out who the bad guy was long before he tore off his cowl (or hood, mask, fake monster costume, etc.). It seldom mattered, either, because the masked persona was usually much more interesting than the person who wore it. This love of the dramatic quickly transferred from the pulps into comics, and persists to this day.

The Monster: It's always fun to just square off against a monster. No heated debates over conflicting ideologies, no political agendas, no devious crimes to solve. Just a monster, a hero, and some violence. However . . . looking beneath the surface of the hero vs. monster story form there is (gasp!) another layer, and this subtext allows for allegory and metaphor to convey everything from racism (sadly, that was rampant during the pulp era) to social commentary (less common then, more common in the generations that followed). The monster could stand for anything. In the sword and sorcery stories of Robert E. Howard, monsters and savages who acted in mindlessly violent ways were stand-ins for Native Americans, blacks, and other ethnic groups that the Texan writer of the 1920s and '30s misunderstood and therefore disliked and feared. The modern reader can, however, edit out the subtext by granting the benefit of the doubt by thinking, Well, if Howard was alive today he might not have been a racist and the monsters might have been ciphers for disease, terrorists, or something acceptably dislikeable.

To be fair, though, a lot of the more horrific monster stories in which the nature of the threat is never clearly or deeply explored are the writers attempting some catharsis for whatever species of paranoia crawling around their brains. By the late forties, books and movies dealt with giant monsters as a way of demonstrating an understandable fear of atomic energy and its likely misuses. In the fifties, the mind-control invasion stories were thin coats of storytelling paint over fears about communism. And so on, up to the current wave of zombie stories that speak to our fears of pathogens like SARS, HIV, and H1N1.

The Supernatural Villain: Supernatural villains flourished in the pulps, especially those pulps that favored fantasy and horror stories. Robert E. Howard's stalwart heroes, Conan the Cimmerian, Bran Mak Morn, Solomon Kane, and King Kull of Atlantis, fought them on a regular basis; and in the Cthulhu stories of H. P. Lovecraft you were far more likely to encounter a villain from beyond the stars or from some other dimension than you were to find anything even resembling a "hero."

The Supervillain: The label "supervillain," however, is often used as a catch-all phrase for most of the villain subtypes we've been discussing. To the true connoisseur of the genre, however, a

---

Using Your Braaaaaiiins!

By the 1960s, during the wave of low-budget horror movies that were changing the face of horrific storytelling and which owed a large debt to the larger-than-life storytelling of the pulp era, social subtext of a more positive and deliberate nature was showing up in the form of new monsters. George Romero's *Night of the Living Dead*, for instance, used flesh-eating ghouls to tell a story about racism and intolerance. This was part of a developing trend in genre fiction—science fiction, fantasy, and horror—to use fantastic storytelling to convey important social issues.

The Victim Protagonist

Horror fiction does not always require a hero. Horror fiction, in fact, sometimes exists in order to let us glimpse the awe and mystery of a very weird, very nasty thing. The protagonist of these stories is more likely some helpless and hopeless character who makes some awful discovery—in a spooky old house, coming out of a magical object, etc.—and then gets eaten by it. H. P. Lovecraft, August Derleth, Robert E. Howard, and others wrote many a tale in which the protagonist is there to be the victim, often chronicling the events leading up to his (or her) own unpleasant demise.

supervillain—be it human, metahuman, or alien—possesses some qualities that made them physically more threatening than just some guy in a weird costume. So Lex Luthor, Fu Manchu, and John Sunlight are technically either evil geniuses or criminal masterminds who don't care if anyone knows who they are, while the Green Goblin and the Octopus are masked villains who want to keep their identities secret. During the pulp era there weren't as many supervillains as there were, say, masked villains. The supervillain truly flourished in the superhero comics, a market that grew out of the pulps and lasted far longer.

WEIRD BOOKS AND STRANGE TALES

Most of the major pulp magazines had a unique flavor—a tone and voice that appealed to different kinds of people. This individuality helped cultivate certain writers, allowing them creative liberties not otherwise found. As a result, those writers were able to dig deeper into their imaginations (and in some cases into mythology as source material) in order to tell ever more complex tales of the struggle of good and evil.

For horror and darker fantasy, *Weird Tales Magazine* was the first and the most enduring pulp, and it's outlasted the end of the pulp era and even the end of the twentieth century. Created in 1923 by J. C. Henneberger, the magazine went on to publish some of the most chilling and horrific tales of horror, and to very effectively wipe out the dividing line between good and evil. Conan was introduced in *Weird Tales*, as were the Great Old Ones of Lovecraft's Cthulhu Mythos, and Seabury Quinn's Jules de Grandin stories. The magazine even featured the short story "The Vengeance of Nitocris" which launched the career of Tennessee Williams.

In its early years it featured stories by Robert Bloch (who went on to pen *Psycho*), Robert E. Howard, H. P. Lovecraft, Ray Bradbury, Manly Wade Wellman, Fritz Leiber, Henry Kuttner, C. L. Moore, and Theodore Sturgeon; and in later years, tales by Brian Lumley, Thomas Ligotti, Gene Wolfe, Ramsey Campbell, Tanith Lee, Nina Kiriki Hoffman, and Nancy Springer.

What made this magazine so popular? Current editor Ann Van-DerMeer shared her thoughts on why the magazine worked so well: "Very simply because *Weird Tales* was the first. The first fantasy magazine dedicated to the strange, unusual, weird, and bizarre. No one had ever seen anything like this before. It was always breaking new ground . . . like 1933, for example, when Margaret Brundage's artwork graced the cover for the first time. She was the first and only female artist to do pulp covers at that time. *Weird Tales* has been the trail-blazer, not afraid to take chances and do what other magazines would not, or could not, do."

When asked about some of the magazine's landmark moments, former *Weird Tales* editor Darrell Schweitzer marks them by specific stories. "Lovecraft's 'The Rats in the Walls' (March 1924) was certainly the strongest American horror story since Poe. Like a bolt of lightning out of a clear blue sky. Another key moment was not the actual discovery of Robert E. Howard (his first story, 'Spear and Fang' is negligible) but the publication of Howard's brilliant 'The Shadow Kingdom' (August 1929), which is the first modern sword and sorcery story. Conan the Barbarian makes his debut in 'The Phoenix on the Sword' (December 1932) and the rest, as they say, is history. Lovecraft's 'The Call of Cthulhu' (February 1928) is also an important milestone. It is one of the most influential pieces of fiction ever published, on a par, at least, with a few Sherlock Holmes stories. Think of the thousands of Cthulhu Mythos stories by other hands, the movies, games, T-shirts, jokes, plush

Cthulhu dolls . . . it all starts there, with that one story. And, Stephen King called Ray Bradbury's *The October Country* 'the Dubliners of American horror,' referring, if anybody doesn't catch the reference, to the seminal mainstream collection by James Joyce. Many of the October Country stories—'The Jar,' 'The Lake,' 'The Scythe,' 'The Wind,' 'The Crowd,' etc., were published in *Weird Tales* in the early '40s."

THE CTHULHU MYTHOS

Howard Phillips Lovecraft (1890–1937) was an American author of horror, fantasy, and science fiction and the creator of a series of stories that dealt with good and evil on a cosmic level. Award-winning horror author James A. Moore, a devoted fan of Lovecraft, brings us up to speed: "The Cthulhu Mythos posits that all life on Earth is merely an accident, a by-product of what was created eons ago as a slave race to the Great Old Ones. Said ancient deities actually being incredibly old and highly advanced alien creatures that wound up on the planet more by luck than by design. Everything that has happened since that time is merely coincidence, and the human race is nothing special, has no unique place in the universe and is effectively stumbling around believing that their existence has meaning when it does not."

Moore goes on to give a who's who of the key players among the Great Old Ones: "Among Lovecraft's most notorious are, of course, Cthulhu, the nominal head of the Great Old Ones, who dwells in a sunken city here on earth in a deathlike sleep that will only end when 'the stars are right.' Hastur, whose name must not be spoken for fear of summoning the creature, Yog Sothoth and creatures that were lesser but no less dangerous to mere humans, such as the Deep Ones, aquatic creatures that were often worshipped in primitive cultures, according to the Mythos and who in turn worshipped Dagon and Mother Hydra, creatures that were connected with Cthulhu. The Fungi from Yoggoth, the Night Gaunts and numerous other creations not only of Lovecraft but of his peers. It wasn't unusual for the various authors he knew to playfully incorporate variations on the names of his creations in their tales and vice versa."

Michael Calandra, *Bride of Cthulhu*

"In 'Bride of Cthulhu,' I strive to capture both the despair and horror of Lovecraft's idea that humans are unaware of a higher reality, perhaps one that is not to their liking."
—Michael Calandra is an artist and book illustrator whose work appears in *Heavy Metal Magazine* and *Art Scene International*.

The Great Old Ones are just one part of a three-way cosmic war that crosses time and dimensions. The other players are the Outer Gods (first called the Other Gods by Lovecraft and later renamed for the role-playing game Call of Cthulhu), and the Elder Gods. Lovecraft scholar J. K. Hardwicke explains: "It really depends on who is interpreting Lovecraft, and these days it's like a bunch of Biblical scholars wrangling over the meaning in an obscure bit of scripture. Most people, however, view the Outer Gods as being separate from the Great Old Ones and more powerful.

"The bottom line is that Lovecraft created a new kind of horror fantasy fiction—one in which man is, ultimately, an insignificant part who at his most useful gets to chronicle the attempts of the rightful owners of this planet to return and claim it . . . the Cthulhu cycle of stories is endlessly compelling and it has a

---

The Necronomicon

In a number of his stories, Lovecraft makes reference to an ancient and evil book of sorcery and unsavory knowledge that he called *The Necronomicon*. It was first mentioned in his short story "The Hound" and the tome is purported to have been written by "Mad Arab" Abdul Alhazred. The book contains accounts of the Great Old Ones and provides spells for summoning them—which is something no sane person would want to do. Of course, sanity isn't a major theme in these stories, so there are various attempts at summoning—both deliberate and accidental, and none of them end well.

Funny thing is, because so many Mythos writers made mention of the book, a lot of later writers and fans believed that the book was, in fact, real, or at least part of real-world mythology. Booksellers and librarians have been barraged by requests for over seventy years, and once a prankster smuggled a card for it into the Yale University Library's card catalog.

Many faux versions of it have been written and published—some openly admitting that they are works of fiction based on a device of fiction, and some claiming that they are, in real point of fact, the actual *Necronomicon*.

---

grandeur that makes it feel like these are stories about real myths rather than wholecloth imaginings."

One of the most entertaining aspects of the Mythos is that Lovecraft openly invited other writers to write and publish these kinds of stories. "Besides Lovecraft," recalls Stephen Mark Rainey, an author and editor of three anthologies of Lovecraftian fiction, "numerous authors have added to the Mythos. Some of the most notable include Robert Bloch, Ramsey Campbell, Lin Carter, Fred Chappell, August Derleth, Robert E. Howard, T. E. D. Klein, Henry Kuttner, Fritz Leiber, Frank Belknap Long, Brian Lumley, Clark Ashton Smith, Karl Edward Wagner, Colin Wilson, F. Paul Wilson, even Stephen King. Of these, August Derleth was most directly responsible for presenting and keeping Lovecraft's work visible to the public by creating Arkham House after Lovecraft's death. Yet Derleth's own contributions to the Mythos are generally considered inferior, and in my opinion, rightly so, as they attempt to force the established tenets of the Cthulhu Mythos into the framework of Judeo-Christian myth, which I feel is a serious mistake."

According to Brian Lumley, the international bestselling author of the Necroscope series and the author of several Mythos novels: "H. P. Lovecraft was unique among horror writers—not that there were too many of those before or in his time. He had a feel—an imagination and an erudition second to none: a cosmic insight into the way horror should be written. But you ask: why does his work inspire devotion? Well, horror fiction has its icons; that is to say, in the fiction itself. We have the Frankenstein Monster, the Wolfman, the Zombie, the Mummy, the Vampire, Golem, and so on. But while it must be admitted that Lovecraft 'admired' Ghouls, he simply put the rest of the players aside and created monsters the likes of which we'd never seen before! . . . There simply isn't anything anywhere in the fiction that looks like—or impacts on the reader's sensibilities—like Wilbur Whately; or like Cthulhu, or the Antarctic's Great Old Ones, or the batrachian Deep Ones under Devil Reef in the ocean off crumbling Innsmouth, or gugs, or ghasts, or gaunts and ghouls. (We'll just have to accept HPL's ghouls); but every other one of these creatures, with that single exception, were Lovecraft's: the extraordinary monsters that he made real, such was his way with words . . ."

Soul of the Monster

"Frankenstein always brings a tear to my eye. He was such a beautiful innocent being who was labeled a monster and then forced into that role. It is the same with King Kong. He was a victim of humanity's mistakes, and was not a monster at all. I felt the same way in *Cloverfield,* and not just for the fact that Clovie was taking down some of New York's more annoying residents. There is also a film from 1972 called *Raw Meat* (or sometimes *Deathline*). It shows these coalminers trapped by a cave-in while building train tunnels. Generations later, they emerge (very mutant and monster like) and kill subway patrons encroaching on their underground home. This movie always saddened me because the mutants are just protecting the only home they know. To them, we are the monsters destroying their normality."—Rebekah McKendry is a writer for *Fangoria Magazine.*

PULP HEROICS

The pulp writers knew how to build tough heroes. They also built them to last, and nearly a century after the start of the pulp era, we're still writing about them, reading them, making movies about them. Some heroes became popular enough to merit their own magazines, and these "character pulps" developed huge fan followings and often resulted in reprints decades later—as with Doc Savage, the Shadow, the Spider, etc.—and even new stories written by modern writers and published as comics, shorts, fan fiction, and conventionally published novels.

One of the things that separates the character pulps from the commingled mass of all pulps is that they were always about the struggle of good over evil, though often the heroes had to resort to some highly questionable practices in order to win the day.

Here are some of the most notable of the many, many heroes of the Pulp Era.

The Shadow: For eighteen years (1931–49) the Shadow was the premier pulp hero in print and on the radio. That he even became a hero is odd, considering that he was not a lantern-jawed brawler, did not wear a white hat, didn't have a teenager sidekick, and psychologically speaking was a complete basket of snakes.

But he was the good guy.

The first version of the Shadow appeared in the February 1929 issue of Street and Smith's *Fame and Fortune*. In this story, Compton Moore was a mysterious figure who donned a green shroud to fight crime. His appearance was marked by a particularly disturbing laughter, that was part mockery and part threat. When Street and Smith started a radio program, *Detective Story Hour*, to capitalize off of the popularity of their magazine characters, actor James La Curto played the Shadow, complete with that mocking laugh. The audience loved it.

However, when Street and Smith decided to copyright the character and launch a series of novels, they handed it over to newspaperman and amateur stage magician Walter Gibson, who made substantial changes to the character and went on to write 282 Shadow novels, sometimes banging out two books per month. Other writers—Theodore Tinsley and Bruce Elliot—wrote the remainder of the series. All of the books appeared under the Street and Smith house name of "Maxwell Grant." And even though the books ended in 1949, the radio show lasted until 1954. There were also a half-dozen two-reel shorts, a serial, and seven feature films, including one with Alec Baldwin in the title role. The Shadow radio program ran from 1937 to 1954 and was marked by the signature call and response: "Who knows what evil lurks in the hearts of men? The Shadow knows!" And, although legendary actor Orson Welles was the radio voice of the Shadow only through 1938, it is his voice that will forever be associated with that character and those compelling words.

Gibson's Shadow was named Kent Allard, though he frequently took the identity of millionaire playboy Lamont Cranston. This persona created the template for a huge number of rich playboy heroes, from Bruce Wayne to Tony Stark.

So . . . who was the Shadow? In Gibson's pulp novels, the Shadow was a master of disguise, a master hypnotist, a ruthless fighter, and a tireless defender of justice and enemy of evil. It's fair to say that the Shadow was the single most important character of the pulp era and the blueprint for the entire comic book industry. Secret identity, costume, hidden lair, and special powers.

What made the Shadow so unique was that unlike the stalwart heroes of pervious years (and of competing pulps), the Shadow used the same methods and tactics as the masked villains he fought. He became a shadowy, frightening monster in order to fight monsters. He descended to their level—and the bad guys did not like it one bit. When they heard that mocking laughter, fear blossomed in their hearts, just as their presence struck fear into the hearts of their victims. They became the victim, and the Shadow became the terrible predator.

It was a terrific switch. Suddenly all of the props and conventions of evil were being used to fight evil. It was as stunning a change as if an angel had dressed like a devil.

The Shadow broke other rules. Instead of being the stand-up guy who wanted to fight fair, he used disguises, psychological torture, hypnosis, and magic (in some stories he had supernatural powers, in others he didn't). He also wasn't very nice. He carried guns and he wasn't above using them.

Also, like the Criminal Mastermind, the Shadow acquired a network of spies and agents throughout the world, many of whom were shady characters themselves. He created his own underworld, but their common goal was the destruction of evil.

When Batman was created a few years later, there was more than a little of the Shadow in the Caped Crusader. And over the years a lot of writers have used the same source material (deliberately or because this model is now commonplace in our creative landscape) to build other edgy characters. Without the Shadow we wouldn't have the Destroyer of the Don Pendleton novels or Marvel Comics' the Punisher. There may even be a bit of the Shadow in James Bond, Jack Bauer, and Joe Ledger.

Doc Savage: Less than two years after the Shadow first saw print, Henry W. Ralston and John L. Nanovic of Street and Smith created another super crime fighter who would be beloved and emulated for generations to come. Clark Savage, Jr., known to the world at large as Doc Savage, debuted in the 1933 novel, *The Man of Bronze*. The writer hired to craft these novels was Lester Dent, writing under the house name Kenneth Robeson. Dent wanted to build a hero who had the physical presence and power of Tarzan and the cognitive genius of Sherlock Holmes, matched with the arrow-straight moral compass of Abe Lincoln and the vast scientific and forensic knowledge of the popular fictional character Professor Craig Kennedy.[1]

By the time the series came to an end in 1949, 181 novels had been published, most of them written by Dent; the rest were written by Harold A. David, William G. Bogart, W. Ryerson Johnson, Lawrence Donovan, and Alan Hathaway.

The defining characteristics of Doc Savage are integrity, brilliance, and the scientific method. Doc was raised to be what he was. If the stories had been written fifty years later, then Doc would have likely been the result of specific genetic design—a perfect human being who was faster, stronger, and smarter than everyone else, but only as smart as the human absolute would allow. Doc's father hired the world's top scientists as tutors for his son, and though this made the young Clark brilliant, it also made him something of an emotional freak—a theme explored later in the series.

Unlike the Shadow, who had confederates but few real friends, Doc had a group of five very close friends, and each of these men was a genius or expert in his own field. Each of them was also hell on wheels in a fight. The five men were civil engineer Colonel John "Renny" Renwick, archaeologist and geologist William Harper "Johnny" Littlejohn, electrical engineer Major Thomas J. "Long Tom" Roberts, lawyer Brigadier General Theodore Marley "Ham" Brooks, and industrial chemist Lieutenant Colonel Andrew Blodgett "Mon" Mayfair. Occasionally Doc's cousin the beautiful, reckless, but far more personable Patricia Savage would join the boys for an adventure.

In the earliest adventures—and as was typical of many of the early pulps—Doc Savage lived up to his surname by savagely killing his enemies with hands, guns, or by any convenient means. He goes through a change of heart, however, that is, sadly, never

---

1. Professor Craig Kennedy is a character created by Arthur B. Reeve and who first appeared in "The Case of Helen Bond." *Cosmopolitan*, December 1910.

really explored or discussed to any satisfying degree, and thereafter he refuses to kill, although villains do have a habit of being killed by their own weapons. Monk and the others are less fussy, and they'll kill if Doc isn't looking.

As the novels went on, Doc developed a method for rehabilitation that is both fascinating and morally questionable. Instead of turning the criminals he captured over to the police, he performed a delicate brain operation on them that caused an alteration in their moral behavior while (apparently) leaving their intelligence and memories intact. These surgically altered criminals were then put through work rehab, taught trades useful to society, and even provided jobs. Most people look at that and say: Moral question? What moral question? It sounds great, and maybe it is. But it suggests that criminality is the result of an imperfection of the brain and not as a matter of choice. That presupposes that man is innately good and criminal behavior is just bad wiring.

"That's a can of worms," said Father Joseph Bremmer of Philadelphia. "It opens the door to social Darwinism, Eugenics,

---

Escape into the Pulps

"Pulp equals escapism and Doc Savage was the ultimate escape. He was introduced during the [Great] Depression, and he was smart, strong, rich, and tough as nails. He was also American. He was the concept of 'American ingenuity' personified. Though he wasn't financially strapped, he had nonetheless suffered a terrible loss with the murder of his father. That event changed his life, but it also gave him a sense of purpose. People who were putting their lives back together, or trying to create a new life in a world where everything they'd known or relied on had crashed down, could relate to that kind of mindset. And, unlike most of the other pulp heroes, Doc had a tight group of close friends who were also smart and resourceful. Those books were as much about the friendship as they were about the hero. And they hold up today."—Larry Ketchersid is the author of *Software by the Kilo* (Jose Media, 2009), and *Dusk Before the Dawn* (Infinity Publishing, 2006).

---

and a mixed bag of other problems. It also begs the question: By whose standard is normal social behavior to be judged? There are cultures where eating human flesh, even the flesh of one's own relatives, is a way of honoring them and adhering to cultural law; and yet here in Philadelphia it would get a person locked up. Stealing is a crime, sure, but a person stealing food from a starving person and a starving person stealing food are hardly the same crime. How does one diagnose a medical criminality in that? And . . . don't get me wrong . . . Doc Savage is a fine role model. But not in all ways, and certainly not when it comes to being the detective, the judge, the lawmaker, the jury, and—by way of surgery—the executioner. I know the writer probably meant well, but as they say, the path to hell is lined with good intentions."

Hugo Danner: In 1930, three years before the creation of Doc Savage, author Philip Wylie published his novel, *Gladiator*, in which he introduced Hugo Danner. Hugo was the son of a scientist who wanted to produce a superman. He concocted a special serum that enhanced his son's physical abilities to above peak human so that Hugo could bend steel in his hands, leap forty feet in the air, lift cars, and resist injury. Though this book has sadly been forgotten, the framework for the superhuman hero was laid down, and we can see very clear signs of him in Doc Savage and Superman. Wildside Press re-released the novel in 2009.

The Spider: The Spider was a deliberate attempt by Popular Publications to cash in on the success of the Shadow. The character wore a black hat and cape, he was a wealthy playboy (Richard Wentworth), he had a network of agents, and he fought racketeers and criminals. Ho-hum.

Or not. If the character had remained as a mere copy he would have probably vanished pretty quickly, but instead he got a substantial thematic makeover by borrowing from another hero: Doc Savage. Writer Norvell W. Page, working under the house name Grant Stockbridge, transformed the character from a monied detective in an opera cloak to a man who adopted the disguise of a fiend, a process that included wearing fangs to scare the bejesus out of the crooks. The scope of his battles changed, and he faced villains who threatened all of mankind.

The makeover was so intense and so frightening that the publishers refused to have accurate paintings of him on the cover. They tried it seven times, but the horrific character was too nasty looking, so they softened his image in the art, but not at all in the writing. The Spider, backed by his Hindu servant, Ram Singh, gorgeous Nita Van Sloan, and rough-and-tumble chauffeur Ronald Jackson beat the living hell out of the bad guys for 118 issues, from 1933 to 1944.

The Avenger: Street and Smith tried to strike gold again with a new character, the Avenger, introduced in 1939. The character, Richard Henry Benson, starts off as a globe-trotting adventurer and self-made millionaire whose family is murdered by the members of a kidnapping ring. The loss so profoundly affects Benson that the muscles in his face go into shock so that he looks like a dead man. His face becomes strangely malleable as a result, however, and he can reshape it in order to disguise himself as other men, which gives him an advantage when he decides to wage war on criminals.

The books were released with the Kenneth Robeson house name in an attempt to snag the Doc Savage audience, though the stories were written by Paul Ernst. The series was very well written, with more subtle character development and interesting plot twists, but it was not as popular as the publishers had hoped. New stories were released in fits and starts and then canceled in 1943.

One of the most compelling aspects of the story was the hero's broken heart and his quest to bring criminals to justice and to find some measure of closure. Benson gathered a crew of other people who had likewise been victims of crimes and together they fought the good fight under the name Justice, Inc.

G-8 and His Battle Aces: G-8 was a World War I flyer and adventurer who appeared in 110 novels published by Popular from 1933 to 1944 by Robert J. Hogan, which, for once, was the author's real name rather than a house name. G-8 and his intrepid crew of pilots faced all manner of enemies, many of them science fiction oriented and a few truly supernatural. These threats were the products of mad scientists working for the German kaiser. Though the novels are a lot of fun, there is a strong thread of anti-German racism that was typical in the years leading up to and during World War II.

The Phantom Detective: Because of the overwhelming success of pulp, publishers looked for other heroes around whom they could build a fan base. The second major player was the Phantom Detective, introduced by Thrilling Publications to the public in February 1933, one month before the debut of Doc Savage. The character went on to appear in 170 issues. Only the Shadow and Doc would star in more stories.

The first eleven stories were published with the house byline of G. Wayman Jones, though they were written by Jack D'arcy. The house name was later changed to Robert Wallace and written by a whole slew of writers, most notably Norman Daniels, Edwin V. Burkholder, Anatole F. Feldman, Charles Greenberg, George A. MacDonald, Laurence Donovan, and C. S. Montanye.

The character was called the Phantom[2] in the stories, and like his contemporaries he was a rich guy (Richard Curtis Van Loan) who donned a costume to fight crime. He was self-educated in forensic science, criminology, and detection, and the Phantom was an escape artist and master of disguise. Unlike the Shadow, the Phantom was liked and respected by police around the world and was often called in to solve cases that baffled regular detectives. He also had a red beacon erected on the roof of the Clarion Building, a clear precursor of the Bat signal.

The Phantom Detective was less threatening than the Shadow, less austere than Doc Savage, and better dressed than any of his contemporaries, generally adopting a Lone Ranger–style mask and a top hat.

The character's charm has not held up as well as the Shadow, Spider, or Doc Savage—very likely because he had very little edge. He had more in common with the high-society amateur detectives like Philo Vance and Nick Charles than he did with the over-the-top pulp heroes. Yet he was popular, and for a long time. He was a decent, civilized man who wasn't consumed by hatred or warped by the need for revenge. If his personality is echoed in today's pop culture it's probably a trace element in shows like CSI.

2. Not to be confused with Lee Falk's comic strip creation, also called *The Phantom*.

Operator #5: Was another of Popular Publications' heroes who appeared in forty-eight adventures between 1934 and 1939. The house name on the books was Curtis Steele, though the stories were written by Frederick C. Davis, Emile C. Tepperman, and Wayne Rogers.

The title character was Jimmy Christopher, a covert U.S. Intelligence agent whose codename was Operator #5. The stories were very fast paced and exciting, and quite violent. Unlike the typical Criminal Mastermind or Masked Villain stories, most of the tales in this series dealt with open or clandestine attacks on the United States by foreign powers—though in an early move to be politically correct those foreign powers were given new names.

Christopher's character was a bit of latter-day swashbuckler, and kept a flexible rapier concealed inside his belt and had a distinctive skull ring—presaging the trademark ring Lee Falk's comic strip Phantom later used to great effect.

Unlike the other pulps, many of the Operator #5 stories were written as chapters of a much larger story, particularly a thirteen-novel run written by Emile C. Tepperman in which the Purple Empire (a very thinly disguised Germany) invades and conquers the United States. It's up to Jimmy Christopher to lead the insurgency in what became known as the Purple Invasion stories. These books are a fascinating exploration of resistance against political and military evil, and with some adaptations would make a very good miniseries or even TV series. Certainly they've been an influence on a variety of later novels, comics, TV shows, and movies up to and including the alien invasion show *V*.

After the Purple Invasion was defeated, the authors began a new series with the Yellow Vulture as the main villain, an obvious stab at Japan. The series was canceled before the storyline could play out, though. Pity.

SWORDS AND SORCERERS

One of the landmark subgenres of the pulps were fantasy stories in which brawny heroes faced all sorts of supernatural threats ranging from armies of the dead to mighty wizards to hordes of apemen. These stories would later be dubbed "sword and sorcery" in 1961 by Fritz Lieber, who coined the term in reply to a letter published in the heroic fantasy fanzine *Amra*. Sword and sorcery differed from the much more common high fantasy in that the principal action centered around personal battles rather than the clash of kingdoms. These stories were usually very violent and initially written by—and for—a male audience. That changed over time with the introduction of female heroes and female writers who could pen a tale of bloody swords and iron thews as readily as their male counterparts.

The roots of the genre go all the way back to swashbuckling tales by Alexandre Dumas and Rafael Sabatini, and to the enchantment of the *Arabian Nights*; but with the advent of the pulps the stories took on elements of darker myth and magic.

Most sources credit Robert E. Howard (1906–1936) with creating the sword and sorcery genre as we know it today. He wrote a large number of thrilling adventures with heroes who were typically gruff, barbaric, antisocial, and violent. It's hard to call most of them "heroes" in the classic sense. Conan, for example, is a thief, murderer, mercenary, assassin, and ultimately a usurper of a kingdom. However he routinely encounters monsters, fiends, and other enemies who are much worse. And although Conan will slit a throat for a few gold coins, he isn't deliberately cruel. The monsters and madmen he faces, however, are; and so Conan became the lesser of two evils and, in a pinch, you'd rather be on his side when the chips were down. Being on the side aligned against Conan was a great way to wind up dead—and in pieces.

Howard also wrote of pirates, Vikings, Arabs, hunters, brawlers, and other manly men whose wayward paths led them into dark alleys, smoky backrooms, dungeons, haunted ruins, and more than a few battlefields. One of his early heroes was the dour puritan Solomon Kane who traveled the world in search of evil, which he would then confront and destroy. Kane was a humorless, inflexible man who dressed in black and was as deadly a swordsman as he was a gunman. In later stories he acquires a juju staff from an African shaman, and this "staff of Solomon" became both a weapon and talisman against evil.

The first of the Solomon Kane stories, "Red Shadows," was published in *Weird Tales* in 1928, and in it Kane goes up against a gang

The Hero in *The Princess Bride*

"My favorite movie character is Wesley, a.k.a. the Dread Pirate Roberts from *The Princess Bride*. The witty one-liners, the amazing swordsmanship, the romance, the dashing good looks—you can't go wrong! Plus, hey, he's a pirate. There's the whole morally ambiguous thing again. He'll kick your ass, get the girl and look damn sexy in skin-tight leather pants all at the same time."
—Ruby Young, a.k.a. Ruby Rocket, is an actress and a model.

of murderers. The story was a huge hit with readers, and soon Howard was cranking out more stories with this grim but righteous hero. In later stories he encounters ghosts ("Skulls in the Stars"), sorcerers ("Rattle of Bones"), vampires ("The Moon of Skulls" and "Hills of the Dead"), slave traders ("The Footfalls Within"), and pirates ("Blades of the Brotherhood"). Howard left several unfinished Kane stories at the time of his tragic suicide at age thirty.

Howard's greatest and most enduring creation is the barbarian antihero Conan of Cimmeria. Introduced in *Weird Tales* in 1932, Howard churned out a number of Conan short stories and novels, featuring the hero at different points of his life—as a raw and savage youth, as a young adventurer, as a middle-aged mercenary, and as a king. The first published story, "The Phoenix on the Sword," was actually a rewrite of a rejected story about another of his characters, King Kull.

Conan was an instant hit with fans who loved the character and could not get enough of his ruthlessness, raw power, and conditional heroism. Howard's lush (though purple) prose and unflinching love of bloody battles left the fans breathless, and by the time of his death in 1936, he'd completed twenty-one Conan stories, seventeen of which saw print in his lifetime. Years later, Sprague De Camp and a number of other authors revised and completed the unfinished Conan stories, rewrote stories with other characters so that they became Conan adventures, and then began a process of adding many new and original stories to what has become a massive library of stories. This includes movies, comics, a TV show, and games.

Conan was and is an enigmatic figure. In many ways he's more villain than hero, and he's spilled enough blood—guilty and innocent—to float a battleship. His armies have sacked towns, with all the murder, rape, and looting that goes with that sort of thing; yet he is the clear hero of the tale. Instead of whitewashing the protagonist, Howard and his followers simply made the antagonists that much darker.

"One of the reasons Conan worked so well then and still works now," says rare book dealer Mercer Arkady, "is that we all know people like him. Sure, not as savage or brawny, but folks who have conditional morality that they can adjust to fit whatever situation they're in. Replace the magic with politics and you could be reading about an undercover cop who has crossed the line, or a mercenary working in the Middle East, or anyone else whose life and experiences have taken them away from ordinary morality. There are a lot more 'Conans' out there than there are Three Musketeers, more's the pity."

Does that make the character evil?

"Evil doesn't seem to apply directly to him," insists Arkady. "If anything, he probably considers himself the good guy trying to survive in a corrupt world. At worst, he would be regarded as a person whose experience makes him believe that the rules of right and wrong don't apply to anyone and therefore not to him. Kind of an artificial and constantly enforced sociopathy."

FRESH PULP

In recent years pulps have begun to make a return. Some have speculated that the economy, the troubled state of the world, and the divisive internal squabbles that have turned American politics into a bad SNL skit have all conspired to make us yearn for the pure escapism of the pulps.

"We're in a moral miasma," posits social anthropologist Norman D. Howell. "Granted things aren't as bad as they were in the middle of the [Great] Depression, but they aren't a whole lot better. When people are losing their jobs, worried about health care, losing family members to war . . . they need something to distract them. But the spin on that is that we're much more cynical in the twenty-first century than we were in the early twentieth. We don't expect heroes to ride in on white horses. We've been betrayed by too many role models and discovered feet of clay on too many cultural icons. The result? We pick up escapism built around characters who are morally ambiguous. Sadly, we can all identify with that . . . but happily most of us want to believe that even if we have to make a few small bad choices it will ultimately lead to something good."

Charles Ardai has been leading the pack with a line of neo-pulps that he publishes under the imprint of Hard Case Crime. The novels he publishes rarely have a spotless hero, and in some entries we have to decide which crook to root for.

Ardai says, "Pulp crime fiction in particular deals with the themes of morality and corruption and justice: How can we live our lives well when there are dark forces marshaled against us and no assurance that goodness will triumph? Also, when is it justified, if ever, to do something awful in pursuit of good ends? If you have to choose between betraying your lover and betraying your partner, which way do you go? If you know you're doomed, do you keep struggling anyway, and if so, why? These are the central themes you see over and over again in pulp crime fiction and they're as involving and disturbing today as they were eighty years ago."

As Ardai sees it, the spotless hero was more the exception than the rule, then and now. "It's funny," says Ardai, "but in the pulp magazines you did occasionally have the pure, square-jawed heroes, combating evil with nary a gray area troubling their psychic makeup. But the conflicted or troubled characters are generally the more interesting ones. You want your heroes to have a bit of dirt in their background, a bit of darkness to add texture and complexity. In the retro-pulp movie, *Raiders of the Lost Ark*, Indy is a more irresistible character for being a bit of a rogue, a sometime grave robber who also rogered his mentor's underage daughter. This makes him less two-dimensional, more human, and also more dangerous; we feel less certain at any given point just what he might do, and that unpredictability is bracing. Same with Rick in *Casablanca*, and doubly so for the heroes and femmes fatale in every film noir and noir novel. We enjoy being unsure about just what the characters' motivations and agendas might be. It's more fun to see a man teetering on the brink and deciding to do the right thing in the end than to see someone who's certain all along of what the right thing to do is and that he will, of course, do it. If virtue is a foregone conclusion, it becomes boring."

The Hard Case pulps have drawn a lot of today's top writers, and bylines include Stephen King, Lawrence Block, Ken Bruen, Christa Faust, and many others.

"When you think of the best American pulp fiction publishers of the past 60 years, you think of Gold Medal, Black Lizard, and Hard Case Crime," says modern pulp and crime novelist Jason Starr. "I wanted to write for Hard Case as soon as I heard about the imprint. My good friend Ken Bruen wanted to write for Hard Case, too, so we came up with the insane idea of co-writing a novel for Hard Case Crime, and Charles Ardai went for it, and the result was *Bust*, which was one of the mostly highly reviewed and successful books for each of us."

"The genre appeals to me most for its tradition of taking the 'now' off the street and throwing it on the page," says Russell Atwood, author of *Losers Live Longer* (Hard Crime Case 2009). "Wrestling with the problems of today, not because you have an answer, but because wrestling with them is part of the answer. Pulp fiction takes notice of the now. In a time when many writers

---

Pulp Heroes and Villains

"Pulps were an escape and entertainment in the pre-1950s and while some sought out tales of true adventure, the average pulp fan was looking for the big 'wow,' the transportation to another reality where the hero had the chance to save the day even if it was by extraordinary means. Some pulp heroes had standards and never crossed their morals lines in order to get the job done. Other heroes could be nearly as bad as the villains in the methods they used, but if it was all in the name of good and protecting the innocent, well then I guess we didn't really care how badly the bad guys got treated, right?"—Daryl Danforth is a pulp magazine collector.

---

are daunted by the complexities of the modern world and so turn to writing historical fiction, pulp fiction writers embrace the terrors of the future. Maybe because being lost and out of sync with your surroundings is such a major theme in the world of noir. The passionless mechanics of the future are just a natural progression of man's corruption from the point of view of the pulp fiction 'hero,' so what else is new?"

11 SPANDEX TO THE RESCUE

Stan Lee

When asked why comics legend Stan Lee pioneered characters who were flawed and complex, he told us: "I simply wanted them to be the sort of characters I personally would be interested in reading about. I've no interest in two-dimensional, cardboard figures. Everybody without exception has some flaws. That's what makes people interesting." (Stan Lee photo by POW Entertainment.)

A Hero Will Rise . . .

So what do Superman, the X-Men, and Buffy the Vampire Slayer all have in common?

A lot, actually.

They're all superheroes; they all appeared on the screen, on TV, and in comics. And they've all faced Dracula.

Superheroes are our advocates for facing any threat that comes our way, from vampire overlords to alien invaders to corrupt governments. They fight the fights we can't fight; they defeat the threats we want to tackle but can't.

Superheroes were created from our need to have something bigger and stronger than us come and haul our collective butts out of the fire. At the same time we wanted these heroes to be more or less human so that we could relate to them while at the same time they served as our proxies. Unless we're corrupt, then down on some private levels we all want to believe that we have the qualities to be heroic. All we need is that one x-factor. Say . . . a bite from a radioactive spider, or a super soldier formula. Or discovering that we're really from another world and, by golly, we're faster than a locomotive and able to leap tall buildings in a single bound.

Superheroes come in all shapes and sizes, all levels of power, all degrees of intensity. Some are superstrong, others can fly, some project power beams from their eyes, and some are just tough hombres in masks and tights. The label "hero" is often misleading. Batman, Green Arrow, Ronin, and the Punisher have no enhanced physical abilities. Daredevil is blind and relies on acrobatics and a radioactive enhancement of his remaining senses. Thor is a god. Superman is an alien. Some are superpowered only because of technology, like Iron Man and the Green Lantern.

Generally the thing that identifies them is less the "super" and more of the "hero." Most of them have a strong moral code and a marked determination to stop crime or deter evil. However, this moral code also comes in different flavors. Batman, for example, refuses to kill, whereas the Punisher has racked up a body count rivaling that of smallpox. While Captain America and Superman have almost inflexible moral and patriotic mind-sets, most characters are focused less on the Constitution and the letter of the law than they are on right and wrong, justice and injustice. Most heroes fight for something—revenge, justice, their friends, their species, human rights (or whatever applies to them); or against something—intolerance, evil, crime, genocide. It's fair to say that the defining characteristic of superhero comics is the struggle against evil.

Most heroes aren't motivated by greed or glory—although this became less true as comic book storytelling matured and became more subtle and realistic. Luke Cage, for example, was originally a "hero for hire," willing to sell his prodigious skills to anyone who could pay his fee. Spider-man, on the other hand, eked out a living selling photos of himself in action (relying on his secret identity of Peter Parker to actually hawk the pics). Later he was "hired" by the Avengers and started making a regular paycheck. Odd thing is . . . Parker could have made millions by selling the patent to the web fluid and web-shooters he created; or from the spider-tracer devices he sometimes used to track criminals. Any construction company in the world would pay through the nose for web fluid: it's strong enough to lift heavy loads and then dissolves completely afterward. Hell, the military would have paid him billions. Iron Man and Reed Richards from the Fantastic Four, at least, did cash in on patents based on their inventions.

Personal motivation is the key to what drives most heroes to fight even when there is no paycheck. Spider-Man feels an over-whelming sense of responsibility as a result of a tragedy arising from an action he did not take. Batman is on a lifelong vengeance trip. Wonder Woman and Thor are destined to be heroes.

Most superheroes try to keep their adventuring persona separate from their out-of-costume self. For some it's a way to keep from being arrested, since vigilantism is illegal. For others it's a way of keeping their family and friends safe from the bad guys who might target them for revenge. And for some having a real life is an important factor in keeping them from becoming lost in their superhero role. The Fantastic Four are rare exceptions in that they've never used secret identities.

Superheroes tend to wear dynamic costumes. We can stretch a point and say that the spandex allows for a great freedom of move-ment. On the other hand, you'd think more of these heroes would have opted for something more physically protective. It's also more fun to see male and female heroes in their tights, their bodies sculpted to physical perfection. Very godlike, very much like the statues of the Greek and Roman deities, because to a very real degree the superheroes have become the gods of modern myth.

Some costumes are functional—again, Iron Man comes to mind. Some have been given recent upgrades to be more protective, such as Captain America's chainmail shirt and Black Panther's vibranium-weave catsuit. Others carry weapons and equipment. Batman is famous for his utility belt, from which he can apparently produce just the right chemical or device no matter how unlikely the circumstance. The Punisher carries guns; the Green Arrow carries a bow and quiver. Daredevil has a balanced billy club, and Thor has his big hammer.

STRANGE VISITOR FROM ANOTHER PLANET

Superman was an outgrowth of earlier pulp heroes like Doc Savage (see chapter 9, "Pulp Heroes"). He was smarter than us by an order of magnitude; he was buffer than us ('cause most of us don't have the waistline or pecs to pull off brightly colored spandex undies as daywear); and they were braver than us because they couldn't be hurt. At first this sounded great, especially to folks who had survived or grown up during the Depression and who wanted to feel invulnerable to whatever else came down the pike; and for those with a global sense who saw the way things were going in Europe and wanted to feel safe if Uncle Adolf ever took a swing at the U.S. of A. That's why Superman, who debuted in 1938, was such a hit. You couldn't hurt the guy. Bullets and bombs were nothing to him, and he could change the course of mighty rivers, bend steel, and all that.

Who wouldn't want to be him?

If Superman squared off against a villain, that villain was going down, plain and simple. He was also strong enough to lift the entire superhero genre. He was a new kind of hero, and he's become a cultural icon. Even people who never picked up a Superman comic or watched the TV shows or movies know who he is. People living in the remotest parts of the world, in caves, or under rocks know who Supes is. How can you not?

The character was created in 1932 by American writer Jerry Siegel and Canadian-born artist Joe Shuster and later sold to Detective Comics in 1938. His debut was in *Action Comics #1* on June 30, 1938, and he's been with us ever since, often in multiple comics at the same time, in movie serials, cartoons, and everywhere else from toothbrushes to Underoos.

In the comics, Superman squared off against villains. Initially they were just crooks, but it soon became apparent that for the comic to have balance the hero has to have enemies who are at least as tough as him, or even tougher. Hence the birth of the first supervillain, the Ultra-Humanite who opposed Superman in *Action Comics #13* in 1939. In a fascinating twist, the Ultra-Humanite was intended to be the polar opposite of Superman. Instead of being a decent and moral human (or at least humanoid) hero with great physical powers, the Ultra-Humanite was a criminal genius whose vast intellect was trapped inside a crippled body. When introduced, the Ultra-Humanite was more or less human; but years later his consciousness was transferred into the body of an albino ape. This amped up the villain's threat level, making him a key opponent of several of DC Comics' heroes.

The need to invent a supervillain speaks to the basic flaw of the Superman ideal. If the hero is too strong, then there is no tension left in the story. This is a storytelling concept that informs everything from pulp fiction to biblical prophecy. After all, if the Antichrist was some no-power schmuck, then the whole book of Revelation would lack drama. And, yes, drama matters, even in religion. It's a "struggle" between good and evil, not a one-sided bitch slap.

Superman was portrayed as invincible, which is cool for five

My Secret Identity 1

Superman's secret identity, Clark Kent, was created by combining the first names of two popular he-man movie stars: Clark Gable (*It Happened One Night, Mutiny on the Bounty, Gone with the Wind*) and Kent Taylor (*Boston Blackie, I'm No Angel, Death Takes a Holiday, The Rough Riders*).

minutes but gets old fast, a factor that came to light when writing scripts for the 1943 Superman radio program. In order to create more story tension (and to give the bad guys some kind of chance) the writers created a kind of Achilles' heel for the Man of Steel in the form of Kryptonite, a mineral from his home planet of Krypton. When exposed to the mineral's radiation, Superman loses his power and becomes weak and vulnerable.

The storytelling value of this was foreseen by Superman's co-creator Jerry Siegel in "The K-Metal from Krypton"; but the story was never published. In that story the mineral not only took Superman's powers away, it gave superhuman powers to ordinary humans. This concept was picked up by the writers of the *Smallville* TV show and became a recurring plot device. Kryptonite entered the comic book continuity in 1949 and was soon a regular feature used to level the playing field for Superman and his enemies. That created tension, and for a while it added a degree of reality to the story because we know that our own heroes are never perfect and constantly invulnerable.

"You can draw some parallels between Superman and Jesus," insists biblical scholar Dr. Jonas Weiland. "Prior to the New Testament God was too big, too abstract a concept for most people to grasp, and in the face of harsh Roman rule and corruption within the Judean government, the people were drifting from adherence to religion. Then Jesus comes along. He's God, but he's in human form. He eats, he drinks wine with his buddies, he has a temper. In short, he's human. Sure, he's also God, but he's an aspect of God we can relate to. Superman, prior to Kryptonite, was fun but he wasn't relatable. Kryptonite gave him weakness, and that made us like him. I doubt that the comic would have survived through the 1950s if they hadn't introduced Kryptonite to the story."

Peter Goldenberg, who has dressed as Superman at genre cons such as Dragon*Con in Atlanta for the last five years agrees. "Because Superman is so iconic a lot of people come up and talk to me about the character. Kryptonite is a common joke among us, and some folks even present me with anything green just to get me to react as if I'm suddenly weak and helpless. It's fun, and I can understand why they do it even though it's the same joke over and over again. . . . They can relate to someone who has flaws and weaknesses. . . . It's why I like Superman so much, and it's why I can relate to him."

Despite the vulnerability, or perhaps because of it, Superman has become a representation of the moral compass in practice. For decades you knew exactly where you stood with him. He was the "big blue Boy Scout" (a nickname hung on him by his fellow superheroes). He never made the wrong moral choice. He was never tempted to the dark side. He was Good with a capital *G*.

THE CAPED CRUSADER

When DC created Batman in 1939 (in *Detective Comics* #27), he was a bit darker and more complex than Superman, though admittedly not a hundredth as dark and complex as he would become. But we'll get to that in a bit. In the beginning, Batman was a pulp-style hero like the Shadow or the Spider: a human with no extra physical abilities who hid behind a mask and costume and fought crime using science, intellect, fisticuffs, and cool gadgets. Batman was us. Batman was street level. Granted, he was a millionaire playboy with a mansion and a cool car, but in an ideal world that was something we, too, could become. We could never become an alien from Krypton. In the landmark *Detective Comics* #33, we find out that Batman is a ruined personality, someone whose childhood was ripped away when he saw his parents gunned down. Suddenly Batman has become darker. He's damaged goods. He broods; he's obsessed. We like that. Oh hell yes we do, because we have been hurt, we have baggage, and we all have some past memories of hurt that we'd like to get payback for.

Batman, perhaps, more than Superman, paved the way for the more interesting superheroes of the next several decades. His humanity and damaged psyche were intriguing, and they gave the writers somewhere to go with him. Unfortunately the writers who came to the book weren't always the cutting edge of insightful storytelling and the character was often played for laughs. Campy fun was great for the 1960s TV show, but it wears thin very fast in comics. Humor is okay, even self-effacing and self-aware humor, but camp is hard to sustain.

However in the late sixties, writer Dennis O'Neil took Batman into darker territory in a deliberate effort to distance him from the fun but silly TV show. With the help of brilliant artist Neal Adams, O'Neil fought to make Batman once more a serious detective and a fearsome avenger of wrongs. In the late seventies, writer Steve Englehart and artist Marshall Rogers did a series of stories that were strong influences on Tim Burton's rather dark 1989 film *Batman*. However, the comic-buying audience was staying away in droves. It wasn't until Frank Miller's landmark 1986 limited series *Batman: The Dark Knight Returns* that the character finally found its true voice. The story takes place in the near future, where a fifty-year-old Batman comes out of retirement to save Gotham from its own self-destructive tendencies toward corruption. This Batman was grim, brutal, and even more badly damaged. He was the perfect Batman for the era, proving that straight storytelling works when camp fails. More important, this Batman dwelt in the moral gray area where a hero sometimes has to venture in order to defeat the blackest villains.

In 1986, the same year as *The Dark Knight Returns*, Dennis O'Neil took over as editor of the Batman titles and steered the character into continually darker waters. He green-lighted the *Batman: Year One* storyline that ran in *Batman #404–407* (February–May 1987), in which Frank Miller continued to deconstruct and then rebuild Batman. In 1988, Alan Moore (*Watchmen, V for Vendetta,* etc.) wrote one of the most powerful and disturbing comics ever: *Batman: The Killing Joke,* in which the Joker kidnaps and tortures Commissioner Gordon in an attempt to drive him insane. The Joker also shoots and permanently cripples Gordon's daughter, Barbara, who until then was the superhero Batgirl. That comic took no prisoners. It was as much a gamer-changer as Miller's *Dark Knight.* No one does that sort of thing. Except in the real world. Talk about breaking the fourth wall!

The Joker used to be something of a joke himself, a caricature rather than a villain of any real substance. Frank Miller and Alan Moore proved that old dogs can learn some vicious new tricks, and if it wasn't for both of them, then Heath Ledger would never have had the chance to close out his all too short but brilliant career with an unforgettable turn as the most disturbing villain in recent screen history. The dark Batman finally got the dark villain he so

My Secret Identity 2

Paul Henri Corentin Féval is also credited with pioneering the hero with a secret identity in his 1842 novel, *Le Loup Blanc*, which featured a tough and resourceful albino hero who wears a costume like Zorro's to fight crime and corruption. This "White Wolf" was the granddaddy of everyone from the Lone Ranger to Batman to Spider-Man.

---

badly needed, and from their encounter we learned so much about how darkness blossoms inside the human soul, and of the strange and terrible shapes it can take as it grows.

The Batman movies, *Batman Begins* (2005) and *The Dark Knight* (2008) genuinely understood this, and the Batman in these films has no trace of camp. He's the dark, conflicted, and very dangerous hero that Bob Kane and Bill Finger almost certainly intended when they created the character back in the thirties.

A TIMELY ARRIVAL

DC may have started the superhero wave, but Marvel caught up fast and has become the six-hundred-pound gorilla in the comics field. They launched with Marvel Comics #1 in October 1939 under the publishing name Timely Publications. That comic introduced the first Human Torch (no relation to the character of the same name who was later a member of the Fantastic Four) and reprinted a story of Namor the Sub-Mariner, a character previously available only through the comic book packager, Funnies, Inc.

These characters were less powerful than Superman but also less human than Batman. Despite his name, the "Human" Torch, created by writer-artist Carl Burgos, was actually an android whose artificial body inexplicably burst into flame when exposed to oxygen. Though nonhuman, the Torch became a defender of humanity, facing down all manner of threats including the Nazis.

The Sub-Mariner, on the other hand, was half-human—the son of a human father and a princess of the sunken kingdom of Atlantis. Namor is superhumanly strong, headstrong, short tempered, and frequently antisocial, and in a lot of ways was the most interesting of the first wave of heroes, largely because he wasn't always heroic. Even now, seventy years after his introduction, Namor is as often a villain as a hero. He's a paradoxical character who doesn't fit comfortably into any world. Though he came to rule Atlantis, he's a white-skinned half-breed in a land of blue-skinned purebreds. When on the surface he's viewed as an alien. Definitely not one of "us." He has wings on his feet, tremendous physical strength, and political views that don't support ours. He's the outsider who wants to be included, but because he can't he tends to throw temper tantrums. Some of those tantrums took the form of waging open war on the Nazis and on America, depending on who pissed him off the most at any given time. He makes questionable choices for allies and has sided with Magneto against the X-Men and the Fantastic Four, with Doctor Doom against just about everybody, and with Norman Osborne (a.k.a. the Green Goblin), during Marvel's Dark Reign cross-continuity storyline of 2008 and beyond.

On the other hand he can be quite heroic, often fighting against ecological threats and supervillains of all kinds. He even joined the X-Men in 2009.

His kind of character—complex, changeable, conflicted—ultimately became the hallmark of Marvel's approach.

In 1941, Timely Comics introduced Captain America, a character who had the street-level physical abilities of Batman and the superhuman moral compass of Superman. The character, created by writer Joe Simon and artist Jack Kirby, was the product of a secret Super Soldier program designed to take ninety-pound 4Fs like skinny Steve Rogers and transform them into combat-ready soldiers who were at the peak of human strength and speed. Cap joined the fight against the Nazis as soon as he could pull on his red, white, and blue spandex, and for years he was the symbol of the larger than life (and yet not too large) American hero.

Because Captain America was more or less a human being, it gave the storytellers a chance to relate to the readers. Cap wasn't an alien, he wasn't a fiery android or a half-breed from Atlantis, and he wasn't a millionaire playboy. He was a tough guy in brightly colored underwear who needed a shield to deflect bullets. People could grasp that concept. Like most heroes of the era, Cap was saddled with a teenage sidekick, Bucky Barnes. Bucky was supposed to draw in a preteen and teenage readership, but mostly he was a pain in the ass who was as useless as Toro (the Torch's sidekick) and Robin (who apparently lived up to his nickname of the "boy hostage" way too often). The writers of Captain America did something innovative, however, when they had Bucky get wounded in action. That hadn't happened before to a hero's sidekick. It took Bucky out of the game and allowed Captain America to get a female sidekick, Betsy Ross, who adopted the identity of Golden Girl.

FAMILY VALUES

The popularity of comics waned in the fifties, but in the early 1960s Timely became Atlas Comics and then evolved into Marvel Comics in 1961 with Stan Lee at the helm. It was Lee and a team of talented artists who created the Marvel Universe as we know it. That universe includes Spider-Man, the X-Men, Daredevil, Thor, the Punisher, Black Panther, Captain America, the Avengers, the Hulk, Iron Man, and many others. For Marvel, though, it all started with the Fantastic Four.

There had been plenty of other team books in comicdom, but the Fantastic Four was different. Their team predated the acquisition of superpowers. Sue and Johnny Storm were siblings. Sue and Reed Richards were dating. Reed and Ben Grimm were college buddies. The book was built around a core of family and friends, and that real-world dynamic made the characters human from the start. No Kryptonite required. They bickered, they hung out, and they had real lives.

When the four of them were exposed to cosmic radiation during an experimental rocket flight, they were forever changed. Reed Richards gained the ability to stretch his entire body like rubber; Sue became invisible and later learned to create force fields; Johnny became a new Human Torch; and Ben morphed into a lumpy mountain of orange rock, losing his apparent humanity but gaining enormous physical strength. Those changes became parallels to the changes each of us undergoes as we grow up and grow older. And although the Fantastic Four adopted combat names: Mr. Fantastic, the Invisible Girl (later Invisible Woman), the Human Torch, and the Thing, these were not secret identities. Everyone knew who they were and where they lived. They were public heroes—a family that fought together to keep the world safe from all manner of scientific threats, ranging from conquerors from the Earth's core to world-devouring aliens to teams of supervillains.

Unlike most other comics at the time, the Fantastic Four went through continual personal drama. Sue and Reed married; they got pregnant and had a child. Sue even miscarried once. Ben was torn up by his new appearance as a monster, and his angst at being a permanent outsider to the human race was a poignant aspect to the story throughout its run—fueled by Reed's frequent attempts to cure him. The book also included an expanding circle of friends and recurring guest stars, and even new members of the lineup. During Sue's pregnancy, the Inhuman Crystal joined the team and became Johnny's first real love interest.

In *issue #4*, Johnny Storm discovered that a homeless man was really Namor, the Sub-Mariner who was suffering from amnesia. The following issue introduced the most famous of all Marvel's villains, Doctor Doom. Other characters introduced through the book include the Silver Surfer, Galactus, the Watcher, Wyatt Wingfoot, the Inhumans (Black Bolt, Medusa, Crystal, Karnak, Triton, Gorgon, Lockjaw, and Maximus the Mad), and many others. What sets many of these characters apart from comics mainstream is the

---

Who Created Whom?

There is a long-standing and heated debate about who created certain Marvel characters. Stan Lee is most often credited as the inventor of the Fantastic Four, Spider-Man, Doctor Strange, etc. Other sources claim that artists Jack Kirby and Steve Ditko invented and/or developed many of these characters and that Lee provided word balloons after the art was completed. There are valid points on all sides of the arguments, and after decades of wrangling no one seems able to give a definitive pronouncement. Either way, those men—writers and artists—created legendary characters and our culture is the better for it.

---

same thing that merits their inclusion in this book: they were damaged, conflicted characters for whom "right and wrong" were debatable and relative points.

THE ROCKY ROAD TO REDEMPTION

The Silver Surfer is a prime example. At heart he is a decent and compassionate man—Norrin Radd—who is given a choice: become the star-spanning scout of Galactus, a demigod who feasts on the vital energy of populated worlds, or have his home planet consumed. He agrees and is transformed into the cosmically powered Silver Surfer. After leading Galactus to many worlds, the Surfer comes to Earth and while preparing the way for the big cosmic chow-down, meets the Fantastic Four. The encounter leads to a process through which the Surfer reclaims his humanity (as far as we can stretch that term for an alien). He recants his ways and defies his patron, ultimately helping to save Earth from total annihilation. This is a classic redemption story, one in which a character descends from a certain moral point and hits rock bottom, has an epiphany, and then is empowered by a new (or renewed) sense of right and wrong.

This is a fascinating concept because the Surfer did actually do great harm, and he did it for years. At the very least he is guilty of conspiracy to murder billions of life forms, which begs the question: is there a point in which the soul becomes so heavy with guilt that no redemption is possible?

Redemption is a tricky theological concept. In a literal sense it means to "buy back" one's life or soul, usually through good acts that ultimately balance the scales. The shortcut of repentance and absolution didn't seem to be an option for the Surfer. Many of our world's religions offer some version of forgiveness of sins. Judaism posits collective salvation for the people of Israel; Christians are redeemed through a belief in Jesus; and for Islam, submission to Allah is the path to redemption. But the Surfer is an alien. Who would he have confessed his sins to (other than the faithful readers), and who would have granted absolution? Different planet, different religion.

Science fiction has long been comfortable with the metaphor of

Menton J. Matthews, *Ars Memoria*

"This is a page from a work in development: *Ars Memoria: Book One*. This is the ending to the encounter between Augustus and Lapis in the first book. It is where Augustus finally subsumes his fear and allows himself to come through a bit more, while Lapis agrees to the challenge he himself has set forth. Both believe they are doing the 'good' thing but only one is doing something one might call 'evil.' Lapis, the killer here, is only doing what is within his nature to do. It's an ending that draws on the story of 'The Scorpion and the Frog.'"
—Menton J. Matthews III is a freelance artist for IDW Publishing, Image Shadowline comics, and others.

other worlds equaling other countries, which (in most) presupposes a respect for their native beliefs or at very least an acknowledgment that our rules don't necessarily apply.

The Surfer did, however, lament his crimes and accept his guilt. So much so that some fans gave him the nickname of the Silver Sufferer. Atonement became the driving force behind the Surfer's action after he defied Galactus. However, lacking a personal Yom Kippur, he set about saving lives, saving worlds, and fighting evil and he's racked up one hell of a tally (if "hell" is the right word to use here).

Rabbi Carol Kasser offers one perspective: "Judaism believes that the soul is born pure and we can always return to that state of purity through atonement. That doesn't mean that we aren't held accountable for our actions, but that by atoning for them, no matter how grievous they were, we can achieve forgiveness. We also believe that each person has within them an evil inclination (yetzer ha ra) and a good inclination (yetzer ha tov) and we struggle to overcome our evil inclinations and foster our good one. That might account for our fascination with evil characters—we recognize some of their feelings and motivations in ourselves so we can empathize with them and maybe even admire them for doing what we ourselves have sometimes wanted to do."

According to interfaith minister Edie Weinstein-Moser, "Redemption is always possible, since my take is that evil is 'live' spelled backward and is a disconnect from life force energy. When people commit so-called evil acts it may be because they feel so estranged from their own Source (call it God, Spirit, Essence, Creator, Allah,

---

Redemption Song

"Redemption is a theme I return to again and again in my writing. I'm fascinated by the depths that the average human can sink to and the heights to which he can ascend. I love the idea that virtually every wrong can somehow be corrected if only by personal sacrifice."—Mike Watt is a writer and filmmaker; he has written for *Fangoria, Cinefantastique,* and *Femme Fatales,* and served as the editor of *Sirens of Cinema.*

---

or Yahweh) and that they live in a state of fear. Remember that Darth Vader still had the heart of Annakin Skywalker beating in his chest, and deep inside he maintained a kernel of love and compassion that needed awakening. And each person who commits destructive acts has core wounds that have been left to fester. I also sense that redemption is related to the twelve step concept of 'making amends' . . . it isn't enough to speak the words, asking for forgiveness. It is more about the actions that result in healing."

Another character on the redemption road was Iron Man, introduced in *Tales of Suspense* #39 (March 1963), and created by writer-editor Stan Lee, scripter Larry Lieber, and artists Don Heck and Jack Kirby. When introduced, Iron Man's alter ego, Tony Stark, was a billionaire weapons manufacturer who was more interested in making a buck than taking responsibility for his actions. When kidnappers seriously injure him, Stark makes a chest plate to keep his damaged heart going . . . and then builds a heavy metal suit around it. Dressed in this armor, Stark escapes and returns to his life, although he continues to refine his armor and uses it to fight against evil, both in solo adventures and as a founding member of the Avengers (along with the Hulk, Thor, Giant Man, and the Wasp).

Later Stark has a real change of heart when he decides that manufacturing weapons makes him part of the problem rather than an active part of a solution. He re-purposes Stark Industries and works to redeem himself, mostly in his own eyes; though he is fully cognizant of the blood on his hands. This story element served as the basis for the movie *Iron Man* in 2008.

Image Comics also explored redemption with Spawn, introduced in 1992 by Todd McFarlane. The character, Al Simmons, was a government agent murdered by his own men and sent to hell. He's resurrected as a powerful creature called Spawn who refuses to serve hell and instead risks his immortal soul to protect the citizens of New York.

A similar hero, Ghost Rider, was introduced in *Marvel Spotlight* #5 (August 1972), created by writer-editor Roy Thomas, writer Gary Friedrich, and artist Mike Ploog. This was a much darker take on the redemption hero in that the first Ghost Rider actually sold his soul to the Devil. Of course, the title character, stunt-cyclist Johnny Blaze, did so to save the life of his mentor, so the act was selfless, which nicely confused things. Ghost Rider manifests as a leather-jacketed biker with a flaming skull for a head and a motorcycle that runs on hellfire. Ghost Rider rebelled against hell and fought the armies of darkness to protect humanity.

Another conflicted soul, Danny Ketch, became the second Ghost Rider when he came into contact with the mystical motorcycle following a murderous attack on his sister by ninjas. The enchantment turned him into a "Spirit of Vengeance," imbuing him with vast supernatural powers. Later we learn that Johnny Blaze and Danny Ketch are brothers, and by 2009 they were teamed up, not against hell but against a traitorous angel, Zadkiel, who had conquered heaven and was waging war on humanity.

"There's often not much of a clear-cut delineation between good and evil in my comics," says Jason Aaron, one of the new breed of writers that have been bringing the complex twenty-first-century cultural sensibility to comics. "Or, if there is, I still try to flip things around somehow. In the current issues of Ghost Rider,[1] I have the heroes out trying to protect the Anti-Christ in order to oppose a renegade angel, who's the main villain of the piece. Those are the kind of things that are interesting to me, as opposed to the traditional guys-in-white-hats vs. guys-in-black-hats scenario. I especially love getting readers to sympathize or identify with a character who does terrible things, like in my Friday the 13th story when I tried to make Jason a sympathetic character, while still being a monster who goes around with a machete hacking up campers."

"Fans that relate to the darker characters," suggests Weinstein-Moser, "may feel it is an outlet for their shadow side that they would never allow out to 'play' in their daily lives. . . . Sometimes people who appear to be the darkest are often the most kind and altruistic people you would ever want to meet, while those who are the innocent little angels are often the biggest control freaks."

"Given that people have dark urges and dark thoughts," asks Rabbi David Schulman, a counselor for troubled teens in Chicago, "is it any wonder that they look for reflections of their own

---

1. Jason shared his views with us in late 2009.

complexity in popular culture? Perhaps those persons who demonstrate violence in the real world are people who cannot find adequate surrogates in fiction or film. Or, indeed, comic books."

Weinstein-Moser offers yet another view. "On the other hand, some people relish the 'evil role' because they feel it gives them power and no one will mess with them. . . . Also, some people identify with the dark energies."

Monsters as heroes became a workable theme in comics, and arguably the most interesting and successful exponent of this was Hellboy, the creation of writer-artist Mike Mignola. Hellboy is a demon who was raised by a kindly scientist and who fights for the U.S. government's Bureau of Paranormal Research and Defense (BPRD), tackling everything from Nazis to creatures out of folklore. Mignola says he loves mining folklore for his source material. "There's so much there. Every country, every culture has legends of monsters and demons. I'm working my way through world culture to craft stories for Hellboy and the BPRD."

World myth, especially those stories dealing with the contact between humans and demons, is seldom the basis for happy stories. Yet this conflict, with all of its pain and misery, is grist for the comic book writer. "From the very beginning," Mignola recalls, "when creating the Hellboy world, I considered all characters in folklore and myth to be toys for me to play with. And while I've changed some of those characters quite a bit to suit my purposes, I have always tried to preserve the traditional aspects of those characters—I do not want to explain that they are really aliens or mutants or anything like that. The trick is to create some kind of mythology for your world where all these things can function and exist. That's very tricky and, for me, it means not going into too much detail . . . there always has to be an element that is beyond human comprehension. . . . Of course to figure out how it all works I *did* have to do a lot of research—I read a lot of different creation myths, looking for parallels, and then made up my own creation myth (revealed in the story "The Island") borrowing bits and pieces from different cultures. My Ogdru Jehad were inspired by seven demons referred in ancient Chaldean magic text—but their origin was sort of a combination of the Egyptian Ogdoad (eight reptilian/amphibian gods who created the world and ruled

Mike Mignola, *Hellboy*

"What's interesting for me is the grey area between good and evil. What motivates the supposedly evil characters? I need to understand them—there has to be a good reason (at least from their perspective) to do the things they do. Even Hellboy's 'destiny' as destroyer of the world—isn't it possible that from a certain perspective this will be a good thing?"—Mike Mignola is the creator of Hellboy.

over it for a while), the Greek legend of Prometheus, and the story of the Watchers—angels sent down to Earth to watch over mankind, but who ended up taking human wives and were punished for it. A lot of different stuff went into that origin. . . ."

Hellboy has so far been featured in two motion pictures in 2004 and 2008, starring Ron Perlman and directed by Guillermo del Toro, and two straight-to-DVD animated films, *Hellboy: Sword of Storms* and *Hellboy: Blood and Iron*. The films touch on the running subplot that Hellboy is destined to one day embrace his demonic heritage and destroy the world—a destiny Hellboy refuses to accept. Yet all of the signs point in the direction of this fate being inevitable. Talk about inner conflict.

Writing about monsters in comics isn't much different from writing about super-powered aliens. At the heart of each story is the human element. When talking about the spin-off stories of the BPRD, Mignola observes, "I think what really works in that book (and most of it these days is thanks to co-author John Arcudi) is how human these extremely non-human characters are. I come up with strange characters and make horrible things happen to them and John treats them like human beings and shows me (and the readers) how they will be affected by the horrible things I do to them. It's a little like a game the two of us are playing."

Readers are willing to play along, happy to wander down whatever dark paths comic writers are willing to lead them.

Another character who walks the line between heaven and hell is John Constantine, star of the *Hellblazer* comic from DC. Created in 1988 by Alan Moore as a supporting character in the *Swamp Thing* comic book, Constantine is a streetwise magician who is more con man than outright hero. He lies, cheats, steals, and otherwise breaks all of the "good guys don't do that" set of rules, but his heart is more or less in the right place. He probably owes more to John D. MacDonald's Travis McGee or TV's Jim Rockford than to Batman or Superman. Sometimes you need a con man to swindle the bad guys out of what they stole. Constantine is a pain in the ass; he's irritable, occasionally offensive, and seldom comes out of a situation with more friends than he had going in, but always with more enemies. He's also fascinating and appealing because we like the idea of someone who isn't afraid to break the rules if that's the only way to take down the bad guys.

"Constantine is everything Batman isn't," observes Gayle Capullo, Ph.D., a lecturer on pop culture and formerly of Temple University. "Batman is sometimes shackled by his own moral restraint, and though we can applaud his integrity in the moment, we also pull back and realize that when he doesn't just kill the Joker we know that the Joker will eventually kill others during some future scheme. In my view, that blood is on Batman, and his restraint ultimately looks like self-indulgence: he likes to win individual battles but overall his regard for the well-being of humanity is questionable. John Constantine, on the other hand, is far less scrupulous and as a result many of the enemies he fights won't be bothering anyone else again."

Constantine is one of a growing number of morally conflicted characters. Readers are powerfully drawn to these damaged and disturbed antiheroes. Jason Aaron agrees: "My Western series, Scalped (Vertigo Comics, a DC imprint), is all about that moral gray area. I love characters that are complicated and morally ambiguous . . . characters who can be a hero one minute and a poor excuse for humanity the next. That to me is real. I like the idea of throwing readers into a big moral quagmire and letting them find their own way out. I think that challenge makes the story more interesting."

Characters like Ghost Rider, Hellboy, and Constantine are sometimes "bad" but they aren't evil, and that's an important distinction. "The difference between bad and evil seems to be a matter of degree . . . a spectrum of behaviors. Can we harbor bad thoughts but not follow through on them? Maybe that's the key. We can live out our darker urges in fantasy—our own, or those created for us by comics and movies and so on—rather than act on them ourselves."

One of the most compelling characters in this moral gray area is the Punisher, who conversely sees things in black and white, and there are legions of fans who wish they could do what he does, but because they can't they can live vicariously through him. Frank Castle is the most violent of comicdom's vigilantes, a former Special Forces soldier whose family was accidentally caught in a gangland gun battle while on a picnic in Central Park. Castle watched his family die horribly, and something inside of him snapped. At that moment, the man Frank Castle had died along with his wife and children, and a fierce killing machine—the Punisher—was born. Wearing austere black except for a white death's head on his chest, the Punisher began waging war against the mob. Any mob. His method is simple: he identifies criminals and then slaughters them. He doesn't engage in witty superhero banter. He has less of a sense of humor than a block of granite, and just about as much warmth. His wrath is almost biblical, and, in fact, a number of writers have borrowed from some of the more violent passages of the Old Testament to craft Punisher tales.

Writer Jason Aaron observes, "My obsession with violence and dark characters probably comes from being raised on the Bible, the most violent book ever written. One of the darkest stories I've ever written was a Punisher Christmas special I did last year (2008), but some of the most disturbing parts of it were stolen right from the Bible."

Is the character a white knight fighting on the side of the angels? Maybe, especially the Old Testament angels, who were big into wrath, vengeance, and punishment. Is the Punisher morally conflicted? Not as far as he's concerned. He's a force of vengeance, not a Byzantine monk struggling with his dark night of the soul. The immoral and vicious acts of the enemy purified the Punisher's sense of purpose, effectively removing all shades of gray.

Having written Punisher stories myself—*Punisher: Naked Kill* (2009) and *Punisher: Last Gun on Earth* (2010), I found it a fascinating challenge to write about him without deconstructing him. To open him up is to destroy him. Not that he would feel the surgery . . . it's just that beneath the hard exterior is more of the same. Remove all of the calluses on his soul and there's nothing left. He is cold punishment, pure and simple.

WITH GREAT POWER

One of the most significant characters created during the early 1960s was Spider-Man, and he matters for two disparate reasons. On one hand he's the most easily accessible superhero because of who he is under the mask: Peter Parker is a nerdy teenage science geek who worries about money, worries about girls, worries about his sickly Aunt May (who is his sole caregiver), worries about his boss (a cheap, loud-mouthed tyrant), and worries about doing the right thing. We can seriously relate to all that. Peter is just a guy. We either know him or have been him; we completely believe in him.

Then comes the second part, and this is probably the defining moment in the moral timestream of comics. After acquiring super-powers from the bite of a radioactive spider, Peter first tries to use those abilities to make some much-needed cash. After being short-changed by a crooked wrestling promoter, he then does nothing when a thief robs that promoter. He could have stopped him but didn't think that it was his responsibility. Later Spider-Man discovers to his horror that this same thief has murdered Peter's Uncle Ben. Had Spider-Man stopped the thief, his uncle would not have died. No question about it. The first issue of the comic closes with an observation that is widely regarded as the single most important statement in comics: "With great power comes great responsibility."

For young Peter, this aphorism became the bearing that allowed his moral compass to turn. However, instead of volunteering to become a policeman, soldier, firefighter, or rescue worker, he opted to become a masked vigilante. He became Spider-Man. The character quickly became one of Marvel's most beloved and bankable heroes, as popular as Superman, and as heavily marketed through toys, games, food products, and anything else you could slap a logo onto.

SUCCESS THROUGH CONFLICT

The success of Marvel's new batch of heroes is directly related to the inner conflict each character faced. That gave the books a soap opera feel, and the melodrama was usually much more interesting than the slugfests with supervillains.

According to Fred Van Lente, one of Marvel's hottest writers and the scripter for *Marvel Zombies 3, 4,* and *5,* X-Men noir, and lead writer on *Marvel Zombies Return,* "The cliché that kept being used in the 1960s, when the Marvel heroes really became a pop

Who Said It First?

The wonderfully apt statement, "With great power comes great responsibility" is the core message of Spider-Man and, indeed, of most superhero comics; but it didn't originate with the comics. Looking back, there is a biblical passage that hits the same mark: "For unto whomsoever much is given, of him shall be much required: and to whom men have committed much, of him they will ask the more." Gospel of Luke, chapter 12, verse 48. And in more secular circles, Franklin Delano Roosevelt made this comment during the Jefferson Day Dinner in 1945: "Today we have learned in the agony of war that great power involves great responsibility."[2]

culture phenomenon, particularly on college campuses, was that their heroes had 'feet of clay.' Unlike the Supermans and Batmans of the world, who enjoyed close relationships with the authorities and were generally beloved by the public, the Fantastic Four, Spider-Man, and the X-Men all, to very varying degrees throughout their careers, were despised and feared by a capricious public and often branded as vigilantes and/or criminals by the cops. So the Marvel heroes have to constantly ask themselves, Is it worth it, constantly putting my neck on the line for people who don't even like me? Generally speaking, they always come around to their basic heroic natures in the end, but it was quite groundbreaking for its time to have superheroes who were constantly denounced for their activities."

BRING ON THE BAD GUYS

It's hard to define a hero without some situation in which he can demonstrate heroism. Since comic books aren't built around tales of people risking their lives to simply do good works, the superhero required an enemy of equal mettle. Hence the supervillain was born.

2. From *Nothing to Fear*, ed. by Ben D. Zevin, p. 464 of the 1961 Popular Library paperback; the book was originally published in 1946 by the World Publishing Company.

Marvel Heroes

"I think the Marvel creators have always seen themselves as telling stories about the struggle between good and evil. It's just Marvel heroes, rather than the more traditional super hero, who's a paragon of righteousness, struggles with what is good and what is evil, just like the rest of us, and so they've tended to be seen as the more believable and more easy to relate to of the major super hero icons."—Fred Van Lente writes Spider-Man, Marvel Zombies and other comics.

Supervillains, like superheroes, don't always have to possess superpowers. Some are powerful, of course, while others are brilliant, well armed, and ruthless. In many ways they're almost interchangeable with heroes in that they frequently have secret identities, hideouts, sidekicks, cool costumes, weapons, bizarre origins, and motivations for doing what they do. What separates them from the heroes are their core needs. Many are criminals, ranging from cheap smash-and-grab thieves all the way up to brilliant criminal masterminds bent on stealing billions. Some are conquerors; others are dedicated to agendas such as racial cleansing, violent xenophobia, and mass murder. Some are ciphers for real-world villains—serial killers, terrorists, gangsters, and dictators. Some are psychotic killers who cross the line from bad to evil.

THE SUPERVILLAIN

The first real supervillains did not debut in comics but in novels of Paul Henri Corentin Féval. First came Jean Diable (a.k.a. "John Devil") in 1862 and then Colonel Bozzo-Corona in 1863. These villains were brilliant, manipulative, diabolical, ruthless, cultured, and well organized. They used henchmen, crafted master plans, and could not be defeated unless the hero was equally smart, savvy, powerful, and relentless. Without these criminal masterminds we would never have had Professor Moriarty, Lex Luthor, or Doctor Doom.

Over the years comics have explored the criminal mastermind

Evil Spandex

The first costumed supervillain was the Lightning from the 1938 film *The Fighting Devil Dogs*, a twelve-chapter serial from Republic Movies starring Lee Powell and Herman Brix. The heroes are a pair of U.S. Marines (not superheroes).

in a variety of ways, sometimes portraying them as the heads of criminal families that, although violent, hold to some standards of honor. Here are some classic villains from DC Comics.

Brainiac: The extraterrestrial android Brainiac is another of Superman's regular sparring partners, debuting in Action Comics #242 (1958). He has appeared in various forms and with a variety of conflicting backstories, but in each case he presents a deadly threat to Superman and the people he's sworn to protect—on Earth and elsewhere.

Darkseid: Every comic universe needs a Big Bad, and Darkseid more than fills the bill. He's one of the New Gods created by Jack Kirby but brought into the DC mainstream as a major player by Paul Levitz. Darkseid's goal is to subvert the universe by eliminating all free will via the Anti-Life Equation. As master plans go, that's pretty darn evil.

The Joker: The Joker is a madman's madman and Batman's ongoing nightmare enemy. A brilliant chemist, subtle planner, and a nihilist beyond compare. His ruthlessness is legendary. He shot and crippled Barbara Gordon (Batgirl) and murdered Jason Todd (the second Robin). *Wizard Magazine*, the comic industry periodical, ranked Joker as the #1 Greatest Villain of All Time.

Lex Luthor: Superman's perennial villain is a brilliant scientist who possesses no superpowers of his own. His intellect, however, is staggering, and his corruption knows no limits. Introduced in 1940, Luthor is always a terrific fallback villain for Superman writers because there's no end to the schemes he has cooking. His agenda has basically two bullet points: Take over the world and kill Superman. You have to admire that kind of focus.

Rā's al Ghūl: This Batman villain's name translates from Arabic as "The Demon's Head" and since his introduction in 1971 has risen to become a major player. Presented as erudite, brilliant, and even possessing nobility, Rā's al Ghūl is also a terrorist and assassin. But he's an idealistic terrorist and assassin, whose ultimate goal is to achieve environmental balance, even if he has to eliminate most of humanity to accomplish it. Liam Neeson portrayed the villain as a thoughtful (if deadly) intellectual in Christopher Nolan's 2005 film, *Batman Begins*.

Two-Face: Harvey Dent was once the district attorney of Gotham City and a hero in his own right—morally straight and honorable. Then he was badly injured and terribly deformed in an accident that also unhinged his mind. From that point on he was evil and vile. The tragedy of this character has been showcased in various Batman comics, but was most poignantly presented in Aaron Eckhart's brilliant portrayal of both sides of Dent in *The Dark Knight* (2008).

Creating Demon Characters

"I'm of the 'If it ain't broke, don't fix it' school. When I was researching *Daimon Hellstrom, the Son of Satan* (for Marvel Comics), I discovered in his origin way back in the 1970s that he was studying to become a priest before he dropped out of seminary. I love that kind of outrageous juxtaposition super hero comics specialize in. So when it came time for Daimon to join the cast of *Marvel Zombies 4: Midnight Sons*, I came up with the idea of putting him in a Jesuit cassock—except the pentagram on his chest burns right through it, as the cloth cannot disguise his demonic heritage. I have fun doing that, mining the essence of a character for choice nuggets."—Fred Van Lente has written *Marvel Zombies 3, 4 and 5*, and was head writer on *Marvel Zombies Return*.

Here are some Classic Villains from Marvel Comics.

Apocalypse: An ancient and almost immeasurably powerful villain who first appeared in *X-Factor #37*. Apocalypse focuses his vast intellect on changing the course of evolution to craft a master race that he has control over. He created a timeline in which Apocalypse has conquered much of the world, which temporarily replaced the main Marvel Universe.

Doctor Doom: First introduced in *Fantastic Four #5*, Victor Von Doom is one of the world's most brilliant scientists, the ruler of an Eastern European nation (Latveria), a sorcerer of great skill, and a certified wacko. He's fought virtually every Marvel character and allied himself with many of Marvel's top villains. And though he often loses (otherwise the Fantastic Four would be dead and gone decades ago), he always comes back stronger and more devious than ever.

Galactus: This world-devouring demigod is not exactly evil. He is so ancient and alien that he considers himself above concepts like "good" and "evil," and considering that he is something of a force of nature, he just might be correct. He has been thwarted by several Marvel characters, but seldom actually defeated.

Kingpin: Though not superhuman, the Kingpin is immensely powerful for a human and a superb martial artist, and as a result he's been able to give Spider-Man and Daredevil a run for their money. Wilson Fisk is a criminal mastermind almost unparalleled in Marvel. He has run several vast criminal empires and each time he's defeated he rises again, stronger and more dangerous.

Magneto: This mutant powerhouse was introduced in the X-Men but has since become a force throughout Marvel's complex universe. Once Marvel's writers got a real handle on his character, he transformed from a prating villain into a complicated hero of the harassed and disenfranchised mutant evolutionary subculture. A survivor of the Holocaust, Magneto fiercely and violently defends mutants from the hatred and bigotry of humans. His motives are not hard to question; his methods are.

Doctor Octopus: Another Spider-Man villain and also a world-class mad scientist. Dr. Otto Octavius designed a set of mechanical arms controlled via a brain-computer; however, a radiation leak caused the arms to become fused to his body. The same accident warped his mind and turned him evil.

Norman Osborne: Whether he's presented as the Green Goblin or as businessman/scientist Norman Osborne, he's one of the most devious and feared villains in Marvel. Originally a Spider-Man villain, Osborne was reintroduced during Marvel's cross-continuity Secret Invasion storyline and fired the shot that killed the evil Skrull queen and thus saved humanity. For a while (during the Dark Reign crossover event), Osborne was the world's greatest hero, though he secretly formed a cabal of villains and worked tirelessly toward a goal of covert global dominance.

The Red Skull: The Red Skull is a name shared by several different violent madmen in Marvel Comics. Originally presented as a Nazi and agent of Hitler in *Captain America Comics #1* in 1941, the Red Skull has been the sworn enemy of Captain America since World War II. One Red Skull is responsible for the murders of the parents of Peter Parker (Spider-Man); another engineered the "apparent" murder of Captain America. All versions of the Red Skull have been vicious and unrelentingly evil.

Sabretooth: Victor Creed is a mutant supervillain who first appeared in *Iron Fist #14* (1977) who possesses great strength, a mutant healing factor akin to Wolverine's, and superhuman senses. He works as an assassin and has become a regular enemy of Wolverine's. Where as Wolverine struggles to suppress his bestial nature, Sabretooth delights in it.

Ultron: A sentient robot created by Dr. Henry Pym who has evolved to become one of the most dangerous villains in all of Marvel. Ultron's primary goal is the destruction of the Avengers, and to accomplish this he's willing to destroy the rest of the world. He's also virtually indestructible and immensely powerful. Not a comforting combination.

Venom: The creature known as Venom is actually an alien symbiote who first appeared as a new costume for Spider-Man and later
overwhelmed and possessed the criminal Eddie Brock. Once the
symbiote bonds with a human host it becomes a creature of
enormous superpower and incredible viciousness.

MEANWHILE, BACK IN THE REAL WORLD

There have always been fans and will always be fans, bless their
geeky hearts. Fans become emotionally and psychologically
invested in the characters—both heroes and villains. They debate
them endlessly, in person, at conventions, and on the tens of
thousands of comic book message boards and forums. The perception of folks who are outside of the comics world is that fans
and fanboys are socially inept and deeply insecure people who use
comics as a way of hiding from the real world. That view is as
shortsighted as it is unfair. Fans come in all shapes and sizes, all
personality types, all economic levels, all degrees of social confidence.

At a recent Dragon*Con—a genre convention that draws upward
of forty thousand people—we interviewed a number of devoted
fans who showed up in costume. Sure, there were some shy social
outcasts who haven't moved out of their parents' basement yet
(though it's fair to say you could find plenty of those anywhere),
but there was a huge cross-section of people. This cross-section
included a doctor who was about to take over as chief of surgery
for a V.A. hospital, an interstate trucker, a soldier just back from
his second tour in Afghanistan, an underwear model and her tattoo
artist boyfriend, a grandmother, a third-grade teacher, a NASA
rocket propulsion chemist, a radio DJ, a high school track and field
coach, and a lawyer. In short, a cross-section of America.

While cruising the crowds at the con—where one in three people
wears a costume all weekend long—we noticed that there were
nearly as many villains and monsters represented as heroes and
monster-hunters. The fascination to emulate darkness was everywhere to be seen, with perhaps a slight emphasis toward vampires.

We asked people there, and at other events, why they choose
these characters, particularly the darker ones.

Eternal Flame

"I think people (especially Americans) are fascinated by creatures who are eternally fit. Vampires never have to have hip replacements or bifocals, get on Social Security or Medicare. In today's youth-oriented society, that's quite a coup."—Charlaine Harris is author of the Sookie Stackhouse novels upon which the HBO series *True Blood* is based.

"Who doesn't want to be a vampire?" was the question fired back by Regina Wilkes, a real estate broker from North Carolina who came dressed as Anne Rice's Queen of the Damned. "Vampires are everything we're not: immune to disease, eternally young, unnaturally beautiful."

What about the cost of being a vampire? Preying on the innocent, killing, and drinking blood. "Sure, from a moral human standpoint we'd all like to say that we'd never do that sort of thing," says Linda Poliarski, an insurance claim processer from Atlanta who came dressed as Drusilla from *Buffy the Vampire Slayer*. "But believe me, when you hit thirty, or forty, and you start seeing those crow's feet at the corners of your eyes and the first varicose veins in your inner thigh . . . don't even try to tell me that you wouldn't kill to be young and healthy forever."

Even if that meant killing?

"Sure," she said. "The survival instinct is a lot older than human laws or codes of morality."

Joe Flint, a BMW dealer from Alberta, Canada, agrees wholeheartedly. "Put ten people in a lifeboat for a week or so with no food. They'd regress to savagery right quick and the weakest would be lunch. Count on it." He came to the con dressed as a Predator (from the popular series of science fiction flicks). "I know I would. If it was me or someone else, then sorry, but it sucks to be them. That's how human beings are built."

Emulation with the baser desires and urges of fantasy characters is not necessarily the driving force for most fans. Apart from those who do it just for the pure fun of it, there is often a conscious or unconscious need to experience a life different from the one we lead, as Vincent Ferrante, creator/writer of the Monarch Comics character, Witch Hunter, points out. "These archetypes mirror aspects of ourselves that either frighten us or we are uncomfortable dealing with. By giving them an identity separate from us, we can deal with them better in a more indirect way, being able to face them without having to look in the mirror. Plus they're fun."

HORROR IN THE FUNNYBOOKS

The struggle against evil in comics isn't confined to the spandex crowd. Horror comics have been around at least as long and have often delved more openly and at times more deeply into the nature of evil and how it is fought. Often in the horror comics that struggle isn't won by the good guys. Quite often, in fact. Writers of horror comics frequently explore the triumph of evil, or the failure of good—either separately or as these themes collide in a single tale.

And, like superhero comics, the illustrated horror story has evolved over time as storytellers probed deeper into the psyche or into the darker aspects of the human experience. Writing styles matured, too, and some of the most sophisticated writing in comics can be found in modern horror books.

EC COMICS

Entertaining Comics, more commonly known as EC Comics, is the cornerstone of the horror comic genre even though they have long since ceased publishing these books. EC was an American publisher of comic books specializing in horror, crime, satire, military, and science from the 1940s through the mid-1950s, and their lineup included seminal books like *Tales from the Crypt*, *Shock Suspense Stories*, *Crime Suspense Stories*, *Weird Science*, *Weird Fantasy*, *Weird Science Fantasy*, *The Haunt of Fear*, and *The Vault of Horror*.

The EC stories were known for terrific if lurid artwork and twist endings of the kind later identified with the TV show *The Twilight Zone*. At its peak, EC was churning out ten titles a month, each with multiple stories.

EC pulled no punches with gore and violence and were truly shocking to read, until censorship forced the company to soften its approach. The issue was made public in 1948 with the publication of articles Judith Crist's "Horror in the Nursery" (*Collier's*, March 27, 1948) and Dr. Fredric Wertham's "Are Comics Horrible?" (*Newsweek*, May 3, 1954). These articles condemned horror comics as being dangerous to the minds and development of children. The articles supported the findings of a Senate sub-committee in which themes in comics were linked (however tenuously) to juvenile delinquency.

EC's response was to drop the horror books and begin publishing *Mad Magazine*, which thereafter mocked the system and conventions that created it.

Warren Publishing picked up the horror comic baton in the 1960s and ran with it for twenty years with *Eerie, Creepy*, and *Vampirella*. These stories often blended elements of horror, science fiction, noir mystery and fantasy, and included some of the era's top writers and artists.

Marvel has published a fair number of horror books in their standard and MAX lines, *Tomb of Dracula, Werewolf by Night, Blade, Man Thing, Brother Voodoo*, as well as a number of horror and SF anthology books like *Tower of Shadows, Creatures on the Loose*, and others. Among Marvel's most popular horror books are those featuring the Marvel Zombies—standard superheroes like Wolverine and Spider-Man who have become flesh-eating ghouls.

DC offered up *Secrets of Haunted House, Secrets of Sinister House, House of Mystery, House of Secrets, Ghosts*, and *Phantom Stranger*, among others. More recently, DC's Vertigo line offered more adult fare with books like the award-winning fantasy-themed *The Sandman* by Neil Gaiman, and Warren Ellis's insanely entertaining *Preacher*.

Preacher is one of the most influential comics of the twenty-first century and certainly one of the most respected. The titular character, Jesse Custer, is a down-on-his-luck minister in a nowhere town in Texas. A demon takes possession of Custer and while possessed he slaughters his entire congregation. Later, when freed of the demonic force, Custer is emotionally destroyed by guilt and filled with anger toward God for allowing the tragedy to happen. Also, a child is born who is the offspring of an unholy union between a demon and an angel. God, disgusted with everything, abandons heaven when the child is born, and Custer, furious with the state of affairs, goes on a cross-country trek to find God. Because of his connection to the demon, Custer possesses extraordinary powers that allow him to command absolute obedience from anyone who hears his words. Along the way he's joined by Cassiday, a hard-drinking Irish vampire, and Tulip O'Hare, Jesse's old girlfriend.

Jesse and his friends encounter all forms of resistance, both natural and supernatural, and are thrust into a series of encounters including a secret holy organization called the Grail, the KKK, various murderers and assassins, and the Saint of Killers, a killer whose inner rage and hatred is so intense that when he's sent to the underworld the force of it causes hell to literally freeze over. This enrages the Devil, who Saint of Killers ultimately murders. The comic was never for the faint of heart but also never hid behind cheap shots or exploitive elements that had nothing to do with the plot. The story always moved forward, and always into very dark, very complex moral and spiritual territory. Highly recommended for anyone who doesn't mind getting their hands bloody while turning the pages.

Dark Horse has become a big player in horror comics, both with original characters like Hellboy and licensed monsters like Angel—an extension of the Joss Whedon TV show; moreover, books that have a groovy horror/SF crossover appeal like Aliens and Predators.

And IDW made a big splash with popular comics such as Steve Niles's *30 Days of Night*, which was later adapted into film and also spawned a number of sequels. The comic company also owns Dark Horse Entertainment, a hugely successful movie and television production company responsible for the Hellboy films, *Sin City*, *The Mask*, *Mystery Men*, and *30 Days of Night*.

The Dark Horse films, like the comics they're based on, often deal with the fight against evil and often by heroes who are themselves morally conflicted or who are forced to make bad choices in order to defeat evil.

THE COMIC CODE AUTHORITY

As a result of the 1950s Senate hearings and protests from vocal but deeply misinformed critics, comic book publishers were bullied into censoring their own content. The Comics Magazine Association of America (CMAA) was established and instituted the Comics Code Authority (CCA). In a stunning move to ignore the First Amendment, the Comics Code seal of approval would only be given to a new wave of sanitized comics. Here's what the code specified:

▸ Crimes shall never be presented in such a way as to create sympathy for the criminal, to promote distrust of the forces of law and justice, or to inspire others with a desire to imitate criminals.

▸ If crime is depicted it shall be as a sordid and unpleasant activity.

▸ Criminals shall not be presented so as to be rendered glamorous or to occupy a position that creates a desire for emulation.

▸ In every instance good shall triumph over evil and the criminal punished for his misdeeds.

▸ Scenes of excessive violence shall be prohibited. Scenes of brutal torture, excessive and unnecessary knife and gunplay, physical agony, gory, and gruesome crime shall be eliminated.

▸ No comic magazine shall use the word horror or terror in its title.

▸ All scenes of horror, excessive bloodshed, gory or gruesome crimes, depravity, lust, sadism, masochism shall not be permitted.

▸ All lurid, unsavory, gruesome illustrations shall be eliminated.

▸ Inclusion of stories dealing with evil shall be used or shall be published only where the intent is to illustrate a moral issue and in no case shall evil be presented alluringly, nor so as to injure the sensibilities of the reader.

- ▶ Scenes dealing with, or instruments associated with walking dead, torture, vampires and vampirism, ghouls, cannibalism, and werewolfism are prohibited.

- ▶ Profanity, obscenity, smut, vulgarity, or words or symbols that have acquired undesirable meanings are forbidden.

- ▶ Nudity in any form is prohibited, as is indecent or undue exposure.

- ▶ Suggestive and salacious illustration or suggestive posture is unacceptable.

- ▶ Females shall be drawn realistically without exaggeration of any physical qualities.

- ▶ Illicit sex relations are neither to be hinted at nor portrayed. Violent love scenes as well as sexual abnormalities are unacceptable.

- ▶ Seduction and rape shall never be shown or suggested.

- ▶ Sex perversion or any inference to same is strictly forbidden.

- ▶ Nudity with meretricious purpose and salacious postures shall not be permitted in the advertising of any product; clothed figures shall never be presented in such a way as to be offensive or contrary to good taste or morals.

"The motivations for the Code may have been morally sound," posits J. David Jonssen, a comic book scholar from Ontario, "but they were coming from an ultra-conservative and very close-minded viewpoint. It's the kind of limited thinking that maintains that to deny all access to a thing will protect a person from it. It's foolish. Unfortunately the power was on the side of the conservative view, and the comics industry was severely impacted."

The Comic Code went through a number of revisions, sometimes to block newly perceived threats to the minds of our nation's youth (ahem), but also to soften it as a result of the lobbying of the sane and well balanced. The comic fandom newspaper *Newfangles* cited several examples:

- ▶ The sympathetic depiction of criminal behavior . . . [and] corruption among public officials . . . as long as it is portrayed as exceptional and the culprit is punished.

- ▸ Permitting some criminal activities to kill law-enforcement officers.
- ▸ The suggestion but not portrayal of seduction.
- ▸ Vampires, ghouls and werewolves . . . when handled in the classic tradition such as Frankenstein, Dracula, and other high caliber literary works written by Edgar Allan Poe, Saki, Conan Doyle and other respected authors whose works are read in schools around the world. (issue 44, February 1971)

Zombies were still prohibited, but Marvel Comics did an end run around that rule by calling them "zuvembies."

MARVEL FLEXES ITS MUSCLES

In 1971, the United States Department of Health, Education and Welfare approached Marvel Comics editor-in-chief Stan Lee to do a comic about drug abuse. This was in direct violation of the Comics Code, but Lee felt that getting an antidrug message out was far more useful than pretending the problem didn't exist. He scripted a three-part Spider-Man story in which Peter Parker discovered that his best friend, Harry Osborne, was addicted. Nothing in the comic glamorized drug use and yet the Comics Code Authority refused to approve the story. Lee, undeterred by the rebuke and backed by the U.S. government, went ahead and published the story without the Comics Code seal.

It would be nice to report that this bold move on Lee's part shattered the prohibition of the Comics Code and incited a rebellion in defense of free speech, but Marvel's biggest rival, DC Comics, criticized Lee and Marvel and defended the integrity of the Comic Code Authority.

As the seventies burned away and the cynical eighties rolled in, the strength of the Comic Code waned. Monsters of all kinds began appearing in comics, as did corrupt politicians, crooked cops, drug abusers, sex offenders, and other kinds of monsters.

Comic book scholar Jayne DeMarnez says, "The effect was not a destruction of society and the abandonment of all values. Just the opposite, because with the freedom to tell of realistic crime, monstrous behavior, and other forms of corruption and evil the comic book storytellers were able to more clearly demonstrate good and noble behavior. When the Code was in full force it was like trying to explain Yin and Yang by only showing the white. The message is weakened to the point of being counterproductive."

By the 1990s, Marvel and DC, along with a few other companies that still nominally supported the Code, began publishing comics without Code approval for adult readers, and sold directly through comic book stores. The softer-edged comics that carried the Code were sold in more mainstream and less specialized markets. Then in 2001, Marvel Comics withdrew from the Code entirely and instead instituted its own rating system, which is more along the lines of advisories for age-appropriate comics buying.

So where does that leave the struggle for good and evil in comics?

"It's in the story," says Brad Byers, owner of several comic book stores in the United Kingdom. "It's always been in the story. The nature of comics has been to explore the human experience through sequential art. Super heroes are just that: heroes. They fight villains. That's good and evil, pure and simple. The horror comics don't always have a happy ending, but then again neither does life. At worst, these comics use allegory and metaphor to tell of dangers in our own world. At best, they are cautionary tales in which the nature of a threat left unchecked is depicted. Ever heard the expression 'forewarned is forearmed'? That's horror comics right there."

12 CHILDREN SHOULDN'T PLAY WITH DEAD THINGS

Rob Sacchetto, *Zombie Todd*

"I've been doing zombie portraits for years. Not just zombie fans, but musicians, filmmakers, people's pets, their kids . . . everyone seems to have a secret desire to see themselves as a flesh eating monster. And as much as zombies can be played for laughs, it doesn't blunt the edge of horror that keeps the zombie genre going strong."—Rob Sacchetto is the original Zombie Portraits artist and the author/illustrator of *The Zombie Handbook* (Ulysses Press 2009).

BE AFRAID . . . BE VERY AFRAID

In an interview on the BBC program *The Monitor* in 1964, the great spookmeister director Alfred Hitchcock said that "people like to be scared when they feel safe." That's pop culture in a nutshell.

Psychologist and pop culture analyst Martin Sulkman explains: "Experiencing fright under controlled situations—a horror movie, a hair-raising book, a roller-coaster ride or a haunted funhouse— these frightening experiences give people the opportunity to see how they might handle fear or violence should it ever come their way. It's crisis by proxy."

Neurologist Andrea Lankhmer adds, "It is also an addictive thing. A controlled addiction, perhaps, but there's no denying that some people crave the chemical rush that occurs during the deliberate fear of horror entertainment. . . . Modern filmmakers know this, which is why they have sudden bursts of sound and things jumping out at frequent intervals throughout. The key is to initiate a stress reaction and then maintain it for the duration of the entertainment experience. . . . They don't want the audience to crash until afterward, which makes the body feel as if it has actually experienced the real terror or real action."

Dr. Sulkman also points out, "There is a strong and marked similarity—psychologically and physiologically between the way the body experiences fear and pleasure. Similar parts of the brain are put into play, and there are similar chemical releases."

"While watching a horror film or playing a frightening video game, like Resident Evil or Silent Hill," says Dr. Lankhmer, "data is gathered from your senses—particularly ears and eyes—to the amygdala, a subcortical nuclei linked to emotional or affective behaviors and feelings such as anger and fear. Those shocks and horrors energize us, excite us, and stimulate us. Quite a few people

---

Fear Itself

In modern speech the word "fear" refers to emotion; but in Old English "fær" refers to the specific "peril or danger" and not the emotional reaction.

---

crave that specific hormonal cocktail and keep going back for more, more, more."

The "safe" environment aspect of horror movies, scary video games, or a book with real bite is that we know that we can always shut our eyes or close the book if it gets too intense; or hit the reset button if we die. The knowledge that we have control over the amount of horror that we experience through entertainment allows us to feel powerful and makes it safe to go deeper into the darkness.

The late L. Sprague DeCamp, a fantasy writer best known for bringing the Conan stories back from obscurity in the 1960s, once said[1]: "It is not difficult to understand why we choose thrilling experiences as entertainment. It is immensely satisfying when we can experience fear and come out of it without a mark or a missing limb. This is vastly different from the fear (which may in many physiological ways feel the same) that is experienced during a plane crash, while being hacked to death by a real serial murderer, or getting shot at in combat. Those circumstances are largely beyond our control and that kind of fear is in no way entertaining. At least, not to the sane."

Skin Art

Go to any horror convention and you'll see some of the most amazing horror art around . . . and it's walking around. Horror skin art has grown to become a major part of the horror sub-culture, and it's far more than someone getting a grinning devil or a skull and crossbones tatted on their arm—these are works of art. Impressive in their detail and scope, often photo-realistic, and designed to delight the eye rather than shock the mind.

"It's a new form of beauty," says Brooklyn tattoo artist Miguel Jimenez. "We've moved into a time when people want to use the beauty of their bodies, of their exposed skin, to tell stories and share ideas. If some of those ideas are dark, then that's just honesty because beneath the skin we're all dark."

---

1. Sprague was a close friend and mentor and we often discussed the psychology behind genre entertainment.—Jonathan Maberry.

It calls to mind the Jack London quote that you see in just about every tattoo parlor in the world: "Show me a man with a tattoo and I'll show you a man with an interesting past."

In an editorial, *Rue Morgue Magazine* former editor-in-chief Jovanka Vuckovic had discussed the reaction people have to her own extensive body art. " 'Why would a pretty lady like you want to cover yourself with monsters and horrible images?' the curious observer has often asked about my tattoos. . . . It appears they (the unmarked general public) can understand the reasoning behind memorial or uplifting symbolic pieces, but not horror, not the grotesque. It's simple, really. Horror fans are a dedicated bunch. We attend festivals, conventions and zombie walks. We read horror books, play horror video games, listen to horror music, wear horror clothing and buy horror-inspired art. In fact, the mere existence of this magazine is evidence that many of us are much more than fans—we live the genre, we collect things that give meaning to our obsession and, perhaps more than any other type of fan, we get tattooed—the ultimate way of celebrating that which we adore."

Jovanka's personal collection includes portraits of Vincent Price (from *Theatre of Blood*), Lon Chaney (*London After Midnight*), Boris Karloff (*Frankenstein*), Elsa Lanchester (*Bride of Frankenstein*), Christopher Lee (*Taste the Blood of Dracula*), Max Schreck (as Count Graf Orlock, *Nosferatu*, 1922), Andy Brooks (Bob Clark's *Deathdream*), H. P. Lovecraft, Edgar Allan Poe, two images from Guillermo del Toro's films (Santi from *The Devil's Backbone* and the Pale Man from *Pan's Labyrinth*), a Cthulhu (drawn for her by Mike Mignola), a zombie, a hanya, a crawling eye, a tentacled, toothy Venus fly trap, a flaming jack-o'-lantern (in tribute to Washington Irving's *Sleepy Hollow*), the number thirteen, a flaming skull, wrist tattoos of gashes and staples (also in tribute to Karloff, with whom she shares a birthday), the words PURE EVIL tattooed on her knuckles, and a sleeve tattoo of Blade Runner on her left arm in tribute to her all-time favorite film. She insists that this is "just for starters."

"We stop each other on the street," she says of others with skin art, "in coffee shops and at various events and share our tattoos, showing our solidarity as horror fans in doing so. For people who grew up outcasts and misfits (I've noticed many of us genre junkies

Jovanka Vuckovic, *Skin Art*

"By getting a horror tattoo, fans become members of a somewhat private sect that treats the genre almost as if it were a religion."—Jovanka Vukovic is the former editor of *Rue Morgue Magazine.*

have that life experience in common), there is a sense of belonging involved in this exchange. . . . Sleeves are rolled up, collars are stretched, shoes are discarded, pants are dropped. I can't say there's any other unofficial club I belong to that unites strangers so quickly and so powerfully than that of the horror tattoo collector."

Nick Cato, author of *Don of the Dead* (Coscom, 2009) is another devotee of horror-themed skin art. "I have a tattoo of Kyra Schon, who played the little zombie girl in the original *Night of the Living Dead*; it was my first, and to this day my favorite. The film was released the year I was born (1968) so it acts as a 'birthmark' of sorts and *Night of the Living Dead* is the film responsible for getting me into the genre. I first saw it when I was seven years old on late-night TV. In 1997 I got to show it to Kyra at a horror convention and she freaked out; she loved it so much she even started a Kyra Schon tattoo page on her website, which she named me the 'Founding Father.' I have six tattoos, including an image from H. G. Lewis's classic 1970 shlocker, *The Wizard of Gore*. They remind me of the love I had (and still have) for the horror genre."

Brendon Casper, who bills himself as a "frequent flyer" who has attended more than two hundred horror cons from the UK to California, says, "I've been seeing horror tats increase in number every year. You see them on men and women, young and old, fit or fat. The art makes everyone beautiful. I used to say that I would never get one, but after seeing so many mind-bogglingly beautiful pieces of art on human skin . . . I think I'm going to take the plunge."

But the connection goes beyond the skin, she insists. "There is also a deeper connection, I think, between the art of tattoo and horror. Both were once outlaw cultures, barely respected as art forms. In that way they seemingly go hand-in-hand. Of course, both have now ingratiated themselves with the mainstream."

Exotic dancer Belinda Letwin, who performs under the stage name Baybee Bloodbath, has horror art from her chin to her toes, and she says that the art changed her life. "I was a very shy— painfully shy kid, and even into my early twenties I always wore baggy clothes and a lot of Goth makeup to hide from the world. My inner world was always dark, and I didn't get comfort from fairies and angels or any of that. I felt more at home with darker images. Not exactly devil worship, but a deep attachment to monsters because my own thoughts were rarely pretty. Then I saw the show *Miami Ink* (on cable TV's TLC channel) with this gorgeous black-haired woman, Kat Von D[2] who was covered in tattoos. I was floored, and I think I fell in love. I wanted to be her, or at least I thought I did. After I worked up the nerve to go to a tattoo place I realized that it wasn't that I wanted to be Kat, I wanted to be like her. Bold, unafraid of being who I am, and unafraid of letting people see what went on inside my thoughts. That was five years ago, and now I have skin art everywhere. I have all of the Clive Barker Cenobites on my thighs; I have dark angels and demons on my back, and werewolves and vampires biting my breasts. And lots more. . . . I've never felt more powerful."

Skin art also allows each person to make a bold statement: "The way I see it," Jovanka says, "my body is like a hot rod I can customize to my own specifications. In a way it's a statement, but not in the rebellious teenage sense. Rather, it's a testament to my devotion to the genre as well as the art of tattoo. I love both more than anything I've ever loved, and it's a thrill they can commune so easily in my skin. . . . To me, those grotesque images are beautiful, a joy to look at and a joy to wear."

"I have done loads of horror-themed tattoos," says professional tattoo artist Susan Ricciardi, "including portraits of movie characters (Regan from *The Exorcist*, Pinhead from *Hellraiser*, Michael Meyers from *Halloween*, etc.); and I've also done a great deal of vampire-themed tattoos, including a set of bite marks on a man's neck. For what's on me, my favorite tattoo is my Day of the Dead[3] piece, and I plan to continue that theme down my right arm in the future."

Jovanka Vukovic sums it all up with a smile that is both wicked and wistful, "Finally, like they've done all my life, my beloved monsters will keep me company in the cold embrace of the grave."

2. Katherine Von Drachenberg was part of the cast of *Miami Ink* during its first season, before spinning off into her own show, *L.A.Ink*, also on TLC. She is also the author of *High Voltage Tattoo* (Collins Design, 2009).

3. From the Mexican holiday, not the George Romero flick.

GAMES WITHOUT FRONTIERS

The concepts of "games" and "horror" don't seem like they would fit comfortably into the same sentence, let alone the same activity. However, horror gaming has developed into a massive global industry. They exist in a variety of formats, from old 64-k dinosaurs like the Atari 2600 released in 1977 (for games like Combat and Pac-Man) to 1989's 16-bit Sega Genesis (Altered Beast and Sonic the Hedgehog) to 1994's 32-bit PlayStation 1 (Silent Hill and Resident Evil), all the way to today's ultra-powerful Wii, Xbox 360, PlayStation 3 (with cutting-edge games like Silent Hill 2, Fatal Frame 1/2, Manhunt, and The Thing).

For horror fans there is an entire sub-genre of games that put the player right in the middle of the action. Dubbed "survival horror games," these games increase the vulnerability of the player by giving him fewer weapons, less ammo, and fewer resources, and amping up the nature of the threats. In one of these games a character is less likely to get pummeled by an anime-style kung-fu master with weird hair and far more likely to have the flesh torn from his bones by a ravenous zombie. The graphics and mood provide the atmosphere, and the direct interaction makes the play feel more real than watching a monster movie. The character has to solve complex puzzles—usually built around discovering and navigating avenues of escape, rescuing the helpless, finding weapons, and surviving. Attacks can come at any time, and plot twists abound.

The term "survival horror" was coined for the first Resident Evil game (known as Baiohazā do in Japan where it was developed), released in 1996 and has since been used as a catch-all for any of these games. In order to draw in the legions of fans devoted to the non-horror-action games, designers have incorporated more hunt-and-fight elements. This has annoyed some horror purists (and no matter what you do, you'll always annoy some purists), but the sales continue to climb.

Horror games have translated into films with varying degrees of success. Notable among those already released or in advanced stages of development are *Resident Evil* (2002), *House of the Dead* (2003), *Resident Evil: Apocalypse* (2004), *Alone in the Dark* (2005),

Doom (2005), *BloodRayne* (2006), *Forbidden Siren* (2006), *Silent Hill* (2006), *BloodRayne II: Deliverance* (2007), *Resident Evil: Extinction* (2007), *Resident Evil: Degeneration* (2008), *BloodRayne III: Warhammer* (2010), *Resident Evil: Afterlife* (2010), *Dead Space* (2011), and others.

"It's interesting," observes video game reviewer Tommy Kang, "that when they make a movie from a game we players are all jazzed at first, but although the script may follow the basic story-line, we're often disappointed because it's not the way we would have played the game."

"I've become a huge fan of Persona Three," says architect Blair Rovin, "one of the Japanese console games that are cornerstones of the whole gaming industry. This one is based around the hunt for creatures that feed on the minds of humans. The central game character is a teenage boy with special powers who can invoke a 'persona,' a physical manifestation of his ideal inner self. This persona then fights the evil 'Shadows'. . . . I got hooked. Now I play it on lunch hours at work. The people around me think I'm goofing off, but really in the kind of corporate world in which I live—and most people live—where else could we get the chance to fight evil?"

"The characters I am most drawn to can go either way: good or bad," says Daniel Toska, another devoted gamer. "In games like Persona Three you encounter situations where you have to decide whether to kill or not kill a character, and when you first go in you don't know if that's the right or wrong thing to do. You have to make tough decisions and hope they're the right ones. Sometimes the game character is forced into situations where the decision he makes is good and bad at the same time. He's a kind-hearted character, but he's sometimes caught up in the pull of destiny, and things spiral out of his control. Is that good or evil? Moral or immoral? When we play these games we're constantly exploring those questions."

Sarae Thomas, who has been involved with gaming for over twenty years, shares her opinions. "Fatal Frame and Resident Evil are my favorites. I believe in ghosts, so the ghost-chasing theme of Fatal Frame is a big draw. And as for the zombie-themed Resident Evil? Well . . . I would not put it past our government or some big corporation to produce zombies if there was either a military use or a buck to be made."

"For me, it's more fun to be the good guy," muses writer and longtime gamer Rich Weiss. "I would rather relate to a character with superpowers who can right wrongs and protect people. If only we could have these powers for ourselves in real life."

RPGs

Role-playing games (RPGs) are also vastly popular with the horror crowd. In these games, players take on characters in an interactive story overseen by a game master (GM) who creates the worlds the characters inhabit and interacts with NPCs (non-player characters). The GM also poses complications such as politics, traps, battle, and puzzles, as well as other dangers. The difference over a computer game is that the players' actions can lend to and affect the overall story to a greater degree than in a computer RPG. Most die-hard players agree, however, that computers aren't yet subtle, imaginative, or devious enough to replace a flesh and blood GM.

These games can be played in the real world with boards, figures, and dice; on computers using a combination of typing and some joystick work; and in virtual locations like Second Life, which allow for tabletop-type interaction. Good RPGers can play in any environment, regardless of their experience with a similar background. Combat in some games is purely storytelling, other times it is heavily rule scripted.

"All RPGs deal with good and evil, just like life," says Tony Finan, a longtime gamer and horror film aficionado. "The games I find most rewarding are the ones that play in the gray areas between. Just as real life isn't black and white, a good game isn't, either. Just as a lot of fiction explores moral dilemmas, so too can a game adventure."

Most players in horror games prefer to be the hero, but that shifts a bit when designing a game or preparing an adventure, as Finan explains: "As I mostly GM, rather than play, I like exploring the subtleties of good and evil. Maybe with an emphasis on the evil, because it lets me release my inner demons every so often. . . .

And One for the Good Guys . . .

"I like being the good guy, the monster hunter. I had a hard life and I came from an abusive home, so I've seen what darkness looks like when it manifests in the real world. When I play games, I want to be the force for good that stops evil in its tracks. I know that's not as popular in horror gaming as being the bad guy, but it's incredibly satisfying."—Noah Baker is a comic book dealer from Quebec.

I don't really derive joy from being evil. Sneaky and under-handed yes, but not evil."

Mike McPhail, a member of Military Writers Society of America (MWSA) and editor of the military science-fiction anthologies *Breach the Hull* and *So It Begins* (Dark Quest), gives it another spin. "I've played the Alliance Archives MRPG since 1986. Although it is military sci-fi, the setting and characters are based strongly in reality, and as such, good and evil are generally a matter of which side you're on. But, as in reality, that line blurs from person to person to a point where there is no such distinction as good/evil, just the hell of combat, and the fight for survival; this while trying to operate within the military chain of command."

For people outside of the gaming world the attraction is sometimes hard to understand. "Oh, people clearly don't get us," agrees Yuki Kazuki, a video game designer who prefers RPGs for his own recreation. "You see it a lot at comic book stores, where a bunch of us might gather to play; or at cons held in hotels. We'll all be clustered around tables, playing for hours and even days on end, and the people who aren't there for the con look at us like we're from Mars . . . they can't get away fast enough. It's even worse with the horror games. Our own families think that we're damaged goods if we like being a vampire or a werewolf in a game. They think that we want to do harm, that we would transform if we could. That's absurd. I mean . . . okay, sure, I'd go for being a vampire in a heartbeat if there was a chance, but it doesn't mean I'd turn evil."

KEEPING IT REAL

Live action role playing (LARP) attracts yet another large chunk of the gaming community. And these stories tend to edge more in the direction of adventure fantasy than horror. Even so, many horrific elements pop up, such as monsters, evil magic users, curses, and transformations into monsters.

LARPers dress up as their characters and act out the stories. With some limitations. "We may swing some swords or pull guns," says Mindy Schwartman, who does both Old West and Steampunk LARPing, "but no one's getting carted off to the E.R. or the morgue."

"We do take it seriously, though," adds her husband, Mark. "Sure, there's a part of us that is acting as guide to keep things from ever getting out of hand, but at the same time we're doing more than putting on costumes. Serious players know as much about their worlds and characters as do the folks who do the high-end Civil War re-enactments."

The outcome of each player's actions is generally mediated by predetermined game rules, or voted on by consensus among players. Event game masters decide on the setting, create challenges, select the rules to be used, and facilitate play.

"Apart from the sense of community you get," says Sante Fe LARPer Boris Morescu, "when you become the character you really feel the power. It's transformative. When you are a hero, you feel

---

The Gray Area

"Some LARPs deal with good vs. evil as a very black and white issue: you are a hero fighting hordes of demons. Pretty easy to take a moral side. But other live action experiences like Seventh Kingdom offer more gray, more of the complex and in-depth political intrigues. I seem to be drawn to games that allow for a gray area. They allow me to explore my own gray area and kind of play-test certain moral situations in a fantasy environment, rather than messing up my own life."—Tara M. Meacham is marketing director for Seventh Kingdom, an IGE (interactive gaming environment similar to an LARP).

heroic. When you are a sorcerer, you can feel the magic flowing through you. And, when you are the villain you can understand why they do what they do. That includes motivations and justifications."

Novelist and attorney Michael Ventrella recalls, "I became involved with gaming back in college in the late seventies in the days when Dungeons and Dragons had just been released... I wrote the adventures and acted as 'Dungeon Master.' In 1989, a group of us avid gamers decided to try writing rules for a live action fantasy medieval game.... We called the group NERO (New England Roleplaying Organization), and after I wrote an article about it for *Dragon Magazine*, we grew tremendously. Years later, I broke off from them and started the Alliance LARP, which has chapters all over the United States. My rule books and players' guides sell fairly regularly on Amazon.com and in gaming stores."

"I started out doing tabletop role playing," remembers Connie Berger, a costume designer for LARPs who travels the convention circuit. "That was fun at first, but everything is spoken. It's hard to believe that you're a warrior-queen if you're wearing an old Zork T-shirt and sipping a Dr Pepper. Then when LARPing got rolling in the late seventies, early eighties, a lot of my friends moved into doing the live action stuff. At first we were buying costumes, or fudging them from Salvation Army racks; but now there are people like me who make highly detailed, high-quality stuff."

"I don't really believe in good or evil," admits David Hill, a freelance writer in the Philadelphia area who has written for a handful of role-playing games. "I believe in spectrums, I believe that case dictates. Sometimes, the best people in the world can do deplorable things. Sometimes, a 'bad person' does good things for various reasons. Sometimes, a person with the best intentions can be forced into a situation where he or she has to choose a lesser of two evils. Often, the lesser is not really clear, and either choice is still 'bad.'"

Horror LARPs abound. There are zombie games of all kinds—many of which are unpublished and unofficial but well attended; and several notable games that draw on the supernatural writings of H. P. Lovecraft, among them Cthulhu Live and Cthulhu Calling. And, of course, vampires are well represented in games like the World of Darkness.

Cthulhu Calling . . .

"Call of Cthulhu is the epitome of horror gaming. It is based on the works of H. P. Lovecraft and others (the 'mythos' as it is known) and deals with the theme of tremendously powerful cosmic beings returning to Earth after millions of years of absence to reclaim the planet. The majority of RPG material is set in the 1920s, because that is when Lovecraft did most of his writing. The players take the part of investigators who, in the course of the adventure, discover Things Man Was Not Meant To Know and must work to thwart evil human cultists (and the monsters they summon) who are bent on bringing the old gods back to take over (and presumably destroy) the world."
—Elzbeth MacIain is a veteran gamer.

COSPLAY

Appearing in costume at cons and other events is called "costume play," or Cosplay for short, and it has become a major feature at all cons. There are costume contests, parades, continual photo ops, Cosplay websites, calendars, and pin-ups, and fan bases built around specific Cosplayers who have become celebrities in their own right. One of the most well-known and popular Cosplayers is Ruby Rocket (a.k.a. actress, model, and seamstress Ruby Young) from Southern California, who discussed the subculture with us. "People are so drawn to it because it allows them to transform themselves into their favorite characters. You can be the brave Jedi or the evil Supervillain for a day. It definitely brings out another side of their personalities."

When asked if it was more fun to be a good or evil character, she said, "I think the in-between section is the best. There are too many pitfalls set up for those that are solely evil or purely good . . . Most of my costumes are heroes but there have been some villains I greatly enjoy, as well. The villains just don't get as much screen time, though, so I think the hero is forefront in most peoples' minds. However, good versus evil is something that plays out every day . . . We always hope that good will prevail and I think seeing that played out on screen helps us basically cope with the evils of the every day."

Liana Kerzner, another internationally famous Cosplayer, adds, "The fascination with good and evil makes life seem simpler because we're trying to figure ourselves out as a people. Because we want heroes to save us, but the way villains break the rules is absolutely romantic. Identifying with the good and evil characters in movies is cathartic—it's a safe emotional investment because it's just a film . . . the audience knows who to cheer for. How can that not be fascinating?"

And Erin Montemurro, a graphic designer, avid costumer, and comic book collector, offers this perspective: "Good versus evil is the nature of all that we see in life, it is something we mimic from childhood, for example, cops and robbers. It is the truest sense of judging everything as black and white. It is simplicity."

The selection of character is sometimes a reflection of the inner life or secret desires of the Cosplayer, and sometimes it's a reaction

Cosplay Fun Facts

▶ Most people think Cosplay began in Japan, but it started in America at science fiction conventions in the 1990s.

▶ A Japanese man coined the term "Cosplay" at World Con (World Science Fiction Convention) in California.

▶ In May 2009, 337 people broke the world record for the largest gathering of Cosplayers.

▶ There are Cosplay restaurants in Japan. Each has a theme and the wait staff dress in costume according to said theme.

▶ Cosplay is so popular at some conventions that it is nearly impossible to use the bathrooms because so many people crowd them to dress in costume. Some conventions rent out dressing rooms in advance to avoid this problem.

▶ Two well-read magazines on the subject are *Cosmode* and *Dengeki Layers*.

▶ Some modeling companies are using Cosplayers for their ads rather than traditional models.

to the desires of others as Liana points out: "Most of my newer costumes are challenges or requests. Or they're done because a particular creator is coming to town. So that creates a pretty wide and random repertoire of characters."

When asked their personal preference for good or evil characters, we got these answers:

Liana said, "I seem, with some notable exceptions, to gravitate toward bad-girl heroines and villainesses that make some sense in the context of their worlds. Ms. Marvel's a drunk. Power Girl smashes gender stereotypes by being brash, impulsive, violent, and a computer programmer to boot. Batwoman's the first lesbian Batman family character. . . ."

Cosplay

World-class Cosplayers Liana K., Riki LeCotey, David Ross, Ruby Rocket, Rachael Lavin, Ron and Ken Baron, Danielle Ackley-McPhail, and Erin Montemurro.

"One of the characters I portray at cons is Namor the Sub-Mariner," says David M. Ross, Cosplayer and professional wrestler ("The Amazing Darkstone"). "I have always found him to be a bit of an enigma because he is a hero at times and a villain at times. The moral ambiguity makes him unpredictable and it also suggests that there is a great conflict within him . . . I've never seen anyone else portray Namor at a convention . . . I don't think most people understand him. They don't have insight into this confused, angry and 'lost' antihero. I do. I get him . . . In wrestling as in comics and movies, people can respect, admire, or even revere a villain because they're conflicted, multidimensional. A great villain can be appreciated and respected on many different levels, whereas heroes have a much more limited range and if they do not work well as a hero, they generally go unappreciated. Heroes, sad to say, can sometimes be boring."

"On the villain side," Liana muses, "Knockout's morality makes absolute sense on the planet she comes from, but on Earth it's less than virtuous. Poison Ivy may be a villain to people, but she's fighting for the planet and sees humanity as a parasite and a destructive force. To this day, I'm still not sure if Frank Cho's take on Shanna the She Devil is a heroine or a villainess, and that's what I like about her!

"But then there are the characters that are fun because they're just *so* good or *so* bad. There is nothing complex or conflicted

---

Hunter: The Vigil (Roleplaying Game)

"Hunter: The Vigil by White Wolf Publishing is a wonderful exploration of good and evil. In Hunter, you play characters who hunt the monsters that terrorize your average people. On the surface, it looks clear-cut, black and white. You kill the monsters, you save the world. However, there's a lot of room for philosophical debate. When you kill a monster, you're still killing. Oftentimes, those monsters were once human. Some maintain human lives. And if you're trying to kill to protect people, is it also all right to kill humans who hurt people?"—David Hill is a freelance writer in the Philadelphia area.

What Makes a Better Story—Good Triumphs or Evil Triumphs?

▸ *Erin Montemurro:* "Good triumphs over evil allows you to leave the theater or put down the book having a sense of closure. I do believe that the hero should struggle in all aspects in order to find success."

▸ *Liana Kerzner:* "It completely depends on the story. Popular culture is focused on the protagonist of a story winning. Every so often you get a great story like *Silence of the Lambs* wherein an evil character triumphs and it makes sense. However, that's extremely hard to do . . ."

▸ *Ruby Rocket:* "Just as in movies, we ultimately want to see good triumph, I think. We want to have a sense that this crazy world we live in isn't just going in the gutter . . . in real life we don't see good truly winning that often. And if they do win it doesn't last for very long. No matter what, in the end, evil always end up alone."

---

about Cheetara from Thundercats, for instance, although I see her as more of a tomboy than some might . . . But getting into her headspace is interesting. There a kinetic drive to her virtuousness that her name implies. She's mystical. It's a different part of the Cosplay mosaic that's fun to play in. The Queen of Hearts, on the other hand, well, she's just nasty. And that's fun sometimes. But it's only fun because I know I hate her. She's the embodiment of stupid rules that everyone follows without knowing why, so that character is a good way to vent any subdued brattiness."

Erin's take was a little different: "I have both villains and heroes. Although some of the characters do 'bad things' they all represent a strong female character. Strength of character is something I look up to, and the strength each character represents has inspired me to build that costume."

Some Cosplayers do lose themselves in the personas of the characters they portray. We asked Liana about how often that happens, or if it's a phenomena to embrace. "Ideally that's every event. That's the difference between costuming and Cosplay. But you

Fans vs. Geeks

A lot of folks are confused over the difference between the fan subtypes of geeks and nerds. Being a geek myself, I can answer that question. A geek will show up to the midnight release of a new Harry Potter film; a nerd will show up dressed as Harry. A true, self-respecting nerd will also have the costume right to the proper stitching on the Hogwart's school patch and the grain on the phoenix-tail wand. A geek won't do that, but he will be able to fairly judge if it was done well.

---

really have to know when to draw the line and when to turn it off, because it's a safety issue. That being said, it gives people more of a thrill if they can believe they're talking to the character instead of a person dressed up . . . Some characters are easier than others. A very glamorous, manipulative character like Poison Ivy is easier to play in photos than someone like Shanna, who, if I were being completely true to the character, would punch the photographer, then break his stuff. You have to use common sense. If someone asks me my name, I'll give them the character's name instead of my own. Little touches here and there make a world of difference. Ms. Marvel is fun that way, because I can announce that I need a drink when I'm getting tired and it gets a laugh. Knockout calls men 'pups.' Power Girl is known for putting people in headlocks. You need to do your homework. If I'm dressed as Leia, other Star Wars Cosplayers will address me as 'Princess,' and they expect me not to look confused. Ditto for comic book artists approaching and saying 'I drew you!' It's expected that you'll know who they are."

13 REAL EVIL

David Cousens, *Hyde in the Shadows*

"The story of Jekyll and Hyde is one of the most interesting representations of good versus evil as it represents an internal struggle between the two, where good and evil are actually both part of the same person. I love characters that have a duality to them; characters that are all good or evil are not as interesting as the shades of grey."—David and Sarah Cousens are UK illustrators whose clients include Macmillan Publishing, Kingfisher Publishing, *Digital Arts* magazine, and Letraset.

SERIAL KILLERS

Depending on who you ask, serial killers[1] are either born with evil or environmental circumstances dictate their actions, or a combination of both. But no matter who you ask, no one aspires to be a

---

1. The U.S. Bureau of Justice Statistics defines a serial killing as "[involving] the killing of several victims in three or more separate events."

Vampires Are Serial Killers

"Probably the most significant vampire story we published in *Weird Tales* was 'Midnight Mass' by F. Paul Wilson, which is gripping, visceral, and pretty basic. I am a bit of a fundamentalist when it comes to vampires, preoccupied with an idea so old-fashioned that it is shocking. Are you ready for this? Vampires as evil. Vampires are, after all, predatory serial killers. . . . When Anne Rice spoke of vampirism as 'the dark gift,' my reaction was that this was the 'gift' of becoming like Jeffrey Dahmer forever."
—Darrell Schweitzer is an author, anthologist, and former editor of *Weird Tales*.

serial killer . . . except for the serial killers, who work hard to perpetuate evil.

Most serial killers have several traits in common, including the need to control others and a lack of remorse for their actions; but there's no generic profile for a serial killer—that's why serial killers are so evil. Serial killers don't kill out of passion or without forethought. Serial killers kill for the thrill of killing or because they feel a compulsive need to kill. But like ice cream, serial killers come in a wide variety of flavors and no two are alike—that's what makes serial killers so difficult to catch.

We've all heard of (and feared) the most famous of the serial killers: Jack the Ripper, Charles Manson, Ted Bundy, the Boston Strangler, the BTK Killer, Jeffrey Dahmer, David Berkowitz, and others. But for every serial killer who's been caught, there are others still out there hiding in the shadows, and with them comes the good guys who strive to catch the killers and prevent them from hurting others.

Hunting serial killers is a difficult task, one that requires dedication, know-how, and perseverance . . . and a bit of good luck thrown into the mix. Thanks to the hard work of the FBI, the police, the profilers, and other law enforcement personnel, many serial killers have been caught and taken off the streets. But it's a never-ending battle of good versus evil, a battle that will continue as long as humankind exists. A battle for life . . . and death.

HUNTING THE HUNTERS

It takes a lot to hunt the hunters, the serial killers who revel in death. According to John Douglas, former unit chief of the FBI's National Center for the Analysis of Violent Crimes, "Serial killers don't look like one-eyed monsters but look like your next door neighbor, and areas with runaways, prostitution, a drug culture, and street people are fertile grounds for someone who is inclined to perpetrate a violent crime against others. About a dozen serial killers are arrested each year in the United States and the solution rate is only around 64 to 67 percent nationwide. The problem in our country is that we have over 17,000 law enforcement agencies, but we don't always have 100 percent participation in solving the crime among the agencies, which becomes an even greater problem if the offender becomes mobile."

So what's it take to hunt the hunters? Television shows like

The Myths About Serial Killers

"There are a number of myths about serial killers floating around, such as that they always prefer the same type of victim, they're always white males, they're smarter than the average person, they're all insane, they're all psychopaths, etc. . . . but the truth is that serial killers are as diverse as any other designated population, and if you examine the cases in other countries you will see that South African serial killers tend to be black, Japanese serial killers tend to be Asian, etc. . . . Some are married, with families, others are single loners. Some are educated, others aren't. Some are organized predators, others are psychotic. Some kill in a solitary manner, others operate in teams. . . . Some write letters to police or newspapers, but many do not. Some but not all revisit crime scenes; some leave distinct signatures. Some are sexually motivated, but others are greedy, bored, angry, or driven by some other personal issue."—Dr. Katherine Ramsland is professor of forensic psychology and author or coauthor of over nine hundred articles and thirty-seven books, including *The Human Predator* (Berkley, 2005), *The Unknown Darkness* (Diane Publishing, 2003), and *The Devil's Dozen* (Berkley, 2009).

Criminal Minds, CSI, and *Fringe,* and movies such as *Natural Born Killers* (1994) and *The Bone Collector* (1999) make it look easy, but in real life identifying and locating serial killers is difficult. Wouldn't it be great if we could solve these cases in a mere hour or two, the time it takes to watch a television show or movie, or in the time needed to read a book like Thomas Harris's *Silence of the Lambs* (St. Martin's Press, 1999) or J. T. Ellison's *All the Pretty Girls* (Mira Books, 2007)? Unfortunately, real life is never as easy as fiction. It takes a patient and confident person to hunt a serial killer. After all, it can take weeks, months, or years to identify, locate, and capture an unknown subject.

While we don't often hear about the good guys who hunt evil, they work tirelessly to keep the streets safe. According to Peter Vronsky's 2004 book *Serial Killers: The Method and Madness of Monsters,* investigative profilers such as Sherlock Holmes[2] and C. Auguste Dupin[3] existed long before the FBI developed their system to analyze serial killers in the late 1970s.

Today, most people refer to FBI personnel who develop psychological profiles of serial killers as "profilers," but the word actually refers to an aspect of the job and not a job title. The profiler is called in to assist local, state, federal, or foreign law enforcement agencies when the agencies have exhausted all leads.

A profile is formed from the evidence collected at the crime scenes, including photos, witness statements, and police and medical examiner reports. Profilers search for similarities and patterns among killings and attempt to determine the type of person who committed the crime. What's the killer's sex, age, race, socioeconomic status? Is he outgoing or a loner? What's his method? How often does he kill? What's his motive—is it the mission or the killing of specific types of people that drives him? Does he derive pleasure from the killings? Is he motivated by sex? Does he get a thrill from watching other peoples' fear or pain? Is he motivated by a need for control? Does he believe someone is ordering him to

2. Arthur Conan Doyle's London detective who appeared in numerous novels and short stories since the late 1880s.
3. Edgar Allan Poe's detective who appeared in *The Murders in the Rue Morgue, The Mystery of Marie Rogêt,* and *The Purloined Letter* (1841–44).

On Profiling Serial Killers

"It is the ability to make order out of chaos, to take a complex horrific crime scene and distill it down into its essential parts. To then take information and explain it in a cogent articulate way so that almost anyone can then understand the dynamics of the crime. It is the ability to look at everything that happened within the totality of the crime. To analyze all the important aspects such as victimology, motive, access, organization and planning, cause of death, injury severity, post offense behavior, and body disposal among other scene considerations and then interpret what that means is very rewarding, and recognizing that only a handful of people in the world can do this type of complex analysis."—Mark Safarik retired from the FBI after twenty-three years, serving the last twelve as a senior profiler in the FBI's Behavioral Analysis unit, and is now the executive director of Forensic Behavioral Services International.

kill? Does he murder to acquire material gains? Or does he kill for compassionate reasons—to alleviate perceived suffering.

To determine a serial killer's motive one must examine the victimology. Why this victim? What happened? How did the crime occur? "I look at victimology like a doctor performs a patient history," says FBI former unit chief John Douglas. "But my patients are dead, so I rely on forensic evidence to identify a subject. However, a profiler is only as good as the information that was analyzed. If the investigation wasn't done properly or all the evidence is not present, then the profiler will be wrong in his analysis. That's why it's important for the different agencies to cooperate."

A killer's modus operandi (MO) is developed through learned behavior and by trial and error. If something doesn't work for the killer, then the killer adapts. If the MO works, then the killer stays with that MO.

From the MO, a profiler attempts to determine the killer's signature (something done that is unnecessary to commit the crime but emotionally necessary for the killer). For example, a serial killer might stab someone postmortem or pose the body—neither

---

Profiling Isn't Just for Serial Killers

Television shows like *Criminal Minds* portray profilers as people who spend all their time working to catch serial killers. According to John Douglas, profilers just don't focus on catching serial killers. They work on all types of crime, including arsons, terrorism, extortion, product tampering, kidnappings, child molestation, and bombings. They also help establish probable cause and obtain search warrants by telling law enforcement what to look for, that is, souvenirs and newspaper clippings. Prosecutors enlist profilers to help with jury selection, preparing witnesses, and ways to cross examine the killer.[4] Profilers also testify in court, not about a profile, which is an investigative tool and cannot introduced as evidence, but about the modus operandi or type of murder.

---

is necessary to kill the victim, but the killer derives emotional satisfaction from the act. The MO combined with the signature and victimology leads to a profile, an investigative tool used to refocus or reinforce an investigation.

Some television shows like *Profiler* and *Criminal Minds* make profiling and catching killers appear easier than it really is. In *Profiler*, a psychic detective assists with the investigations and makes it seem that identifying and catching an unknown subject (UNSUB) is the result of some kind of psychic event rather than the hard legwork of interviewing suspects, reviewing evidence, and studying victimology. Other television shows complicate matters for law enforcement and make it easier for serial killers to get away with murder . . . at least for a while. Today's serial killers have access to a vast store of information on forensics thanks to television shows like *Bones*, *NCIS*, *Dexter*, *CSI*, *Forensic Files*, *Crime 360*, or *Medical Detectives*, where viewers get a behind-the-scenes look at forensic science. There are also many books on forensics, websites, and courses at universities, all excellent sources for a serial killer to gather the latest and greatest information on forensic

4. The method is based on what the case tells the profiler about the killer.

techniques, information that will enable him to minimize the trace evidence left behind at a crime scene and delay arrest.

Some serial killers wear gloves to avoid leaving fingerprints, use condoms during rapes, and bleach away blood evidence or dispose of evidence away from the crime scene. Although these precautions minimize the forensic evidence left at a crime scene and make it more difficult for law enforcement to catch serial killers, it is nearly impossible to outwit forensic science.

For over twenty years, police have used DNA evidence left behind at a crime scene to positively identify a suspect and tie him to the crime. With the advances in genomics, it's now possible to provide a physical description of a serial killer based on genetic evidence recovered at a crime scene, evidence that does not match any suspects with profiles already in the system. Granted, genomics won't reveal the name of the killer in this instance, but it can assist law enforcement in narrowing the pool of perspective suspects. In 2003, police in Baton Rouge, Louisiana, used genomic testing to reevaluate their suspect profile after reaching a dead end in their search for a serial killer, which led to an arrest and a conviction. In the future, genomics will undoubtedly play a bigger role in profiling.

These factors—combined with evidence from the murders,

Apprehending Dexter

"Criminals always make mistakes, and Dexter makes many. [Dexter, the main character in the television show *Dexter*, is a serial killer who justifies his crimes by murdering criminals who avoided apprehension.] If a detective followed Locard's Principle (criminals always take something from a scene, and they always leave something behind) and the simple MOM formula: M = motive, O = opportunity, and M = means, Dexter would quickly be captured. The MOM theory is simple; find the person with all three elements and you'll have your killer. Dexter always has the motive, opportunity, and the means to commit the crime."—Lee Lofland is a retired police detective and the author of *Police Procedure and Investigation, A Guide For Writers* (Writers Digest Books, 2007) and the wildly popular blog *The Graveyard Shift*.

---

previous interviews with serial killers, and knowledge of prior crimes—enable the profiler to create a set of criteria to describe the serial killer. Often these criteria are accurate; occasionally they are not and must be reworked as the killings progress. But what's common among all the serial killing cases is the tireless dedication of the law enforcement personnel who hunt the hunters and stop the hunt before serial killers claim the lives of more innocent victims.

SERIAL KILLER HALL OF FAME

David Berkowitz (Son of Sam): David Berkowitz terrorized New York City from July 1976 to July 1977, murdering six people and wounding seven others using a handgun. In a letter written to the police, Berkowitz said he was "the Son of Sam" and that demons ordered him to kill. Upon his arrest in 1977, Berkowitz confessed to the murders and was sentenced to 365 years in prison. Books about Berkowitz include *Son of Sam: The .44-Caliber Killer* by George Carpozi (Manor Books, 1977), *Son of Sam: Based on the Authorized Transcription of the Tapes, Official Documents and Diaries of David Berkowitz* by Lawrence D. Klausner (McGraw-Hill, 1980), *Confessions of Son of Sam* by David Abrahamsen (Columbia University Press, 1985), and *A Serial Killer: David Berkowitz Son of Sam/Son of Hope* by Stephen and Kenneth Cender (1st Books Library, 2001). And in 1999, Spike Lee presented his take on David Berkowitz in the film *Summer of Sam*.

William Bonin (Freeway Killer): Although truck driver William Bonin confessed to raping and murdering twenty-one boys during the late 1970s, he was convicted of raping and murdering only fourteen. Bonin's accomplices for some of the crimes were Vernon Butts, Greg Miley, and James Michael Munro. Bonin was put to death by lethal injection in 1996. His story is told in the 2009 film *Freeway Killer*.

Boston Strangler: Between 1962 and 1964 more than eleven women were sexually assaulted and strangled to death in Boston, Massachusetts. Although Albert DeSalvo (a man already jailed for life) confessed to the murders, the police never charged him due to a lack of evidence.

Ian Brady and Myra Hindley (Moors Murderers): Notorious in England, Ian Brady and Myra Hindley jointly tortured and murdered five children between 1963 and 1965.

Ted Bundy: From 1974 to 1978 Ted Bundy raped and murdered thirty-five to forty women across the United States. He also mutilated the bodies and kept the body parts in his apartment. Bundy confessed to killing twenty-eight, but some estimates put the deaths in the hundreds. No one knows for sure how many women Bundy murdered except for Bundy, who refused to reveal that information prior to his execution in 1989. Howard Chua-Eoan called Bundy the "devil" in his Time.com article, "The Top 25 Crimes of the Century," and we'd have to agree.

David Jospeh Carpenter (Trailside Killer): Incarcerated for fourteen years for attacking a woman with a hammer, David Joseph Carpenter turned to murder a mere two years after his release from prison. A park in Marion County, California, was Carpenter's hunting ground and the place where he shot and raped his victims from 1979 to 1981. Carpenter was convicted of seven murders and sentenced to death.

Richard Trenton Chase (Vampire Killer of Sacramento): Drinking the blood of his victims was part of Richard Trenton Chase's modus operandi. Chase killed six people in Sacramento, California, in 1978.

Andrei Chikatilo (Rostov Ripper, Butcher of Rostov, or The Red Ripper): This Russian sexually assaulted and murdered over thirty women and children between 1978 and 1990.

Daniel Conahan Jr.: Conahan's six male victims were mutilated and slain in Florida in the mid- to late 1990s.

Mary Ann Cotton: Suspected in the murders of fourteen or more family members, mainly by arsenic poisoning, Cotton was convicted of murdering her husband, two stepsons, and her baby in 1873. She was hanged that same year.

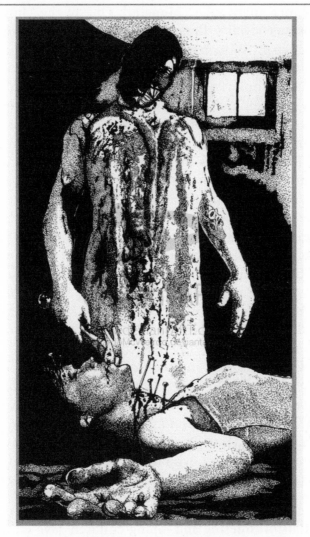

Jacob Parmentier, *Shhhh Quiet*

"I would have to say that the majority of my work depicts evil in its finest form. Whether it's a sadistic murderer taking pleasure in the awful deed he has just committed, or just the details that lead up to the act itself. Generally evil appears to be winning in most of the work I produce. Sad to say, that's true more often than not in this world."—Jacob Parmentier is an artist, illustrator, and graphic designer whose work has been featured in various horror genre publications and on Internet websites.

Jeffrey Dahmer (Milwaukee Monster): One of the United States' most notorious serial killers, Jeffrey Dahmer murdered at least seventeen men in Wisconsin from 1978 to 1991. But the killing wasn't enough for Dahmer. He also dismembered, cooked, and ate parts of his victims. Police discovered body parts in Dahmer's refrigerator, freezer, and closet, and under the bed. They also discovered headless torsos stored in chemical-filled drums. For close to a year, neighbors had smelled odors originating from the apartment, but Dahmer always managed to concoct an excuse for the smell and the neighbors bought it.

Convicted of fifteen murders after a failed attempt to plead not guilty by reason of insanity, Dahmer was sentenced to fifteen consecutive life terms. In 1994, he was beaten to death in prison.

The public was fascinated with Dahmer and his crimes as evidenced by the multitude of books on the subject, including Edward Baumann's *Step into My Parlor: The Chilling Story of Serial Killer Jeffrey Dahmer* (Bonus Books, 1991), *Milwaukee Massacre: Jeffrey Dahmer and the Milwaukee Murders* by Robert J. Dvorchak and Lisa Holewa (Robert Hale, 1992), Richard Tithecott's *Of Men and Monsters: Jeffrey Dahmer and the Construction of the Serial Killer* (University of Wisconsin Press, 1997), *The Jeffrey Dahmer Story: An American Nightmare* by Donald A. Davis (St. Martin's Press, 2006), and *The Man Who Could Not Kill Enough: Secret Murders of Jeffrey Dahmer* (Titan Books, 1992), written by investigative reporter Anne E. Schwartz, who followed the story from the beginning. Films include *The Secret Life: Jeffrey Dahmer* (1993), *Dahmer* (2002), and *Raising Jeffrey Dahmer* (2006).

Gilles de Rais: Murdering and raping children gave Gilles de Rais great pleasure in the 1440s. Estimates place his victim count between several dozen and several hundred.

Nannie Doss (Jolly Black Widow): Considered by some as the original Black Widow, Nannie Doss killed four husbands and several infant children between 1920 and 1954. She also was accused of murdering her mother and several other family members.

Marc Dutroux (Monster of Belgium): Dutroux liked them young and female. He abducted, then raped, tortured, and killed six young

A Serial Killer with Morals

"Gary Evans is an anomaly in the world of contemporary serial killing, in that he preyed on friends and those in his life he believed had wronged him. He was also a person who hated those who killed kids or women. He hated drug dealers—thought they were the scum of society, along with rapists and pedophiles. So here we have a serial killer with morals, it would seem. Go figure."—M. William Phelps is the award-winning author of fourteen nonfiction books, including *Every Move You Make* (Pinnacle 2005), which examines this serial killer who confessed to murdering five victims.

girls in his soundproof dungeon and torture chamber in Belgium in 1995.

Pedro Rodriques Filho (Pedrinho Matador or **Little Peter the Killer):** Filho claims to have killed more than a hundred people in Brazil, including his father. A tattoo on his left arm reads *Mato por prazer* (I kill for pleasure). He was sentenced to 128 years' imprisonment, but under Brazilian law the maximum a person can serve is thirty years.

Albert Fish (Gray Man): A cannibal, a molester, and a sado-masochist, Albert Fish admitted to molesting more than four hundred children, confessed to killing six, and alluded to murdering dozens more between 1910 and 1934. Fish drank his victims' blood and ate their flesh. He also enjoyed hurting himself, mainly with needles. Of course, his victims suffered, too, before their deaths—a process that gave Fish much pleasure, for Fish possessed a raw penchant for harming others, one he couldn't ignore. Fish pleaded guilty by reason of insanity, but the jury found him guilty and sane. He was electrocuted in 1936.

Thomas Harris's renowned fictional character Hannibal Lecter, featured in *Red Dragon*, *The Silence of the Lambs*, *Hannibal*, and *Hannibal Rising*, was based on Albert Fish. Numerous shows and magazines have parodied Hannibal Lecter, and at the 1992 Academy Awards, Billy Crystal made his entrance wearing a straitjacket and a mask, a costume straight out of the movie *Silence of the*

Silence of the Lambs

▸ Won the top five Oscars—Best Picture, Best Director, Best Actress, Best Actor, and Best Screenplay (adapted).

▸ Fortunately for Jodie Foster, who played Clarice Sterling and won Best Actress for the role, Michelle Pfeiffer turned down the part when it was offered.

▸ Real-life FBI profiler John Douglas coached Scott Glenn for his role as Jack Crawford, the character based on Douglas.

▸ Hannibal Lecter (remarkably portrayed by Anthony Hopkins) was nicknamed Hannibal the Cannibal.

▸ The despicable character Buffalo Bill had a cherished dog named Precious.

Lambs. In addition, Harold Schecter examines Albert Fish in his book, *Deranged: The Shocking True Story of America's Most Fiendish Killer* (Pocket Books, 1990) as does M. Heimer in *The Cannibal* (Pinnacle, 1991). Films include *Serial Killers: Real Life Hannibal Lecters* (2001), *Albert Fish* (2006), and *The Gray Man* (2007).

John Wayne Gacy (Killer Clown): It's hard to imagine a likeable family man, who was active in his community and ran a successful business, as a serial killer. But that's exactly who John Wayne Gacy was. Gacy drugged, sodomized, raped, and strangled his victims, then he buried their bodies either in a crawl space under his garage, under the house, or dumped them in rivers near his home outside of Chicago. Both Gacy's wife and his neighbors noticed awful odors at his home, but Gacy insisted a dead animal was responsible for the smell, and neither the neighbors nor Gacy's wife thought to question the issue any further. Nor did they know that Gacy had been convicted of raping a young boy in 1968 and was jailed for ten years for the crime, a crime that gave Gacy the thirst for additional rapes and ultimately murder. When police discovered the bodies, Gacy confessed to murdering thirty-two people. The police also found drivers' licenses and jewelry belonging to the victims in Gacy's house.

Medical experts testified that Gacy suffered from a mental disorder, and the defense argued that Gacy was insane at the time of his murders. However, after two hours of deliberations, the jury found Gacy guilty—it was difficult to believe that a man who planned his murders and remembered the murders in detail could possibly be insane at the time of the murders. Gacy was executed in 1994.

While in prison Gacy occupied himself by painting. According to an Associate Press article in the June 6, 2004, *St. Petersburg Times*, some people enjoy Gacy's clown paintings for their merit, regardless of who painted them—they've been displayed in numerous galleries. But others abhor Gacy and his art and have purchased his paintings just so they could burn them. In addition to clown paintings, Gacy painted a wide range of subjects including Elvis Presley and Mickey Mouse.

For more information on John Wayne Gacy, check out these books: *Buried Dreams: Inside the Mind of a Serial Killer* (Bantam, 1986) by Tim Cahill, *Killer Clown: The John Wayne Gacy Murders* (Grosset & Dunlap, 1983) by Terry Sullivan with Peter T. Maiken, and *The Man Who Killed Boys: A True Story of Mass Murder in a Chicago Suburb* (St. Martin's Press, 1986) by Clifford L. Linedecker.

For film buffs, both the 1992 movie *To Catch a Killer* and the 2003 movie *Gacy* recount John Wayne Gacy's life and crimes. The 2010 film *Dahmer vs. Gacy*[5] is a horror/comedy where famous serial killers are cloned and genetically altered to create super killers. John Wayne Gacy and Jeffrey Dahmer are in a race to kill everyone and ultimately fight each other to the death.

Luis Garavito (the Beast): During a five-year period in the 1990s, Garavito lured Colombian children into his clutches by promising them food and drink. Garavito confessed to 140 murders but was convicted of raping and murdering 189. Surprisingly, Garavito received only a thirty-year sentence, the maximum allowed under Colombian law, a sentence that was reduced to twenty-two years.

---

5. In production at the time of this writing—release title may differ.

Murderabilia

It seems natural to despise serial killers. After all, they are evil. Ironically, there are people out there who are fascinated by serial killers, not because they desire to understand what makes serial killers tick, but because they actually revere serial killers like one would idolize a movie star or a sports figure. And we're not talking about serial killers' mothers or fathers, who may continue to love their children regardless of their crimes.

Buyers today can find murderabilia[6] on the Internet and by writing to killers in prison. There's a market for this stuff among collectors, including letters, photos, artwork, and more. John Wayne Gacy's and Charles Manson's artwork sell for thousands of dollars to collectors.

To the families of the murder victims, murderabilia brings back the pain of losing their loved ones. Some debate that the sale of murderabilia is a product of a free marketplace and should not be banned, whereas others argue that it's a sick way to make money. The sale of murderabilia has been banned in a handful of states under the Notoriety for Profit Law; however, entrepreneurs find clever ways to circumvent the system. We imagine that as long as serial killers exist there will be those who value murderabilia.

Edward Gein: Although Edward Gein was convicted of only two murders and doesn't meet the true definition of a serial killer, people categorize him as one. During the late 1950s near Plainfield, Wisconsin, Gein murdered women and robbed the graves of those whom he felt resembled his deceased mother. But murder and grave robbing didn't give Gein the satisfaction he desired. He used his victims' skin to create a body suit and a mask, which he then wore around the house. With the bodies he took from graves, he made furniture upholstered with the corpses' skin. When authorities raided Gein's home they discovered all kinds of items created from human body parts—skin lampshades, skull cap bowls, flesh socks, a nipple belt, and more. In addition, Gein stored organs in the refrigerator and in shoe boxes.

6. A term used to describe murder memorabilia.

Gein spent ten years in a mental institution before he was competent to stand trial. In 1968, Gein was found not guilty by reason of insanity. He lived in a mental institution until he died from cancer in 1984 at the age of seventy-seven.

Edward Gein influenced the creation of several fictional characters, most notably Norman Bates in the film *Psycho* (1960), James Gumb (otherwise known as Buffalo Bill) in the film *Silence of the Lambs* (1991), and Leatherface in *The Texas Chain Saw Massacre* (1974). *Three On a Meathook* (1973), *Deranged* (1974), *Maniac* (1980), *Nekromantik* (1987), and *Nekromantik 2* (1991) are other films whose fictional characters were "inspired" by Gein. The "true" story of Edward Gein is told in the 2000 film *Ed Gein*.

Films weren't the only media influenced by Gein. Bands such as Ed Gein (a metal punk band) and Ed Gein's Car are named after Gein, and the Seattle grunge Band TAD wrote a song titled, "Nipple Belt," which was on their 1989 debut album *God's Balls*. Gidget Gein (Brad Stewart) was a former bass player for Marilyn Manson's band whose stage name was derived from the TV show character Gidget and Ed Gein.

Harvey Murray Glatman (Lonely Hearts Killer): Twice Glatman posed as a photographer to lure models; the third time he lured his victim into a blind date, a date that ended in death. Each time Glatman photographed, raped, and murdered these women. A fourth victim doomed Glatman to his own fate, an execution in 1959, when a policeman heard Glatman accidentally shoot the woman while attempting to restrain her inside his car.

Christman Gniperdoliga: It is said that from 1568 to 1581 this German murdered close to a thousand people—that's approximately one person every 4.7 days.

Belle Gunness (Lady Bluebeard): Indiana authorities are uncertain as to the exact number of people murdered by Gunness but place the number between twelve and fourteen based on body parts discovered buried in shallow graves around her house. Some figures place the number as high as forty. Belle Gunness disappeared in 1908 and no one knows what happened to her.

Saeed Hanaei (Spider Killer): Saeed Hanaei was an Iranian construction worker who strangled to death at least sixteen prostitutes in 2000 because he believed prostitutes corrupted other people and were a "waste of blood." Maziar Bahari's 2002 documentary *And Along Came a Spider* explores the murders of these women and the murderer.

Robert Hansen: This serial killer loved to hunt . . . humans that is. During the 1980s, Hansen flew women in his private plane to his cabin in Alaska where he raped them and then released them. The only catch was that Hansen was on the hunt and his victims were the prey. Hansen confessed to killing more than seventeen women but cut a deal with the prosecutors that resulted in a conviction on four counts of murder. In exchange for the reduced sentence, Hansen led the authorities to the gravesites of his victims and would serve a sentence of 461 years plus life in a federal prison instead of a maximum security prison. He would not be afforded an opportunity for parole. *Butcher, Baker: A True Account of a Serial Murderer* (Onyx, 1991) by Walter Gilmour and Leland E. Hale recounts Hansen's life and his murders.

The Harp Boys: Known as America's first serial killers, cousins Micajah and Wiley Harp began killing in the late 1700s throughout Kentucky and Tennessee. They butchered their victims and often cut open the stomachs and filled them with stones before dumping the corpses in bodies of water. Micajah confessed to killing twenty people, but some believe the true number of victims is between thirty and forty. Harp's Head Road near Dixon, Kentucky, is named for the road where Micajah Harp's head was displayed after authorities killed him in 1799.

Donald Harvey (Angel of Death): This orderly believed he was ending the suffering of those he murdered, and working in a hospital gave him the perfect opportunity to commit his crimes without detection. Ultimately, authorities caught up to Donald Harvey and he was convicted of committing thirty-six murders over a seventeen-year period. However, Harvey admitted to killing approximately eighty-seven people. William Walen, Harvey's court-appointed defense attorney, and Bruce Martin examine the life of

Harvey and his horrific crimes in their book *Defending Donald Harvey: The Case of America's Most Notorious Angel-of-Death Serial Killer* (Emmis Books, 2005).

Hillside Stranglers (Kenneth Bianchi and Angelo Buono): These two cousins posed as undercover police officers from October 1977 to February 1978 and persuaded women and teenage girls to enter their unmarked car. Once they captured their prey, the pair tortured and raped the women and then strangled them and dumped the bodies on hillsides in Los Angeles.

Jack the Ripper: Who hasn't heard of Jack the Ripper? The serial killer who strangled and mutilated prostitutes in London during a nine-week period in 1888. The true number of victims remains disputed but ranges from five to seven, or more.

Generations later Jack the Ripper still fascinates the public. There are dozens upon dozens of nonfiction books, novels, songs, television shows, and films featuring Jack the Ripper, including the 2001 movie *From Hell* starring Johnny Depp. Jack the Ripper also has been featured in numerous comic books and manga. For the video enthusiast, Jack the Ripper appears in games dating back to the original PlayStation and Nintendo64. The newest video game with Jack the Ripper is the 2009 release, Sherlock Holmes vs. Jack the Ripper.

Edmund Kemper III: Fourteen was the age Edmund Kemper III took the life of his first victims when he murdered his grandparents. He later preyed on female student hitchhikers, killing six between May 1972 and February 1973. Instead of leaving the bodies behind, Kemper dissected the bodies and dumped the parts in the hills of California. But first Kemper sexually assaulted the corpses. Kemper also murdered his mother and a family friend.

Ken and Barbie Killers (Paul Bernardo and Karla Homolka): This married couple raped, tortured, and killed women together in the early 1990s. Although Paul admitted to Karla that he was the Scarborough rapist,[7] she stayed with him. Bernardo and Homolka

---

7. He committed more than fourteen rapes in the Scarborough, Ontario, area, later confirmed by DNA evidence.

claimed that Brett Easton Ellis's 1991 book *American Psycho* inspired them. The film *Karla* (2006) examines this couple and their crimes.

Peter Kürten (Vampire of Düsseldorf): This sadist terrorized Düsseldorf, Germany, from February to November 1929. Kürten stabbed, burned, sexually assaulted, and murdered females, mainly young girls. Investigators believed Kürten drank the blood of his victims, and the press nicknamed Kürten the Vampire of Düsseldorf. He was convicted on nine counts of murder and seven additional attempted murders in 1931 and was executed in 1932 via guillotine in the yard of the Klingelputz Prison. Anthony Neilson's 1991 play *Normal: The Düsseldorf Ripper* portrays the fictional life of Kürten. The play was later adapted into a 2009 film titled *Angels Gone* (English title) and *Normal* (Czech Republic title).

Robert Joe Long (Classified Ad Rapist): This predator used classified ads to gain access to homes with household goods for sale in Florida in the early 1980s. Once inside, he raped women. Soon rape no longer satisfied his desires and he turned to murdering women, mainly prostitutes. Long confessed to eight counts of murder and described his crimes in detail to the police. In addition to two death sentences, Long received thirty-four life sentences plus an additional 693 years in jail. On appeal, Long lost and was sentenced to death again. Amazingly, one potential victim, Lisa McVey, survived. She details her story (with coauthors Joy Wellman and Susan Repogle) in the book *Smoldering Embers* (Expanding Horizons, 2006). Other books on the subject include Anna Flowers's *Bound to Die: The Shocking True Story of Bobby Joe Long, America's Most Savage Serial Killer* (Pinnacle, 1999) and Bernie Ward's *Bobby Joe: In the Mind of a Monster: The Chilling Facts Behind the Story of a Brutal Serial Killer* (Cool Hand Communications, 1995).

Henry Lee Lucas: No one knows the true extent of Henry Lee Lucas's murders. Estimates range from five to five hundred, with Lucas supposedly confessing to approximately 350 murders, some of which were disproven. Some sources state he confessed to three thousand murders between 1975 and 1983, but many of those confessions were not considered believable for a variety of reasons. In

1960, Lucas was convicted of murdering his mother and sentenced to twenty to forty years in jail. A suicide attempt during his incarceration resulted in Lucas's admission to a mental hospital, but Lucas was paroled after serving only ten years. A year later, Lucas attempted to kidnap a girl at gunpoint and spent an additional five years in prison. Upon his release, he teamed up with Ottis Toole (see page 350 for more on Toole), and together they engaged in a killing spree across the country. Lucas used a knife to kill his victims or he strangled them, but sometimes he used other methods to avoid creating a pattern and elude the authorities.

It wasn't until Lucas was arrested for possession of a deadly weapon and began confessing murder after murder that the police realized the true evil they had captured. At his trial in 1985, Lucas was sentenced to death for the murder of a woman identified as "Orange Socks." However, it was later determined that the evidence convicting Lucas of the murder was slim and not enough to warrant the execution. Because Lucas was convicted of additional murders and was diagnosed as paranoid schizophrenic, George Bush (governor of Texas at the time) commuted Lucas's death sentence to six consecutive life sentences on June 26, 1998.

While in jail, Lucas confessed to killing Adam Walsh, the six-year-old son of John Walsh, creator and host of *America's Most Wanted*. Adam Walsh disappeared in 1981 outside a mall in Florida, and a nationwide manhunt ensued. Lucas later recanted his confession. In 2001, at the age of sixty-four, Lucas died in prison of natural causes.

Henry Lee Lucas has been featured in several documentaries, including *Myth of a Serial Killer—The Henry Lee Lucas Story* (1997) and *Drifter: Henry Lee Lucas* (2009). Two films based on Lucas's confessions, albeit loosely, are *Henry: Portrait of a Serial Killer* (1990) and *Henry: Portrait of a Serial Killer, Part 2* (1997). In addition, the 1988 play *The Road*, written by David Earl Jones, was based on Lucas's murders, and the song "While You Sleep, I Destroy Your World" by the band Nailbomb is dedicated to Lucas. For more information on Henry Lee Lucas, check out the following books: *The Confessions of Henry Lee Lucas* (Pocket Books, 1991) by Mike Cox and *Hand of Death: The Henry Lee Lucas Story* (Prescott Press, 1985) by Max Call.

Real vs. Fictional Serial Killers

▶ "Real life serial killers are unpredictable in every sense of the word. Just when we think we have one figured out, he or she changes his or her behavior (even just a little bit), adding another layer of mystery to what makes a person keep killing. . . . On television, in books and movies, serial killers are over the top—they do things that real serial killers simply would never do. I am speaking more of the cat-and-mouse than the actual method of murder. Most real-life serial killers will only tempt police and leave clues when they honestly think they are going to get away with it. For the serial, it is no fun if there is no chase. In fiction, we tend to see predictable behaviors that ultimately allow the protagonist to catch the killer, i.e., that 'mistake.'"—M. William Phelps is a crime/serial killer expert, investigative journalist, and the award-winning author of fourteen nonfiction books.

▶ "In pop culture they usually make serial killers diabolical, like Hannibal Lecter[8]—so smart, so intelligent. Hannibal Lecter is too smart, way too sophisticated. Serial killers are portrayed as if they are Doctor Jekyll and Mr. Hyde with two distinct personalities. It's not like that at all. . . . Buffalo Bill[9] was a composite of three different killers (Ted Bundy, Ed Gein, and Gary Heidnik). In real life you never really see anyone who has all those elements in one personality."—John Douglas is a former unit chief of the FBI's National Center for the Analysis of Violent Crimes and author of *Mind Hunter: Inside the FBI's Elite Serial Crime Unit* (with Mark Olshake; Pocket Books, 1997).

Pedro López (Monster of the Andes): Pedro López confessed to stalking, raping, and strangling over three hundred girls in Peru and Ecuador in the late 1970s and early 1980s. López was sentenced to life in prison for his deeds.

Lee Boyd Malvo and John Allen Muhammad (DC Snipers): This sniper team killed ten random victims in and around the

8. From *Silence of the Lambs*.
9. Also from *Silence of the Lambs*.

Washington, D.C., area over a three-week period in 2002. Three others were wounded.

Charles Manson: Like many serial killers, Charles Manson's crimes didn't begin with murder. Burglary and robbery were the crimes Manson committed in his teens. After a stint in reform school and various juvenile facilities for an assortment of crimes, Manson was incarcerated for a violation of his parole, but that didn't deter Manson from forging a treasury check. Again Manson was jailed, this time for ten years. At the completion of his term, Manson requested to remain in prison, but the request was denied. Perhaps only Manson knew what was to come next—the brutal murder of seven people over the course of several days.

Manson loved to write music on his guitar and listen to his favorite groups, including the Beatles, who he idolized. When the Beatles released their song "Helter Skelter," Manson saw true meaning in the lyrics, lyrics that reinforced his belief about an impending racial war, a belief he shared with his followers (unrelated people referred to as his family).

On July 31, 1969, Manson's family stabbed Gary Hinman to death, who Manson knew through the music business. Next Manson ordered his family to the Tate residence where they murdered four people, including Sharon Tate, the pregnant wife of Roman Polanski. These murders were brutal; the victims were stabbed a total of 102 times and also shot multiple times. A fifth person was not stabbed but shot to death. The following night Manson's family stabbed and killed two more victims. At all three crime scenes, the perpetrators left messages such as the word "war" carved into a victim's flesh. The words "helter skelter" and "political piggy" were written on the walls with blood. Had the family not been caught, they claimed to have a list of celebrities they intended to murder, including Elizabeth Taylor, Richard Burton, Frank Sinatra, and others. If Charles Manson and his family intended to shock the world, they certainly succeeded.

Following a highly publicized nine-and-a-half-month murder trial that required the sequestering of the jury for 225 days, the longest trial in American history at that time, Charles Manson and four of his followers (Charles "Tex" Watson, Patricia Krenwinkel,

Susan Atkins, and Linda Kasabian) were convicted of the seven murders. A fifth accomplice, Leslie van Houten, was convicted of two murders. Manson and his followers were sentenced to death, but in 1972 the death penalty was abolished in California and the sentences were changed to life imprisonment.

Prosecutor Vincent Bugliosi's book (with Curt Genry), *Helter Skelter: The True Story of the Manson Murders* (Bantam Books, 1995) provides a thorough look at these shocking murders. Other books on the subject include John and Rod Kenner's, *The Garbage People: The Trip to Helter-Skelter and Beyond with Charlie Manson and the Family* (Amok Books, 1995) and Bob Murphy's *Desert Shadows: A True Story of the Charles Manson Family in Death Valley* (Sagebrush Press, 1993).

The 1976 television show *Helter Skelter* was a fictionalized portrayal of the investigation leading to the capture of Manson and his family, and the film *The Six Degrees of Helter Skelter* (released on DVD in 2008) takes viewers on a tour of the locations related to the Manson murders.

In the music industry, Marilyn Manson, the lead singer of the heavy metal band by that name, derives his stage name from a combination of Marilyn Monroe and Charles Manson. Several songs written by Charles Manson have been recorded by rock groups, and many other songs refer to him. There was even an opera written about Manson titled *The Manson Family: An Opera* (Polygram Records, 1992).

Today, more than forty years after Manson's crimes, a fascination with Manson continues to exist. Manson receives fan mail in jail, there's an internet fan club that sells Manson memorabilia, and an Amazon.com search revealed a Charles Manson inflatable "icon" for sale.

Daisy de Melker: Arsenic was the weapon of choice for this South African killer who was hanged for poisoning her son in the 1930s. She also was suspected of poisoning two husbands, but the charges could not be substantiated. The 1993 four-part TV miniseries *Daisy de Melker* chronicles these events.

Ivan Milat: Between 1989 and 1992, Ivan Milat stabbed and shot to death seven backpackers in Australia. After police discovered

Do the Names We Give to Serial Killers Inform the Public Perception of the Killer?

"The public when informed of a serial killer and aspects to the crime has already nicknamed him. Sometimes it is similar to the one that sticks and other times not. And in some cases the killer names himself (Zodiac, BTK, etc.). The nickname may caution, upset, or make the public curious. . . . Naming of course gives publicity but it can also lead to information—an informed citizen may know what a symbol means, what a name really means. A name also can create a more cautious awareness. . . . As good as all that can be, names are glorifying to the serial killers. They give publicity and in many cases too much spotlight! That being said, they will continue being named and they will continue providing fear, information and caution."—Dr. Cynthia Lea Clark, Psy.D., Ph.D., MHt., has done over seventy interviews with serial killers and mass murderers.

---

weapons and items belonging to his victims in Milat's home, Milat was convicted of the murders and received seven sentences of life imprisonment (and an additional six years for assaulting another individual). Milat appealed his conviction, but the appeals were dismissed. *Wolf Creek*, a 2005 Australian horror film, was based loosely on Milat's crimes.

Herbert Mullin: The brutal slaughterer of thirteen people is what defined Herbert Mullin, who claimed he received permission to murder his victims from the victims themselves, messages that were communicated telepathically. Mullin also claimed he received telepathic messages from his father telling him to kill. It was determined that Mullin was legally insane when he committed three of the murders and legally sane when he committed the other ten. No one seems to dispute that Mullin suffered from paranoid schizophrenia, and Mullin was convicted of ten murders and sentenced to life in prison.

Charles Ng: With his partner Leonard Lake, Charles Ng videotaped and photographed the torture, rape, and murder of their victims in northern California. Ng and Lake kept their victims in a small concealed room contained within a bunker located on the property near the cabin where Ng and Lake lived. Inside the cabin, police discovered military equipment, weapons, and a diary detailing the pair's crimes (which they referred to as "Operation Miranda"). Bodies and evidence of the murders were found nearby on the property. Evidence implicated the pair in more than twenty-five murders; however, Ng was charged with twelve murders based on the collected evidence. He was convicted of killing eleven and sentenced to die. After the police arrested Lake, he committed suicide using cyanide pills he had secreted in his shirt collar.

Dennis Andrew Nilsen: London was the killing ground for Dennis Andrew Nilsen between 1978 and 1993 when Nilsen strangled and drowned fifteen men and boys. The need to dispose of the bodies led Nilsen to cut the bodies into pieces and flush the parts down the toilet, which ultimately clogged the waste disposal system and drew the attention of the authorities. Nilsen was convicted of six murders and two attempted murders and was sentenced to life imprisonment.

Clifford Olson: Clifford Olson confessed to murdering eleven children in British Columbia in 1982 and was sentenced to serve life. According to his July 2006 internal parole records, Olson led the authorities to the victims' bodies in exchange for $100,000 paid in trust to his wife and children. Jon Ferry and Damian Inwood's 1982 book *The Olson Murders* (Cameo Books) and Ian Mulgrew's *Final Payoff: The True Price of Convicting Clifford Robert Olson* (Seal Books, 1990) provide a more in-depth portrait of this serial killer and the circumstances surrounding his body exchange deal.

Dr. Marcel Petiot (Dr. Satan): As if it wasn't hard enough escaping Nazi-occupied France, some Jewish refugees found their death at the hands of Dr. Marcel Petiot after he promised (for a price) to help them find refuge in South America. According to Marilyn Z. Tomlin's 2007 article in *Crime Magazine* titled "Dr. Petiot Will See You Now," police and pathologists were unable to explain how Petiot killed his victims. However, it is believed that Petiot dismembered the bodies and then used fire and quicklime to dispose of the remains. Petiot was found guilty of murdering twenty-six people (although he admitted to killing sixty-three) and was executed by guillotine in 1946. The Belgian band Univers Zéro recorded a song titled "Docteur Petiot" on their 1977 album *1313*.

Alexander Pichushkin (Chessboard Killer): Russia's most infamous serial killer, Alexander Pichushkin, first killed at the age of eighteen out of jealousy but didn't kill again until 2001. Pichushkin lured his victims—mostly elderly men who played chess with him in a Moscow park—to a quiet area and then attacked them with a hammer; however, sometimes he drowned his victims. According to Pichushkin's testimony, his original goal was to kill sixty-four people, one for each square on a chessboard, but that changed, and he believed he would have killed indefinitely had he not been caught in 2006. Varying sources state that Pichushkin confessed to between sixty-one and sixty-three murders; he led the police to the bodies of many of his victims. Pichushkin was convicted on forty-eight counts of murder and sentenced to life imprisonment. Although many wanted to see Pichushkin put to death, Russia had suspended capital punishment, making life imprisonment the greatest punishment available under the law at the time.

Robert Pickton: This Canadian ran a pig butchering business on a seventeen-acre farm near Vancouver and murdered women, including a significant number of prostitutes, beginning in the mid-1980s

---

Monster of Florence

"Of any list of serial killers the Monster would just about top the list for pathology, brutality—and aptitude. Using a word like 'aptitude' may seem strange, but here was a killer who coolly murdered 14 people over a period of 11 years in public areas and got away with it, despite the biggest and most expensive criminal investigation in modern Italian history. Over a hundred thousand men were investigated as part of the case—and they still didn't catch him."—Douglas Preston has published twenty-two books, including *The Monster of Florence* (Grand Central Publishing, 2009), which he coauthored with Italian journalist Mario Spezi.

---

until his arrest in 2002. Apparently Pickton ran his victims' bodies through a wood chipper and then fed the pieces to his pigs. According to a January 25, 2007, article by Deborah Jones in *The Australian*, Pickton was upset that he could kill only forty-nine women before he was caught because he had wanted to kill fifty.

After a twenty-one-month search of Pickton's farm, Pickton was charged with twenty-six murders, and convicted of six, in 2007. Because of the enormity of the evidence, the number of murders, and the anticipated difficulty the jury would have to comprehend everything at once, the case was divided in two parts. The British Columbian Crown agreed not to try Pickton on the additional twenty counts unless Pickton won the appeal of his original conviction because he already faced life in prison without the eligibility of parole. Pickton's appeal was denied, but his legal proceedings continue. As if Pickton's true life horror was not enough shock, a 2005 American horror movie, *Killer Pickton*, was released in Australia in 2007—legal complaints by the Canadian government forced its withdrawal.

Jesse Pomeroy: The year 1874 was when Jesse Pomeroy began mutilating and murdering young children. Although Pomeroy does not fit the criteria defined earlier for a serial killer, he is considered one because he began murdering in his midteens and it is assumed he would have continued throughout his life had he not been caught. Pomeroy was sentenced to life in solitary confinement and died in 1932. Due to his age he was spared death by hanging.

Dorothea Puente: Elderly and disabled individuals who checked into Dorothea Puente's boarding house were victims of this serial killer's greed. Puente cashed her boarders' Social Security and disability checks and used the money for herself. Those who complained were murdered,[10] and she continued to collect their checks and cash them. Police became suspicious when social workers reported people missing and neighbors complained about the smell

---

10. We'd make a sick joke about that old roach motel commercial where roaches check in but they don't check out, but we won't—we're talking about serial killers after all, and there's nothing funny about them.

coming from the backyard where Puente buried her victims. Puente was tried on nine counts of murder, but convicted for three after the jury failed to reach a verdict on the other six. She was sentenced to life in prison without parole. For more details, check out William P. Wood's 1994 book *The Bone Garden: A Chilling True Excursion into the Dark Heart of a Female Serial Killer* (Pocket Books) and Carla Norton's *Disturbed Ground: The True Story of a Diabolical Female Serial Killer* (HarperCollins, 1994).

Dennis Rader (BTK[11] Killer): Ten people were tortured and murdered by Dennis Rader between 1974 and 1991 in Kansas. In 1993, investigators assigned to the case collected DNA samples from over two hundred suspects in the BTK killings but failed to identify Rader as the killer. Rader sent letters to the authorities and signed them BTK, which he based on his modus operandi; however, Rader was not apprehended until 2005 when—according to a March 6, 2005, *New York Times* article by Monica Davey— "Suspect in 10 Kansas Murders Lived an Intensely Ordinary Life"—police caught the BTK killer by using a computer disk that BTK sent to the media and DNA evidence. BTK also sent a slew of other items to the media, including letters and other objects related to the killings. For his crimes, Rader received ten consecutive life sentences. It's quite likely that Rader would have received the death penalty if the law were different at the time he committed his murders, but Kansas did not reinstate the death penalty until three years after Radner's last murder.

John Douglas's *Inside the Mind of BTK: The True Story Behind the Thirty-Year Hunt for the Notorious Wichita Serial Killer* (Jossey-Bass, 2007) offers an extensive look into the life and crimes of Rader. And films on this subject include *The Hunt for the BTK Killer* (2005), *B.T.K. Killer* (2005), and *B.T.K.* (2008).

Richard Munoz Ramirez (Night Stalker): Ramirez stalked people at their California homes, then raped, murdered, and burglarized his victims from 1984 to 1985. Sometimes, Ramirez mutilated his victims. Ramirez was convicted in 1989 of forty-three crimes,

11. Stands for bind, torture, and kill.

including thirteen counts of murder and five attempted murders, and was sentenced to death.

Raya and Sakina: The first Egyptian women to be executed, Raya and Sakina murdered seventeen people, and their own husbands, from 1919 until their capture three years later.

Angel Maturino Resendez (Railroad Killer): This illegal alien, originally from Mexico, crossed Texas and five other states via train to find and kill his victims until he was apprehended in 1999. Some victims he shot, others he bludgeoned to death with objects he found at the scene. In addition, some female victims were raped prior to death. Resendez was charged with the murder of seven, suspected in many others, and convicted for one. He was executed in 2006, at which time he begged for forgiveness.

Gary Ridgway (Green River Killer): A means to pleasure and empowerment—that's how Gary Ridgway viewed his victims, mainly prostitutes or runaways he strangled, raped, and tortured in Washington State during the 1980's and 1990's. According to Terry McCarthy and Nathan Thornburg in their 2002 *Time* magazine article "River of Death," Gary Ridgway killed many of his victims in 1983, sometimes five women a month. All told, Gary Ridgway

---

The Fascination with Serial Killers

"The fascination with serial killers seems multifaceted: an attempt to understand what makes them tick, so-to-speak, by reading about or seeing what they do; learning how to avoid becoming a victim, and so forth . . . some have theorized that we have become so interested in them because of our desire to feel compassion for the victim, or perhaps to feel a sense of relief that the victim was not oneself or someone close to us. In many ways our interest in serial killers is a mystery itself—one might not be so fascinated if they saw in real life, or even in photos, the atrocities created by such people . . . Serial killers are bad people, simply and plainly put, that we should never idolize in our fascination with them."
—Gary C. King is the author of numerous true-crime books, including *The Murder of Meredith Kercher* (John Blake, 2010).

---

murdered at least forty-nine women, but that number may be low—some authorities believe he may have killed ninety women.

In an attempt to confuse the police, Ridgway would occasionally dump the bodies with assorted items such as cigarette butts and trash. Ridgway, a former truck painter, was arrested in 2001 after DNA evidence linked him to four murders; however, Ridgway pleaded guilty to forty-eight counts of aggravated murder and received life in jail instead of the death penalty in exchange for his assistance in locating his victims' remains. According to a November 2003 article on CNN.com, "Green River Killer Avoids Death in Plea Deal," Ridgway admitted to the killings in court. He also stated that he killed prostitutes because he believed he wouldn't get caught because no one would look for a missing prostitute—guess he just wasn't as smart as he thought.

The Search for the Green River Killer by C. Smith and T. Guillen (Penguin Books, 1991) and *The Riverman* by Robert Keppel (Pocket Books, 1995) have detailed information on Ridgway and his killings. David Reichert's book, *Chasing the Devil: My Twenty-Year Quest to Capture the Green River Killer* was used to create the 2008 TV mini-series *The Capture of the Green River Killer*, and the 2004 TV show *The Riverman* was a fictionalized account of real FBI interviews with Ted Bundy that occurred in the hopes of gaining insight into the mind of the Green River Killer.

Dayton Leroy Rogers (Molalla Forest Killer): In the 1980s, Molalla Forest in Oregon was the dumping ground for six of Dayton Leroy Rogers's victims. Rogers bound his victims in the nude then tortured them with a knife or a hacksaw before death relieved their pain. The year 1989 found Rogers convicted of seven murders and sentenced to death. Although it is believed Rogers killed an eighth victim, no evidence was found linking him to the crime. After his death sentence was overturned twice on appeal, Rogers was sentenced to death once again. Gary C. King's 1992 book *Blood Lust: Portrait of a Serial Sex Killer* (NAL/Dutton) gives a more in-depth look into this serial killer.

Daniel Harold Rolling (Gainesville Ripper): A knife was the weapon of choice for Daniel Harold Rolling who brutally murdered five students in Florida over three days in August 1990. All of the victims were posed in sexual positions, several were raped, and others were mutilated. Rolling was dubbed the Gainesville Ripper because his murders were similar to those of Jack the Ripper. Rolling received the death penalty for his crimes and was executed in 2006.

Michael B. Ross: Six teenage girls lost their lives at the hands of Michael B. Ross when he kidnapped, raped, and strangled them in Connecticut between 1982 and 1984. Ross admitted to his crimes and was sentenced to death. He appealed the death sentence but the sentence was upheld; he was executed in 2005.

John Arthur Shawcross (Genesee River Killer): Rochester, New York, was the killing ground for John Arthur Shawcross, who strangled to death (and often beat and mutilated) eleven women from 1988 to 1990 and then dumped the bodies near the Genesee River. Sentenced to 250 years in prison, Shawcross died of a heart attack in 2008.

Dr. Harold Frederick Shipman (Dr. Death): Although convicted of murdering fifteen of his patients with fatal doses of heroin, most of them elderly, this British doctor may have killed many more with numbers ranging from sixteen to more than 450. Officials, however, placed the number between 215 and 260, according to a January 13, 2004, BBC News report. Jailed for life, Shipman was found hanged in his cell in 2004.

Lucian Staniak (Red Spider): Lucian Staniak's modus operandi was to strangle or stab women, then rape and/or mutilate the bodies. He confessed to murdering over twenty people in Poland from 1964 to 1967, but he was convicted of only six. Sentenced to death, Staniak was sent to an asylum instead when it was determined he was insane at the time of the murders.

Peter Stumpp (Werewolf of Bedrug): In Germany in the 1500s, Stumpp murdered sixteen or more people. He strangled, bludgeoned, and ripped apart their bodies, often mutilating the remains. Stumpp also admitted to eating the brains of some of his victims. For his crimes, Stumpp suffered a horrible death at the hands of society. Hot pincers tore away his flesh, and his extremities were crushed with an axe. Finally, he was decapitated and burned.

The supernatural villain Ubel Griswold in Jonathan Maberry's Pine Deep trilogy[12] is based on Stumpp. And, the lyrics of the song "The Werewolf of Bedburg Peter Stumpp" by the band Macabre describe Stumpp's crimes, capture, and death.

Ahmad Suradji: This Indonesian man believed ritual slayings would give him supernatural powers. With the help of his wife, Suradji killed forty-two females over a period of eleven years by burying them up to their waists, then strangling them. Once the victims were dead, Suradji ingested their saliva. After admitting to the murders, Suradji was convicted and subsequently executed by firing squad in 2008. His wife received a life sentence for her role in the crimes.

Peter William Sutcliffe (Yorkshire Ripper): For almost six years in the mid-1970s, Peter William Sutcliffe succeeded in committing his ritualistic murders. A ball-peen hammer was his weapon of choice, which he used to hit his victims over the head. Then, with a knife and a Phillips-head screwdriver, Sutcliffe stabbed his victims repeatedly in their chests and abdomens. All told, Sutcliffe murdered thirteen women in England and admitted to those killings. He was sentenced to life imprisonment after it was decided Sutcliffe was sane at the time of the murders; however, after a physical altercation at the jail, Sutcliffe was transferred to a mental hospital.

Dr. Michael Swango (Doctor of Death): To do no harm was not the oath this doctor adhered to. It is believed Swango is responsible for murdering thirty to sixty of his patients; however, he was convicted of murdering only four, three in New York and one in Ohio. Swango administered poison or overdosed his victims. For more information about Dr. Michael Swango we recommend *Blind Eye—The Terrifying Story of a Doctor Who Got Away with Murder* by Pulitzer Prize–winning author James B. Stewart (Simon & Schuster, 1999).

---

12. *Ghost Road Blues* (Pinnacle 2006), *Dead Man's Song* (2007), and *Bad Moon Rising* (2008).

Maria Swanenburg: A Dutch murderer in the 1880s who used arsenic, Maria Swanenburg was convicted of killing three and was suspected of attempting to kill between fifty and ninety others. She was sentenced to life imprisonment and died in 1915.

Ottis Toole: Together with Henry Lee Lucas, Ottis Toole murdered and cannibalized his victims. Although Toole claims he murdered

---

Male vs. Female Serial Killers

"Males can kill at will, without much thought or even rage put into it. For the male serial killer, the desire to kill is wired deeply in a broken psyche from childhood, generally some sort of trauma in the form of sexual abuse or sexual fantasies relating to violence, such as a father who took the child to porno movies or forced him to watch as he took a prostitute. It doesn't take much for that 'demon,' if you will, to emerge and begin a rampage later in life in the male. There are endless triggers. Male serials are also prone to use more violent means of killing—i.e., throat slashing; vicious, multiple stabbing; blunt objects; etc. Males will also torture their victims.

"For the female serial killer, the act of murder is far more complicated and emotionally motivated. She will plan her crimes for months, maybe even years, generally focusing on someone who reminds her of her abuser, or the person in her childhood who 'wronged' and/or hurt her. She uses all of her strengths as a means to achieve her goals: sexuality, charm, humility, shyness, the simple fact that she is a seemingly harmless female. Whereas the male will kill with any object or weapon available to him, the female chooses poison, fire, or a means of killing that may seem not as violent. She rarely chooses extreme violence when killing and almost never allows her victim to know what she is doing. Remember, for the female serial the murder is more passionate and deeply ingrained in the emotional wreckage of her life up to that point. She uses murder as a way to deal with trauma; whereas the male serial will use murder as a way to feed the desire to kill. Killing, for a male serial, is generally in response to an inner identity. For the female, serial murder is a response to trauma."—M. William Phelps is a crime/serial killer expert.

---

his first victim at age fourteen, that he killed four others prior to meeting Lucas, and that he killed hundreds with Lucas, Toole was convicted of only three murders and sentenced to death in 1984, a conviction that was changed to six consecutive terms of life imprisonment after Toole was diagnosed with paranoid schizophrenia. In 1983, Lucas confessed to the 1981 kidnapping and killing of six-year-old Adam Walsh, one of the most widely publicized cases in the United States; however, doubt about the confession caused the case to remain open. Toole died in a prison hospital in 1996.

Henry Louis Wallace (Charlotte Strangler): Beginning in 1992 and lasting until his arrest in 1994, Henry Louis Wallace raped and strangled (and sometimes stabbed) African American women he knew in Charlotte, North Carolina. Wallace confessed to the murders stating he committed them for sex. At a later date, he stated he was coerced into confessing and that he did not commit the murders. Wallace was sentenced to death in 1997 for nine murders.

Fred and Rose West: Over a twenty-year period, this English couple lured runaways with the prospect of a job and then proceeded to rape, torture, and kill them. When authorities searched the couple's home, they discovered remains belonging to the Wests' daughter, who had been missing since 1987. Eight additional bodies were found on the property, and two bodies were discovered at a former home. Rose was convicted of ten murders and sentenced to life; however, Fred committed suicide in jail while awaiting trial in 1995. It is believed that the Wests may have been devil worshippers and that the killings were sacrificial. Over a half dozen books were written on this couple including Howard Sounes's *Fred and Rose: The Full Story of Fred and Rose West and the Gloucester House of Horrors* (Little, Brown, 1995) and John Bennett's *The Cromwell Street Murders: The Detective's Story* (The History Press, Sutton Publishing, 2005).

Randall Brent Woodfield (I-5 Killer): Woodfield was convicted of murder, attempted murder, and two counts of sodomy and was sentenced to life in prison plus 125 years. Woodfield is suspected of thirteen or more murders along I-5—the interstate that runs along the west coast of the United States.

Aileen Wuornos: This prostitute used a .22-caliber gun to murder seven men in Florida; each of the victims was shot multiple times. Wuornos initially claimed the murders were in self-defense and that the men attacked her, but later she stated she murdered out of fear resulting from several past rapes and that the men didn't hurt her. A jury found Wuornos guilty of first-degree murder and recommended she be sentenced to death. Wuornos then confessed to five additional murders and received an additional five death sentences. She was never charged for the seventh murder because the body was not found. In 2002, Wuornos was executed. Films about Wuornos include *Overkill: The Aileen Wuornos Story* (1992), *Aileen Wuornos: The Selling of a Serial Killer* (2002), and *Monster* (2003) where Charlize Theron amazingly transforms into this serial killer and gives a riveting performance without sensationalizing Wuornos or her story. Theron won an Oscar for her role and the film was nominated for over a dozen awards. For more about Aileen Wuornos and her crimes, check out *Dead Ends* (Warner Books, 1992) by Michael Reynolds.

Yang Xinhai: In China, over a period of four years, Xinhai murdered sixty-seven people, raped twenty-three women, and seriously injured ten others. Xinhai confessed to his crimes and was executed in 2004.

Zodiac Killer: The year was 1966 and fear was not yet in the air when the Zodiac Killer claimed his first victim in San Francisco, California. But that didn't last for long. One by one the Zodiac Killer murdered couples near or in their cars while taunting the authorities and the media with cryptograms and letters containing unpublicized details about the murders. At times, the Zodiac Killer insisted newspapers publish his letters on the front page or a killing spree would ensue. The Zodiac Killer also expressed plans to bomb a school bus, but the attack never occurred.

Police investigated over 2,500 suspects but were unable to identify the Zodiac Killer, and the cases were never solved. Perhaps if the authorities had the forensic technology available today they would have been able to definitively identify the Zodiac Killer from the narrowed suspect pool. They certainly didn't fail to identify the Zodiac Killer from lack of trying.

The murders stopped abruptly several years after they started, but the letters to the media continued until 1974. Sources state that the Zodiac Killer claimed to have murdered between seventeen and thirty-seven people; however, evidence places the number murdered at five. Is it possible the Zodiac Killer is still alive? No one knows the answer.

Robert Graysmith's book *Zodiac* (Berkley, 1997) takes an in-depth look at the murderer who terrorized San Francisco and is reported to be the basis for several movies, including *The Limbic Region* (1996) and *Zodiac* (2007).[13] The film *The Zodiac Killer* (1972) takes a look at who this murderer could be, and *The Zodiac* (2006) examines the impact of the murders from a different perspective—that of the friends and families of the victims.

The Zodiac Killer turns up in television, too. Michael R. Perry's killer Avatar in the show *Millennium* was originally the Zodiac Killer, but the name was changed at the insistence of network executives. The Zodiac Killer also appears on *Cold Case Files* (episode 51), *Unsolved Mysteries* (two episodes with air dates of September 20, 1996, and December 27, 1996), *America's Most Wanted* (air date March 8, 2003), *Nash Bridges* (episode titled "Zodiac"; air date November 1, 1996), and *Criminal Minds* (air date March 22, 2006) where an unidentified suspect is compared to the Zodiac Killer.

Fiction also features the Zodiac Killer. In David Baldacci's 2004 novel *Hour Game* (Grand Central Publishing), a murderer commits his crimes using a similar modus operandi as the Zodiac Killer. And the graphic comic, *Killer Komix* (Headpress 1992), contains a fifty-page piece about the Zodiac Killer by Steven Friel, aptly titled "The Zodiac." In addition, numerous songs make reference to the Zodiac Killer, including those by the San Francisco punk band the Zodiac Killers.

---

13. Also based on *Zodiac Unmasked: The Identity of America's Most Elusive Serial Killer.*

APPENDIX A:
THE OFCS TOP 100
VILLAINS OF ALL TIME

Reprinted with the permission of the Online Film Critics Society, ofcs.org.

1. Darth Vader (David Prowse/James Earl Jones [voice])—*Star Wars*, etc.
2. Hannibal Lecter (Anthony Hopkins)—*The Silence of the Lambs*, etc.
3. Norman Bates (Anthony Perkins)—*Psycho*, etc.
4. Hans Gruber (Alan Rickman)—*Die Hard*
5. Frank Booth (Dennis Hopper)—*Blue Velvet*
6. Rev. Harry Powell (Robert Mitchum)—*Night of the Hunter*
7. HAL 9000 (Douglas Rain [voice])—*2001: A Space Odyssey*
8. The Wicked Witch of the West (Margaret Hamilton)—*The Wizard of Oz*
9. Graf Orlock (Max Schreck)—*Nosferatu*
10. Khan Noonien Singh (Ricardo Montalban)—*Star Trek II: The Wrath of Khan*
11. Alex (Malcolm McDowell)—*A Clockwork Orange*
12. Keyzer Soze (mystery actor's name withheld)—*The Usual Suspects*
13. Harry Lime (Orson Welles)—*The Third Man*
14. Amon Goeth (Ralph Fiennes)—*Schindler's List*
15. Michael Myers (a.k.a the Shape) (Nick Castle)—*Halloween*
16. The Joker (Jack Nicholson)—*Batman* (1989)
17. Nurse Ratched (Louise Fletcher)—*One Flew Over the Cuckoo's Nest*

18. Mrs. Iselin (Angela Lansbury)—*The Manchurian Candidate*
19. The shark (himself)—*Jaws*
20. John Doe (Kevin Spacey)—*Se7en*
21. T-800 (Arnold Schwarzenegger)—*The Terminator*, etc.
22. Annie Wilkes (Kathy Bates)—*Misery*
23. John "Jack" Daniel Torrance (Jack Nicholson)—*The Shining*
24. Frank (Henry Fonda)—*Once Upon a Time in the West*
25. Salieri (F. Murray Abraham)—*Amadeus*
26. Hans Beckert (Peter Lorre)—*M*
27. Chad (Aaron Eckhart)—*In the Company of Men*
28. The alien (himself)—*Alien*, etc.
29. Uncle Charlie (Joseph Cotten)—*Shadow of a Doubt*
30. Freddy Krueger (Robert Englund)—*A Nightmare On Elm Street*, etc.
31. Col. Walter E. Kurtz (Marlon Brando)—*Apocalypse Now*
32. Noah Cross (John Huston)—*Chinatown*
33. Alex Forrest (Glenn Close)—*Fatal Attraction*
34. Gunnery Sergeant Hartman (R. Lee Ermey)—*Full Metal Jacket*
35. Roy Batty (Rutger Hauer)—*Blade Runner*
36. Mr. Smith (Hugo Weaving)—*The Matrix*
37. Dracula (Bela Lugosi)—*Dracula* (1931)
38. Christian Szell (Laurence Olivier)—*Marathon Man*
39. T-1000 (Robert Patrick)—*The Terminator 2: Judgment Day*
40. Mr. Potter (Lionel Barrymore)—*It's a Wonderful Life*
41. Pazuzu (Mercedes McCambridge [voice])—*The Exorcist*
42. Captain Hank Quinlan (Orson Welles)—*Touch of Evil*
43. Norman Stansfield (Gary Oldman)—*Leon* (The Professional)
44. Max Cady (Robert De Niro)—*Cape Fear* (1991)
45. Auric Goldfinger (Gert Frobe)—*Goldfinger*
46. King Richard III (Ian McKellan)—*Richard III*
47. Bruno Antony (Robert Walker)—*Strangers on a Train*
48. Albert Spica (Michael Gambon)—*The Cook, the Thief, His Wife and Her Lover*
49. Phyllis Dietrichson (Barbara Stanwyck)—*Double Indemnity*
50. Patrick Bateman (Christian Bale)—*American Psycho*
51. John Ryder (Rutger Hauer)—*The Hitcher*
52. Tommy DeVito (Joe Pesci)—*Goodfellas*

53. Eve Harrington (Anne Baxter)—*All About Eve*
54. Rhoda (Patty McCormack)—*The Bad Seed*
55. Tommy Udo (Richard Widmark)—*Kiss of Death*
56. Arthur "Cody" Jarrett (James Cagney)—*White Heat*
57. The queen (Lucille La Verne [voice])—*Snow White and the Seven Dwarfs*
58. Mrs. Danvers (Judith Anderson)—*Rebecca*
59. Max Cady (Robert Mitchum)—*Cape Fear* (1962)
60. Jack D. Ripper (Sterling Hayden)—*Dr. Strangelove*
61. Dr. Evil (Mike Myers)—*Austin Powers: International Man of Mystery*, etc.
62. Travis Bickle (Robert De Niro)—*Taxi Driver*
63. Catherine Trammell (Sharon Stone)—*Basic Instinct*
64. Leatherface (Gunnar Hansen)—*The Texas Chainsaw Massacre*
65. Gordon Gekko (Michael Douglas)—*Wall Street*
66. Minnie Castevet (Ruth Gordon)—*Rosemary's Baby*
67. Mountain men (Bill McKinney and Herbert "Cowboy" Coward)—*Deliverance*
68. Alonzo Harris (Denzel Washington)—*Training Day*
69. Jane Hudson (Bette Davis)—*What Ever Happened to Baby Jane?*
70. Cruella De Vil (Betty Lou Gerson [voice])—*101 Dalmatians*
71. The evil Maria (Brigitte Helm)—*Metropolis*
72. The truck driver (Carey Loftin)—*Duel*
73. Booth (John Malkovich)—*In the Line of Fire*
74. Erik (Lon Chaney)—*The Phantom of the Opera*, (1925)
75. Wendy Kroy (Linda Fiorentino)—*The Last Seduction*
76. Henry (Michael Rooker)—*Henry: Portrait of a Serial Killer*
77. Don Logan (Ben Kingsley)—*Sexy Beast*
78. Roat (Alan Arkin)—*Wait Until Dark*
79. Mr. Blonde (Michael Madsen)—*Reservoir Dogs*
80. Aguirre (Klaus Kinski)—*Aguirre, the Wrath of God*
81. Tyler Durden (Brad Pitt)—*Fight Club*
82. Catwoman (Michelle Pfeiffer)—*Batman Returns*
83. Archibald Cunningham (Tim Roth)—*Rob Roy*
84. Mrs. Robinson (Anne Bancroft)—*The Graduate*
85. Major Heinrich Strasser (Conrad Veidt)—*Casablanca*
86. Biff Tannen (Thomas F. Wilson)—*Back to the Future*, etc.

87. Ed Rooney (Jeffrey Jones)—*Ferris Bueller's Day Off*
88. Roger Smith (himself)—*Roger & Me*
89. Little Bill Daggett (Gene Hackman)—*Unforgiven*
90. The monster (Boris Karloff)—*Frankenstein*, etc.
91. Ming the Merciless (Max von Sydow)—*Flash Gordon* (1980)
92. Henry Morrison/Jerry Blake/Bill Hodgkins (Terry O'Quinn)—*The Stepfather*
93. Mystery Villain (actor's name withheld)—*Primal Fear*
94. Jack Wilson (Jack Palance)—*Shane*
95. Mark Lewis (Carl Boehm)—*Peeping Tom*
96. Captain William Bligh (Charles Laughton)—*Mutiny on the Bounty* (1935)
97. The Lord of Darkness (Tim Curry)—*Legend*
98. Krug (David Hess)—*The Last House on the Left*
99. Clare Quilty (Peter Sellers)—*Lolita*
100. Dr. Caligari (Werner Krauss)—*The Cabinet of Dr. Caligari*

APPENDIX B:
SPIRIT SUPERSTITIONS

Not surprisingly, there is an abundance of superstition and lore regarding deaths, ghosts, ghostly phenomena, and anything associated with the dead. Superstitions have given us one way to explain what seems to be inexplicable, and to protect ourselves from the ruthless whims of fate.

Animal omens

▸ A large black snail appearing on the doorstep of a home may be the spirit of a deceased family member.

▸ In certain African tribal societies, a white bird flying into a prayer hut bears the spirit of an ancestor who brings blessings.

▸ The cry of an owl symbolizes death. Where it builds a nest, ghosts will haunt for as long as the bird stays.

▸ The crowing of a rooster signals wandering ghosts that it is time for them to disappear until nightfall.

▸ A big black moth in the house means a deceased one is just visiting reincarnated through that moth.

Binding a ghost or spirit

▸ Tie seven, fourteen, or twenty-one knots into a rope, while naming the soul you wish to restrict. Bury this outside the home to keep that spirit out, or burn the rope to release the spirit into another existence.

- In Malaysia, sacred water combined with incense is said to expel the grasshopper demon.

- Pinching a possessed person and blowing on his or her head banishes the unwanted spirit and returns the human spirit to its body. This tradition also comes from Malaysia.

- If someone is possessed with the spirit of sickness, have him or her drink coconut juice, followed by a bland diet for at least one week. This person should try to maintain emotional and digestive balance from that time forward to keep the malevolent spirit away.

- In the sixteenth century, a common recipe for banishing unwanted spirits was to fast, pray, and drink wine mixed with holy oil, and carry appropriate religious charms or relics.

- Scatter dill mixed with salt, fennel, and mullein all around the area in which the ghost or spirit is believed to reside.

- Burning frankincense and myrrh may not completely banish spirits, but it helps to give them peace and rest.

- Hang a garlic wreath over your doorway. Whenever a spirit plagues you, bite a piece—then toss it away from the house. This carries the spirit with it.

- Gather knot grass by the waning moon. Take this to the area where the ghost abides and tie one knot in it. Bury this to confine the spirit to the grave.

- Burying a person's shadow in a specific location prior to his or her death will prevent the spirit from leaving that spot.

- In Denmark, there is a tradition that you can pin a ghost to a location using a wooden post. If the post is pulled up, however, the ghost will be freed.

Preventing ghosts

▸ Closing the eyes of the dead before burial keeps their spirits from wandering.

▸ In Greece, dancing around the burial site of an enemy was a way to keep that person's spirit from returning for revenge.

▸ Wash the threshold of your house immediately after a dead body is removed. This keeps the spirit of that person from returning.

▸ Within the burial site, always place a cross of iron. This will keep the spirit of that person in the grave.

▸ Egyptians wrapped their mummies in sweet spices so the soul smelled pleasant to the guardians of the next world, who would then allow the soul to enter its new existence.

▸ Provide the body with things that it loved in life—a few coins, some good wine, and so on. This brings contentment to the spirit.

▸ In Spain, to guarantee that the soul rests peacefully, people at the wake danced seven times around the body.

▸ In India, placing a sprig of basil in the coffin provided the spirit with a peaceful journey.

▸ Open all the doors and windows in the area where the person died so the spirit can have quick passage.

▸ If a person did not receive a proper burial or cremation, give him or her one. This will stop a haunting.

Protection from the dead

▸ Lodestone is a protective talisman against spirits. This may be due to its association with iron.

▸ Plant houseleeks on your roof. The Latin name for this plant, *sempervivium*, means "ever living," and the dead cannot bear its presence.

▶ Cover all your mirrors immediately after a death. This keeps a spirit from using them as a portal or getting confused.

▶ Jump into running water, or cross it. A spirit cannot follow you there: moving water represents life.

▶ The Aztecs considered jimsonweed a sacred plant that would protect from ghosts any area where it grew.

▶ Bonfires and other light sources drive away malevolent spirits.

▶ In the Middle Ages, people left candles near their beds to drive away spirits.

▶ On Hallows specifically, people carried turnips with candles inside—the original of the jack-o'-lantern—for protection.

▶ Place a sprig of rosemary inside a seashell. Bind it within, using a red thread. Carry this with you as an amulet against ghosts.

▶ Hang rowan and St. John's Wort over the doorway of your home, and no malicious spirits can enter therein.

▶ Write the letters *AGLA* in the center of a hexagram and carry this token with you. The hexagram repels evil spirits and misfortune. Cabalists used this formula to banish spirits.

▶ Angelica and nettle worn or carried as an amulet will protect the bearer from evil spirits.

▶ Bathing in fennel water, or drinking it, protects one against the spirit of disease.

▶ In Greece, growing violets in or around a home was considered an effective ward against wandering spirits.

Seeing or attracting ghosts

▶ Mayas of the Yucatan draw a chalk line from the grave to the hearth of the deceased's home. The spirit can then find its way back to visit, whenever it wishes.

▶ If you know a spirit's true name, you can evoke it.

▶ Ghosts are more readily seen and contacted at midnight (the time in between day and night), and on the anniversary of their death.

- ▸ Medieval spell books say that burning a mixture of aloe, musk, saffron, vervain, and pepper in a cemetery will allow you to see the spirits that reside there.

- ▸ In the Middle Ages, some felt that washing a clean piece of steel in mugwort juice would summon a spirit.

- ▸ Write the name of the spirit you wish to evoke on parchment and burn it while repeating sacred words to help draw the spirit to you.

Reprinted by permission of Stephanie Lechniak-Cumerlato, founding partner of Haunted Hamilton, www.hauntedhamilton.com and www.ghostwalks.com.

Top 10 Vampire Movies of All Time

1. *Nosferatu* (1922)
2. *Dracula* (1931)
3. *Bram Stoker's Dracula* (1992)
4. *Interview with the Vampire* (1994)
5. *Shadow of the Vampire* (2000)
6. *From Dusk Till Dawn* (1996)
7. *Near Dark* (1987)
8. *Let the Right One In* (2008)
9. *The Lost Boys* (1987)
10. *Cronos* (1993)

Top 10 Werewolf Movies of All Time

1. *An American Werewolf in London* (1981)
2. *The Howling* (1981)
3. *Dog Soldiers* (2002)
4. *Ginger Snaps* (2000)
5. *Wolfen* (1981)
6. *The Company of Wolves* (1984)
7. Tie: *The Wolf Man* (1941) and *The Wolfman* (2010)
8. *Bad Moon* (1996)
9. *Silver Bullet* (1985)
10. *Underworld* (2003)

Top 10 Demon Movies of All Time

1. *The Exorcist* (1973)
2. *The Omen* (1976)
3. *The Exorcism of Emily Rose* (2005)
4. *Pumpkinhead* (1988)
5. *Hellbound: Hellraiser II* (1988)
6. *Hellboy* (2004)
7. *Rosemary's Baby* (1968)
8. *Hellraiser* (1987)
9. *Curse of the Demon* (1957)
10. *Demons* (1985)

Top 10 Ghost Movies of All Time

1. *The Shining* (1980)
2. *Poltergeist* (1982)
3. *The Sixth Sense* (1999)
4. *Ghostbusters* (1984)
5. *The Ring* (2002)
6. *The Others* (2001)
7. *Kwaidan* (1965)
8. *The Uninvited* (1944)
9. *Below* (2002)
10. *The Blair Witch Project* (1999)